Jane Austen and Sigmund Freud: an interpretation

130 Ashley Gardens, Thirleby Road, London SW1P 1HL

e-mail dr.julian.wilmot.wynne@zen.co.uk

Dear Librarian,

Since I have recently learnt from a user of your library that it has not yet acquired a copy of my book *Jane Austen and Sigmund Freud - an interpretation*, I hope you will accept the enclosed for your shelves.

    With my compliments,

    yours sincerely,

Jane Austen and Sigmund Freud
an interpretation

'In the realm of fiction we find the plurality of lives which we need.'

(Sigmund Freud, 12.79)

Julian Wilmot Wynne

First published in Great Britain in 1998 by
Plume Publications
130 Ashley Gardens, Thirleby Road, London SW1P 1HL

19277

British Library Cataloguing in Publishing Data
A catalogue record for this book is available from the British Library

ISBN 0 9534023 0 4

Book Production managed by Amolibros, Watchet, Somerset

Printed and bound in Great Britain by Professional Book Supplies, Oxford

CONTENTS

Acknowledgements

Acknowledgement is here made for brief quotations
from the following to owners of copyright therein:

George Allen and Unwin, P.M.Spacks, *The Female Imagination*. Athlone Press
Ltd., J.David Grey, *Jane Austen Handbook*. Baltimore University Press, Alistair
Duckworth, *The Improvement of the Estate*. Blackwell Publishers, Norman Page,
The Language of Jane Austen; Rush Rhees, Preface, Ludwig Wittgenstein, *Blue
and Brown Books*, *On Certainty*, *Lectures and Conversations on Aesthetics, Psychology and Religious Belief*, *Philosophical Grammar*, *Philosophical Investigations*,
Tractatus. Geoffrey Warnock, *Berkeley*. Bohra, T.V.Reddy, *Jane Austen and the
Matrix of Matrimony*. Christian Bourgois, Denise Getzler, trad. *Mansfield Park*.
Butterworth & Co Ltd., Bertrand Russell, *The Problems of Philosophy*. Jonathan
Cape Ltd., R.W.Clark, *Freud: the Man and the Cause*; José Ortega y Gasset, *On
Love...*. Carcanet Press: 'H.D.' *Tribute to Freud*. Chatto and Windus, Laurence
Lerner *The Truth-Tellers*; A.Walton Litz, *Jane Austen, A Study of Her Artistic
Development*; Charles Rycroft, *Psychoanalysis and Beyond*. Chicago University
Press, Wayne C.Booth, *The Rhetoric of Fiction*; Claudia L.Johnson, *Jane Austen,
Women, Politics and the Novel*; Susan Morgan, *In the Meantime, Character and
Perception in Jane Austen's Fiction*; Philip Rieff, *Freud: The Man and the Moralist*.
Cambridge University Press, D.W.Hamlyn, *Metaphysics*; Jocelyn Harris, *Jane Austen's Art of Memory*. Cresset, Geoffrey Gorer, *The Danger of Equality and Other
Essays*. Wm.Dawson & Sons, L.P.Hartley, *Address*. André Deutsch, K.C.Phillipps,
Jane Austen's English. Dover Publicatons, Heinrich Wölfflin, *Principles of Art
History*. Gerald Duckworth & Co Ltd., Graham Hough, *The Dream and the Task*.
Everyman, P.Washington, Introduction, Sanditon and Other Stories. Faber and
Faber Ltd., W.H.Auden, *Collected Shorter Poems*; T.S. Eliot, *Selected Essays*; *Collected Poems*; Ezra Pound, *Literary Essays*. Fontana Press, William James, *Varieties
of Religious Experience*; C.G.Jung, *Memories, Dreams, Reflections*; Frank Kermode,
Renaissance Essays; David Lodge, *The Novel Today*; David Pears, *Wittgenstein*;
Richard Wollheim, *Freud*. Free Press, *A Critical History of Western Philosophy*.
Julian Friedmann Publishers Ltd., L.L.Whyte, *The Unconscious Before Freud*. Galaxy Books, C.S.Lewis, *The Allegory of Love*. Gallimard, Isaiah Berlin, *Karl Marx*;
Georg Groddeck *Le Livre du Ca*. Greenwood Press, Henry James, *The House of
Fiction*. Hambledon Press, Maggie Lane, *Jane Austen and Food*. Hampshire Co.
Council, Audrey Hawkridge, *Jane Austen in Hampshire*. Harper & Row, D.Van
Ghent, *The English Novel, Form and Function*. Rupert Hart-Davis, Leon Edel,
Literary Biography. Harvard University Press, J.M.Masson (ed.) *The Complete
Letters of Sigmund Freud to Wilhelm Fliess*. Harvester Press, John Halperin, *The
Life of Jane Austen*; Margaret Kirkham, *Feminism and Fiction*; B.J.Paris, *Character and Conflict in Jane Austen's Novels*. Hodder & Stoughton, Joan Hodge, *The*

ACKNOWLEDGEMENTS

Double Life of Jane Austen. The Hogarth Press, J.Laplanche and J.-B.Pontalis, *The Language of Psycho-Analysis*, (Introduction, Daniel Lagache); Leonard Woolf, *Beginning Again.* Imago, Ernst Kris, *The Origins of Psychoanalysis*; Hanns Sachs, *Freud: Master and Friend.* Johns Hopkins University Press, Deborah Kaplan, *Jane Austen Among Women.* Kimber, Margaret Llewelyn, *Jane Austen, A Character Study.* Longman Ltd., Stella Gibbons, *Cold Comfort Farm*; Robert Liddell, *The Novels of Jane Austen*; A.P.Rossiter, *Angel With Horns.* Macmillan Publishers Ltd., Marilyn Butler, in *Northanger Abbey: A Casebook*; Geoffrey Gorer, *Five Approaches of Literary Criticism.* David Lodge, in *Emma: A Casebook*; Laura G.Mooneyham, *Romance, Language and Education in Jane Austen's Novels*; Leroy W.Smith, *Jane Austen and the Drama of Women*; B.C.Southam, in *Jane Austen's Achievement*; Tony Tanner, *Jane Austen*; Tara Ghoshal Wallace, *Jane Austen and Narrative Authority*; Michael Williams, *Jane Austen*; Ludwig Wittgenstein, *Remarks on the Foundations of Mathematics.* Mercury, Lionel Trilling, *The Liberal Imagination.* Methuen, Albert Einstein, *Relativity*; Catherine Belsey, *Critical Practice*; Malcolm Bradbury, in *Emma, A Casebook*; Wendy Craik, *Jane Austen, the Six Novels*; Elizabeth Wright, *Psychoanalytic Criticism.* The Nation & Athenaeum, Virginia Woolf, 'Jane Austen at Sixty'. New York State University Press, Jane Nardin, *Those Elegant Decorums.* Nouvelle Revue Française, André Gide, *Oeuvres.* Open University Press, Nigel Wood (Introduction) and Mary Evans ('Henry Crawford and the sphere of love in *Mansfield Park*'), '*Mansfield Park*'. Oxford University Press, *The Oxford Illustrated Jane Austen*, ed. R.W.Chapman, with revisions by Mary Lascelles and B.C.Southam; *Jane Austen's Letters to her Sister Cassandra and others*, ed. R.W.Chapman; John Bailey, *Introductions to Jane Austen*; Lord David Cecil, 'Sir Charles Grandison'; R.W.Chapman, *Jane Austen: Facts and Problems*; Mary Lascelles, *Jane Austen and her Art*; Harry Levin, *The Gates of Horn*; Charles Rycroft, *The Innocence of Dreams*; Arthur Sherbo (ed.) Hesther Piozzi, *Anecdotes of the Late Samuel Johnson.* Peter Owen, Barbara Hardy, *Jane Austen.* Paladin Books, Anton Ehrenzweig, *The Hidden Order of Art*; H.Stuart Hughes, *Consciousness and Society*; Bryan Magee, *Modern British Philosophy.* Pan, W.S. Maugham, *The Summing-Up.* Penguin Books Ltd., A.J.Ayer *Wittgenstein*; Bruno Bettelheim, *The Uses of Enchantment*; Ronald Blythe, Introduction, *Emma*; Jorge Luis Borges, *Labyrinths*, J.A.C.Brown, *Freud and the Post-Freudians*; John Ciardi, in *Aspects of Alice*; William Empson, *Seven Types of Ambiguity*; Margaret Doody, Introduction, *Sense and Sensibility*; Margaret Drabble, Introduction, *Minor Works*; H.J.Eysenck, *The Decline and Fall of the Freudian Empire*; Ifor Evans, *A Short History of English Literature*; E.M.Forster, *Aspects of the Novel*; Robin Fox, *Kinship and Marriage*; G.S.Fraser, *The Modern Writer and His World*; Eric Harth, *Windows on the Mind*; Werner Heisenberg, *Physics and Philosophy*; Henry James, *Selected Literary Criticism, The Wings of the Dove*; Ernest Jones, *Sigmund Freud, Life and Work* (abridged and ed. by Lionel Trilling and Steven Marcus; James Joyce, *Ulysses*; G.S.Kirk, *The Nature of Greek Myths*; F.R.Leavis, *The Great Tradition*; Peter Lomas, *The Limits of Interpretation*; Brian McGuinness, *Wittgenstein, A Life*, Anthony O'Hear, *What Philosophy Is*; Paul Roazen, *Freud and His Followers*; Charles Rycroft, *Critical Dictionary of Psychoanalysis*; Anthony Storr, *The Dynamics of Creation*; Robert Thomson, *Pelican History of Psychology*; George Watson, *The*

Literary Critics; Richard Wollheim, *Art & Its Objects*, Introduction, *The Image in Form: Selected Writings of Adrian Stokes*; Andrew Wright, *Jane Austen's Novels*. Pennsylvania University Press, Alison G.Sulloway, *Jane Austen and the Province of Womanhood*. Pennsylvania State University Press, James Thompson, *Between Jane Austen and the World*. Phaidon, E.H.Gombrich, *Meditations on A Hobby-horse*. Picador, William McGuire (ed.) *The Freud / Jung Letters*; Vladimir Nabokov, *Lectures on Literature*. Pitkin, Victor Lucas, *Jane Austen*. Prentice Hall, Mark Schorer, Edmund Wilson & Ian Watt in *Jane Austen, A Collection of Critical Essays*. Princeton University Press, Erich Auerbach, *Mimesis*; Northrop Frye, *Fearful Symmetry*; Karl Kroeber, *Styles in Fictional Structure*; Marvin Mudrick, *Irony as Defense and Discovery*. PMLA, Edgar Shannon, 'Emma: Character & Construction'. Rodopi, C.C.Barfoot, *The Thread of Connection*. Routledge, M.R. Ayers, *Locke*, Andrew Cairncross, Introduction, *2 Henry VI*; Denis Donoghue 'A View of Mansfield Park', Robert Garis, 'Learning, Experience and Change' & J.I.M. Stewart, 'Tradition and Miss Austen', in *Critical Essays on Jane Austen*; C.G.Jung, *Analytical Psychology: Its Theory and Practice, Modern Man in Search of a Soul*; A.R.Lacey, *A Dictionary of Philosophy*; Karl Popper, *Conjectures and Refutations*; Roger Sales, *Jane Austen and Representations of Regency England*; B.C.Southam, *Jane Austen: The Critical Heritage*. Royal Society Obituary Notices, A.G.Tansley. Schocken, Ernst Kris, *Psychoanalytic Explorations in Art*. Scrutiny, D.W.Harding, 'Regulated Hatred: An Aspect of the Work of Jane Austen'; Q.D.Leavis, 'A Critical Theory of Jane Austen's Writings'. Secker and Warburg, Thomas Szasz, *The Myth of Mental Illness*; Lionel Trilling, *Beyond Culture*. Seuil, Jacques Lacan, *L'Ethique de la Psychanalyse, Le Moi dans la Théorie et dans la Technique de la Psychanalyse, Les Quatre Concepts Fondamentaux de la Psychanalyse*; Paul Ricoeur, *De L'Interprétation*. Signet editions, Elizabeth Hardwick, Afterword, *N.A.*. Twayne, John Lauber, *Jane Austen*. University of Victoria Press, Juliet McMaster, Literary Monographs, no. 18. Virago, Steven Marcus, *In Dora's Case*. Weidenfeld and Nicholson, Park Honan, *Jane Austen: Her Life*. Yale University Press, Edward J.Ahearn, *Marx and Modern Fiction*; Susan Gilbert and Sandra Gubar, *The Madwoman in the Attic*; Oliver MacDonagh, *Jane Austen, Real and Imagined Worlds*.

I am also glad to have the opportunity to express my thanks here to Mr and Mrs Nigel and Sanja Poleščuk Higgins for friendly support, to le Comte et la Comtesse Christian et Diane de Maynard for an amicable arrangement, to Professor and Mrs Charles and Jean Wynne for *l'incontournable*; and to Professor Catherine Belsey, Ms Gill Davies, Professor John Day, Mme Catherine Delafontaine, Mme Victoria Diehl, Ms Barbara Kirby, Mr and Mrs Richard and Elaine Montgomery Knight, Dr Nigel Llewellyn, Dr and Mrs Richard and Annette Marlow, Ms Jane Northcote, Mr Stephen Parkin, M. Jean-Louis Puech, Mme Thérèse Renne, Dr and Dr Nicholas and Jenny Richardson, Mr and Mrs Lionel and Louise Williams de Rothschild, Mr Leo Salingar and Ms Alexandra Zahorski, for encouragement at various times in the process of producing this book.

PREFACE

'..It will have to become possible to talk about these things without being stamped as a trouble-maker . . . there is work enough to do for the next hundred years.'

Sigmund Freud in 1898 (*SE* III.278)

This book may be figuratively described as effecting an introduction between Jane Austen (1775-1817) and Sigmund Freud (1856-1938).

To many admirers of the first-named writer, the encounter proposed will appear patently preposterous—doomed from the start, in fact; to some actually offensive; and to a few indeed almost sacrilegious.

Even to those who register no such initial reaction, the idea that these two could possibly have anything whatever to say to each other may not be transparently obvious. A brief indication is thus appropriate here of the various aims this book sets itself, and the interrelations between those aims. All of this is expanded in the Introduction, but it seems opportune to make quite clear at the outset one aim that this book does not set out to accomplish. I therefore certify that no attempt is made in it to psychoanalyse Jane Austen.

My overall objective is to foster, in two categories of readers otherwise perhaps unlikely to coincide, concern with each others' pursuits: on the one hand, readers of Jane Austen (especially re-readers); on the other, those interested in understanding the unconscious, and the instrument Sigmund Freud designed for its examination.

A specific thesis is to be defended, under the supposition (not altogether uncontentious, I am aware) that things happen, outside literature, which can give it meaning: namely that the preoccupations of these two writers, very far from being worlds apart, are essentially similar.

This, already, calls for a little further expansion.

For some people, the most remarkable fact about the universe is that in an out-of-the-way corner of it there should exist beings who are aware—of anything at all—who consciously 'realise' something, in their minds and out, conceive and build bicycle sheds or civilizations. For others, it is an equally astounding fact that those same beings should know something without knowing that they know it.

Jane Austen—whose admirers agree in regarding as probably the most intelligent woman of whom we have record—has been almost exclusively associated with the first of these two facts. I am quite sure this is wrong, and that her chief artistic interest is in the other, maybe even profounder fact.

The point this book seeks to make, then, is a historical rather than a critical one in the strictly evaluative sense; its upshot should nevertheless be the essentially critical one of supplying better reasons for reading or re-reading an author. To an expected retort that in Jane Austen's case there already exist perfectly good reasons, one may first reply that perfection should perhaps not have come quite so soon; and furthermore that to admire need not interfere with breathing. Indeed, whilst it is a contribution to 'the history of ideas' only by the way, this inquiry's properly critical edge is directed rather towards the reasons on offer in the received account of her art. Which brings me to my third main aim.

Before we can see how Freud's work illuminates Jane Austen's—let alone understand why, contrary to all apparently sane likelihood, it should do so— a *complete* break must be made with the idea of Jane Austen, and of her oeuvre, as she and it are commonly pictured. To that picture I refer throughout as 'Janeism'. This may appear an indefensibly tendentious ploy; but the term is accurate in so far as it designates all commentary which, while purporting to be about Jane Austen's work, in fact constantly refers home not to a body of writing but to a person, and to a world ('Jane Austen's England')—not critical counters, but symptoms of a collective exercise in romantic imagination. In this sense, I shall show, every single one of my predecessors, without exception, is a Janeite.

Any cross-disciplinary study brings upon itself a quandary: works that attempt to bridge the gap between two classes of readers 'cannot offer to each what each lacks' (Freud, 13.49). But behind the capacity of this book to exasperate the two sets of readers at whom it is directed, lies the essential interrelatedness of its aims. For as we shall see from Chapter I on, the grounds for supposing new and better reasons are needed for reading Jane Austen—grounds which come from grasping Freud's importance for language and literature (Part 1)—turn out to be inseparably bound up with understanding why the old ones all need ditching (Part 2). I want to do something better in this book than merely replace the reigning interpretation; I want to make sense of it.

And thus we come to my fourth main objective: to bring Jane Austen Studies in line with at least some of the gains in understanding art achieved by contemporary critical theory (which is in the process of displacing, elsewhere, practically all the received account stands for). These gains involve an essentially simple but profound reversal of assumptions—something notoriously hard to present. Avoid being snooty, but remain firm. Here goes:

A book is a configuration of words, not of things. An apparently obvious fact, this, but whose full implications are proving almost as hard for our collective conscious to adjust to as the theory of relativity. All a book can do is refer. The question may then be asked: what does it refer to? The answer is that rather than referring from individual words to individual things outside the book, it works from the pattern as a whole to some other patterned thing. What thing is that? Well, because books issue from and are directed to minds, the contents of books are far more like the contents of mind than like the contents of the world, despite the misleadingly 'real' look of the furniture.

A word, to end with, about the overall formal aim of this inquiry: to keep as many even potentially sympathetic Jane Austen readers as unruffled for as long as absolutely possible. That has seemed supremely worthwhile. Thus, to be sure of carrying such readers with me, objections are constantly anticipated as we go along (sometimes, for reasons of economy, in footnotes). In order to avoid the drearily systematic, the reading experience is varied from chapter to chapter; so after the general point Chapter I makes about the interest of Freud for language, psychoanalytic and other theory is presented as the need for it arises. The interpretative principles are all both cumulative in presentation and retroactive in application.

Naturally, I do not expect the point of all this to be immediately accepted; if it were, there would be no occasion for the book.

J.W.W.

Abbreviations, and a note on presentation

Jane Austen

For the novels, references are to volume, chapter and page: e.g. (I.14.121), using conventional abbreviations (*S & S*; *P & P*; *MP*; *E*; *NA*; *P*; *MW*) from the six-volume *Oxford Illustrated Jane Austen*, ed. R.W.Chapman (see References.)
Readers using other editions may refer to a chapter-numbers repertory, p. xxx.

For the letters, abbreviation *L*, then page no.: e.g. (*L* 346), from *Jane Austen's Letters to her Sister Cassandra and Others*, ed. R.W.Chapman (see References.)

Sigmund Freud

Where possible, references are to the fifteen-volume Pelican Freud Library, by volume and page: e.g. (15.135); otherwise to the twenty-four volume *Standard Edition of the Complete Psychological Works of Sigmund Freud*, translated and edited by James Strachey, abbreviated *SE*: e.g. (*SE* XVII.161).
Permission to quote substantially from this has been graciously accorded by Sigmund Freud Copyrights, The Institute of Psycho-Analysis and the Hogarth Press.

F/F = *The Complete Letters of Sigmund Freud to Wilhelm Fliess, 1887-1904*, translated and edited by Jeffrey Moussaieff Masson, Belknap Harvard 1985.

F/J = *The Freud/Jung Letters*, edited by William McGuire, translated by Ralph Mannheim and R.F.C.Hull, abridged by Alan McGlashan, Picador 1979.

L & P = *The Language of Psycho-Analysis*, by J.Laplanche and J.-B.Pontalis, translated by Donald Nicholson-Smith, The Hogarth Press 1985.

Jones = Ernest Jones: *Sigmund Freud, Life and Work*. Where possible, reference is to the Penguin ed. (1964), abridged by Lionel Trilling and Steven Marcus; otherwise to the original three-volume ed., by year: e.g. (1953), (1955), (1957).

Of the many ways in which authors may comment on what they quote, two sheerly typographical ones are used throughout this book, justifying a brief note here.
   (1) Since its didactic aim is to give readers (even those familiar, in one sense, with Jane Austen's work) all the help it can to notice—literally to *see*—the recurrences of words in different contexts across a novel, this point is made visually by frequent recourse to bold type. (The alternative solution—italics—encounters the snag that the novelist herself often uses them, so constant wearying reminders would be needed to distinguish between the two cases.)
   (2) Various conventions exist in typography for the use of dots (other than the single one used as a full stop.) At the start of a quotation two dots denote a 'lead-in', drawing attention to the fact that what is quoted has been taken from its context in a larger whole. At the close of a quotation, when they do not simply signal that it is to be completed further on, they denote a rhetorical 'suspension' on the part of the commentator. (Both of these are distinct from 'ellipsis'— omission of words not germane to the point which is the occasion for its being quoted—always represented here by three dots.)

INTRODUCTION

'..creative writers are valuable allies and their evidence is to be prized highly, for they are apt to know a whole host of things between heaven and earth of which our philosophy has not yet let us dream.'   (14.34)

- 1 -

Whilst it may be true that, strictly speaking, there are no bad reasons for liking a writer's work, it should be allowed that there are better or worse.

The reasons given in the existing critical literature for liking Jane Austen are perhaps not all equally bad, but the position which will be argued for in this book must here be clearly stated: few of those reasons are really good, and most could hardly be worse; indeed—to make now the first of a series of stands necessitated by the inertness of contemporary Jane Austen Studies— it will contend that her oeuvre has been *fundamentally* misunderstood.

This extravagant and implausible point of view—which the present work seeks to support, first by exposing a complex set of interrelated logical and factual errors, and then by suggesting new criteria of meaning in Jane Austen's writing—must appear all the more indefensible and extreme when we take into account the decidedly exalted company in which, from very early on, she is found mentioned.

Readers familiar with Jane Austen's critical reputation cannot easily forget the striking manner in which Lord Macaulay (this is 1843) interrupts an excursus on Fanny Burney's characters:

> Shakspeare [sic] has had neither equal nor second. But among the writers who, in the point we have noticed, have approached nearest to the manner of the great master, we have no hesitation in placing Jane Austen, a woman of whom England is justly proud... [etc.][1]

Discussing dramatic presentation a few years later, G.H.Lewes declares:

> ..instead of telling us what her characters are, and how they feel, she presents the people, and they reveal themselves. In this she has never perhaps been surpassed, not even by Shakespeare [sic] himself.[2]

---

[1] Thomas B.Macaulay: 'Madame d'Arblay' in *Critical and Historical Essays*, Longman 1857, II.312.

[2] G.H.Lewes: 'The Novels of Jane Austen', *Blackwood's*, July 1859.

That this comparison—which even the Jane Austen fanatic might excuse us for thinking just a little strained—was due to no mid-Victorian craze, but has continued to be made late into the present century, is attested by remarks to the same effect from critics as various as Ifor Evans, G.S.Fraser and Margaret Drabble; in that order:

> ..The complete control of her world gives her work a Shakespearian quality.[3]
> ..Jane Austen's world is one in which the soul can breathe . . . it gives one a Shakespearean sense of life's gravity, order and fullness.[4]
> ..There would be more genuine rejoicing at the discovery of a complete new novel by Jane Austen than any other literary discovery, short of a new major play by Shakespeare, that one could imagine.[5]

From Macaulay to Margaret Drabble, then, Jane Austen's name has regularly been linked with that of an author who enjoys a sort of axiomatic primacy in world literature; some of her admirers might feel that to be compared with Shakespeare (after all, they could say, you can't get much better than that) obviates the need for critical writing on her work at all.

However, if criticism (even of the classics) continues to be necessary, that is not for the authors themselves but for us, since it is our reading which does not stay the same; constant reassessment is one of the things the critical attitude means: even classic Shakespeare's relevance has proverbially not just survived, but has been enhanced by, several revolutions in thought:

> ..whole ranges of facts, previously unnoticed or dismissed as irrelevant, can suddenly be seen to pertain to the work of art. These transformations can occur in a variety of ways as a result of changes in criticism, or as a result of changes in the practice of art, or as a result of changes in the general intellectual environment . . . we might cite the grammaticality of Shakespeare's sentences, which has over history been regarded as a matter primarily of philological interest. Recently, however, critics have suggested that the syntactical incoherence of certain speeches, in e.g. *Macbeth*, may be of significance as expressive of deep and disordered trains of thought.[6]

By exploring possibilities of interpretation in one particular instance—the work of Jane Austen—this study aims to lend plausibility by its example to a more general contention: namely that the whole range of facts and ideas assembled under the name *psychoanalysis*, may be said to constitute an

[3] Ifor Evans: *A Short History of English Literature*, Pelican 1940, p. 238.

[4] G.S.Fraser: *The Modern Writer and His World*, Pelican 1970, p. 151.

[5] Margaret Drabble: Introduction, *Minor Works*, Penguin 1974, p. 8. Jane Austen, we may recall, is the first name to figure on F.R.Leavis' list of the 'successors of Shakespeare' (*The Great Tradition*, Pelican 1967, p. 145).

[6] Richard Wollheim: *Art and Its Objects*, Peregrine 1975, pp. 104/5.

exacting challenge for the understanding of literature. Partly for the reasons most usually given (the most radically original theory of human minds formulated in the 20th century might be expected to have some effect on our view of the whole products of those minds); but perhaps mainly, as the above quotation suggests, because it is what we had not noticed—or rather, what we left unnoticed, something in the very texture of the stuff literature is made out of: language itself—this, it has progressively become clear, was the basic matter on the understanding of which Sigmund Freud established a new discipline, a profession, and a way of seeing.

- 2 -

Our reasons—those to which we admit—for *dis*liking an author's work are seldom any good whatever: personal incapacities to engage with some part or other of our culture's accumulating baggage (into the midst of which, whether we liked it or not, our cradle was thrust) always exasperatingly unhelpful in a teacher, can be of absorbing interest only to our very closest friends.

The work of Sigmund Freud has hardly touched Jane Austen at all.[7] Right across the board—from articles in learned journals, via blurb on the back of the latest paperback reprint of her novels, to the pre-release write-ups of television or film adaptations—our idea of Jane Austen (her 'image') has been.. well, perhaps the right word is 'protected'.

At this early stage, a rudimentary demonstration is called for. In what still claims to be the fullest survey available of Jane Austen's vocabulary, under the word 'conscious' we find 'The negative *unconscious*, meaning "unembarrassed", occurs',[8] followed by an illustrative quotation: 'Emma could look perfectly unconscious and innocent' (*E* II.5.189).

In 1816 (the year *Emma* was published), 'conscious' included among its connotations what we now call *self*-conscious, so the negative term certainly admitted the meaning given here. But this does not exhaust its meaning; and that is the very least that should be said: when Marianne Dashwood apostrophises the trees at Norland as ' "unconscious of the pleasure or regret you occasion" ' (*S & S* I.5.27) is this because those trees are unembarrassed?

No. As when Elizabeth Bennet, refusing Darcy's first proposal, declares that though she is sorry to occasion pain, it is ' "most unconsciously done" ' (*P& P* II.11.190), or as when we are told that Mr Woodhouse is dismayed by John Knightley's critical remarks about Mr Perry, to whom 'he had, in fact, though unconsciously, been attributing many of his own feelings and expressions' (*E* I.12.107) so, when applied to the Norland trees, the word bears a

---

[7] With a handful of exceptions (see Appendix). This early opportunity is taken to acknowledge the hints of Tony Tanner, who in his *Jane Austen* (Macmillan 1986, p. 77) wrote that the suggestion 'Jane Austen was an early Freudian' would be a 'rare thought'.

[8] K.C.Phillipps: *Jane Austen's English*, André Deutsch 1969, p. 82.

meaning for which the closest synonyms are the modern 'unaware', or 'inwardly insensible'.

This demonstration may cause some Jane Austen readers surprise; though it is hard to believe many have not noticed the word in their reading of the novels.[9] Nevertheless, this is the first occasion (as far as I know) to bring together onto a single printed page, out of numerous examples, even three.[10]

But it is more than merely the novelist's use of a word that we shall pursue in this book, whose main thesis is that she turns out to be one of those 'valuable allies' in the quotation heading this Introduction. Jane Austen, it will be argued, anticipated by structural representation of complex mental states the dynamic unconscious which was to find its first ordered conceptualisation a century later, in the work of Sigmund Freud.

A corollary to this thesis will be that it has needed the advent of a psychoanalytically-based aesthetic to see what Jane Austen was doing, and how she was doing it.

- 3 -

Philip Rieff has called Freud's work 'perhaps the most important body of thought committed to paper in the twentieth century';[11] H.J. Eysenck takes a different view: psychoanalysis is 'psycho-babble', and the whole thing can be dismissed as 'a historical curiosity'.[12]

There is nothing radically new in the second of these two assessments: as early as 1914, Freud himself wrote that he often saw in newspapers: '..now psychoanalysis is dead, defeated and disposed of once and for all..' (15.93).

Be that as it may, in view of so spectacular a divergence of opinion, of the fact that 'Psychoanalysts differ widely among themselves as to which aspects of Freud's thought they wish to remember and commemorate',[13] and of the relative voluminousness of his writing, the reader may welcome some indication as to which parts of it this study will be turning to account.

---

[9] Neither the word nor some notion of what it refers to were unknown in the late 18th century. The idea had been teetering on the edge of Western consciousness for centuries, perhaps millennia, before a Scot (Lord Kames, whom readers of Boswell may remember: ' "Sir, we have Lord Kames." JOHNSON: "You *have* Lord Kames. Keep him; ha, ha, ha!" ' [*Life of Samuel Johnson*, Everyman I.344]) was the first to use the adjective in something like its modern sense, in *Essays* (1751) (L.L.Whyte: *The Unconscious Before Freud*, Julian Friedmann 1979, p. 103). The interested reader will find an account of how 'conscious' (literally 'knowing with') acquired its present meaning, in Hobbes' *Leviathan*, I.7. It is worth noting that J.F.Herbart, whose influence on the young Freud is well-documented, was Jane Austen's almost exact contemporary: he was born in May 1776, five months after her; that same year saw the publication of *Philosophische Aphorismen* by Ernst Platner, who is credited with the first use in German of the adjective *bewusstlos* and even the noun *Unbewusstsein*.

[10] The word does not figure either in the *Letters* or in the works conjecturally written before the six novels; 'unconsciously' appears (scratched out) on the 'Sanditon' MS; on the one occasion Jane Austen uses the word 'conscious' in surviving letters (*L* 261), and the two when she uses 'consciousness' (ibid., 144 & 497), the meaning is clearly 'aware' and 'awareness', not 'embarrassed' and 'embarrassment'; in the novels, she sometimes appears to be playing with the double meaning. All these are significant facts to which we shall return.

[11] Philip Rieff: *Freud: The Mind of the Moralist*, Chicago 1959, p. x.

[12] H.J.Eysenck: *The Decline and Fall of the Freudian Empire*, Penguin 1985, p. 208.

[13] Charles Rycroft: *Psychoanalysis and Beyond*, Chatto and Windus 1985, p. 261.

Chapter I aims to give that indication (demonstrations and argument from Chapter II onwards being moreover intended to continue to derive some of their force from points made there.)

It should however be said that the founder of psychoanalysis was himself in a sense opposed to any such approach, claiming in 1932 that, although its structure was unfinished, it nevertheless presented 'a unity from which elements cannot be broken off at the caprice of whoever comes along' (2.173).[14]

Others must judge how far the interpretative model which this work draws from Freud's oeuvre is eclectic in a pejorative sense—based, that is, on an unrepresentative selection of his ideas—but at least on this point the view of his oeuvre presented here need not be unfavourably contrasted with that of other, more practised interpreters: Charles Rycroft calls Freud's achievement 'a collection of miscellaneous ideas, insights and intuitions propounded over a span of fifty years', and concludes with the happy simile that these heterogeneous elements have proved to be 'more of a quarry than an edifice';[15] Professor Rieff's view is: 'There are truths in these texts, but no truth'; he goes so far as to say that Freud's thought was 'created piecemeal, and *fortunately* never integrated into one systematic statement';[16] even Ernest Jones thought psychoanalysis could be profitably studied 'only as a historical evolution, never as a perfected body of knowledge';[17] and finally Freud himself, wishing to correct what is still a popular misconception, distinguished his own work from that of Alfred Adler by underlining that psychoanalysis never claimed to provide a complete theory of human mentality, but only expected

..that what it offered should be applied to supplement and correct the knowledge acquired by other means. Adler's theory, however, goes far beyond this point . . . [it] was from the very beginning a 'system'—which psychoanalysis was careful to avoid becoming.   (15.110/112)

- 4 -

..the work of analysis involves an *art of interpretation*, the successful handling of which may require tact.   (15.224/5)

Simply to take for granted that the work of Sigmund Freud is of axiomatic interest—to anyone at all, let alone to readers of the work of Jane Austen— would be question-begging at the very outset. In order for it to appear less

---

[14] He once referred in proprietary mood to '*my* psychoanalysis' (letter, Jones [1964], p. 634, my italics).

[15] Rycroft, op. cit., p. 11.

[16] Rieff, op.cit., p. x (my italics); cf. 'I have assuredly not dug up more than a fragment of truth' (in the same letter as n. 14). The modesty in this (which may surprise some, since it goes against another popular misconception of Freud) will be further illustrated in the following; at the age of 70, writing of his work as 'beginnings' and 'suggestions' he says: 'Something will come of them in the future . . . I cannot myself tell whether it will be much or little' and that psychoanalysis 'seems destined to give valuable *contributory help* in the most varied regions of knowledge' (15.255, my italics).

[17] Jones (1964), p. 26. This study quotes psychoanalytic writings other than Freud's only occasionally; the reason for this is given in Chapter I, p. 11.

so, a completely new space needs to be cleared where these two can meet. With that end in view Chapter I will be concerned with stating and meeting, in what it is hoped will appear logical order, objections often raised in such circles against Freud and his work. And since within their ranks there is an exceedingly knowledgeable subset whose potential suffrage one may have reason not lightly to alienate from the start, this Introduction will already have a word of reassurance tailored especially for them.

There are plenty of books about psychoanalysis and literature, but most of them either assume a considerable degree of familiarity with psychoanalysis, or else operate with its concepts on a level too elementary for anything very interesting to emerge.

This study has a different aim: namely to bring to the fore words, expressions, sometimes whole passages in Jane Austen which appear to have gone unnoticed in the critical literature, and only then to suggest ways in which psychoanalysis might set about attributing some meaning to them. The first part of Chapter I prepares the way for that exploration by reviewing Freud's writings from a very specific point of view: that of the literary reader, whose interest inevitably focuses first on questions of language.

The second part of Chapter I, reaping gains (it is hoped) from the first, moves towards elucidating the final term in what was called 'a psychoanalytically-based *aesthetic*'. For a big jolt that aesthetics received in the 20th century—a jolt to which literary criticism, and within that, Austen Studies, must sooner or later come to terms—is attributable to the work (in for a penny, in for a pound) of another Viennese of genius: Ludwig Wittgenstein.

Wittgenstein's main field was not aesthetics (nor was it Freud's, ostensibly), but their writings display constant kinship of preoccupation.[18] Asking, for example, an old question—'What is the proof that I *know* something?'—Wittgenstein's new first move is to exclude one answer, for he replies: 'Most certainly not my saying I know it';[19] elsewhere this state of affairs is explained thus: 'The word "know" doesn't denote a state of consciousness.'[20] And the odd fact that you know Jane Austen wrote *Emma* even when you are not consciously thinking of her, or it, might be an example of a lesson he draws:

> The aspects of things that are most important for us are hidden because of their simplicity and familiarity. (One is unable to notice something—because it is always before one's eyes.) [21]

Readers need have no apprehension that they are to be terrorised by squads of technicalities, philosophical or psychoanalytic. As far as the former goes, it

---

[18] Exploring why this is so will not directly concern us, but as that kinship is present at every turn (as will be obvious to readers familiar with either of the two) parallels are indicated from time to time, in footnotes.

[19] *On Certainty*, Blackwell 1969, ¶ 487.

[20] *Philosophical Grammar*, Blackwell 1974, p. 71.

[21] *Philosophical Investigations* (henceforth abbreviated: *P.I.*), Blackwell 1968, ¶ 129.

it will be obvious that since philosophy for Wittgenstein includes exploring the nature of representation, his inquiries have repercussions on understanding what sort of thing a novel, say, (the genre in which Jane Austen mainly worked) might be. As for psychoanalytic terminology, it will be introduced gradually and only when called for; as we shall see from Chapter I on, one of the *least* well-founded objections brought against psychoanalysis is that it seeks to impress by a factitiously esoteric vocabulary.

But—and here the promise to anticipate, as we go along, various parties' objections, is honoured for the first time—to some this may sound, *already*, too complicated to have much to do with the simple activity of reading novels; in particular Jane Austen's (proverbially, at the simplest level, 'a good read')?

If so, it may be necessary to have a reminder that reading itself—reading anything at all—is a complex act. Jane Austen readers, furthermore, are today in the iron grip of a highly complex interpretative model.

Complex and, it will be argued, mistaken: as we shall discover in Chapter I part 2, most of the worst common reasons for liking Jane Austen are based on what, it now turns out, reasons exist for thinking a novel actually *cannot* be. That is why a brief review must be made there (section 3) of the misapprehensions characteristic of the way her oeuvre has so far been seen.

Other readers may feel that the reigning interpretative model does not deserve the high compliment paid it, in those pages, of rational opposition.

The answer to this, which Chapter I as a whole reflects, is that before you can cure the patient you should identify the disease. Lionel Trilling thought opinions held of Jane Austen's work 'almost as interesting and almost as important to think about as the work itself';[22] although this goes rather far, the present study takes it seriously enough to add to the many accounts of her work which involve discussing other accounts of her work. Apart from any lesson to be learnt from taking apart a powerful belief-system to see how it gained its ascendancy (in this area such a thing has not to my knowledge been attempted before[23]) it may be agreed that the process by which conclusions are reached counts quite as much as the conclusions themselves. Before operating, one must distinguish the bit of the organism that does not work from the bit that does. For naturally the reigning model does work (after a fashion) or it would not have survived. What for some will seem a painful operation may perhaps be slightly palliated with humour—the only anaesthetic available—but there was no way of softening what had to be some very deep

---

[22] *Beyond Culture*, Secker and Warburg 1966, p. 31.

[23] A hearing is given to critics evenly spread over the last five decades: some are quoted because their assessments (no less interesting or important for belonging to the earlier part of this period) have had immense influence, or because their critical formulas have not been improved upon—indeed some have acquired something like classic status; others are quoted from the later part of this period in order again to anticipate an objection: to show that the attitudes evoked are still alive and kicking.

incisions, since in the event practically the whole thing has to go; each chapter attempts to replace a different rotten constitutive organ.[24]

So now: why is the operation needed at all?

Freud thought analysis 'cannot avoid wounding cherished prejudices' (15. 179).[25] Certainly an understatement. The only way the incoherence of the reigning interpretative model in Jane Austen Studies can be exposed, is by judicious employment of a little rhetorical overstatement. Thus:

It would perhaps not be too much of an exaggeration to say that most critics, approaching a novel by Jane Austen, describe it as if it were something rather like a box: according to this model, each box has things 'in' it; and understanding these things consists of tracing where they came from ('outside' it): a task hampered only by our not knowing more about the author.

The paradigmatic case for the model in question is the *Mansfield Park* 'Problem', to which A.W.Litz gave classic formulation when he said he found the 'moral indignation' in this novel so 'disproportionate to its subject . . . that it is natural to seek the source for this indignation outside the novel'.[26]

The question implored in 'natural' is to engage us in both parts of Chapter I; but 'seek the source' establishes a precedent that should be noted now.

Among ploys in the box approach the most inconsequential is to leave readers the task of accomplishing the act of faith—i.e., as to the relevance of a given datum—themselves: in a word, 'background'.. And here commentators might appear to be competing in a bizarre Lewis Carroll-like game: which of us can take Jane Austen by the hand, run furthest away from the boxes, and still get her to lob things into them? Thus one of the recent spate of biographies[27] includes an extremely long description of the battle of Trafalgar. Not, as you might perhaps at first surmise, because the biographer has unearthed evidence to suggest the novelist herself took part in that action (though she is sometimes all but reproached by her detractors for not doing so), no, but because he has ascertained that one of her brothers.. well, *almost* did.

Now: no one doubts that Miss Jane Austen dearly loved a sailor; but if the whole naval thing was of such perennial importance to her, how does it come about that the navy is totally absent from four out of the six novels?[28]

---

[24] A further consideration would be, adapting a classic dictum on philosophy, that those who do not know the history of literary criticism are condemned to repeat it–*for ever*.. And the way biography itself, literary or otherwise, seems almost set to displace fiction as the most popular prose genre, suggests that the anti-biographist plea to be submitted in this study has wider application than Janeism.

[25] Cf. '..the whole of your previous education and all your habits of thought are inevitably bound to make you into opponents of psychoanalysis' (1.40).

[26] *Jane Austen: A Study of Her Artistic Development*, Chatto and Windus 1965, p. 117.

[27] Park Honan: *Jane Austen: Her Life*, Weidenfeld and Nicholson 1987, Chapter 13.

[28] There is one allusion to it in Chapter 19 of *S & S*: the navy figures among the professions Edward Ferrars did not adopt. Muddle about necessary and sufficient conditions continues to feature widely in the critical literature: e.g.: The 'family background [sc. two naval brothers] *no doubt accounts for* Austen's enthusiasm and knowledgeable presentation of naval affairs'; 'Recollection of those theatricals [of 1787] *would provide Austen with* a key episode' etc. (John Lauber: *Jane Austen*, Twayne 1993, pp. 1 and 3, my italics).

At this early point, any possibility of misunderstanding must be strenuously avoided. 'Authors never use their experience when writing their books': the statement looks as if it ought to be palpably false; but the thought is muddled, rather, behind even such an apparently harmless sentence, and it will take some time to untangle why it cannot even be stated. Large programmes such as 'the elucidation of works of art and the correction of taste'[29] are now felt to beg too many questions; an unavoidable initial task for criticism is to find what we cannot argue about.[30]

As a first step, then: a very large proportion of Jane Austen 'criticism' is based, it must uncompromisingly be spelt out, on in all senses *un*-critical recourse to family legend, letters, etc.; it is rare to find any consideration given to questions about how much is needed, and to make what sort of case. To resort to two criteria used in logic for assessing the truth of sets of statements, Janeism may have a sort of internal *coherence*, but the *correspondence* on which it is founded, common sense must sooner or later in all conscience acknowledge, is hopelessly incomplete. More or less conscious neglect in exercising such common sense probably stems from understandable reluctance to believe that any information about a much-loved author (perhaps especially because there is so little of it) can actually be useless; moreover the biographical data looks as if it *must* be important, must indeed be 'the material', because of a treacherous likeness to the work.

Here is another bit of the organism that must go: a critic informs us that when Jane Austen was young, 'the central issue of her life must have been whether she was going to grow up or to remain a child';[31] but unless he has access to occult sources of information (unsurprisingly, this turns out not to be the case: what is known about her childhood may be written on a postcard) is it responsible to assert in so very matter-of-fact a style what in no way involves matters of fact?[32]

The advantage of having some facts (on the again not uncontentious supposition that it is they which make statements true or false) should be that

---

[29] T.S.Eliot's programme for literary criticism, *Selected Essays*, Faber 1951, p. 24.

[30] As a first move in untangling, readers may consider the analogy of another class of fictions: are we the authors of our dreams (including all their horrors)? On the one hand, as Freud in Humean mood says, 'All the material making up the content of a dream is in some way derived from experience' (4.69); on the other hand, 'dreams scarcely ever take over ordered recollections from waking life, but only details selected from them', which moreover 'they tear from the psychical context in which they are usually remembered in the waking state' (4. 108). A first example of Freud/Wittgenstein 'coincidence': Freud's insistence on the essentially collective character of mind may be related to questions Wittgenstein asks (e.g. in *The Blue and Brown Books*, Blackwell 1972, p. 49) about the possibility of private language.

[31] Bernard J.Paris: *Character and Conflict in Jane Austen's Novels*, Harvester 1979, pp. 174/5. Cf., in the same vein of gratuitous hypothesis: 'I don't think her superb intelligence brought her happiness' (Elizabeth Hardwick, Signet ed. of *N.A.*, 1965).

[32] Every decade brings new confident assertions about her early life and writing: 'Jane Austen started writing at the age of eleven' (Margaret Llewelyn: *Jane Austen, A Character Study*, Kimber 1977, p. 15); 'By her early teens she already spent much of her time writing' (Lord David Cecil in 'Sir Charles Grandison', O.U.P. 1981, p. viii); 'Austen did no fiction writing while fulfilling her domestic duties' (Deborah Kaplan, *Jane Austen Among Women*, Johns Hopkins U. P., 1992, p. 102), and so on.

one can then discuss their significance. But as the seam that this inquiry aims to uncover has not (to my knowledge) been worked, what constitutes 'the facts' turns out to be itself problematical.

For this reason, as the very point of departure of the present study scarcely coincides at all with that of the existing critical literature, we shall hardly have occasion to engage with it at all, after Part 2 of Chapter I.

At some point the question must be confronted: *why*—amongst all possible bad reasons for liking authors—has biographism had such a field-day in Jane Austen Studies? A first attempt to answer this is also made in Part 2 (section 5). Returns must at all events be constantly diminishing: there is almost certainly nothing more to come, and (with due proportion) one may say that for her admirers all the little we know merely conspires 'to place upon the rack again our strained and aching wonder'.[33]

- 5 -

So now: what, it may be asked, is 'an interpretation'?

At the simplest level, to interpret is simply 'to say something about something'.[34] The problem, as everybody knows nowadays, is how—or, more disturbingly, whether—you can separate what you choose to call 'the facts' from interpretation of them: to talk about the whole universe is impracticable; to select anything smaller constitutes an act of interpretation.[35]

On the one hand it would be foolish to ignore that Jane Austen is in a context of cultural facts. How much do we need to know, of that context, in order to catch all her meaning?

A large question. Mr Rushworth's £12,000 a year (now roughly the average British wage) probably does not halt us for long: we imagine what a colossal income that is in *Mansfield Park*, or we get out our conversion tables, remembering what we have so often been told: that the novel is essential social history.. (But there are other facts most readers do not arrive at Jane Austen with: must we have read *Sir Charles Grandison* ? —and *Lovers' Vows* ?)

On the other hand, the authors of many critical books on Jane Austen appear to resemble those Blake-scholars Frye characterised with accurate cruelty as being 'less interested in what he wrote than in what he read';[36]

---

[33] Henry James, 'The Tempest', *Selected Literary Criticism* Peregrine 1968, p. 343.

[34] Paul Ricoeur: *De L'Interprétation*, Seuil 1965, p. 30. Connotations of the forced or arbitrary in the English are absent in the German *Deutung*, 'explanation' or 'clarification', cognate with *Bedeutung*, that simply means 'meaning'. Freud, sensitive to our resentment ever since childhood of others knowing things about us which we do not, was critical of *wilde Psychoanalyse*–'coarse' psychoanalysis–viz. ploys adopted by those 'who justify their power by appealing to their "superior knowledge" ' (*L & P* 481). Naturally, some regard their own minds as so private and sacred that they deny human mentality can be the field of specialist knowledge at all.

[35] Even the divine word needs interpretation, as Spinoza (for whom prophets were 'interpreters') saw: since 'Scripture, like Nature, gives no definitions of the things of which it speaks', the task is to find the *right* method of interpretation, and to separate the meaning of texts from their truth (*Theological-Political Tractatus*, 1670, ch. VII). Readers may wonder on what grounds psychoanalysis is affirmed to be the right method for elucidating Jane Austen's meaning; the reason should be clear by the middle of Chapter 3.

[36] Northrop Frye: *Fearful Symmetry*, Princeton 1969, p. 6.

the present study, by contrast, makes at least a bid for the possibility of starting, as it were, from the results end first.[37]

All Jane Austen readers are, whether they know it or not, already used to making at least one complex act of interpretation, namely in understanding her irony: a figure of style which goes beyond mere horizontal equivalence of meanings (viz., if two men ride a horse, one must ride behind). This inquiry interprets the two levels operating within her irony in very different terms from that of the received account; however, this is less a new theoretical position in itself than a redefinition, consequent on applying the psychoanalytic 'fundamental rule' (to which we shall return in a moment) of facts whose mere existence any reader may check.

Of all Jane Austen readers, the one who might be assumed to have known the texts best would be the editor of the Definitive Edition. To illustrate the way facts can be ignored, here is a passage from *Sense and Sensibility* (1811) with, in bold type, a sentence removed in the second edition (1813): Mrs Jennings is telling Marianne that the letter necessitating Col. Brandon's sudden departure is from 'a very near relation':

> '...We will not say how near, for fear of shocking the young ladies.' Then lowering her voice a little, she said to Elinor, 'She is his natural daughter.'
>
> 'Indeed!'
>
> 'Oh! yes; and as like him as she can stare. I dare say the Colonel will leave her all his fortune.' **Lady Middleton's delicacy was shocked; and in order to banish so improper a subject as the mention of a natural daughter, she actually took the trouble of saying something herself about the weather.**
>
> When Sir John returned, he joined most heartily in the general regret on so unfortunate an event.. [etc.] (I.3.66)

R.W.Chapman's 1923 comment on this was: 'a sentence was deleted in the interests of propriety'; and twenty-five years later: 'In the first edition . . . Mrs Jennings does mention a natural son [sic]; but this was expunged in the second'.[38]

Psychoanalysis has one 'fundamental rule': the necessity not to hold back any idea from communication, even if one feels 'that it is too disagreeable or

---

[37] Something must dictate one's calling a particular set of data, 'results'; those who say this is itself question-begging must explain how it is that anyone finds what no-one is seeking.

[38] *S & S*, 1923 ed., p. xiv, and *Facts and Problems*, O.U.P. 1948, p. 119. The futility of this (given the allusion 4 ll. earlier) is remarkable–as, it must be said, is subsequent Oxford editors' failure, to date, to notice and correct it (in 1996 Peter Washington described Chapman's ed. as 'magisterial': Introduction, Everyman ed. of 'Sanditon and Other Stories', p. xxiii). We might also inquire why Chapman changes the child's sex.. Anyway, 'Harriet Smith was the natural daughter of somebody.' (*E* I.3.22). Perhaps someone noticed the ploy of having Lady Middleton change the subject by mentioning the weather had been used a few pp. earlier (I.12.62).

. . . judges that it is nonsensical or too unimportant or irrelevant to what is being looked for' (15.135).

Freud was early struck by the significance *latent* in patients' talk: his remark about one of them—'Nor is her conversation . . . so aimless as would appear' (3.112)—may bring a particular character to the seasoned reader's mind: the present study applies in a thoroughgoing way the principle everyone needs in order to savour all the ironies in Miss Bates' ramblings. If for example going beyond Chapman's remark that Jane Austen 'permitted herself the licence' of making Easter 'particularly late' in the year Fanny Price returns to Portsmouth (*MP* III.14. 430, ed. n. p. 554), we were to pursue the question and ask *why*, a possible answer—'Oh! that's just background: local colour'—would have one fatal drawback: it will not wash for a moment with those for whom a key feature in their experience of reading and re-reading the novels is the sudden flash of enlightenment as yet another detail one had previously thought gratuitous takes its place in the design.

The lesson to be learnt is that just like a village such as the one Miss Bates inhabits, a work of art has its own internal economy: *Hamlet* is not 'a random set of facts about Hamlet';[39] thus the brief demonstration above, concerning Jane Austen's use of the word 'unconscious', should be taken to mark a conviction that any general theory of meaning in a work of literary art must begin with study of the words actually used in that work, together with exploration of the dynamic relationships between them.

The leading characteristic of interpretation that begins 'from the results end first' should be that it draws the work together: parts of an individual work, and also works that make up the oeuvre. The facts that the reading proposed here aims to integrate, are the extremely numerous words in Jane Austen's novels which even on their own are rarely if ever quoted in the critical literature, and certainly never assembled to support any other interpretation. The coherence of an interpretation then reflects the coherence claimed for the work.

Before we leave—for the present—the question of what constitutes an interpretative act, it may be pointed out that the present study's subtitle is '*an* interpretation': the article is an indefinite one: naturally, in the last analysis interpretation can be no more than what art itself is: ineluctably historical. This book does aim to leave the reader with an enhanced sense of synthesis,[40] and a refreshed sense of what is in Jane Austen's novels should entail a clearer awareness of what is not; nevertheless the demonstrations make no claim to constituting a systematic account of the novelist's total lexical field. The reading offered may appear just as preposterous as the biographist one (intended to be corrective, it is perforce one-sided); but it may well

---

[39] Wollheim, op. cit., p. 107.

[40] Cf. 'psycho-synthesis is . . . achieved during analytic treatment' (*SE* XVII.161).

turn out to be nothing like preposterous enough. The little jolt intended to Jane Austen Studies is only a first step towards evolving an interpretative model capable of comprehending the whole text. Freud may have found that 'neither Charcot nor Bernheim offered a satisfactory explanation for the unruly facts they had discovered';[41] but he rarely made any more immodest claim than that of having elaborated a theory which fitted the facts *better* than anything then available—and more of them.[42]

If this is only *an* interpretation, the essential indefiniteness of the article bears a further sense, of which Freud himself (contrary yet again to a common misconception) was aware, and notably with regard to literature. He concludes a study of a contemporary novella thus: 'We have probably often aroused a suspicion that what we claimed was the author's meaning was in fact only our own' (14.106/7).

Projection (the mechanism in question here) is so universal a human phenomenon that Freud's answer to 'an objection concerning first principles' (*L T P* 262) is necessarily 'a measured one': it is to seek confirmation in the *context*: a key term for this study, throughout which meaning is always first tested in the context of associations within the individual novels, each of which possesses its own delicate economy, each thus setting a particular interpretative challenge.

Only later (Chapters 3 and 4) shall we begin tentatively relating this to the larger web of associations within the context of the oeuvre, the sense of which cannot emerge other than gradually, in the course of our (re-)readings: reticences in the reader's mind should be progressively dispelled by a realisation that the text itself is very far from reticent.[43]

Finally, the following facts may be borne in mind: that Jane Austen was an Englishwoman (rather than 'a Mohammedan Indian', let us say[44]); that her present-day reader belongs in certain key ways to the same *Weltanschauung* as hers; that psychoanalysis may be regarded as one of the great-grand-offspring of the Romantic movement (which had some of its constitutive roots in England); and, most important, beyond these marks of conscious collectivity,

---

[41] Rieff, op. cit., p. 8.

[42] 'Whether or not you accept the conclusions of *Totem and Taboo*, I hope you will admit that a number of very remarkable, disconnected facts are brought together in it into a consistent whole' (12.203).

[43] Freud did not ask prospective patients to bring with them conviction of the truth of psychoanalysis; far from it: 'The attitude we find the most desirable in them is a benevolent scepticism' (1.282).

[44] A neurologist told Freud: 'analyses of Mohammedan Indians which he had carried out showed that the aetiology of their neuroses was no different from what we find in our European patients' (15.88: 1914); by 1935 Freud had come to the conclusion that e.g. the so-called latency period was particular to societies which make 'the suppression of infantile sexuality a part of their system. This is not the case with the majority of primitive peoples' (15.221). As early as 1899 (4.310), he had acknowledged that the fact of historical matriarchy called for a qualification of generalisations about fathers being authority figures in the history of human civilization. It is highly ironical, then, that Freud's own disclaimers concerning the universal applicability of his theories—which played into the hands of the 'culturalist' school—have themselves been subject to demurrers, in so far as 'Oedipal triangles' are found wherever desire and law conflict in the human child.

'the content of the unconscious is in any case a collective, universal property of mankind' (13.381).[45]

- 6 -

And now a promise made earlier must be honoured: reassurance for a key subset of compulsive Jane Austen *re*-readers whose knowledge of her work is only equalled by their acquaintance with 'Jane' herself.

Actually though, being already converts to the validity of this study's main contention—that every blessed detail is important—they should in a sense be my closest allies. If Janeites, or those of Janeite tendency, can find it in them to forgive me for unearthing meaning where it had not previously even been sought, for one impertinence no dispensation need be requested of them, because I shall not be committing it.

The very title of this book will in the eyes of some convict its author of a wish, yes, to *besmirch* the venerable person there named:

> ..there are twenty-five elderly gentlemen living in the neighbourhood of London who resent any slight upon her genius as if it were an insult offered to the chastity of their Aunts.[46]

In the years since Virginia Woolf wrote this the number has grown, but the 'as if' clause (we shall return to it) is still as significant: to imagine an other-than-English Jane Austen is pointless, but one wonders whether a native of any other country could produce the reaction that the theme of this inquiry met with when mentioned to an admirer of the novelist: 'Jane Austen and *Freud*! *..The unconscious*? But..[incredulous frowning] did she *have* one, then?'

A widespread view in England is probably something to the effect that if Freud 'discovered' the unconscious, he would have done better (given what is known to be 'in' it) to have covered it up again, let well alone, let sleeping dogs lie. It happens that someone gave Freud just such a piece of advice (a few years after Virginia Woolf's warning), and his rather neat answer was this:

> ..if the instincts are causing disturbances, it is a proof that the dogs are not sleeping; and if they seem really to be sleeping, then it is not in our power to wake them. (*SE* XXIII.231)[47]

---

[45] Thus Freud in the year of his death, hoping perhaps to correct what is still, over half a century later, a misapprehension about C.G.Jung's contribution to psychological theory: e.g. 'The collective unconscious is a purely Jungian conception' (R.Thomson: *Pelican History of Psychology*, p. 259). Freud on one occasion (13.220) calls the existence of a collective mind 'the basis of my whole position'; he is found exploring what he calls endopsychic myths in his correspondence with Fliess, from 1897 (e.g. F/F 286; Jung was at that time a second-year medical undergraduate).

[46] 'Jane Austen at Sixty', *Nation and Athenaeum*, Dec. 15 1923.

[47] He here means sexual instincts. Freud was not unacquainted with the attitude of those who see sex as 'something mortifying and humiliating to human nature' (12.120); but if one may go by the following extract from a newspaper cutting there is something peculiarly English in the equation sex = nastiness: reporting on the opening of a sex-shop in a certain town, the paper asked people living nearby what they thought of the venture; one 71-year-old man's view was : 'Sex is bad enough without having it encouraged in this way'.

Naturally such an ironic rejoinder is not calculated to pacify orthodox Jane-ites, who may be heard continuing to mumble, in aggrieved undertone: *Why can't they leave (our) Jane alone?*

Let them be reassured, then: the guarantee is here issued that 'their' Jane will be left very much alone: 'mine' indeed cannot but appear somewhat unfamiliar; we have been too familiar with *her*, to the detriment of familiarity with her work.

- 7 -

The main result of showing up that work in an unfamiliar light will be to raise new questions about it. It is impossible to indicate the range and nature of these briefly—they take unexpected directions in the course of the inquiry—but something must be said here about one of them.

A question touched on above—what we need to know in order to read—suggests a related one: what an author needs to know in order to write. And this book's findings will certainly raise what may be called the Inevitable Question of what Jane Austen knew, in two senses: where (on earth) she got it from—herself? her reading? something in the *Zeitgeist*?—and how conscious she may herself have been of the effects attributed here to her work.

As far as the first of these senses goes, the novelist's place in the history of ideas will not engage us much in this inquiry. Others have charted in great detail the criss-cross footprints left in the sand of the eighteenth century's collective conscious as it leads up to Jane Austen; but earnest mappings of this kind yield scant critical interest,[48] and obstruct understanding the evocation in her work of an area where we are certainly *not* driven by 'ideas'.

Regarding the second sense of the Inevitable Question—did she know what she was doing?—it will progressively become clear that several questions are concealed here, and it is again only by painstaking separation of strands in the tangle that critical headway can be made. At each stage of the inquiry, the sorts of ways in which that Question is profitably askable—because, at that stage, at least partially answerable—are clearly indicated.[49]

Division between disciplines can be over-rigorous—the condition known as administrators' fetish—but at some point perhaps one should declare what Faculty (as it were) one is working for. Some readers may feel that both sen-

---

[48] For one (to me blindingly obvious) reason: partly a question of definition, perhaps, but I think it could be said that the novelist herself was wholly uninterested in ideas as such; almost the only one to figure in her letters is the problem of representation in (her own and others') imaginative prose.

[49] In the text; and—since we need to understand what are non-critical questions in order to see the contours of what are—the non-critical ones are sketched in occasional footnotes. Readers who conclude that Jane Austen *was* conscious of the effects described might take account of a principle familiar in art-history but perhaps rather alien still to literary consciousness: 'the effect of picture on picture as a factor in style is much more important than what comes directly from the imitation of nature' (Heinrich Wölfflin, *Principles of Art History*, Dover 1950, p. 230). Those who conclude that she was *not*, would be led to ask whether the unconscious itself can be credited with creativity; Freud's own pronouncements on this subject seem to be contradictory.

ses of the Question really belong among the concerns of a neighbouring Faculty: that of the Psychology of Creativity. Without saying dogmatically that the research carried on there is irrelevant to ours, it seems important to state clearly the view that the present inquiry supposes, which is that their (in themselves fascinating) concerns have no *necessary* relation to literary criticism (their critical relevance has in each case to be argued for, that is, not taken for granted)—any more, to anticipate what is likely to present itself as a further mode of the Question, that there is any necessary relation between the psychological structures which this study reveals to be depicted in Jane Austen's novels, and the psyche from which they sprang. If criticism that battens on biography is severely hampered by there not being enough bio to graph about, this must *a fortiori* be true with regard to psycho-biography, a perilous genre even when far more information is available about the psyche in question. Freud thought applications of psychoanalysis 'are always confirmations of it as well' (2.180/1); whether or not he was right remains to be seen, but even he might have agreed that, as so far exploited, this application of psychoanalysis is at once the least illuminating and the most facile: nothing is easier to do, with a handful of notions; nothing further from engagement with the internal coherence of a work of art.[50]

Texts, like persons, have possibilities of synthesis within, and in a sense texts like patients come to us for analysis: their sovereign individuality must not be betrayed. As analysts are obliged to wait for patients to *say* something ('If we are patient enough, the patient will. . .sooner or later..' *L & P* 7) the patient text knows something analysts do not—knows a particular version of what analysts know in a general way. Contrary again to a widespread misapprehension, Freud was against structuring an analysis according to a preconceived plan: he early insisted that 'It is not in the least our business to "understand" a case at once' (8.185), and much later—at the age of seventy— looking back over the history of psychoanalysis, he underlined that it had been 'impossible to treat a patient without learning something new' (15. 361);[51] in literary criticism, it is the text that knows, and we who learn.

*

---

50 The view that psychoanalysts are 'more interested in utilizing books for documentary purposes than in analyzing their intrinsic nature' (Harry Levin: *The Gates of Horn*, O.U.P. 1963, p. 22) has still some validity; Leon Edel, commenting earlier on a study characterised by 'a kind of "psychologising" which can have meaning only to those who have worked with these concepts at a clinical level' gave classic formulation to what remains the key question to ask about any psychoanalytically-inspired criticism: 'does this interpretation . . . tell the layman anything about the novel, as novel?' (*Literary Biography*, R.Hart-Davis 1957, pp. 70/1). The crux of divergence between the questions asked resides in the fact that art can be an object of study for other disciplines, where aesthetic merit may be irrelevant, psychology being only one of these; thus for example Q.D.Leavis' *archaeology* of Jane Austen's work, intrinsically very interesting (showing germs for all the novels to be present in the *Juvenilia*) has no critical upshot at all: despite bundling together 'origins, alterations and ultimate purpose' (*Scrutiny* x, 1941, p. 84) she never says what the novels are about.

51 One of his objections to the Swiss school was that there, in his view, 'the investigation of *individuals* was pushed into the background' (15.124).

So much for questions. As far as substantive results are concerned, the en-counter this study proposes should have the upshot of broadening ways of thinking about both oeuvres here juxtaposed; indeed part of the argument—that what appear to be two very different kinds of writer belong essentially to the same historical process—can be made by that sheer juxtaposition.

Regarding Jane Austen's, nothing less is at stake than a complete reas-sessment of the nature of her writing: of what her novels are *about*. Despite the romantic tosh which screen 'adaptations' are in the process of reducing her work to, it will be argued that the three novels treated in this volume represent three successive revolutions in the genre, indeed that it would not be too wide of the mark to call the overall tenor of her oeuvre subversive: certainly quite as subversive as Freud's.

To put it in a nutshell, both undermine belief in the coherence of the indivi-dual: in fictional terms, of the character. Character-creation (to return to where we began, with Macaulay & Co.) was for the Victorians central to literature, as it was to education; Shakespeare is still in the process of recovering from that bias. To divide our experiential field into individuals may be 'natural'—one of the facts of life, almost—but the facts of art require different criteria: as will become clear, seeing Jane Austen in terms of her characters constitutes so misleading an account of her work that it is per-haps no better justified in her case than in Shakespeare's.

Whilst Jane Austen needs no defenders, Freud is not in the same case: he wrote his last word only sixty years ago, and it is too early to say which parts of his work will be remembered—indeed still unclear at what court its status might be decided, what sort of knowledge, or of truth, it purveys. In what follows, that uncertainty of the warrant for psychoanalytic interpreta-tion will never be lost to view.[52]

Although this study should enhance Jane Austen's status in European litera-ture, giving fresh meaning to Frank Kermode's thought about the *patience* of the classic,[53] there is a final (indeed an ultimate) sense in which, although Sigmund Freud can help us to understand Jane Austen, he cannot help her, even if we wanted him to: she has been patient with us, but this patient has no more to say: her analysis is over; she is not coming back next week; since 18th July 1817, there has been no possibility of transference, and therefore no cure.

---

[52] If art, purveying not factual, practical or logical propositions but imaginative ones, is part of truth—though we must ask of what world Jane Austen's work is true—the possibility arises that the boot might pass onto the other foot; Jane Austen's contribution to analytic theory (and any upshots for that theory which this inquiry may suggest) is a matter for specialist assessment, but something of that kind does in fact arise, toward the end of the present volume.

[53] *Renaissance Essays*, Fontana 1973, p. 178.

A repertory of chapter-numbers

The three Jane Austen novels to which reference is most frequently made in this study were each originally published in three volumes, with chapter-numbers starting afresh from '1' in each new volume. Readers using editions which do not observe these divisions may find the following repertory of use in enabling them to find at least the chapter referred to, after a quotation.

Sense and Sensibility	*Pride and Prejudice*	*Mansfield Park*
Vol. I 1—22	Vol. I 1—23	Vol. I 1—18
Vol. II 1 = 23	Vol. II 1 = 24	Vol. II 1 = 19
2 = 24	2 = 25	2 = 20
3 = 25	3 = 26	3 = 21
4 = 26	4 = 27	4 = 22
5 = 27	5 = 28	5 = 23
6 = 28	6 = 29	6 = 24
7 = 29	7 = 30	7 = 25
8 = 30	8 = 31	8 = 26
9 = 31	9 = 32	9 = 27
10 = 32	10 = 33	10 = 28
11 = 33	11 = 34	11 = 29
12 = 34	12 = 35	12 = 30
13 = 35	13 = 36	13 = 31
14 = 36	14 = 37	
Vol. III 1 = 37	15 = 38	Vol. III 1 = 32
2 = 38	16 = 39	2 = 33
3 = 39	17 = 40	3 = 34
4 = 40	18 = 41	4 = 35
5 = 41	19 = 42	5 = 36
6 = 42		6 = 37
7 = 43	Vol. III 1 = 43	7 = 38
8 = 44	2 = 44	8 = 39
9 = 45	3 = 45	9 = 40
10 = 46	4 = 46	10 = 41
11 = 47	5 = 47	11 = 42
12 = 48	6 = 48	12 = 43
13 = 49	7 = 49	13 = 44
14 = 50	8 = 50	14 = 45
15 = 51	9 = 51	15 = 46
	10 = 52	16 = 47
	11 = 53	17 = 48
	12 = 54	
	13 = 55	
	14 = 56	
	15 = 57	

CHAPTER I

Part 1: Sigmund Freud and Freudianism

'Psychoanalysis has little prospect of becoming liked or popular. It is not merely that much of what it has to say offends people's feelings [but that it] involves a number of hypotheses—it is hard to say whether they should be regarded as postulates or products of our researches— which are bound to seem very strange to ordinary modes of thought and which fundamentally contradict current views.'   (*SE* XXIII.282)

- 1 -

Shortly before Freud wrote *New Introductory Lectures* (1932) he was awarded the Goethe Prize by the city of Frankfurt; shortly after, he was to be elected a Foreign Member of the Royal Society in London; and in between these two events another occurred in which he found almost equal cause for gratification: the Nazi party organised a public burning of his books in the centre of Berlin. (Progress, he felt: 'In the Middle Ages they would have burnt *me..*'.[1])

Despite these tributes in varied style to an oeuvre which had rocked the intellectual world, Freud's impression in 1932 was that just a few formulas 'have become generally familiar, among them some that we have never put forward—such as the thesis that all dreams are of a sexual nature..', but that most of psychoanalysis, including what may perhaps be regarded as its nub, the theory of dreams, '..still seems about as foreign to general awareness as it was thirty years ago' (2.36).

About ten years later (by which time Freud was dead) Ortega y Gasset noted: 'It is lamentable that psychological research of the past hundred years has not yet flowed into the general cultural stream'.[2]

At the beginning of the 'fifties, Jones published *Sigmund Freud: Life and Work*, and the *Standard Edition of the Complete Psychological Works of Sigmund Freud* began to appear. Yet in 1961 Jung wrote in his autobiography:

> the contemporary cultural consciousness has not yet absorbed into its general philosophy the idea of the unconscious and all that it means, despite the fact that modern man has been confronted with this idea for more than half a century.[3]

---

[1] Jones (1964), p. 618 (my italics).

[2] *On Love... Aspects of a Single Theme*, trans. Toby Talbot, Jonathan Cape 1964, p. 37.

[3] *Memories, Dreams, Reflections*, Fontana 1961, p. 193.

1

And three decades or so after the *New Introductory Lectures*, Paul Roazen, a political theorist, wrote about Freud because he felt that his work had 'not yet become part of the common discourse of my professional colleagues.'[4]

Some attempt must be made to explain how this has all come about.

'Freudian' explanations content themselves with pointing to what Freud wittily called 'my unpleasing discoveries' (*SE* XX.273). But the view that resistance to the outrageousness of psychoanalytic contentions is itself proof of their validity[5] clearly will not, as it stands, quite do.[6] For the non-orthodox it is maddeningly high-handed to be told yet again that, of course, 'no one wants to get to know his unconscious' (6.219); not the less maddening, 'of course', if even partly true. But if today's educated public remains uninformed about Freud and the significance of his work (the above demonstration could, one suspects, be extended into recent decades without much difficulty) the reason may lie in nothing even as interesting as resistance..

To take a different tack, one could invert Gibbon's civil way with the truth of Christianity, and say the 20th century rejected psychoanalysis, having perceived it to be false. But perhaps falsehood is not so invariably identified, and rationally discarded, as that explanation would suggest.[7]

A more profitable approach to the problem might be sought in Freud's particular form of expression. Rieff refers to a 'labyrinth of implication', to 'exquisitely complex silences', etc;[8] and of *The Interpretation of Dreams*—'the book that begins our century', by common consent his masterpiece—Freud himself, in his Preface to the 2nd edition, says it was 'very far from being an easy one to read' (4.46); in 1907 he goes so far as to call it 'an abstruse book' (14.34). He seems to have foreseen that his work would resist accurate summary, but gave merely a general explanation for that: 'A theory which is novel, which lacks simplicity and which runs contrary to our habits of thought can hardly gain in clarity from a concise presentation' (6.218).

One thing is certain: a version of his thought has gained some currency, but the result of reading anything written by him—be it ever so casually—is invariably to impress upon one the considerable difference between Freud and

---

[4] *Freud and His Followers*, Peregrine 1969, pp. 14/5.

[5] It is sometimes said that Freud would have been very cross if he had won e.g. the Nobel Prize; but we need not take too seriously his ironic asides to this effect: 'What, already gaining recognition after scarcely ten years? There must be something wrong with it..' (F/J 80); he was delighted to be awarded the Goethe Prize.

[6] Though this was for centuries a standard criterion in Western theology: from the 'I believe because it is absurd' (?Tertullian) to Luther's position that the scandalousness of Christianity proved its divine inspiration.

[7] If little genuine Freud can be found in Freudianism, the general phenomenon of which this is an instance, is not itself new: (some) Marxists sometimes say Marx has been betrayed by Marxism; even about the inerrant Christian authenticity of (some forms of) Christianity doubts have been known to be uttered. Jesus of Nazareth is not, on the best evidence, the author of the pronouncement 'God is Love' (which appears in the so-called 'First Letter of John', 4.8: a text most N.T. scholars no longer regard as authentically Johannine); nevertheless that is arguably the commonest summary of his teachings (the example is chosen for its formal similarity to the anarthrous 'Everything is Sex' often attributed to Freud.)

[8] Rieff, op. cit., pp. xii and 359.

Freud*ianism*: as Rieff grimly put it in 1978 for the third edition of his prize-winning study, 'Vulgar Freudianism has *buried* Freud'.[9]

Whatever the ultimate reasons for this may be, copious quotation from Freud's work in what follows[10] should enable the English-literary reader to see that the whole problem is closely bound up with the encounter proposed in this study. After all, it is well known that there is no sex in Jane Austen..

In the English-speaking world, however—and especially Britain, which has produced a large proportion of the Jane Austen critical literature—the sheer availability of Freud's work cannot help us toward any explanation of why it is not more read: the 24-vol. *Standard Edition* is still 'the fullest and most authoritative collection published in any language' (including German, incredibly), and to judge from the number of reprints made of the generous 15-volume Pelican selection culled out of that, it must at least be widely bought.

- 2 -

Daniel Lagache opens his Introduction to the magnificent, 489-page *The Language of Psychoanalysis* with a revealing word: 'Aversion to psychoanalysis sometimes takes the form of disparaging comments about its terminology'; those who contest the originality of Freud's achievement often express scepticism about the intellectual honesty of coining what they regard as a whole 'new' terminology: pseudo-technical jargon, it is said, invented more to impress the uninitiated than to designate a genuinely new field.

Bertrand Russell once said he thought the signal mark of Albert Einstein's genius was a 'faculty of not taking familiar things for granted';[11] Freud's contribution was likewise to say something fresh about what, in a sense, everyone already knows. A typical formula is 'There has not, in my opinion, been enough astonishment over this fact' (1.236: here the fact that we almost all forget our early childhood experience), and he continued to the end to be astonished by, and look afresh at, very varied manifestations of a single 'very remarkable psychological problem': namely, that a person's thought can be 'kept secret from his own self' (15.288). Psychoanalysis starts from a fact

..which defies all explanation or description—the fact of consciousness. Nevertheless, if anyone speaks of consciousness we know immediately and from our most personal experience what is meant by it.[12]   (15.388)

A valuable feature of 'Laplanche & Pontalis' is that it assembles definitions almost wholly by quotation from Freud; this, with frequent discussion of the

---

[9] Rieff, op. cit., p. xxiv (my italics).

[10] Whatever else applications of psychoanalysis are (apart from being confirmations, that is) they cannot help being illustrations of it; the answer to difficult problems of interpretation is invariably to be found 'locked in Freud's words' (Richard Wollheim: *Freud*, Fontana 1971, p. 240).

[11] In a BBC radio broadcast of 1955.

[12] Cf. 'We all *know* what light is; but it is not easy to *tell* what it is..' (Boswell, op. cit., II.27 [April 11, 1776]).

original terms, allows even the reader with only little German[13] to grasp how extraordinarily *un*technical Freud's language is. Unlike some of his cleverest followers, the founder of psychoanalysis wanted to be widely understood: *das Ich* is just the everyday personal pronoun 'I', but the Latin *ego* is now alien to most people's image of themselves; likewise the concept of 'anaclisis' is central to the theory of object choice, but the process of its English naturalisation must inevitably be hampered by the strangeness of the word.[14]

Given this accusation of dependence on over-technical language, it is ironic that Freud should almost equally often be excoriated for what appears to be the opposite vice: terminological or conceptual vagueness. The period during which the foundations of psychoanalysis were being laid coincided with another revolution: the one taking place in the conceptual bases of classical physics; and though Freud was uninformed about the implications of Einstein's work,[15] by the end of his life he was able warrantably to point out (15.389) that the fundamental processes 'dealt with by other sciences, by chemistry or physics for example' were scarcely more knowable than those of which psychology treats. He had earlier countered the charge of imprecision by protesting that it rested on a misconception of the history of science:

> Zoology and botany did not start from correct and adequate definitions of an animal and a plant; to this very day biology has been unable to give any certain meaning to the concept of life. Physics itself, indeed, would never have made any advance if it had had to wait until its concepts of matter, force, gravitation, and so on, had reached the desirable degree of clarity and precision. (15.242)

- 3 -

The intellectual status of Freud's thought, his case at the court of the philosophy of science, will engage us shortly; in this attempt to meet common objections made to psychoanalysis we must first give a brief airing to what Freud called 'resistances other than purely intellectual ones' (15.268). In the *Outline* he expressed a wrily-judged understatement: '..in psychology, unlike physics, we are not always concerned with things which can arouse only a cool scientific interest' (15.432); *Civilization and Its Discontents* opens pithily with: 'It is not easy to deal scientifically with feelings' (12.252).

---

[13] My own case, as it is suitable at this point to make clear.

[14] The original *anlehnen* simply means 'to lean on'. Some terms were freshly coined, usually for the good reason that the phenomena they designated had not been brought under one collective heading before: 'parapraxes', for example (*Fehlleistungen*, literally 'faulty functionings'); others–e.g. *Eros*–were deliberately chosen from a dead language so as to betoken preoccupations which go beyond the clinical. James Strachey, the *SE* translator, records that Freud did not specially like 'cathexis' (*SE* III.63, n. 2); nevertheless the *SE* received Freud's imprimatur–having himself translated five books (including, from the English, J.S.Mill) he knew what the difficulties were–and after his death Anna Freud continued to supervise the work.

[15] After meeting Einstein, Freud wrote to Ferenczi: 'He understands as much about psychology as I do about physics, so we had a very pleasant talk' (12.344 n.).

Perhaps at this stage it may be salutary to reflect that psychoanalysis is a rather paradoxical discipline: an attempt to assemble a body of knowledge about the essentially unknowable; a lucid map of the inexorably ambiguous; a reasoned view of the irrational—or what seems such.

And the least rational but also most comprehensible cause of resistance to psychoanalysis is no doubt attributable to the still very widespread ignorance and fear of mental diseases, with their peculiar status of being both less tangible than physical diseases in their effects on the person who is unwell, while at the same time drawing the energies both of that person and of those who surround him or her in a way that inescapably recalls the most frightening aspect of certain physical scourges: contagion.

We may accept one of the first axioms of psychoanalysis: that mental illnesses are not due to previous deficiences in mental synthesis, but rather disorders of the whole (and otherwise quite healthy) personality; we might even agree that 'unconscious wishful impulses [are] the core of our being' (4. 763), especially if we are allowed to go on calling them *sub*conscious impulses (more accessible, just under a little lid, as it were). But when Freud puts these together, telling us that 'our civilization is built up entirely at the expense of sexuality' (15.309); that for humankind sexuality is largely a matter of *ideas*; that our culture is characterised by an almost total 'alienation between physical and psychic sexuality' (F/F 82); that only a hair's-breadth separates the sick from the healthy; that normality is simply the successful repression of perversion; and that, in this ward, illness, for sick people, *is* their sexuality (hysteria, for example, being a sort of 'equivalent of coition' 10.102)..—when Freud tells us all this, he has made demands on our credulity which have proved fatally excessive.

The Introduction tried to reassure those apprehensive lest a distasteful 'psychobiography' be sprung on them; they will perhaps be willing now to hear that the promise made there put the cart before the horse.

Psychoanalysis is accused of 'pathologising' everything: we are told Freud said not that everything was sex but that everything was illness.[16] Russell's phrase about Einstein should again help correct a misconception: Freud refused to take the *normal* for granted; it is the normal which needs explaining, given that the normal, when you look at it closely, is.. —well, yes: *odd*.

The very title of an early book, *The Psychopathology of Everyday Life*, neatly makes the point; but in all his work he breaks down barriers between the concepts 'normal' and 'abnormal':[17] discussing a common phenomenon, he insists that 'the exclusive sexual interest felt by men for women is also a problem that needs elucidating and is not a self-evident fact' (7.57 n.).

---

[16] In *The Myth of Mental Illness*, Thomas Szasz, Secker and Warburg 1962.

[17] Cf. '..the Demonstrator . . . asked me where some nerve was and I did not know. He told me; whereupon I remonstrated, for it was in the wrong place . . . I complained of the abnormality, and he, smiling, said that in anatomy it was the normal that was uncommon' (W.S.Maugham: *The Summing-Up*, Pan 1976, p. 48).

'Pathologisation' would then really better be renamed *normal*isation' in the relativistic schema according to whose terms Freud reinterprets the whole range of our behaviour, sleeping and waking.

Concerning the former, a good deal of art produced over the last two centuries, and the unselfconscious way in which the adjectives 'mad' or 'crazy' spring to our lips when we refer to our dreams, helped Freud: by 1924 he was saying not only that dreams were a part of 'normal' mental life, 'which yet may in fact be regarded as pathological products that can regularly appear under healthy conditions' (15.177) but—even more forthrightly—that 'the close affinity of . . .psychosis to normal dreams is unmistakeable' (10.215).

As for application of his relativising project to waking life—a trickier pill to administer—the way he is seen early on in his work redrawing the map of what were thought three mutually antagonistic domains (neurotic/psychotic, perverted, and normal) may again be analysed in linguistic terms: what is felt in reading as a slight pause before certain words, accompanied by a distancing formula—in 1901 'what is called normal sexual intercourse' (5.131); in the 1905 Dora case 'the act of kissing, which is looked upon as normal' (8.86); in the *Three Essays* of the same year 'what passes as the normal constitution', 'what is known as normal sexual life' (7.86/7) and 'what are called perverts' (7.43); even to the inverted commas round the first word in the 1908 essay ' "Civilized" Sexual Morality and Modern Nervous Illness' (12. 29-55)—which subtly undermines any lingering a priori attitudes the reader might have—so that by 1920, describing how a patient became acquainted as a girl with the facts of life, he is able to produce a fine rhetorical effect: she received this knowledge, he comments, 'with mixed feelings of lasciviousness and frightened aversion, in a way which may be called normal..' (9.381).

This irony should serve to show the literary reader that Freud's whole oeuvre is what has recently been called 'deconstruction': the first formulas to this effect are somewhat timid: in 1901 he advances what hardly anyone would disagree with: 'the borderline between the normal and the abnormal in nervous matters is a fluid one . . . we are all a little neurotic..' (5.343). In 1907 he brings the more coloured word 'pathological' into his account: the frontier between normal and pathological is 'in part a conventional one and in part so fluctuating that each of us probably crosses it many times in the course of a day' (14.69). By the 'twenties, he is able to go a step further: 'neuroses and psychoses are not separated by a hard and fast line, any more than health and neurosis' (15.176); by the end of his life he was throwing off statements which forty years before would have been unacceptable: the ego of every human being, he says, 'approximates to that of the psychotic in some part or other and to a greater or lesser extent' (*SE* XXIII.235).[18]

---

[18] He liked to quote literary predecessors in the idea: 'a person who does not lose his reason under certain circumstances can have no reason to lose' (Lessing: *Emilia Galotti*, quoted 14.126).

The upshot of all this should be that if a 1912 article (on *The Resistances to Psychoanalysis*) is quoted—'it was no small thing to have the whole human race as one's patient' (15.272)—the idea may now strike the reader as less tendentious. Neurotics 'are people much like others . . . they fall ill of the same complexes against which we healthy people struggle as well'. Indeed 'the only difference..'—here is the rub—is that '..healthy people know how to overcome those complexes without any gross damage *demonstrable* in practical life' (7.188 my italics). As usual, Rieff finds the apt form of words: our world, he says, is 'made up entirely of latent and manifest patients'.[19]

- 4 -

As the plan of this half of the chapter is to deal in logical order with obstacles to granting psychoanalysis the status at the very least of an interesting interpretative tool, it would be question-begging not to mention at this point a reserve (rather than a resistance) sometimes uttered about the relation of Freud, the man himself, to this 'world'.

'Until Ernest Jones wrote his biography, the public at large had little idea of the magnitude of Freud's personal achievement'.[20] But even Jones, noting that 'few if any psychoanalyses are complete' (so it would be unreasonable to suppose Freud's *self*-analysis was) states his essentially pathographical intention early on, albeit cautiously: '*Perhaps* we shall have occasion to *suggest* how the incompleteness *may* have influenced *some* of his conclusions.'[21]

Freud established a discipline 'first of all for himself';[22] and psychoanalysis is certainly 'linked with Freud's personal development in a way in which scientific doctrines rarely are with the intimate lives of their founders'.[23]

What is never made clear by detractors is on what grounds such a peculiarity is *necessarily* prejudicial to the respectability of psychoanalytic theory.[24] As Roazen points out,[25] Freud at times voluntarily indicates the autobiographical nature of his discoveries; and readers of *The Interpretation of Dreams* cannot easily forget the page (4.179): moving, momentous even in its consequences—yet at the same time characteristically wry—on which its author announces: '..Thus it comes about that I am led to my own dreams, which offer a copious and convenient material, derived from an approximately

---

[19] Rieff, op. cit., p. x. 'No healthy person . . . can fail to make some addition that might be called perverse to the normal sexual aim' (7.74); 'sexual perversions are very widely diffused among the whole population, as every one knows except medical writers on the subject' (8.85). The criterion for *perversion* (complement to *normal*) is never a *social* consensus: e.g. homosexuality 'is not considered abnormal because it is condemned, not does it cease to be a perversion in those societies where it is very widespread and accepted' (*L & P* 308).

[20] Ibid., p. 67.

[21] Jones (1964), p. 283, my italics.

[22] Rieff, op. cit., p. x.

[23] Ibid., p. 65.

[24] Let alone to its truth; Freud's own view was that 'the fact that a theory is psychologically determined does not in the least invalidate its scientific truth' (15.45).

[25] Roazen, op. cit., p. 252.

normal person..'.[26] If doubt about the validity of Freud's thought is placed at the door of its source in his own psyche, the effectiveness of the accusation loses something of its edge when one learns Freud made no secret of it; as he wrote in 1897: 'the most important patient for me was myself' (F/F 279).[27]

But in any case, to impugn the status of a body of thought on such grounds might if applied generally turn out to establish a perilous precedent: David Pears' view is that (even) philosophical theories 'are a product *of the imagination*';[28] whether you regard the bewitching power of that faculty as good or evil is another matter: it may be that 'Ideas are not conscious inferences from experience, but orderings of experience, achieved largely unconsciously'.[29]

- 5 -

In the attempt to define the nature of Freud's thought, and of the instrument he forged single-handed to enable others to see what he had seen, the central claim of psychoanalysis—that it provides a new, unifying approach to areas of subject-matter not themselves new—perhaps makes it a branch of philosophy; not a science, but capable of becoming one.[30] Freud's own view was that his invention derived nothing but disadvantages from what he thought of as 'its *middle position between* medicine and philosophy' (15.268, my italics).

Even from the medical point of view—to which we now turn, ignorance of the facts having made assessments in this area egregiously bellicose—one could almost qualify the therapy offered by psychoanalysis as a philosophical one in a more popular sense: patients learn to become philosophical *about themselves*. We may recall a famous phrase at the end of *Studies in Hysteria*: the therapy aims merely at 'transforming your hysterical misery into common unhappiness' (3.393); Freud once wrote in a letter that a person should not strive '..to eliminate his complexes but to get into accord with them; they are legitimately what directs his conduct in the world.'[31]

A ploy such as Professor Eysenck's (who bases his assessment on only one aspect of psychoanalysis, its therapeutic interest) will therefore be seen to be lopsided. It must at all events be made quite clear that Eysenck's views on what Freud wished psychoanalysis to be remembered for do not correspond to the published statements of its founder: 'psychoanalysis was . . . first and foremost an art of interpreting' (11.288); 'In the first resort . . . an art of

---

[26] He once ventures a diagnosis: he is, he says, 'an obsessional type' (F/J 75).

[27] 'Freud made his own mind his chief laboratory' (Hanns Sachs: *Freud: Master and Friend*, Imago 1945, p. 5).

[28] David Pears: *Wittgenstein*, Fontana 1971, p. 16 (my italics).

[29] Descartes hatched the 'dream of rationalism . . . that would occupy the West for centuries' *literally* in a dream: rational intellect claimed to be creating science, but 'was not the active principle behind its development' (Whyte, op. cit., pp. 87 & 44). Freud often quoted Cromwell's dictum: 'A man never mounts so high as when he does not know where he is going' (Sachs, op. cit , p. 67).

[30] This has been suggested by e.g. Rieff, op. cit., p. 25 f.

[31] Jones (1955), p. 188.

interpretation' (15.135); 'Psychoanalysis is a method of research' (12.219), etc., etc.: examination of Freud's own terms gives a more accurate view of the question; and actually, his therapeutic claims are decidedly modest.[32]

This can hardly be overemphasised: in the *Outline* he goes so far as to put the word 'cure' in inverted commas (15.407), but much earlier than this— thirty years earlier—he had clearly stated that therapeutic success was not a primary aim: 'we endeavour rather to enable the patient to obtain a conscious grasp of his unconscious wishes' (8.278).

In 1925 he says of psychoanalysis: 'Its *original* significance was purely therapeutic' (15.264, my italics), in the sense that in early days analysts 'could do no more than discover the unconscious material that was concealed from the patient, put it together and, at the right moment, communicate it to him' (11.288). But the discipline (not unexpectedly) evolved, notably in the direction we have seen, of relativising certain concepts. It should further be remembered that a hundred years ago psychiatry was in an unashamedly rudimentary state—as Freud himself recalls with grim humour when he evokes crowds of neurotics '..whose number seemed further multiplied by the way they hurried, with their problems unsolved, from one physician to another' (15.200).

He foresaw the progress which was to come in medical treatment of simple mental disorders (the future, he thought, might well enable doctors to exercise influence by means of chemical substances on 'amounts of energy and their distribution in the mental apparatus'.) However, at that time there was as he put it 'nothing better at our disposal than the technique of psychoanalysis'; and because of this felt that 'in spite of its limitations, it should not be despised' (15.416).[33]

---

[32] Eysenck never explains why the non-therapeutic aspect of Freud's work entails the attempt 'to shunt him into the hermeneutic cul-de-sac' (op. cit., p. 10), or for that matter why hermeneutics is to be regarded as by its nature unscientific. A sizeable question is already begged by the title of his book (*Decline and Fall of the Freudian Empire*), an empire supposing obedience to an emperor; given the wide diversity of temperaments, talents and nationalities among the first analysts, perhaps it is remarkable, rather, how few left Freud's side.

Eysenck's thesis that the basis of psychoanalysis is attributable to a 'personality change' in its creator (owing to 'an addiction Freud developed to cocaine', ibid. p. 38) should perhaps go unanswered: 'When we cannot understand something, we always fall back on abuse. An excellent way of making a task lighter' (8.190).

The most striking aspect of Eysenck's approach is the unendearing contempt he betrays for his reader's intelligence, as attested by the aunt-sallies set up for easy demolition: e.g. 'Having read this book, ask yourself to whom you would go for advice if you had to deal with a head-banging child, or an enuretic one, or with a compulsive hand-washer—Shakespeare, Goethe, Proust, or the hard-nosed behaviourist who could practically guarantee to cure the disorder in a few months? To ask the question is to answer it' (ibid., p. 11). Eysenck tells us he has read hundreds of books on Freud (he quotes from only nine *by* Freud, and nothing from the metapsychological papers, the book on Jokes, *Civilization and Its Discontents*, the *Outline*, etc.); I do not recall any passage recommending recourse to these authors in therapy.

Finally, for a scientist of his reputation, Eysenck's notions of verification are occasionally plain embarrassing: on the Oedipus complex he quotes another psychologist, C.W.Valentine, who writes 'I can find no evidence whatever in the observations on my own children for . . . an Oedipus complex' (ibid., p. 97); Eysenck declares he has 'also failed to find any evidence for either the Oedipus complex or early sexual desires in my own five children.' It is hard to believe this is intended to be taken seriously (cf. Georg Brandes, who declared there was nothing to be had from dreams, and gave as proof that he had twice dreamt he was a woman.. F/F 407).

[33] 'It is worth remarking how small a modification was made necessary in Freud's hypothesis [on 'sexual chemistry'] by the discovery of the sex hormones' (7.138, ed. n.) As early as 1895 he wrote: 'I have always conceived of the processes . . . in the neuroses in general, as an intoxication' (F/F 180).

It should also be oftener made clear that he had few illusions of this situation lasting: analysis as a treatment for neurosis, he says, is 'only one of its applications; the future will perhaps show that it is not the most important one' (15.351).[34]

- 6 -

Is psychoanalysis a science? The question recalls those, similar in form, asked about other areas of human activity—e.g. *Is photography an art?*—questions which need taking to pieces before they yield anything much more interesting than aimless dogmatism and territorial jealousy.

The first observation that must be made is that psychoanalysis is a very recent phenomenon. In 1925, Freud calls it 'the *young* science' (15.232, my italics); in the year before his death he is still speaking of it as 'the *new* science' (15.390, do.). The 'perpetual incompleteness' (15.263) of science in general struck him forcibly: he emphasises that it assumes 'the *uniformity* of the explanation of the universe; but it does so only as a programme, the fulfilment of which is relegated to the future' (2.194); psychoanalytic work was only, in his view, '*gradually being accumulated into* a new scientific discipline' (15.131, my italics).[35]

Second, an area of inquiry cannot itself properly be called scientific or otherwise; the term is applied rather to methods used in approaching any field. And delineating these has turned out to be unexpectedly problematic: a standard reference work defines *philosophy of science*—somewhat hesitantly, it could be said—as 'the study of how science works, or *should work*'.[36] Modern science had hardly got going before Hume pointed out a difficulty (to say the least) in the notion of predictiveness, and dividing disciplines into scientific and non-scientific on that criterion is less straightforward than was once thought. The last words of *The Interpretation of Dreams*, as many have noticed, are 'the past': this might give a hint as to the discipline closest to

---

[34] This point of view was not an isolated one: the definition Freud gave for the 1923 *Handwörterbuch der Sexualwissenschaft* was: 'Psychoanalysis is the name (1) of a procedure for the investigation of mental processes which are almost inaccessible in any other way, (2) of a method (based upon that investigation) for the treatment of neurotic disorders' (15.131); for the 13th edition of *Encyclopaedia Britannica* (1926) he states 'the future will probably attribute far greater importance to psychoanalysis as the science of the unconscious than as a therapeutic procedure' (*SE* XX.265); at the age of eighty-one he wrote 'My work lies behind me . . . No one can predict how later epochs will assess it. I myself am not so sure..' (Jones [1964], p. 634) etc., etc.

Freud 'was extremely averse to interfering with other people or striving to influence them' (ibid., p. 70): the early history of psychoanalysis—abandonment of hypnosis, electrical treatment, etc., in favour of listening—bears this out. 'We refused most emphatically to turn a patient who puts himself in our hands in search of help into our private property, to decide his fate for him, to force our own ideals upon him' (*SE* XVII.164).

[35] James Strachey, than whom few can have known Freud's work more intimately, calls psychoanalysis the *first instrument* for the scientific examination of the human mind' (PFL, Introduction, p. 17, my italics); Whyte calls it a 'protoscience' (op. cit., p. 124); Jacques Lacan speaks of 'la science du désir' (*L'Ethique de la Psychanalyse*, Seuil 1986, p. 373) and 'un espoir de science' (*Les Quatre Concepts Fondamentaux de la Psychanalyse*, Seuil 1973, p. 23). Psychoanalysis is indeed so new that in English there still seems no absolutely standard way of writing *the word*: it is the Institute of *Psycho-Analysis* (hyphen and new capital letter for the second word), Pelican includes the hyphen in its Lacan translations but omits it in the PFL vols.; the text of Hogarth's English ed. of *L & P* keeps the hyphen but crops the second capital—and so on.

[36] A.R.Lacey: *A Dictionary of Philosophy*, R.K.P. 1986, p. 215.

psychoanalysis, which could indeed well be described as a sort of archaeology; it would be almost a good joke to say *that* discipline was predictive.

The author of one of the most interesting examinations of the philosophical
status of Freud's work concludes that the function of types of explanation in
psychoanalysis 'is not reducible to that of laws in an observational science,
though it is comparable to them in its own order'.[37] That careful formula is
similar to the one with which Bryan Magee characterises the most lasting
result that the linguistic analysis phase had on British philosophy: the recognition that 'each field of discourse has its own appropriate logic'.[38]

Organised thought obviously depends both on theory and on observation;
what is at stake is the exact nature of the interaction between the two.[39]
Karl Popper recalled trying to bring home to Viennese physics students this
interaction by starting a lecture with the injunction to ' "Take pencil and
paper; carefully observe, and write down what you have observed!" They asked, of course, *what* I wanted them to observe.'[40] Psychoanalysis was perhaps
not so very different, but one very particular temporal factor must be taken
into account: progress in knowledge requires new or improved methods;

> ..Then come the new facts thus discovered, followed by the organization
> of the old and new knowledge in a theory of them. The theory may then
> lead to speculation, a glancing and guessing at questions and answers
> beyond existing means of observation. It is extremely rare for one and the
> same man to be equally successful in all these phases. [Freud] devised
> the instrument, provided the organizing theory, and ventured on stimula-
> ting speculations beyond the actually known.[41]

The rider to this, the bulk of competent opinion might concede, is that though
the years since Freud's death have seen huge accumulations of observation,
additions of fundamental significance to psychoanalytic theory have been
scarce.[42] And this is another area in which Freud's own contributions to the
problem—of which he turns out to have been aware—show up the specious-
ness of those terribly *knowing* allusions (in a tone of pitying superiority) to
his lack of intellectual sophistication. For whilst on one occasion he refers to
'clinical facts, which have long since lost their novelty but which still await
theoretical discussion' (11.390), on another (7.332), he freely admits—with
what only resolute bad faith will deny is surely rather engaging waggishness

[37] Ricoeur, op. cit., p. 365.

[38] *Modern British Philosophy*, Paladin 1971, p. 8.

[39] Freud was unsure how they interacted in his case (see this chapter's head-quotation); already in1895 he writes: 'it is very difficult for the ego to put itself into the situation of mere "*investigation*" ' (*SE* I.374; n.b. 'difficult' may be Gibbonian irony).

[40] *Conjectures and Refutations*, R.K.P. 1978, pp. 46/7.

[41] Jones (1964), pp. 69/70.

[42] Lacan (for many *the* successor, whom breathless would-be-gallophile bandwaggonery gives almost equal status as to Freud)is on oneoccasion quite clear:'Je ne prétends pas mieux faire que de vous conduire à la lec- ture des oeuvres de Freud' (*Le Moi dans la Théorie et dans la Technique de la Psychanalyse*, Seuil 1973, p. 55).

—that he is publishing speculative theory because, having reached his seventieth year, he feels he no longer has the time to wait for clinical support..

The important point is that he almost invariably *declares* the sort of status he wishes attributed to a given idea: in 1925 for example he announces a recapitulation of his extraordinary 'primal horde' theory by calling it 'the following hypothesis, or, I would rather say, vision..' (15.252);[43] and other expressions could be quoted to bear out his lifelong conformance to the letter of a remark made in 1908: 'I have never put forward inconclusive opinions as though they were established facts' (4.47).

That Freud had a 'nervous craving to remain in the realms of science'[44] is not in doubt; but if we are surprised to find Jones admitting that 'to be tied down to exactitude and precise measurement was not in his nature',[45] it should be made quite clear that Freud himself doubted whether he had 'the scientific mind': as he wrote to Jung in 1911,

> I can see from the difficulties I encounter in this work [*Totem and Taboo*] that I was not cut out for inductive investigation, that my whole make-up is intuitive, and that in setting out to establish the purely empirical science of $\psi\alpha$ I subjected myself to an extraordinary discipline.[46]

Naturally he knew that 'knowledge derived from revelation, intuition or divination' should not be regarded as scientific (2.194); he nevertheless held intuition in high esteem, referring on one occasion to 'the interpretative *art* of psychoanalysis', in which the analyst must 'catch the drift of the patient's unconscious with his own unconscious' (15.136); elsewhere he gives this capacity far wider application: *everyone*, he says,

> ..possesses in his own unconscious an instrument with which he can interpret the utterances of the unconscious in other people.   (10.137/8)[47]

This is an extremely significant statement, and will have a number of important results for the present inquiry.

Overdependence on intuition naturally makes for credulity[48] (Freud long remained under the spell of numerological theories concocted by his early friend Fliess); and credulity rarely goes with carefulness. The evidence is that he wrote very fast, and to be such a prolific letter-writer argues great verbal

---

[43] He approved R.R.Marett's description of it as 'a Just-So story' (12.154).

[44] Peter Lomas: *The Limits of Interpretation*, Pelican 1987, p. 5.

[45] Jones (1964), p. 62.

[46] F/J 251 (the two Greek letters are his shorthand for 'psychoanalysis'.) He made a startling late avowal – 'If I had my life to live over again, I should devote myself to psychical research rather than to psychoanalysis' – to which perhaps too much seriousness has been attributed (Jones [1955], p. 392).

[47] He elsewhere calls this phenomenon strange, but 'descriptively speaking, the fact is incontestable' (11.198).

[48] W.H.Auden, though an enthusiast, wrote of Freud 'often he was wrong and, at times, absurd' ('In Memory of Sigmund Freud', *Collected Shorter Poems*, Faber and Faber 1966, p. 168). Among more far-fetched speculations are a link between the latency period and the glacial epoch (15.384), and the enthralling idea (9.291) that the Wolfman's predilection for intercourse *more ferarum* may have been hereditary.

facility, especially in someone so much of whose time was occupied with patients.[49] However, even his severest critics would probably agree that he never wrote a *dull* book: for half a century his head was bursting with new ideas, and he had not always time to think them through before putting them down on paper:

> ..These interrelations are so complicated and at the same time so important that, at the risk of repeating myself, I shall approach them from yet another angle.. (12.320)

There is a breathless feel to passages like this: one senses Freud putting down what he knows, again and again in different combinations to see what it looks like, worrying at an idea as one worries at a recalcitrant knot, pulling out now this strand, now that. In other words, on such occasions we hear Freud thinking aloud; and perhaps this is in the end an endearing trait in a writer only if you have been already half-won-over to the interest of listening in on the workings of an original mind.

However that may be, if a body of thought is judged according to the number of new doors it opens, then the claim that there were certain questions which he regarded it 'as greatly to the credit of psychoanalysis that it should even have reached the stage of *raising*' (9.336/7) surely entitles him to the lightest compliment we can pay his work: that of our open-minded attention, even in areas where a previous generation dismissed him as absurd.

- 7 -

It may already be clear, from this attempt to answer objections often raised in literary circles that a salient feature of Freud's work is the light it sheds on the understanding of language and meaning.[50]

However, even if we go to the other end, as it were, of Freud's oeuvre—to his anthropological writings—we find the same situation as the one outlined so far: indications that his intellectual sophistication may have been underestimated. The wording in the last passage quoted from Freud ten lines up is strikingly similar to the concluding formula in a passage from a contemporary anthropologist's excursus on one of his discipline's most vexed questions: the incest problem. Freud's theory on this was ridiculed by many, but Robin Fox considers this ridicule misjudged, pointing out that in this area Freud

---

[49] Up to ten hours a day at some periods; it may just be noted that for parts of his professional life he was supporting about a dozen people.

[50] That Wittgenstein took Freud seriously is unsurprising then: he told Rush Rhees that Freud was 'someone who had something to say' (*Lectures and Conversations on Aesthetics, Psychology and Religious Belief*, Blackwell 1966, p. 41). This may be put in the perspective of Wittgenstein's rather delicate reading-palate: Theodore Redpath once told me Wittgenstein had told him (in the late 'thirties) 'I no longer need *Faust*.' Ricoeur (op. cit., p. 351) notes the remarkable fact that it should be British philosophers who have recognized the special character of psychoanalytic language.

..was stressing what most anthropologists have stressed—that we had to become non-incestuous to become human. What he is saying is that the business of becoming so may have been painful, bloody and traumatic, and have left its mark . . . although we might be dubious about the theory, it has the merit of stating the mechanisms involved . . . I would not be as prepared as most of my colleagues to ridicule Freud. He was probably wrong about the details, but he asked the right questions.[51]

If, taking a longer perspective than today's modish tiltings at Freud, such an assessment were to prove just, we might find ourselves obliged to adopt a less condescending attitude to those 'stimulating speculations beyond the actually known'.

At all events, the accusation sometimes levelled at psychoanalysis—that it claims to explain everything—will, again, hardly correspond to the experience of anyone who has actually read anything by Freud.

Perhaps indeed he foresaw what exorbitant requirements would be made of his invention: in a 1915 letter he writes: 'too heavy a burden is laid on analysis when one asks of it that it should be able to realize every precious ideal'.[52]

Throughout his work he states explicitly and often that there are 'narrow limits to what a psychoanalysis is called upon to explain' (9.346), constantly referring to 'mysteries' and 'obscurities': we hear of 'the mystery of homosexuality' (9.398) and 'mysterious masochistic trends of the ego' (11.283); 'the theory of bisexuality is still surrounded by many obscurities' (12.295 n.) and there is 'the chaos of the obscurer processes of the mind' (9.214); duality of the sexes is 'an ultimate fact for our knowledge' (15.422); he declares that 'the whole nature of sexual excitation is completely unknown to us' (7.125). If in an early book he avers 'our knowledge of unconscious processes has scarcely begun' (6.236), the changes on epistemological dead-ends ring through the introductory paragraph of his last work, too: having isolated two poles—the 'scene of action' (viz., the brain) where mental life is played out, and 'acts of consciousness' that 'cannot be further explained by any sort of description'— he declares 'Everything that lies between is unknown to us', and our hypotheses start out 'from these ends or beginnings of our knowledge'; the oldest psychical province, 'the obscure id' (15.433) contains the instincts, 'which originate from the somatic organization and . . . find a first psychical expression here in forms unknown to us' (15.376), etc., etc.

---

[51] Robin Fox: *Kinship and Marriage*, Pelican 1984, p. 61. Ironically, the demolition-job which e.g. *Totem and Taboo* suffered at the hands of the first generation of structural anthropologists, lends symbolic support to its principal contention: the sons continue to kill the fathers..

[52] Jones (1964), p. 433. 'In no other field of scientific work would it be necessary to boast of such modest intentions. . . No reader of an account of astronomy will feel disappointed and contemptuous of the science if he is shown the frontiers at which our knowledge of the universe melts into haziness' (2.34)

Freud's statement that 'the sexual life of adult women is a "dark continent" for psychology' (15.313) has become famous; less well-known—and this too may come as a surprise to those content to live on a fibre diet of received ideas about psychoanalysis—is Freud's demurrer, in the middle of his essay on Leonardo: 'Pathography does not in the least aim at making the great man's achievement's *intelligible..*' (14.223, my italics).

- 8 -

Given the tenor of the last two quotations, readers might be excused for feeling that if Freud himself placed such *a priori* restrictions on the possibility of psychoanalysis elucidating two lines of inquiry—art, and female psychology, at the intersection of which Jane Austen, artist and woman, had her being— mere common sense might tell us that the encounter announced in the Preface could hardly be fruitful.

In the present climate of opinion, to underestimate the difficulties of canvassing such a project would be rash: Freud is branded misogynist so often, and so matter-of-factly, that anyone seeking to explain or defend risks facing the charge of being shifty or paradoxical. And his writings on aesthetics have been subjected to contempt only second to his anthropological theories. But some attempt must be made, and I'll begin with the women.

Freud's theories about female psychology were (for obvious reasons) speculative; and, to his credit, he almost invariably said so: for example, the 33rd of his *New Introductory Lectures* opens with the words:

> LADIES AND GENTLEMEN, —All the while I am preparing to talk to you I am struggling with an internal difficulty. I feel uncertain, so to speak, of the extent of my licence..   (2.145)

and ends with what, in the light of this study's general contention about Jane Austen, opens an inviting perspective:

> If you want to know more about femininity, inquire from your own experiences of life, or turn to the poets..   (2.169)

Accounts based on superficial acquaintance with Freud's writings sometimes give the impression that it was only with this work (1932) that he began to take women seriously as subjects. However over thirty years before, in one of his very first books, we find what again for our present purposes is a highly interesting suggestion: a brief tribute—and paid, one may venture to point out, in the same uncondescending tone—to 'women, with their subtler understanding of unconscious mental processes' (5.208 n.).

His Johnsonian comment on women's inferior intelligence—'The fact itself is disputable and its interpretation doubtful' (12.231)—is sometimes quoted as a late (sc. too late) recognition: it was written in 1927. But at least as early as 1913 Freud had come to the conclusion—a very radical conclusion, for its

15

time, one suspects—that '..strictly speaking, the differences between the sexes can lay claim to no special psychical characterization' (15.48).

Now: it is easy enough to spot self-contradictions in Freud, and not unnaturally, instances of this are to be found in his remarks on female psychology: for example, at one point in ' "*Civilized*" Sexual Morality. . .' he refers to a woman who, 'being a woman, possesses a weaker sexual instinct [sc. than a man]' (12.43); yet observations only six pages later, about the difficulty society has in its task of channelling the female sex-drive into monogamy, seem to be made on the contrary assumption.

Most if not all men's attitudes to women are ambivalent (though whether more so than women's to men might be tricky to ascertain); most men however do not write essays about women and sexual matters, their muddles being left to be experienced by others in conversation and behaviour. If we return to Russell's characterisation of Einstein's genius (p. 3), and to the modification suggested thereof as applied to Freud (it is the normal which we take for granted), would it not be at least as hard today to be sure we know what behaviour, attitudes etc. might, in a woman, be 'normal'?—let alone to disentangle the assumptions that cluster round that word from those, still more problematic, attached to the word 'natural' ?

Feminist thought has seen that a first step needed in understanding what women are and can be is to be sought in analysing how they have been represented. Freud's writing unquestionably played an important rôle in initiating that search; in this area too his thinking was more sophisticated, less crass, than it is commonly represented as being.

For example, in *Group Psychology..* he certainly comes near declaring that a woman's deepest desire is to be mastered; but it might be more often noted that he sets this in the context of a people's desire to be ruled: a perspective which may at the very least give pause for thought.

In classical psychoanalytic theory 'active' and 'passive' are forms of particular drives, not characteristics of men and women, respectively; when Freud pursues a 'secret kinship' which seemed to exist between masculinity and sadism on the one hand, and femininity and masochism on the other, he concludes by admitting that, in spite of the interest of the subject, 'I must add that we have made no progress along that path' (2.137). His interest in contrasting effects of nature and nurture in women may be seen from the way the word 'conventional' returns (italicised here) in texts from 1905, 1920 and 1932: phenomena of sexual overvaluation can be best studied in men, because their erotic life alone has become accessible to research;

> That of women—partly owing to the stunting effect of civilized conditions and partly owing to their *conventional* secretiveness and insincerity—is still veiled in an impenetrable obscurity.   (7.63)

When he describes the subject of his 1920 Case by saying that she had her father's tall figure—

> ..her facial features were sharp rather than soft and girlish, traits which might be regarded as indicating a physical masculinity. Some of her intellectual attributes also could be connected with masculinity: for instance, her acuteness of comprehension and her lucid objectivity..

etc., etc.—feminist hackles may almost be *heard* rising through this description, till Freud quietly adds '..But these distinctions are *conventional* rather than scientific' (9.379). By 1932 he comes to the pioneering conclusion that 'There is only one libido', to which 'we cannot assign any sex'; then

> ..if following the *conventional* equation of activity and masculinity, we are inclined to describe it as masculine, we must not forget that it also covers trends with a passive aim. (2.165/6)

He then acknowledges that he does not claim more than average validity for these assertions; 'nor is it always easy to distinguish what should be ascribed to the influence of the sexual function and what to social breeding.'[53]

Mention has been made of the ironic effect inverted commas round a word in a title can produce: the word in question, it may be remembered, was 'civilized' (closely related, for Freud, to 'conventional'); indeed, that this too was one he very often uses, and that it appears again in the title of one of his profoundest essays (*Civilization and Its Discontents*, 1930) is not surprising, given that the overall direction of his thinking over fifty years was from the repressed, at the beginning of his inquiry, towards the forces of repression, at its end. Within that general movement of thought, if the fact is repeatedly underscored that, as he puts it in 1929, 'woman finds herself forced into the background by the claims of civilization' (12.293), this is because, as he had thirty years before shown himself aware, 'the undoubted intellectual inferiority of so many women can rather be traced back to the inhibition of thought necessitated by sexual suppression' (12.51).

Whether or not we endorse the general thesis—a person's sexual behaviour *'lays down the pattern* for all his other modes of reacting to life' (12.50)—of which the particular cultural thesis about discouraging girls' sexual curiosity is only one instance (though arguably a subtle and far-reaching one), it will be seen that delving into the origins of adult women's problems again attests to Freud's habit of asking the right questions.

This section has aimed to show that the context in which his remarks about female psychology appear, is never irrelevant; to quote them out of context is like quoting a Dr Johnson retort (' "The woman's a whore, and there's an end

---

[53] Freud is here in 'a no-win situation': until 1924 (7.314) broadly assuming symmetry, he had not separated treatment of the two sexes–which is more 'sexist', assuming symmetry or assuming difference?

on't" '[54] is no doubt the apt case) without indicating that as it happens John-son's view of the matter is not dissimilar to Freud's:

> ..I do not deny, Sir, but that there is some original difference in minds; but it is nothing in comparison of what is formed by education . . . Where nothing has been put into the brain, nothing can come out of it . . . Our manner of teaching cramps and warps many a mind which if left more at liberty would have been respectable in some way . . . You teach your daughters the diameters of the planets, and wonder when you have done that they do not delight in your company! [etc.][55]

The last of these quotations may have reminded the reader of the Miss Bert-rams of Mansfield Park (Jane Austen stands half way between Johnson and Freud, in more than one sense). If so, they will not have failed in their effect, for this study aims to show that Jane Austen's vision of women is as essen-tially demythologising as Freud's: indeed, we could apply to Jane Austen what Rieff writes of Freud: he 'taught us in an unique and subtle way how to grow unsentimental about ourselves'.[56]

And this is particularly true of Freud's view of women: can 'liberating wo-men (as he did children) from sentimentality and prudery'[57] be regarded, in the last analysis, as a fundamentally misogynistic act?

A final point (since with this section on Freud and Woman we are nearing the end of this chapter's first half) is that *our picture* of Freud, too, has be-come a mythical one. This returns us to the question with which we started— why Freudianism has buried Freud—and to a possible answer: unsubtle Freudianism is very easy to knock down; if Freud has gained the reputation of being a misogynist, this may be because, thus branded, he is made to play a useful mythical rôle. Demythologising 'Jane' might have the effect of bringing the two a little closer together.

- 9 -

In approaching now the last area in Freud's thought to be considered in this chapter as having provoked unconsidered objections, readers are reminded that the task of nuancing by constant recourse to his writings the 'common-sense' reluctance to believe they can possibly illuminate Jane Austen's work, will occupy us throughout the inquiry. This chapter aims to do no more than prepare the ground for the specific interpretative challenge presented by each of the novels. The following excursus should be taken in that perspective.

---

[54] Boswell, op. cit., I.477.

[55] Respectively: ibid. I.611; *Johnsoniana*, vol X of J.Croker's 1848 ed. of Boswell's *Life*, p. 10; Hesther Piozzi: *Anecdotes of Samuel Johnson*, O.U.P. 1974, p. 133; and ibid., p. 67.

[56] Rieff, op. cit., p. xiii.

[57] Ibid., p. 182.

The view that Freud made any substantive contribution to the understanding of art has been the subject of severe reserves by otherwise sympathetic commentators. 'In spite of his reverence for art', writes Peter Lomas, 'Freud, like Plato, believed the imagination to be inferior to intellect.'[58] Freud's order of *the highest goods of humanity*: 'research, art, love, ethical and social sense' (15.151) might justify that view, as would his confession in *The Moses of Michelangelo* that he must always *understand* the effect that a work of art has on him: 'Whenever I cannot do this, as for instance with music, I am almost incapable of obtaining any pleasure' (14.253).[59] This led Trilling to question Freud's capacity to respond fully even to literature (the art-form in which he was no doubt most at home); Rieff declares 'For the work of art as such, Freud cared very little';[60] and even Wollheim—whom pro-Freudian zeal inspires to devote nearly two pages in *Art and Its Objects* to an explanation of the dream-theory—whilst acknowledging the importance that Freud (and Wittgenstein) have for him, concludes '..though their writings specifically on aesthetics are, judged by the high standards that they themselves impose, disappointing'.[61]

On a rare occasion when Freud allows himself to look upon psychoanalysis with a certain complacency, he goes the whole hog and trumpets 'the profundity of its hypotheses and the comprehensiveness of its connections' (1.437).

Germane at present will be the second part of that assessment, for this study, undaunted by the negative reactions just quoted, aims to apply Freud's thought to an elucidation of Jane Austen's novels by following up a hint of Trilling's to the effect that the parts of Freud's work most applicable to aesthetics are perhaps to be sought elsewhere than in the essays he devoted specifically to it.[62] That perspective will engage us in a moment; but three general observations must first be made about Freud on art.

First, Freud and his aesthetically-minded critics do not share the same kind of interest in art: he is concerned with causes, they with results. Revealingly, he thinks 'the two problems which probably interest [non-specialists] most' are: 'the nature of the artistic gift [and] the means by which the artist works —artistic technique' (15.249), and says he can throw no light on these. To the view that psychoanalysis has been unable to provide 'a satisfactory theory of aesthetic value; but then neither has any other approach. It contributes rather to an understanding of the creative process, both before and in

---

[58] Lomas, op. cit., p. 42.

[59] Of *The Magic Flute* he writes: '..the whole thing rather drags, without any really individual melodies' (Jones [1964], p. 169).

[60] Rieff, op. cit., p. 121.

[61] Wollheim, op. cit. (1975), p. 171.

[62] *The Liberal Imagination*, Mercury 1961, p. 42. 'There is an intimate connection between all mental happenings . . . which guarantees that a psychological discovery even in a remote field will be of an unpredictable value in other fields' (6.46); so 'Find out all about dreams and you will have found out all about insanity' (4.723n).

language'[63] it should be added that as far as Freud is concerned psychoanalysis makes no *attempt* to provide any such theory.

For this reason, the next observation about Freud on art is that he would probably have agreed with the negative assessments so far quoted: here again (though one might ask in passing who else of comparable scientific attainments has made such varied ventures into the field of aesthetics) the view that he thought he had solved all its problems is simply unsupported by the evidence.

Five examples: he interrupts an excursus on story-telling to exclaim: 'All this is nothing new, and has doubtless long been fully taken into account by students of aesthetics' (14.375); he acknowledges almost all the ideas in his Dostoevsky essay come from a book he has just read (14.460); he writes to Jones in English about *The Moses.* . . : 'It is a fun and perhaps no bad one';[64] two pages before the end of the *Leonardo* essay: 'I am far from over-estimating the certainty of these results' (14.228; in a letter he suggests it was merely 'a private amusement'[65]); and finally, quite aware that Nietzsche's ideas anticipated his own, he says he forgoes all claims to priority in instances '..in which laborious psychoanalytic investigation can merely confirm the truths which the philosopher recognized by intuition' (15.73).

Third general observation: any interest that Freud on art may possess is complicated by another factor: his own aesthetic gifts, and his (conscious and unconscious) attitudes to these.

'Somewhere inside me there is a feeling for form' he writes to Fliess (Sept. 1899, F/F 373), and though he invariably refers to 'the artist' in the third person (e.g. *'We laymen* have always been curious to know . . . from what sources that strange being, the creative writer, draws his material..' 14.131, my italics), when he avers that 'it still strikes me as . . . strange that the case-histories I write should read like short stories' (3.231) there is perhaps some disingenuousness. His oeuvre includes a wide diversity of forms of writing, and in the instance of the case-histories—each of which is indeed 'as good as a novel'—he may almost be said to have invented a new genre. A convincing argument has been made out for regarding *Dora* (1905) as a minor 'modernist' masterpiece,[66] and as it has been remarked that Freud was Freud's most interesting patient, he was arguably also the most creative person he knew—quite possibly without knowing that.

From the present chapter's ranging over the whole of Freud's oeuvre, readers should have gathered how quotable he is; one might say of his lucid prose what Maugham says of Hume: '..if you have no philosophical training its

[63] Elizabeth Wright: *Psychoanalytic Criticism*, Methuen 1984, p. 5.

[64] Quoted by R.W.Clark in *Freud: The Man and the Cause*, Jonathan Cape 1980, p. 359.

[65] Ibid., p. 345.

[66] Steven Marcus: 'Freud and Dora', in *In Dora's Case*, Virago 1985. The subtitle on the first draft of Freud's *Moses...* is 'a historical novel' (Jones [1957], p. 206).

implications will doubtless escape you; but no one with any education at all can fail to understand exactly what the meaning of each sentence is.'[67] For those who differ on a particular point Freud's work possesses the signal (and rare) advantage that everyone knows what it is they disagree about.

Is it plausible to suppose someone, himself possessed of such varied literary gifts, insensitive to the particular character of aesthetic effect? Anthony Storr's view is that use of phantasy for a better understanding of reality 'is alien to Freud; and so is the notion that the achievement of aesthetic form might serve a similar function'.[68] But this assertion appears to be incompatible with a passage where, discussing 'expressive intensification' in dreams, he writes that art historians have drawn our attention to the fact that

..the earliest historical sculptures obey a similar principle: they express the rank of the persons represented by their size. A king is represented twice or three times as large as his attendants or as his defeated enemies. (4.754)[69]

This leads us back to the question as to *where*, in his writings, the interest of Freud on art is to be sought. And the answer is: *everywhere*.

The whole of Freud's oeuvre is about representation, language and meaning; that conviction is the dynamic for all the present study's demonstrations.

Psychoanalysis came into being through his first refusal to take something for granted: namely, the theory current in the 1880s that the minds of those suffering from various illnesses (e.g. hysteria) were structurally different from those of the so-called 'healthy';[70] indeed the psychoanalytic revolution might almost be defined in terms of the way Freud took Pierre Janet's insight that hysteria was 'a malady through representation',[71] transforming it into a way of seeing which proved to be of far wider application. The popular sense of 'hysterical' includes even today some notion of theatricality, and Freud's conclusion that 'If hysterical subjects trace back their symptoms to traumas

---

[67] Maugham, op. cit., p. 24. There are haunting brief images—e.g. the 'lost provinces of . . . mental life' (15. 406)—and striking longer figures: e.g., speaking of concealing from children the part sexuality and aggression are to play in their lives, '..sending the young out into life with such a false psychological orientation, education is behaving as though one were to equip people starting out on a Polar expedition with summer clothing and maps of the Italian lakes..' (12.327 n.).

[68] *The Dynamics of Creation*, Penguin 1976, p. 179. Psychoanalysis is often characterised as 'content-bound' (Ernst Kris: *Psychoanalytic Explorations in Art*, Schocken 1971, p. 105); one of the present study's aims is to show that this characterisation is by no means a necessary outcome of applying Freud's insights.

[69] Freud's critics have perhaps been over-willing to take him at his word when (14.253) he avers a relative lack of sensitivity to fine art other than sculpture; of representations being superimposed in the phenomenon of *condensation*, he writes: 'One might arrive at similar representations in a drawing, if one tried to illustrate the way in which a general concept is formed from a number of individual perceptual images' (4.437). I do not recall seeing it remarked that this could be described as the nub of cubism.

[70] As late as 1902 we find William James opining that 'most psychopaths have feeble intellects' (*The Varieties of Religious Experience*, Fontana 1974, p. 43).

[71] Pierre Janet: *L'Etat Mental des Hystériques*, Paris 1894, quoted *L & P* 195.

that are fictitious', then 'the new fact which emerges is precisely that they create such scenes in *fantasy*' (15.75), is an entirely typical example of the aesthetic terminology required by the nature of the subject. It can hardly but interest readers of *Mansfield Park* that one of the earliest psychoanalytic patients referred to her day-dreaming as her 'private theatre' (3.74).

The importance of language in this overall metaphor cannot be over-emphasised: another early patient referred to therapy as 'the talking cure' (3.83, in English); ever since then, the psychoanalytic session has consisted essentially in 'a *linguistic relation*' (*L & P* 179).

It may well be that Freud's most seminal insight is to the effect that everything human must mean something, thus attributing to apparent nonsense a new sort of serious sense: cf. 'my whole purpose is to collect everyday material and turn it to scientific use' (5.211).

His point of departure was that dreams, for example, *could not* be 'senseless'; he moved on to the thesis that 'a neurosis never says foolish things, any more than a dream' (8.190); and from there, given his relativising programme, it was but a step to 'the constant meaningfulness of everyday life':[72] we are all incurable symbolists, constantly figuring forth unconscious preoccupations in our behaviour, linguistic and gestural, because symbolism is not particular to dreams, but is characteristic of all unconscious ideation and 'is to be found in folklore and in popular myths, legends, linguistic idioms, proverbial wisdom and current jokes' (4.467).[73]

As a bridge to the second part of the chapter, a concrete example of this perpetual meaningfulness: the following passage recounts what 'A friend who has learnt to read signs' told Freud about a tiny but telling bit of 'business' introduced by the actress Eleonora Duse into a part she was playing:

> ..It is a drama of adultery; she has just had an altercation with her husband and now stands apart deep in thought, before the seducer approaches. During the short interval she plays with her wedding ring, takes it off her finger, puts it on again, and then once more takes it off. She is now ready for the other man.

Freud compares this with a similarly revealing passage in a novel by Theodor Fontane; and then comments that the ring '..leaves one once again with the impression of how hard it is for a psychoanalyst to discover anything new that has not been known before by some creative writer' (5.261).

On that note, we turn to Jane Austen.

---

[72] Rieff, op. cit., p. 118.

[73] Freud is here on the brink of the semiotic thesis: as early as Dec. 6 1896 he outlined a rudimentary model of the psyche in which there are layers of registration of signs (*Niederschriften*, F/F 207); Lacan ([1973], p. 46) says this pre-empts the whole of modern linguistics (and incidentally until a quite recent edition the O.E.D. defined *semiology* as 'a branch of pathology concerning symptoms'.)

Part 2: Jane Austen and Janeism

Jane Austen, it may reasonably be supposed, had read none of the works of Freud.[1] If she had come across the passage just quoted from *The Psycho-pathology of Everyday Life*, she might have retorted that the figure of the ring was not wholly new: a similar piece of behaviour occurs in Richardson's *Sir Charles Grandison*,[2] published a century and a half before Freud's book:

> Miss Grandison played with her diamond ring; sometimes pulling it off, and putting it on; sometimes putting the tip of her finger in it as it lay on the table, and turning it round and round, swifter or slower.[3]

Had she gone on reading in the Freud, she might have been amused by the description of a patient who returns to the doctor's room, giving as a reason

> ..that she wants to collect the umbrella she has left behind there; but the doctor sees that she is in fact holding it in her hand.   (5.332)

since almost exactly a century before, she had herself included an almost identical idea in a story: Lord Osborne

> ..came back after the others were out of the room, to 'beg her pardon', & look in the window seat behind her for the gloves which were visibly com-pressed in his hand.   (*MW* 336)

Moreover that episode clearly contains an early idea for the better-known moment in *Persuasion* (II.10.236) when Wentworth

> ..begged their pardon, but he had forgotten his gloves, . . . crossing the room to the writing table . . . he drew out a letter from under the scatter-ed paper, placed it before Anne with eyes of glowing entreaty fixed on her for a moment, and hastily collecting his gloves was again out of the room.

Among the questions that this little demonstration raises in the reader's mind,[4] the most pressing will very likely be whether, and in what sense, Jane Austen knew what she was doing: a question which, as was forecast, will periodically force its unwelcome attentions on us. However, it is not our present concern, which in this second part of the chapter will rather be how far her readers know what *they* are doing.

---

[1] Attempts to discover whether Freud had read any Jane Austen have been unfruitful; at time of writing no inventory seems available even of the books he brought with him to London.

[2] Her favourite novel, it appears (J.E.Austen-Leigh, *Memoir* 1871, ed. cit., p. 331.)

[3] *Sir Charles Grandison*, 1754, letter XLI.

[4] Just as Jane Austen's use of the word 'unconscious' might have provoked some reaction in the 20th century, so it may be noted that this is the first time (to my knowledge) these two passages, from 'The Watsons' and *P*, have been brought together in print—let alone related to a body of theory which might be capable of attributing some meaning to such juxtaposition.

Since this study may be classified among the sort that Freud refers to as 'applying depth-psychology to a better understanding of the characters in [a] book or of their actions' (2.170), and since in this part of the chapter points made in part 1 will be echoed (with reference, now, to Jane Austen), a formula used above (p. 2) will serve again—for faced with the almost total absence of psychoanalysis from Jane Austen Studies, here too some attempt must be made to understand how this has come about.

It must surely seem surprising, given the fact that—and spelling out now what may be obvious to some readers—Freud's main concern seems so close to that of the creative writer, of whom he declared that the description of the human mind is the domain

> ..which is most his own; he has from time immemorial been the precursor of science, and so too of scientific psychology. (14.68)

Might not Jane Austen admirers be supposed to welcome any fresh proof of her genius? For is not a key factor in explaining why these novels are so re-readable the psychological finesse they proverbially deploy?[5] If she may be numbered among those whom Freud calls 'the deepest observers of the human mind' (14.35), is it likely that her work takes no account of 'the fact that mental life is the arena and battle-ground for mutually opposing purposes' (1.105)? Is it plausible, just as a first example, that 'there is never any question of self-contradiction in [Fanny Price's] character'[6] ?

Some critics have shown awareness of what we may for the moment call a 'symbolic' dimension: C.C.Barfoot refers to Mary Crawford's glance past Fanny to Edmund (*MP* I.15.143) as 'spacial [*sic*] symbolism';[7] of Fanny and Mary on Edmund's arm at Sotherton, Juliet McMaster comments 'There is . . . an emblematic quality in this threesome';[8] and Tanner alludes to the (*locus*

---

[5] One exception to this judgment is known to me: 'Jane Austen goes relatively deep morally, but scarcely skims the surface psychologically' (Wayne C. Booth: *The Rhetoric of Fiction*, Chicago 1961, p. 163).

[6] Andrew Wright: *Jane Austen's Novels*, Penguin 1962, p. 129.

Readers interested in the–itself non-critical–question of one direction not taken, or taken inappropriately, in Jane Austen Studies, are referred to the Appendix (pp. 213-5) where the little commentary inspired by Freud's thought is reviewed. A brief linguistic point may however be made here, to indicate the level of critics' familiarity with psychoanalytic concepts: a tiny significant detail, the occasional recourse by Jane Austen specialists to the word '*subconscious*' (abandoned by Freud as misleading by the late 1890s, and outside professional anglo-saxon psychoanalysis for at least half a century) sometimes muddled up with the standard term: Juliet McMaster writes of Emma's 'subconscious love' but of Edmund's 'unconscious courtship' ('Jane Austen on Love', University of Victoria English Literary Monograph No.13, 1978, pp. 58 & 36); similarly David Lodge declares the writer pursues the reality of individual experience deeper and deeper into the subconscious or unconscious' ('The Novelist at The Crossroads', in *The Novel Today*, ed. Malcolm Bradbury, Fontana 1977, p. 86); in neither case is any explanation proffered for the duality.

Freud's view was this: 'If someone talks of subconsciousness, I cannot tell whether he means the term topographically–to indicate something lying in the mind below consciousness–or qualitatively–to indicate another consciousness, a subterranean one. . . *He* is probably not clear about any of it. The only trustworthy antithesis is between conscious and unconscious' (15.298, my italics; see also *L & P* 430/1).

[7] *The Thread of Connection; Aspects of Fate in the Novels of Jane Austen and Others*, Rodopi 1982, p. 47.

[8] McMaster, op. cit., p. 35.

classicus) wilderness, of which 'the gate—perfect image for the rigid restrictions imposed by the conventions of civilized life—is locked'.[9]

Most such references are to *Mansfield Park*—not unexpectedly, since the theatricals in this novel obviously bring questions of representation to the fore. But the passages concerned are in any case regarded as occasional setpieces, conspicuous by their rarity, and as a result, remarks about them are correspondingly isolated and fugitive, since they are invariably unconnected with the critic's preoccupations.

Whether the limits of critical consciousness of such episodes (which sees them as just that: episodic, so constituting only one dimension) is witness to a widespread lack of consciousness of—reticence of or resistance to—psychoanalytic vision, readers must be left to judge; this study will attribute to them the status of a much more widespread phenomenon, a thoroughgoing presence in the texture of Jane Austen's work. But when J.I.M.Stewart tells us 'Miss Austen doesn't start out from . . . a Freudian resolution so to exploit "art" as to make her own perplexities widely interesting and palatable',[10] when Joan Hodge refers to 'those happy days before Freud',[11] or when even Tanner, despite enlightening suggestions made elsewhere, assures us that he is not going 'to deviate into the follies of would-be psycho-sexual criticism',[12] one may feel psychoanalysis has some way to go before it is admitted even into the ante-room of Jane Austen Studies.

Finally, just as it is more than the occurrence in Jane Austen's novels of the word 'unconscious' that is to be discussed in what follows, 'symbolic acts' (of which a considerable number may be found) however significant on a first level, are really only the beginning of the story.

For the symbolic, or—as it will be preferable to call it from now on—*figurative* act, forms part of fictional characters' behaviour; and behaviour is no more the only ingredient of a book than it is of life.

The sole ingredient of Jane Austen's novels—indeed, except for odd effects like the blank page in *Tristram Shandy*, of all novels—is language. And the most radical error so far promulgated of the nature of Jane Austen's work is the view that her language is non-figurative.

This disastrous misapprehension appears in one of the first properly critical studies devoted to her work: in 1939 Mary Lascelles writes that 'close observers' of Jane Austen's ways '..must have noticed that she is, so to speak, *shy* of figurative language, using it as little as possible',[13] in 1995 Maggie Lane

---

[9] Tanner, op. cit., p. 161.

[10] 'Tradition and Miss Austen', in *Critical Essays on Jane Austen*, ed. B.C.Southam, R.K.P. 1968, p. 135. Cf., a generation later: 'In spite of Freud and his followers, I detect no trace of anxiety in her' (Jocelyn Harris: *Jane Austen's Art of Memory*, C.U.P. 1989, p. x).

[11] *The Double Life of Jane Austen*, Hodder and Stoughton 1972, p. 152.

[12] Tanner, op. cit., p. 49.

[13] *Jane Austen and Her Art*, O.U.P. 1939, p. 111.

tells us 'What is lacking is imagery, figurative use of language, symbol';[14] and in the half-century between these two, very various types of critic have repeated the same assertion: thus for Wendy Craik, in all the novels (except, she says, *Persuasion*) 'there is an absence of even casual imagery so complete as to be remarkable';[15] Norman Page, speaking of Emma's arrow (*E* III.11.408) mentions 'the rarity with which such figures are used', concluding 'Her language does not habitually draw attention to itself';[16] and Tanner declares: 'We quickly notice how very few metaphors Jane Austen uses, [she] it seems aims at a total transparency'.[17]

- 3 -

'A picture held us captive.'[18]

Janeism[19] has its source in a picture of a life. Everyone's idea of Jane Austen is, whether they know it or not, derived from J.E.Austen-Leigh's *Memoir*: the first (and only) extended piece of biographical writing by someone who knew the novelist, set down fifty-three years after her death by her nephew (now seventy-one; he had been aged eighteen at the funeral): a sketchy cartoon portrait fleshed out in pastels from family legend another forty-three years after the *Memoir*,[20] then embroidered upon (very extensively) by Elizabeth Jenkins (1938), Marghanita Laski (1969), Cecil (1978), John Halperin (1984), Honan (1987), and the colour-supplements. All commentators, sooner or later, find their way back to the life, and the internal logic of Janeism— repetitive, condescending, inert—is left just where it was.

Its first characteristic ploy, faced with a sort of puzzle, or paradox, is to exclaim upon the smallness of the life, but the greatness of the art: Ian Watt compares 'the apparently superficial nature of the subject-matter with the absolute command of experience implied by the way it is presented',[21] and Alistair Duckworth speaks of 'Jane Austen's ability to carry major themes on apparently trivial vehicles'.[22]

The second move is to justify its own critical condescension:

..no-one expects Jane Austen to be as interesting as Stendhal. A book about a dull, stupid, hemmed-in sort of life, by a person who has lived it,

---

[14] *Jane Austen and Food*, Hambledon Press 1995, p. xv.

[15] *Jane Austen, The Six Novels*, Methuen 1965, p. 29.

[16] *The Language of Jane Austen*, Blackwell 1972, pp. 10 and 46.

[17] Tanner, op. cit., p. 64.

[18] Wittgenstein, *P.I.* ¶ 115.

[19] A unique phenomenon in literary criticism. Biographers sometimes refer to their subject by first name only (Leon Edel and his 'Henry'), a few writers (Colette, Alain) use one as a *nom-de-plume*, and in French scholarship there is the case of 'Jean-Jacques', but only with 'Jane' does everyone know whom you are talking about.

[20] W. & R.A.Leigh: *Jane Austen: Her Life and Letters*, Smith, Elder & Co 1913.

[21] Ian Watt: Introduction, *Jane Austen, A Collection of Critical Essays*, Prentice Hall, Inc. 1963, p. 4.

[22] Alistair Duckworth: *The Improvement of the Estate*, Baltimore 1971, p. 171.

will never be as interesting as the work of some author who has compre-
hended many men's manners and seen many grades and conditions of
existence.[23]

..a preoccupation with 'the strictly ordinary' is perhaps no more than
might be expected of a realistic novelist who was also a woman with a
strong affection for family life.[24]

So: Jane Austen's work must be limited, because her life was.

Building on these sturdy foundations, commentators insist (third move) on
the source in the life of everything found in the work: from the general principle—Austen-Leigh in 1871 differentiates the *Juvenilia* from the mature
work by declaring that the latter present 'faithful copies of nature'[25]—to the
particular instance: Tanner in 1966 tells us how it comes about that, as
'typically', Fanny Price's amber cross had a real origin:

> ..*for* Jane Austen herself was fond of the 'gold chains and topaze crosses'
> which the young Charles Austen had sent to his sisters from the Mediter-
> ranean in 1801: her symbolism is firmly grounded in the actual.[26]

The interpretative model so far delineated is a fairly simple one, and can if
required produce its distinguished pedigree in the history of a kindred language-game: 'playing, whose end . . . was and is, to hold, as 'twere, the mirror
up to nature'; its results are numerous and complex.

First of all, the *relation* between the reader (this side of the mirror) and the
character (other side) is assimilated to relation*ships* between persons on this
side: characters, according to this model, are susceptible of being perceived
according to the same criteria as persons. As Austen-Leigh has it,

> ..the Dashwoods and Bennets, the Bertrams and Woodhouses, the
> Thorpes and Musgroves . . . have been admitted as familiar guests to the
> firesides of so many families, and are known there as individually and
> intimately as if they were living neighbours.[27]

Much virtue in 'as if': again about a century after the *Memoir*, B.C.Southam
described this as 'a cult of appreciation in which biographical details and

---

[23] Ezra Pound: *Literary Essays*, Faber and Faber 1960, p. 464.

[24] Page, op. cit., p. 7.

[25] *Memoir*, ed. cit., p. 304.

[26] Tanner, op. cit., p. 158 (my italics). This approach sometimes reaches comic extremes: 'There were in
Chawton the same inherent tendencies towards social convergence and personal repression as in Highbury
. . . In all, it seems fair to say that Chawton in the late winter of 1812/3 *provides an anticipatory verification* of
Emma' (Oliver MacDonagh: *Jane Austen: Real and Imagined Worlds*, Yale U.P. 1991, p. 143, my italics).

[27] *Memoir*, ed. cit., p. 273. Cf. 'There actually is a Fullerton near Salisbury, but it is twice the nine-mile
distance given [in *NA*] This village and Mottisfont Abbey a few miles south, are in Hampshire, so that both
Catherine Morland and Jane Austen may have known them' (J.David Grey: *Jane Austen Handbook*, Athlone
1986, p. 384); 'Hypothetical scene-setting at Steventon during the festivities [1787 theatricals] conjures up a
Jane of twelve years (Fanny Price?)' (Nigel Wood, Introduction, '*Mansfield Park*', Open U. P. 1993, p. 2).

literary commentary were easily and uncritically mingled'.[28] But the past tense was optimistic: practically all the critics quoted in this chapter are more recent than Mr Southam.

The most popular response in the liturgy of this cult is what may be called the 'blank page heresy': speculation about the lives of characters imagined as stretching into those handy sheets that printers sometimes thoughtfully supply at the end of a volume. Thus in the year of Southam's warning, Robert Garis tells us 'Knightley has scolded Emma for years, and will continue to do so';[29] a decade later Paris asserts Mr and Mrs Darcy 'will get along well, as long as each continues to feed the other's pride'.[30] Hodge does not agree: in her view, those marriages stand a better chance of success than

..Henry Tilney's, with his doting Catherine. Did he manage to educate her before the two of them degenerated into a Mr and Mrs Bennet? And similarly, when Fanny realised how much more intelligent she was than her beloved Edmund, had she the sense to keep quietabout it?[31]

Garis and Paris, Hodge and even Lodge (a 'New' Critic—well, almost new[32]), who says of this way of interpreting and evaluating Jane Austen that it has severe limitations, for under its influence criticism

..very easily degenerates into gossip, at which level it is incapable of explaining why we should consider Jane Austen an important writer.

However, he seems to admit this reluctantly, for out comes the value conferred by the mirror: 'It is a *natural* response, and one which we can never entirely suppress—probably we should not try to..'; a few pages earlier he had referred to the Prince Regent's librarian as 'a well-meaning but somewhat conceited and fatuous man, who might have stepped from the pages of one of Jane Austen's own novels'.[33]

If one were respectfully to point out that such is not, actually, the case—because characters in novels are entities made of ink on the page and sparks in the brain, and such things do not 'step'—*if* one said such things as these, one would perhaps lay oneself open to the charge of structuralist terrorism..

*

---

28 Introduction, *The Critical Heritage*, R.K.P. 1968, p. 2.

29 'Learning Experience and Change', in *Critical Essays on Jane Austen*, ed. B.C. Southam, R.K.P. 1968, p. 75.

30 Paris, op. cit., p. 139.

31 Hodge, op. cit., p. 59.

32 It is important to note that the blank page heresy continues to thrive in a period of critical approaches which one could think made it redundant. Thus in a 1993 essay: '..we might conjecture that in marriage to [Fanny, Edmund] will ... learn the limits of conventional morality..' etc, and further that these characters 'will live "civilized" lives, but without, as far as anyone can judge, any hints of creative neurosis' (Mary Evans: 'Henry Crawford and the sphere of love in *Mansfield Park*', in Wood op. cit., pp. 52 & 54); and in a 'deconstructive' study of 1996, Roger Sales speculates that George and Emma Knightley's post wedding seaside tour provides 'a hint that Emma will still get what she wants when married.' (*Jane Austen and Representations of Regency England*, R.K.P. 1996, p. 135).

33 Lodge: Introduction, *Emma: A Casebook*, Macmillan 1969, pp. 13 and 16 (my italics).

On that note a first pause is opportune in this demonstration, to make a point about the aims and scope of literary criticism, in echo to remarks about those of psychoanalysis in Part 1 of this chapter.

Just as Fox characterises Freud's distinction as being his sense, long before structural anthropology, of the right questions to ask about *anthropos*, so literary criticism is a discipline that should enable us to know which are the pertinent and interesting questions to be asked about books. When Mark Schorer teeters on blank page heresy by asking 'how "happy" is this marriage, with Knightley having to move into old Mr Woodhouse's establishment?'[34] it is hard to know according to the terms of what discipline, literary or psychological, anyone could answer his question; when Halperin suggests £350 was, in 1811, an ample income to marry on—'one wonders how smitten Edward and Elinor really are'[35]—there would seem to be no possible world in which his wondering could conceivably be satisfied.

So: the first, and decisive, incoherence of the interpretative model we are exploring is that it allows wrong questions to be asked; begged, rather.

A powerful tool of propaganda for this model is Chapman's edition: its character-indexes, chronologies, 'identifications' of places, pictures of early 19th century carriages, dress, etc., foster the view that a cardinal interest of Jane Austen's works is in their presenting a faithful portrait of a bygone era.[36]

Not everyone reads the novels in his edition; but the Chapman germ has proved exceedingly infectious. It often betrays its presence in just a word or two: as in his character-index to *Sense and Sensibility* we find

Sir John MIDDLETON (no doubt Baronet). *(S & S, p. 428)*

so fifty years later, on a (non-existent) letter in *Emma*, Page writes:

Presumably Martin had written from the heart . . . [etc.][37]

Such suggestions are properly *impertinent*, for there is no source in existence that we could consult for further information pertaining to these characters.

---

34 'The Humiliation of Emma Woodhouse', in *Jane Austen: A Collection of Critical Essays*, ed. Watt (1963), p. 108. Cf. 'what reason is there to believe that her marriage with Knightley would prevent her from going on as she has done before . . . ?' (Edmund Wilson: 'A Long Talk about Jane Austen', in ibid., p. 39); 'we must trust in Knightley's continuing power to control Emma's penchant for manipulating life' (Litz, op. cit., p. 134).

35 John Halperin, *The Life of Jane Austen*, Harvester 1984, p. 88. Cf. 'One wonders whether Emma—even under the vigilance of Mr Knightley—will not be polished into the same engaging ruthlessness after several years of marriage' (Marvin Mudrick: *Irony as Defense and Discovery*, Princeton 1952, p. 199); 'If Mr. Woodhouse were a woman, would Emma's sacrifice be presented as equally noble?' (Lane, op. cit. [1995], p. 168).

36 Southam's tribute (*MW*, p. vii n.) to a 'style of editing and presentation which characterizes so distinctively' Chapman's 'unobtrusive and scholarly attention' is unapt. Chapman may himself have felt he was leaving readers to read, as he puts it, 'without interference' (*S & S*, p. i), but when, having established that Jane Austen's brother knew a certain J.Langham (who owned a house named Cottesbrooke) he triumphantly declares 'We now know that Mansfield Park may be identified with Cottesbrooke' (*L*, 504), no possibility of appeal is left open—unless it be Vladimir Nabokov's downright 'Mansfield Park never existed, and its people never lived' (*Lectures on Literature*, Picador 1983, p. 10).

37 Page, op. cit, p. 184. Cf. 'As Mr.Price almost certainly knows, he has no chance of intervening in Maria's affairs' (Mary Evans, op. cit., p. 41); 'Cowper was a poet who celebrated rural retirement and domestic pleasures (which should have pleased Edward Ferrars)', Margaret A. Doody, Introduction, 1990 Penguin *S & S*, pp. xvii.

'No doubt' and 'presumably' bring us to another key set of axioms within the Janeite interpretative model.

To begin with, it is supposed—indeed, this is never the subject of any expressed doubt—that the narrative 'voice' (which as a matter of plain fact tells us nothing of Sir John's rank[38]) *is* Jane: i.e. the Miss Jane Austen (1775-1817) who is known to have lived at Chawton and written novels.

This position has the advantage that what is said to be known of the one can be used to repair lacunae in knowledge of the other (and this works both ways): thus it is tacitly assumed that all characteristics (chiefly mental ones: moral outlook, religious principles, etc.) synthesised from *Memoir*, *Letters* and so on, must equally be attributes—even if unstated—of the narrative voice.

Finally, since as we have seen the characters are also credited with certain attributes of living people (mostly dimensions which we do not show, but which may be speculated upon: pasts, futures, etc.) the 'relationship' that the narrator may have with 'her' characters is also 'naturalised'.

Before illustration is given of how these further articles have been integrated into the practice of Janeite faith, another general remark is in order. The commentators quoted are being lent a kind of associationist solidarity to which they cannot in fact pretend: indeed, not all of them are guilty on all counts of the belief-system here synthesised by means of their collective testimony; on the contrary it is their disagreement on points of detail which reveals the unsoundness of the whole edifice. If brief hearings are again given to so many individual critics—some of the fifty quoted so far, and about thirty new ones (it may again be insolently underlined that almost all of these are 'specialists')—this is to afford an idea of how widespread some form of adherence to the phenomenon (which displays, it will be seen, a *complex* symptomatology) has proved. The motivation in quoting remarks typical of its more extreme form—the thick end of the wedge, as it were, to which the more circumspect at the thin end might not subscribe—is purely economical: that of showing how factitious the apparent coherence of Janeism is.[39]

The biographist wedge was already stuck fast in the critical doorway when Lascelles wrote 'the mind of any of Jane Austen's heroines may be a means of communicating her opinions to us': just one example of how easily, if you open just that chink, you can slide between the Miss Jane Austen of the *Letters* and, in this case, Elizabeth Bennet:

> ..our chief reason for accepting her point of view as a reflection of her
> author's is the impression she bears of sympathy between them—an

---

[38] Chapman is often wrong even about his own editions of the novels and letters: he tells us (his ed. of *P & P*, p. 411) reference to someone as 'Uncle' is a vulgarism not used by Jane Austen (untrue: see *E* 465 and *MW* 332); he refers (*P & P*, p. 391) to Jane Austen's 'youthful habit' of putting *ei* for *ie* (inaccurate: *MW* 366 ['peices', 'beleive'] January, and *L*, 493 ['cheif'] 22 May 1817; the novelist died two months later).

[39] 'My aim is: to teach you to pass from a piece of disguised nonsense to something that is patent nonsense' (*P.I.* ¶ 464).

impression of which almost every reader would be sensible, even if it had not the explicit confirmation of Jane Austen's letters. Yet [Lascelles unblushingly adds] as she is presented to us in *Pride and Prejudice*, she is but a partial and sometimes perverse observer.[40]

Almost fifty years later, Halperin objects: *Fanny Price*, he says, 'is as much part of Jane Austen's personality as Elizabeth Bennet'.[41] The door is now ajar, for whilst Tanner declares that Jane Austen 'vindicates Fanny Price without qualification', this in no way prevents him from approving other critics' suggestion that.. *Mary Crawford*,

..with her quick wit, her vitality and resilience, is much more like Jane Austen herself than is the shrinking Fanny.[42]

John Bailey opts for *Anne Elliot*, whose claim (*P* II.11.235) about women's capacities for 'loving longest..' etc.

..is, *one cannot but fancy*, nearer to a confession of the deepest and most recent feelings of Jane's heart than . . . [etc.][43]

(Similarly Denis Donoghue, on brother Henry's marriage to cousin Eliza: Jane Austen's feeling on this occasion 'may have found its way into *Mansfield Park*, though [he finds himself constrained to add, as unembarrassed as Lascelles] there is no evidence of direct transcription'.[44])

The shift is sometimes made more subtly: Ronald Blythe's view is that the destruction of Harriet Smith's relationship with Robert Martin leads to one of

..*Jane Austen*'s most celebrated outbursts of snobbery, when she makes Emma say 'a young person, whether on horseback..'etc.[45]

Slidings from author to narrative voice sometimes affect relationships with characters other than heroines. The favourite here is Edmund Bertram, who for Craik 'assists Jane Austen by being a man of sound sense expressed at the right times';[46] but when Schorer goes so far as to refer to 'the author (or, if you wish, Knightley)',[47] the door has been opened as wide as it well can be, and the wedge kicked out of sight.

---

[40] Lascelles, op. cit., pp. 202 and 200.

[41] Halperin, op. cit., p. 235.

[42] Tanner, op. cit., pp. 143 and 154 (my italics).

[43] *Introductions to Jane Austen*, O.U.P. 1931, p. 17 (my italics). T.V.Reddy is driven to a desperate recourse: in this detail 'If Jane was not speaking for herself, she was speaking for her sister' (*Jane Austen and The Matrix of Matrimony*, Bohra 1987, p. 20).

[44] 'A View of *Mansfield Park*', in Southam (ed. 1968), p. 43.

[45] Introduction, 1966 Penguin ed. of *E*, p. 19 (my italics).

[46] Craik, op. cit., p. 112. Cf. '*of course*, she sided with Edmund Bertram rather than Mary Crawford' (Halperin, op. cit., p. 231, my italics); when Edmund tells Fanny of the elopement, 'we hear Austen's voice through Edmund' (Laura Mooneyham, *Romance, Language and Education in Jane Austen's Novels*, Macmillan 1988, p. ix).

[47] Schorer, op. cit., p. 105.

Lascelles thought 'one can confidently deduce *her* likes and dislikes from the distribution of opinions among her characters',[48] and many concur in this: for Fraser 'John Thorpe's praise of Fielding in *Northanger Abbey* suggests that Jane Austen herself disliked Fielding';[49] for Laurence Lerner, the novelist pays the navy 'the most effective compliment in her power, the indirect compliment of having it slighted by one of her silly characters';[50] and for Warren Roberts 'Austen commented on female gentility and took a feminist position by having Mr. Collins read from Fordyce's sermons after tea'.[51]

From the view that characters are bearers of authorial values, there is logically no great jump to the idea that novels in which they figure somehow do the same. Perhaps not all readers would subscribe to Wright's telegram model (or at any rate to the very definite article with which it begins) for *Mansfield Park*: 'The message is: good girls come out best, after all',[52] but Edgar Shannon's view that 'In all her novels, Jane Austen is primarily a moral writer, striving to establish criteria of sound judgement and right conduct'[53] is doubtless held by many people, though they might find it hard to give a precise gloss to Shannon's first word, too.[54] Perhaps some such reserve is behind Jane Nardin's reference, first, to 'Jane Austen's ideas about morality..', then, drawing on a theatrical metaphor as if to cover herself, '..and the techniques she uses to dramatise them'.[55] Southam suggests 'Sanditon' is 'a comedy of ideas';[56] Duckworth discusses what he calls Jane Austen's 'epistemological subversion of the external world';[57] and according to Susan Morgan, in *Sense and Sensibility* the novelist

> ..considers the consequences to behavior of the premise that perception is imperfect. Thus the subject of *Sense and Sensibility*, the problem of action, follows quite naturally from the premises of *Northanger Abbey*.[58]

---

[48] Lascelles, op. cit., p. 47.

[49] Fraser, op. cit., pp. 25/6.

[50] *The Truth-Tellers*, Chatto and Windus 1967, p. 147.

[51] *Jane Austen and the French Revolution*, Athlone 1995, p. 206.

[52] Wright, op. cit., p. 124.

[53] 'Emma: Character and Construction', PMLA LXXI (1956) pp. 637-50.

[54] Cf. '[*MP*] urges the necessity of morality, . . . it lays out certain principles' etc. (Michael Williams, *Jane Austen: Six Novels and their Methods*, Macmillan 1986, p. 86); 'The plot of *Mansfield Park* corroborates Fanny's severity with Mary Crawford' (Claudia L. Johnson: *Jane Austen, Women, Politics and the Novel*, Chicago 1987, p. 111).

[55] *Those Elegant Decorums*, N.Y. State University Press 1973, p. 1.

[56] 'The Seventh Novel', in *Jane Austen's Achievement*, Macmillan 1976, p. 16.

[57] Duckworth, op. cit., p. 26.

[58] *In the Meantime: Character and Perception in Jane Austen's Fiction*, Chicago 1980, p. 110. Cf. Williams, waxing Hegelian about *S & S*: 'a complex debate', he writes, in which readers are offered 'the opportunity of adopting revisions of the argument, and its terms, only to find that the revisions have themselves to be adopted and changed, from the simplest antithetical distinction to the most elaborate combination of unity and opposition' (op. cit., p. 34).

The time has come to make a stand. Coherent interpretation should reflect the coherence of each work, and find the unity of the oeuvre. The synthetic interpretative model to which the critics so far quoted contribute—which, it may be repeated, is permissibly denominated Janeism since all its adherents constantly refer home to a person, rather than to a body of writing—offends in two separate but interrelated ways.

First, it is factually incoherent, for it takes account of too little of the oeuvre to merit the status of a general theory; its attributions of meaning are thus arbitrary. Thus seeking to explain why Emma is the first wealthy heroine, Halperin ascribes this to the novelist's own new financial situation (gains from publication of the first three novels);[59] he does not even mention the question begged by this hypothesis: how is it that subsequent heroines (e.g. Anne Elliot and Charlotte Heywood) are in comparable financial states to Emma's predecessors? Moreover, there is nowhere for this approach to stop: seeking to explain Fanny Price's optical problems, Robert Liddell solemnly informs us: 'Jane Austen herself sometimes suffered from weak eyes'.[60]

But secondly—and this is more fundamentally damaging—the model is *logically* incoherent, since it takes for granted a certain relationship between language (the stuff of literary art) and reality, which developments in aesthetics have given us reason to doubt even possible.

To describe 'Sanditon' as a comedy of ideas (would not this designation be better kept for a Peacock or a Huxley?) is to fail in response to a specific *artistic* invitation; it is to mistake the nature of the language-game at issue, or to have assimilated two language-games;[61] and when we find Jane Austen's novels being discussed in terms redolent of moral philosophy (Morgan, Williams, Johnson, above), something has gone very wrong indeed.

Attributions of didacticism to Jane Austen invariably omit to make a rudimentary distinction—but a crucial one—between intention and result: are we really so certain to agree about what an influential study goes so far as to call 'the overt lesson she sets out to teach in all of her mature novels'?[62]

To identify authors' views through their delegation to characters is to establish an extremely perilous critical precedent; moreover the sheer variety of

---

[59] Halperin, op. cit., p. 273.

[60] *The Novels of Jane Austen*, Longman 1963, p. 83. Cf. Doody, who ends her criticism of Marianne Dashwood with 'Yet her taste is always sound; Jane Austen herself was devoted to Cowper' (op. cit., p. xvii).

[61] Wittgenstein speaks of the necessity of distinguishing an assertion from a fiction or a supposition (*P.I.* ¶ 22). 'What confuses us is the uniform appearance of words [sc., in the two modes mentioned] when we hear them spoken or meet them in print' (ibid., ¶ 11).

[62] Sandra Gilbert and Susan Gubar: *The Madwoman in the Attic*, Yale U.P. 1979, p. 154.
Did any elder son ever move a bookcase in his father's room the less, did any elder daughter ever commit adultery in Wimpole Street the less, after reading *MP*? Have readers ever gone out of their way to avoid relieving feelings of exasperation by an easy quip to a vulnerable spinster, after reading *E*? And does not the burden of proof in this matter lie with those who postulate identifiable results, of any kind?

characters to have been singled out in this way, by different commentators, shows the internal chaos to which such a ploy leads.[63]

Finally, the supposition that some characters carry more of their author's personal opinions than others do, would tend to entail their enjoying indemnity from their author's irony. This is a key point, and we shall return to it.

> With Jane Austen almost less than any other writer except Shakespeare, can one assume that her characters voice her own opinions . . . in company with Shakespeare, who put so many *bons mots* into the mouth of (say) Iago, she allows the most unpleasant or the most stupid of them to say a good thing now and then.[64]

This lucid comment by the novelist L.P.Hartley serves to show what nothing can be gained by hiding: namely, that there have been dissenting voices to some aspects of the model outlined. Faced for example with Malcolm Bradbury's view that the problem of *Emma* is to make us '..care for Emma in such a way that we care about her fate, and like her, but that we in no way subdue our moral feelings about her faults'[65] Graham Hough protests that 'This is not what the experience of the book *feels* like'.[66] Sometimes, a critic starts off with a firmly detached attitude to the work—D.W.Harding declares that Jane Austen 'has none of the underlying didactic intention ordinarily attributed to the satirist..'—only to return at once with greater zeal to (baseless) psychobiography: '..Her object is not missionary; it is the more desperate one of merely trying to find some mode of existence for her critical attitudes'.[67]

Finally, many have drawn a warrant for their own commission of the blank page heresy from Jane Austen's example, pouncing on this, from the *Memoir*:

> She would, if asked, tell us many little particulars about the subsequent career of some of her people. In this traditionary way we learned that Miss Steel [sic] never succeeded in catching the Doctor . . . that the 'considerable sum' given by Mrs Norris to William Price was one pound . . . that Mr Woodhouse survived his daughter's marriage and kept her and Mr Knightley from settling at Donwell, about two years . . . [etc., etc.][68]

or this, from the *Letters*:

> **I can only imagine** that Mr D. prizes any Picture of her too much to like it should be exposed to the public eye. **I can imagine** he wd. have that sort of feeling—that mixture of Love, Pride and Delicacy.   (*L* 312)

---

[63] '—. . .what does Shakespeare say? *Put but money in thy purse.*
  —Iago, Stephen murmured.' (James Joyce: *Ulysses*, Penguin 1969, p. 36).

[64] Address (1965), J.A. Society Reports, Wm. Dawson & Sons 1990, pp. 306 and 305.

[65] Malcolm Bradbury: 'Jane Austen's *Emma*', in *Emma: A Casebook*, ed. cit., p. 166.

[66] *The Dream and the Task*, Duckworth 1963, pp. 44/5.

[67] 'Regulated Hatred: An Aspect of the Work of Jane Austen', *Scrutiny* VIII, 1940, p. 350.

[68] *Memoir*, ed. cit., p. 376.

Ironically, Chapman was perhaps the first to detect the fallacy involved: he points out (and the phrase returns us to the Wittgenstein quotation heading section 3) that if Jane Austen let her imagination continue to work, it was 'not for publication—outside the frame of her picture'.[69]

- 5 -

The reader will now be in a position to understand what was stated in the Introduction: given the preoccupations of the existing critical literature, there will be hardly any further occasion for engagement with it in the rest of the present study, whose point of departure is that Jane Austen's novels are neither moral tracts, nor works of philosophy, nor indeed works of nature, but rather works of art.

But before we explore what this entails, it is worth pausing for a moment to consider why Jane Austen has attracted to such a degree the biographist approach.

There are basically four, very closely related reasons. The first, which goes straight to the heart of the matter, is pinpointed by Liddell when he evokes readers '..who must have a personal story at all costs'.[70]

A personal story: the easiest approach to art. And the *cosiest*, as Katherine Mansfield recognized: every admirer of the novels, she observes, '..cherishes the happy thought that he alone—reading between the lines—has become the secret friend of the author'.[71]

The operation of the second reason is not restricted to 'our' Jane:

> If we could at least discover in ourselves or in people like ourselves an ac-
> tivity which was in some way akin to creative writing.   (14.131)

Thus Freud, in 1908; by 1930 he had come to think the wish to tame genius always means 'reducing the distance that separates him from us', always tending 'in effect towards *degradation*' (14.471, my italics).

This leads directly to the third reason: given the near-adoration in which Jane Austen is widely held, this may surprise, and will no doubt appear the most contentious; however, in view of the cult's peculiar character it can hardly be accidental that its object was a woman.[72]

The very basis of Janeism is sexist, founded on fear of female creativity, compounded with unwillingness to credit women with powers of conception other than those of the womb: those, that is, which require the help of man. Hence the classing of her novels, by some, as works of nature: 'instinctive and charming!' exclaims Henry James; she leaves us, he says, '..hardly more

---

[69] Chapman, op. cit., p. 189.

[70] Liddell, op. cit., p. 142.

[71] In *Novels and Novelists*, quoted in Lascelles, op. cit., p. 219.

[72] Jane Austen excites 'a reverence due, among women, only to the Blessed Virgin' (Liddell, op. cit., p. 147).

curious of her process, and of the experience that fed it, than the brown thrush who tells his story from the garden bough.'[73]

The amount of space taken up with seeking sources for motifs in the work is not only disproportionate to the amount of biographical data available, but greater even than what is found in criticism of male novelists whose dynamic (if one must think in such terms) could perhaps just a mite less unwarrantably be thought of as 'autobiographical' (Proust, Lawrence, etc.).

The final reason to which the success of the Janeite model is owing, less contentious in being more obvious, is of such weight that unravelling its significance will occupy the remainder of this chapter: the phenomenon of Janeism is due above all—justly, it will no doubt be said—to the peculiar, even uncanny feeling of reality her work gives us.

- 6 -

The stand with which this inquiry opened (Jane Austen's work has been fundamentally misunderstood) derives from a more basic contention: that very reality—the one of which we say her work gives us the peculiar, uncanny feeling—is not itself, according to this (in the end, philosophical) contention, a clear, irreducible entity.

The critical literature is full of philosophically *nonchalant* assertions about 'Jane Austen's World', an entity often hunted back to her letters, which we are told (in a characteristic example) 'record the world that was her subject-matter'.[74] However, whatever we conclude Jane Austen's novels to be a representation of—let us call that her subject—surely we must start the critical enterprise further back, and say something about their matter.

Naturally, in order to describe this matter, we can throw over it nets of different-sized meshes:[75] taking the ink for granted now, and noticing as we move further in that the matter of her novels is language, let us acknowledge the need for some discussion of the following question. In what contexts—indeed, in what *sense*—may language be said to represent ..anything whatever?

If study of Jane Austen's language has remained untouched by what has been called the psychoanalytic revolution, it has also shown marked resistance to the contemporary critical revolution (flying flags variously called structuralist, deconstructivist, semiotic, etc.) which has, partly under the influence of Wittgenstein, drawn attention to what we had forgotten: the complexity of the act of reading.

---

[73] 'The Lesson of Balzac', in *The House of Fiction*, Greenwood Press 1957, p. 62. Another echo of what one may call the *Shakespeare-warbling-his-native-woodnotes-wild* complex.

[74] Liddell, op. cit., p. 145. Cf. '..the typical moment of *éclaircissement* towards which all the Austen actions tend, the moment when a key character abandons her error and humbly submits to objective reality' (Marilyn Butler, in *NA: A Casebook*, Macmillan 1976, p. 114); 'her novels preserve, and call attention to, certain formal features proper to comedy in its theatrical sense, and this is used to distance what is represented from life itself' (Margaret Kirkham: *Feminism and Fiction*, Harvester 1983, p. 81); 'the complex class situation in which she lived her life and which her novels evoke' (E.J.Ahearn: *Marx and Modern Fiction*, Yale U.P. 1989, p. 32).

[75] The image is Wittgenstein's (*Tractatus* 6.341).

In this second part of the present chapter, preoccupations recalling factors in the first part are not systematically underlined, readers being supposed capable of seeing them without tiresome authorial intrusion; but in the present instance their attention may permissibly be drawn to a parallel between Freud's refusal to take the familiar for granted, and a thought such as this:

> Don't take it as a matter of course, but as a remarkable fact, that pictures and fictitious narratives give us pleasure, occupy our minds.[76]

The Jane Austen critical literature has taken the way her novels 'occupy our minds' entirely as a matter of course: an excellent example of Wollheim's description of critical approaches in which 'representational properties are not regarded as being . . . problematic'.[77] That, indeed, is the problem.

'Jane Austen's World'—an entity to which commentators so blithely refer (even 'Jane Austen's England')—can have at best merely metaphorical meaning. This idea is probably foreign to the consciousness of most Jane Austen readers; nothing but shock tactics can put it over.

All human beings to have existed so far on this planet have punctuated their lives with a series of physical discharges; the least unmentionable is nose-blowing.

Does any Jane Austen character blow her or his nose? On the roughly two thousand two hundred printed pages of her six main novels, the word 'nose' occurs just three times.[78] If to Miss Bingley (*P & P* III.3.271) it appears that Elizabeth Bennet's ' "nose wants character" ', it must be said that all the other hundreds of Jane Austen's characters appear to want nose..

A corollary to this perhaps startling revelation is that the world she is said to portray turns out to be an almost totally odourless one. Lascelles asserts that Jane Austen 'gives, as a countrywoman would, the country and the season'.[79] Is it not rather remarkable, then—at least for those who endorse this picture of the countrywoman's personal experience going direct into her novels—that a whole host of even agreeable, admissible country smells (*..flowers* might be an example) should be so meagrely represented?[80]

---

[76] *P.I.* ¶ 524.

[77] Wollheim (1975), p. 37.

[78] William Price imagines Portsmouth girls turning up their metaphorical noses at such as him (*MP* II.7.249), and Sir Walter Elliot recalls Mary's nose being red (*P* II.3.142), but that seems to be an 'accidental'.

[79] Lascelles, op. cit., p. 1.

[80] Barton's kitchen 'smokes' (*S & S* 73); Portsmouth 'bad air, bad smells' contrast with 'freshness, fragrance and verdure' (*MP* 332); there is 'mild air' (409); 'smell of spirits' pains Fanny (Mr Price being 'dirty', 389, may imply body-odour); Wingfield ' "thoroughly understands the nature of the air" ' at Southend; London disadvantages include ' "the air so bad" ' (*E* 103); Miss Bates' soup ' "smells most excellent" ' (330); Emma enjoys the smell of nature after a storm (424); Catherine Morland mentions ' "breathing fresh air" ' (*NA* 174), Mrs Clay ' "a poisonous atmosphere" ' (for the doctor to breathe) and Sir Walter ' "foul air" ' (*P* 20): that seems to be all.
This example (of a sense experience hardly found in an oeuvre) is not chosen at random. And excluding the *representation* of a sense, goes a step beyond 'rejection of taste and smell as *constituents* of works of art' (Wollheim: Introduction to *The Image in Form: Selected Writings of Adrian Stokes*, Penguin 1972, p. 27, my italics): gastronomy and perfumery do not constitute art-forms, the rôle of sublimation being insufficient.

In his effort to get us to look afresh at familiar things, not take them for granted, Wittgenstein asks us to think of a picture of a landscape

> ..with a house in it.—Someone asks 'Whose house is that?'—The answer, by the way, might be 'It belongs to the farmer who is sitting on the bench in front of it'. But then he cannot for example enter his house.. [81]

This example highlights succinctly a problem of terminology specific to pictorial representation in our culture. The continuing success in the centuries since the Renaissance of certain figurational schemata in painting has made it almost impossible for Westerners to feel other modes are as 'realistic'. And since it was in the course of the same period that the novel came to be the dominant literary form, we very readily conflate our ways of speaking about the two media: *figure*, we say, and *ground*; *character* and *background*.[82]

The problem is this: the idea of foreground and background in fiction derives from a view of painting which is itself erroneous and misleading as a general theory. We may, if we wish, say that Mr and Mrs Andrews are in the foreground of Gainsborough's picture, and sky in the background; however if you had used the word 'background' to designate the sky in (say) Cézanne's hearing, he would have knocked your head off. If comparative discussion of landscape-painting, covering both Gainsborough and Cézanne, is envisaged— and such discussion would be useful—it cannot be carried out in those terms, and they must be ditched.[83]

We may think of some state as our 'natural innocence' in this area, but there is nothing natural about expression itself; we have simply learnt to 'read' the pointers, or signs, by virtue of which it functions. In *art*, these pointers are by definition *art*ificial; however, the implications of this are more radical: Africans early in the 20th century, unacquainted with photography, were unable to 'read' Western magazine pictures; eventually one of them 'tracing the outlines with his fingers, exclaimed "These are white men!" '[84]

The lesson is that 'The naturalness of a sign is merely a function of how natural we are with it'.[85] In other words, there is no necessary relation

---

[81] *P.I.* ¶ 398.

[82] In one particular area this might be thought to create an extreme of awkwardness; however it is only towards the end of Audrey Hawkridge's *Jane Austen in Hampshire* (No. 6 of the 'Hampshire Papers', Hampshire Co. Council 1995) that we read: 'Jane Austen is undoubtedly Hampshire's most famous author. Yet, far from immortalising the county in her works, she only mentions it in one of them . . . This near-silence on the subject of the place which played such a major rôle in Jane's life may seem strange..'

[83] The point being made here may be easier to grasp in anecdotes from the visual arts: e.g. (1) The late 19th-century Emperor of Japan, shown some recent European portraits by the first envoys to reach his country for centuries, inquired why Europeans all blackened one side of their face. (2) 'Mais M. Matisse..' cried a lady visiting the painter's studio, and viewing his latest nudes, '..les Dames ne sont pas comme ça'; 'Mais ça n'est pas une Dame, Madame..', he is said to have growled, '..c'est un tableau.' Wittgenstein's telling linguistic example concerns the French politician who wrote that 'it was a peculiarity of the French language that in it words occur in the order in which one thinks them' (*P.I.* ¶ 336).

[84] The story is told in C.G.Jung: *Modern Man In Search of A Soul*, R.K.P. 1947, p. 147. A photographer once told me his subjects in countries who had no mirrors (let alone cameras) did not even recognise themselves, at once, when shown photographs he took of them, though they recognised each other.

[85] Wollheim, op. cit. (1975), p. 137.

between experience and language; a thing (a picture, a novel) is not a representation until we see it as such, and what we call 'naturalism' or 'realism', is only possible 'because conventional schemata for representing reality exist which have developed over the centuries'.[86]

Because there are as many realisms as there are ways of 'recognising' representations of reality, one can make mistakes about a particular work or genre, so-called 'Dutch realism' being one of the most treacherous: we think we recognise a still-life of flowers, but then we are told the flowers depicted do not all bloom in the same season, and in fact the work is a hymn to God's plenty; the work's apparent obviousness obscures its (original) meaning.[87]

This is equally true of word-art: in literature (a wholly verbal world) we become so entirely used to the conventions that we forget the complexity of the processes which went into learning the rules of the game.

For literature is a game: a sophisticated language-game involving two sets of people, playing according to rules usually tacit rather than explicit. Or rather a series of such games: ' "understanding" is not one thing; it is as various as the language-games themselves are'.[88]

To make some of this work for us, now: a Jane Austen character we call 'Emma' started life as electrical pulses in the novelist's brain, passed from these into a hand holding a featherful of ink; today it goes through our brains; and because our system of electrics is not dissimilar to hers (likewise the wattage of the appliances into which it is fed: words) our minds are finally enlightened by meaning.

- 7 -

If readers can reconcile themselves when they next read one of Jane Austen's novels to having their vision open on a world of noseless characters, perhaps they may be ready to witness a still more drastic operation: on the 'person', now, assumed to present everything that happens to those characters.

The two words—'Jane Austen'—are used to designate the narrator so automatically, and the single one 'she' resorted to so easily (not merely for ease of reference, moreover, to anticipate a possible quibble) that it may again require some effort to come to terms with the groundlessness of the supposition underlying their use. Without even going so far as to attribute opinions, religious principles, etc., to this narrator, we may pertinently inquire: what justification is there for sticking the female pronoun onto it?

---

[86] Anton Ehrenzweig: *The Hidden Order of Art*, Paladin 1970, p. 20.

[87] 'The notion of meaning supplies no ground for favouring the context contemporary with the text' (M.R. Ayers: *Locke*, R.K.P. 1991, I. p. 4); perhaps, but 17th century viewers did not need to be told the bloomings were 'impossible', as late 20th century city-dwellers do.

[88] Rush Rhees, Preface, *Blue and Brown Books*, Blackwell 1972, p. vii. Different arts involve different sorts of 'belief': in the theatre, there is: '..the actor, who on a stage plays at being another before a gathering of people who play at taking him for that other person..' (Jorge Luis Borges: *Labyrinths*, Penguin 1970, p. 284).

An unsuitable type of expression is a sure means of remaining in a state of confusion. It as it were bars the way out.[89]

The discipline of literary criticism involves elaborating terminology which can take in its long stride the diverse sorts of presences directing our attention in (say) novels, without constantly clamouring for information about their authors; only within that stride does it allow itself to discuss particular cases.

Thus (to begin with the question of sexual identity) we do not, reading *Moll Flanders*, wonder whether it was written by Dani*elle* Defoe; nor, when we reach the last word in the following passage from *The Mill on the Floss*—

..Every one of those keen moments [of childhood suffering] has left its traces and lives in us still, but such traces have blended themselves irrecoverably with the firmer texture of our youth and manhood..[90]

—do we inquire whether Mary Ann Evans had a sex-change in becoming George Eliot. We do not either—to move on from sex to slightly more complex cases—when we read 'Reader, I married him..', scan Yorkshire parish registers for Brontë and Rochester; nor, when we read *Lolita*, suspect Nabokov of being an unreliable paedophile; we do not inquire how Richardson and Burney and Smollett came by their extraordinary caches of letters, etc., etc.

Readers may now understand better the promise made in the Introduction about leaving Jane Austen intact: I shall hardly be touching her at all; and my practically ignoring *her*, in order to concentrate on what she wrote, will be my way of effecting the task which has been so felicitously described as 'prising the text away from the author'.[91]

If it be accepted that the most we can legitimately say of what will henceforth be called the narrative 'presence' is that, being a linguistic construct, it is read as—in the usual sense, and in the sense of interpreted—a voice,[92]

---

[89] *P.I.* ¶ 339.

[90] New American Library ed., 1965, p. 74.

[91] Catherine Belsey: *Critical Practice*, Methuen 1980, p. 16.

[92] Those who still 'feel' something about Jane Austen and her narrative voice may further be reminded: (1) that works published anonymously (hers were) are especially subject to erroneous attributions in sexual identity; (2) that 'I' ('I quit such subjects as soon as I can, impatient to restore every body not greatly at fault themselves..' *MP* III.17) is what linguisticians call a 'shifter'—anyone may use it with exactly equal truthfulness, its sense *shifting* according to user; (3) that in English, participles and adjectives do not agree with the subject—therefore that '..car je suis impatiente de faire retrouver à ceux qui n'ont pas grand'chose à se reprocher..' etc. (p. 497 of the French translation, Christian Bourgois, 1982) is taking an unwarrantable liberty; and (4) that sex is a characteristic of live human beings, not of paper and ink.
We can deal here, while we are at it, with one of the oldest critical solecisms in Jane Austen Studies: Chapman was perhaps the first to venture the tentative remark that she 'hardly ever permits herself a male conversation without female audience' (op. cit., p. 117); Wright asserts forthrightly 'Men do not appear, except in the company of women' (op. cit., p. 18); and more recently Tanner tells us 'It is worth remembering that Jane Austen never describes a scene when men alone are present' (op. cit., p. 59). All three tacitly give the 'significance' to this that he does (sc. 'as though the male world were indeed a "closed book" to her').
The point has now been laboured until it is now as blunt as could well be, but these commentators take no cognizance of the following question: why should a man's thoughts (there are many instances in Jane Austen's novels) be less of a closed book to a female writer, any easier to represent, than words a man utters in exclusively male company?

this will have far-reaching consequences for the way we speak of the relation between it and the characters. (The word 'relation' is used advisedly, for the proprietorial tone of 'My Fanny..' [*MP* III.17.461][93] has given rise to some pretty facile psychologising about the special relation*ship*—parental, maternal even—said to exist in this case: affective surrogates, 'of course, Jane never married..', etc., etc.[94])

The excursus above on the absence of noses and nose-blowing, which may have appeared frivolous, aimed to clarify the limits containing the reader's 'perception' of the lives and habits even of heroines. We can pass quickly over what is usually described as Jane Austen's economical presentation of the human-physical world—shape, form and colour in facial features, dress and so on. More interesting, in a novelist whose main interest is clearly the varied shades of *psychological* colouring, will be to draw the reader's conscious attention to the limited degree to which we are admitted to (again, 'even') the heroines' inner worlds.

That limit is surely quite inconsistent with the realist interpretative model in the last ditch to which this time it has perforce to retreat, that of so-called moral or psychological realism.[95] For although Jane Austen's young women spend 99% of the textual space they occupy thinking about their young (and not so young) men, the terms in which they do so seem invariably to be what might be called *decorous*: beyond generalised appreciations of 'manly' looks (*P* I.7.61), 'air, address' (*E* II.5.190), stature (*MP* I.2.12), etc., the rarer particular allusions never stray beyond visible details such as hands (*P* I.10.91) or mouth (*P & P* III.1.258) towards those invisible parts which must be imagined.

With predictable inertness, the received account here resorts to the rear-guard action of attributing the dearth of sexual imaginings, on the part of heroines, to authorial 'reticence'.[96] Though critics may not now chain the

---

[93] Slidings from novels to letters and back again could be used against those who regard this example as unique, for (apart from borderline cases: 'my heroine', *NA* II.14.232 and 'Sanditon', *MW* 395) on 25 April 1811 we find 'I think she will like **my Elinor**' (*L* 273), on 15 Sept. 1813 'His admiring **my Elizabeth** so much' (*L* 324) and in Dec. 1815 'I am sure you will like to see *my* **Emma**' (*L* 449).

[94] Victor Lucas has the best of both worlds: 'Her books were surely her children, and all those young heroines she created out of herself were the daughters she never had' (*Jane Austen*, Pitkin 1996, p. 15).

[95] Lodge relays with approval Kellogg-and-Scholes' distinction between what is 'true to fact' and what is 'true to experience' (Lodge [1977], p. 84).

[96] 'Life in the Lawrentian sense, the life of the blood and the passions is indeed conspicuously absent in Jane Austen' (Hough, op. cit., p. 47). To judge from the language of two readers separated by just over a century, the absence of sex in Jane Austen must sometimes be made up for in comment on it:

(1) 'The passions are perfectly unknown to her . . . what throbs fast and full, though hidden, what the blood rushes through, what is the unseen seat of life . . .–this Miss Austen ignores.' (Charlotte Brontë, letter of April 12 1850);

(2) 'the dislike of Jane Austen's detractors springs from their sense that she is coolly indifferent to the forward, or the upward, or the inward look which they favor' (Watt [1963], p. 10).

More promising is McMaster's: 'She is not *avoiding* the presentation of strong feelings; she is presenting them by indirection' (op. cit., p. 31), unfortunately not followed up.

There are cases of 'audience participation' in the critical literature: e.g. 'Fanny's apparent innocence and religiosity is an aspect of her sexiness, a veneer of the "angelic" which makes her sexually exciting to men like Crawford, who wish to find in their wives such vulnerable "virtue" ' (Kirkham, op. cit., p. 102).

work to the life as did early reviewers (coolness in descriptions of passion by authors known to be female was thought to be deliberate: a means of forestalling suspicion about their use of personal experiences), most would agree with Karl Kroeber's view about the portrayal of Marianne Dashwood, which amply proves that 'when Austen wished to represent violent emotions, she could do so expertly and effectively. But she did not often wish to..'[97]

One way of explaining the particular case would be to set it in the context of normative limitations to which early 19th women were constrained: this approach,[98] if it were carried through resolutely, would at least possess the virtue of concentrating on the language.

However, if the assumption upon which an inquiry of that kind rested were valid, no place for the present study would exist. And because that assumption has been supposed valid, what is envisaged here has been, even in the 20th century, the subject only of fugitive glimpses, e.g.:

> Jane Austen's simple, lucid, even formally 'correct' language can overlie a deeper complexity of meaning contained within it.[99]
> ..recurrences of a single word or a group of related words, appearing not only frequently but at important points in the story, can hardly be without significance.[100]

As it happens, it was a gauntlet thrown down casually nearly a century and a half ago that is taken up in this study, as will be clear from the last word in Macaulay's approving reference to 'touches' in Jane Austen: 'touches so delicate that they elude analysis.'[101]

For as it was the collective aim of Part 1 of this chapter to suggest, the 'assumption' mentioned above is antipodal to Freud's opposition of sex and civilization. To tie the absence of sexual imaginings in Jane Austen heroines to something similar in their authoress, would be to deny a classical psychoanalytic axiom: sexual curiosity must on the contrary have been *greater* at a time, and for a social class, in which (say) undressing in public was unheard-of. Indeed, Freud thought 'the psychical importance of an instinct rises in proportion to its frustration' (7.257), and that 'The progressive concealment of the body which goes along with civilization keeps sexual curiosity awake' (7.69). If as late as 1912 Freud was able to write of 'the long period of delay, which is demanded by education for cultural reasons, between sexual maturity and sexual activity' (7.255), this must have been truer still in 1812, when

---

[97] *Styles in Fictional Structure*, Princeton 1971, p. 65.

[98] Essentially Leroy W. Smith's in *Jane Austen and the Drama of Women* (Macmillan 1983) marred by constant condescension: e.g. 'Austen exhibits the rising consciousness of women, if not the fully achieved state' (p. 25).

[99] Kroeber, op. cit., p. 25.

[100] Page, op. cit., p. 41; the conviction that 'it is only through a unremitting alertness to her language in action that her meaning can be fully understood' (ibid., p. 2) makes *The Language of Jane Austen* one of the half dozen original contributions to Jane Austen Studies.

[101] Macaulay, op. cit., p. 312.

Pride and Prejudice was published. Indeed, the phrase will make us think of what might be called The Lydia Bennet Problem..

However, to limit recognition of the unsaid, or unmentionable, to places in the text where unusually brazen cases are indeed mentioned, would be to slip back into the old perceptualist trap. If the unmentionable has not been found, it must be elsewhere in the text than where we have looked; and if Jane Austen's novels produce a peculiar, uncanny feeling of reality, it must be by means that are themselves uncanny.

In one of Freud's most compelling essays—'The Uncanny'—from analysis of what is itself an odd word (*unheimlich* in German, related to *heimisch*, which contains the word 'home'; so 'homely'), he concludes the uncanny is 'something which is secretly familiar' (14.368).[102] The essay was written in 1919, but it draws on ideas to be seen in germ thirty years before, in the Fliess correspondence; it is there that we find his first allusion to the Oedipus myth, the peculiar effect of which may be attributed in Freud's view to 'a compulsion which everyone recognises because he senses its existence within himself' (F/F 272).[103]

One of the reasons not only for the popularity of Jane Austen's novels but for that uncanny feeling of reality they give us, may be owing to just some such unconscious or half-conscious recognition, by readers, of the psychical structures her works evoke, in ways this study will present.

If *what* Jane Austen was doing has in a sense always been known, in order to see *how* she was doing it we shall require a quite different theory of meaning to the one current in the critical literature.

- 8 -

The paradigm of psychoanalytic interpretation is the dream; and the various ways in which it is profitable to apply the principles of dream-interpretation to Jane Austen's novels will emerge gradually in the course of this study.

There are obvious differences between dreams and novels (though, as we shall find, some differences are more apparent than real); at present it will be enough to mention five points of similarity.

First, a dream is 'an essentially distorted object'; this fundamental fact (discussed in PFL 4, chapter IV) should be borne in mind with regard to the excursus on noses; for whereas under normal conditions in waking life such

---

102 Particularly interesting is Freud's remark that '..it is in the highest degree uncanny when an inanimate object—a picture or a doll—comes to life' (14.369).

103 G.S.Kirk, sceptical of applying Freudian theory to all myths, acknowledges that some may communicate by access to a faculty more grounded in our biological nature than intellectual equipment required for the access of ideas; see especially 'Myths as Products of the Psyche', in *The Nature of Greek Myths*, Pelican 1974.

organs are readily visible (paradigmatically so: 'It's as plain as the nose on your face'), one peculiarity of dream-images is that they *range* in intensity,

> ..between a sharpness of definition which we feel inclined, no doubt unjustifiably, to regard as greater than that of reality, and an irritating vagueness which we declare characteristic of dreams because it is not completely comparable to any degree of indistinctness which we ever perceive in real objects. (4.442)

Second, though while dreaming we may have bouts of awareness that we are doing so, 'reality-testing' (among 'major institutions of the ego', 11.241) is almost totally suspended. To a certain extent this can also be said to be true when we are 'lost in a book'; succumbing entirely to verisimilitude—failure to distinguish 'between what is merely "represented" and what is "perceived" ' (*L & P* 384, the very nub of Janeism)—is indeed to become unconscious of what is happening, all the more so since 'a dream never tells us whether its elements are to be interpreted literally or in a figurative sense' (4.456).[104]

Third, to pick up the word 'elements', it must be underlined that what we call the dream is only our memory of it; 'elaboration' is going on throughout the dream, but the dream-work is 'under the necessity of combining into a unity' all the sources which have acted as stimuli for the dream (4.323).

We find it almost impossible to recall data unless it is organized in some way; sequence is the most memorable, so what was once a loose 'organization of thoughts' becomes a 'narrative in images' (*L & P* 235).

In this sense (to give another perspective to a question in the Introduction as to the relation between facts and interpretation) it is no doubt right to assert that, strictly speaking, 'there are no "facts" in psychoanalysis, since what happens in it is not someone observing, but someone interpreting'.[105] The dynamic underlying the incoherence in the Janeite interpretative model (the paradigm mentioned in the Introduction was Chapman's *scotoma,* or blind spot[106] about Col. Brandon's natural daughter) is an *inhibition*: reluctance to contemplate a 'presence' incompatible with a certain picture of the novelist. Broadly speaking this is, exactly as Freud said of earlier writers on dreams, because the *manifest* content has absorbed critics' whole attention. The elaboration of an alternative (and corrective) model, based on what may analogically be called a work's *latent* content, will engage us throughout this

---

[104] You see what appear to be human forms painted in grisaille on the wall of a house; having first ascribed them to your imagination, you are then told the house once belonged to a painter; then that your informant is a habitual liar; where does this leave you? E.H.Gombrich asks about the Dutch still-life: 'where exactly is the borderline between reading into and reading?' (*Meditations on a Hobby-Horse*, Phaidon 1963, p. 153)

[105] Ricoeur, op. cit., p. 357.

[106] Cf. '..every unresolved repression in [an analyst] constitutes what has been aptly described by Stekel as a "blind spot" in his analytic perception' (*SE* XII.116).

book—as will, naturally, the formulation of a warrant to use these terms. Furthermore, if this contention is correct, and Jane Austen's most original contribution to the European novel the evocation of psychical structures, we shall also need a different conception of *form* from the received account;[107] as Freud says, *'The form of a dream . . . is used with quite surprising frequency for representing its concealed subject-matter'* (4.446, Freud's italics).

This brings us to the fourth principle of dream-interpretation with the help of which Jane Austen's work is to be explored: namely the 'fundamental rule' (Introduction, p. xxiii). Applying it to an extended fiction involves 'analysis' in an almost chemical sense, for just as Freud analysed sexual impulses by separating them into their component elements, so when he interprets a dream he proceeds 'by ignoring the dream as a whole and starting associations from its single elements' (*SE* XVII.160).

*

Questions, not to say cavils, may already be surfacing in readers' minds.

Concerning this fourth principle, for example: can a novel, like a dream, really be regarded as 'a conglomerate which, for purposes of investigation, must be broken up once more into fragments' (4.581/2)? Is there not something suspect about the injunction to attend not to the novel as a whole but to 'the separate portions of its content' (4.178)?

At the start of Chapter III a first assessment will be made of the question whether applying *any* of these principles highlights necessary distinctions to be drawn between the two sorts of fiction in question: novels and dreams. Readers are asked to reserve judgement about the legitimacy of all these applications until then, after the procedure as a whole has been given a practical trial on Jane Austen's first-published novel.

On this fourth principle, however, this can already be said: as far as any commentary is concerned, Kroeber is right to stress the limited help afforded even by such handy tools as concordances; as he says, 'It is the togetherness that makes the art'.[108] Description of an art so deft as Jane Austen's must always, it goes without saying, appear heavy-handed. Furthermore, to forestall criticism of what cannot but strike the reader as inadequacies in the analyses which follow, no critic can be unaware that linear presentation '..is not a very adequate means of describing mental processes going on in differ-

---

107 From Lascelles–'She is quite incurious about the form of the novel' (op. cit., p. 124)–to Barbara Hardy– 'she introduced no conspicuously new formal devices comparable to Richardson's introspective epistle-writing "to the moment" ' (*A Reading of Jane Austen*, Peter Owen 1975, p. 11). There are many allusions in the critical literature to 'formal perfection' or 'formal artistry' (Lodge [1969], p. 17) or to 'classical' form–e.g. 'her art exacts . . . that the novel shall have a classical precision of structure' (Ifor Evans, op. cit., p. 144); 'the one English novelist who seems to me to achieve classical perfection' (Fraser, op. cit., p. 25), etc., etc. But such references are merely exclamatory, not explanatory.

108 Kroeber, op. cit, p. 18. Cf. Wollheim: '..what we think of as a style has a kind of inner coherence that a mere repertoire lacks' (op. cit. [1975], p. 80).

ent layers of the mind . . . it is a question of forcing a structure which is itself in many dimensions on to the two-dimensional descriptive plane' (9.308/9).

Perhaps it was the sense of this problem which moved Virginia Woolf to coin her celebrated dictum that Jane Austen is of all great writers 'the most difficult to catch in the act of greatness'.[109]

Although psychoanalytic interpretation of art is necessarily 'fragmentary, because it is simply analogical',[110] no excuse is made for recourse in this book to very copious quotation, which constitutes itself a sort of demonstration.

The criteria which have dictated the choice of material quoted are unlikely to be at once clear; indeed the material itself is bound to seem odd and unfamiliar, since it has not been quoted before. By the nature of the demonstration it cannot fail to appear often actually trite; we shall be making constant tacit recourse to one of Freud's most important principles, formulated in the essay on Leonardo: 'Nothing is too small to be a manifestation of hidden mental processes' (14.212); and in the later essay on Michelangelo he alludes to an Italian physician, Giovanni Morelli, who inaugurated a revolution in painting-attribution by a method closely related to the technique of psychoanalysis: 'It too is accustomed to divine secret and concealed things from. . . the rubbish-heap, as it were, of our observations' (14.265).

But the complement to the fundamental rule for the patient, is the rule of 'evenly suspended attention' for the analyst (*SE* XII.111) who controls the motives which usually direct his attention so as to keep in mind 'a multitude of apparently insignificant elements whose correlations are only to emerge later on' (*L & P* 43). Only thus can the density and complexity of Jane Austen's language be roused from the state in which it has slumbered: Freud's rejoinder about awaking sleeping dogs or instincts (Introduction, p. xxvi) finds its literary-critical complement in William Empson's conviction that the English language is perhaps 'uniquely full of metaphors . . . which are not dead but sleeping'.[111]

And only thus, finally, can the fifth principle of dream-interpretation enlighten us as to the nature of Jane Austen's irony. For whilst Freud quoted with approval F.W.Hildebrandt's view that ' "There lies in dreams a marvellous poetry, an apt allegory, an incomparable humour, a rare irony.." ' (4.129), it is hoped the reader will see that irony, far from being a mere heuristic tool for propagating 'Jane's' moral imperatives, serves an indicative function in the very form of the novelist's work, and is indeed the essence of her art.

---

[109] Woolf (op. cit., p. 433) came nearer to the purport of this book than any of her successors, whose post-Freudian baggage might have included the following glimpse: she thought that if Jane Austen had lived longer, 'She would have devised a method, clear and composed as ever, but deeper and more suggestive, for conveying not only what people say, but what they leave unsaid' (ibid., p. 434).

[110] Ricoeur, op. cit., p. 166.

[111] *Seven Types of Ambiguity*, Pelican 1973, p. 45.

PRELUDE

One justification for beginning a reading of Jane Austen with *Sense and Sensibility*[1] is that this novel begins differently from the others. The works that followed it into print all contain in their first sentences a word the slight glint of whose sharper implications lights up its blander surroundings:

> It is a truth universally acknowledged, that a single man in possession of a large fortune, **must**..
>
> About thirty years ago, Miss Maria Ward of Huntingdon, with only seven thousand pounds, had the good luck to **captivate**..
>
> Emma Woodhouse, handsome, clever and rich, **seemed**..

Sense and Sensibility starts with two paragraphs taking up just over a page, devoid of any twinkle of this kind, recounting a situation never recaptured in any of Jane Austen's novels, unless it be in the conjugal felicity glimpsed at the end of them: a Happy Family in a Golden Age, when an 'old Gentleman's days were comfortably spent' amid loving relations; we hear 'his attachment to them all increased . . .their attention to him proceeded not merely from interest but from goodness of heart' and (final marvel) 'the cheerfulness of the children added a relish to his existence'. Even one Jane Austen page without a trace of that famous irony is already a rarity; to find these details on a first page should alert us to the fact that something unusual is going on.

It cannot last: for 'The old Gentleman died', and the whole thing topples; the will is read which, 'like almost every other will, gave as much disappointment as pleasure..'; and by chapter 5, Marianne is wandering alone before the beloved place she must leave next day, crying ' "Oh! happy house!" '

We may never know why, from manuscripts she is thought to have held (three perhaps in some state of finish) Jane Austen chose to revise, or rewrite, or at any rate submit to a publisher this novel first, from Chawton. But there is something apt in its being the first to appear: its opening marks it as a Prelude: to *Sense and Sensibility*, perhaps to her whole oeuvre.

Furthermore, in the theme of dispossession maybe we hear an echo of an early chapter of that book which (not excluding *Sir Charles Grandison*) she doubtless knew best of all. There is however a significant difference: those dispossessed of this 18th century Eden are all women.

---

[1] The first of four novels published in the space of *ca.* four years (Nov. 1811 to Dec. 1815) during her life; of the two that appeared posthumously (she died 18 July 1817), one (*NA*) is probably the one she refers to on 13 March 1817: 'Miss Catherine is put upon the Shelve [sic] for the present' (*L* 484), implying it had been taken down from that 'Shelve'. So what preceding critics treat as the earliest of the six was among the last things she touched.

CHAPTER II

Sense and Sensibility

' "Oh! Elinor, how incomprehensible are your feelings!" '
(Mrs Dashwood, in *S & S* I.15.78)

'I do not wish to arouse conviction; I wish to stimulate thought and
to upset prejudices . . .You should neither believe nor reject . . . [but]
listen and allow what I tell you to work on you.'   (Freud, 1.281)

- 1 -

If *Sense and Sensibility* opens with four dispossessed women, the one who
seems to suffer most from this may be said to get a kind of symbolic revenge
near the end of the novel. Symbolic, and indeed—in the lightest sense of the
word—unconscious: when Marianne's illness scares the Palmers into departure we are told she was kept

> in ignorance of all these arrangements. She knew not that she had been
> the means of sending the owners of Cleveland away.   (III.7.309)

Seemingly insignificant details—three hundred pages apart, and which a
'realist' reading has to relegate to the gratuitousness of 'local colour'—indicate
the sounding of a long echo: in vol.I Fanny Dashwood arrives '..with her child
and their attendants. No one could dispute her right to come; the house was
her husband's..' (I.1.5/6), and when in vol.III Mrs Palmer's departure is fixed
on, '..she set off, with her little boy and his nurse, for the house of a near
relation of Mr. Palmer's' (III.7.308).

Even Marianne's unconscious trees are recalled: we learn her cold was
caught in the part of the grounds 'where the trees were the oldest' (306)—for
which we have been prepared by being told Cleveland boasts '..the fir, the
mountain-ash, and the acacia, and a thick screen of them altogether,
interspersed with tall Lombardy poplars' (302).

Between these first and last extrusions, *Sense and Sensibility* presents no
less than four others, verbal overlappings among which suggest that they all
contribute to the same preoccupation as the above: Col. Brandon, failing to
elope with Eliza, was ' "banished to the house of a relation far distant" '

48

(II.9.206); when Lucy's secret engagement is revealed, the Steeles are ousted: Fanny ' "declared they should not stay a minute longer in the house" ' (III.1.259); repercussions of the affair include ' "a most unhappy rupture:—Edward is dismissed for ever from his mother's notice. He left her house yesterday" ' (ibid. 268; Robert calls it ' "the breach" ', 299); finally we learn that Willoughby's refusal to marry (another) Eliza to please Mrs Smith had ' "ended in a total breach . . . I was formally dismissed from her favour and her house" ' (III.8.323).[1]

Except for the first-mentioned of these four dispossessions—Col. Brandon's, long before, redeemed when 'five years ago', his brother's death ' "left to me the **possession** of the family property" ' (II.9.208)—all are recounted in vol. III of *Sense and Sensibility*; by that time, the preoccupation (only some dimensions of which the present demonstration aims to indicate) may already have imprinted itself upon the reader's mind.

For if we return now to vol.I, we note that three departures are described as having no such justification as those just inventoried; their disconcerting character is indeed that they are unexplained: at I.13.66 the Colonel leaves with no explanation; at I.15.77, Willoughby leaves, with an explanation that satisfies hardly anyone; at I.19.104 Edward leaves, in an atmosphere of ambiguity. This time it is the spacing of the three departures which indicates that they are somehow related: Willoughby's declarations of fidelity in I.14 (the eve of his departure) take place '**about a week** after Colonel Brandon had left the country' (72); Edward arrives '**about a week** after [Willoughby's] leaving the country' (85) and 'remained **a week** at the cottage' (101).

Overlapping with this series, there is another: not now of departures, but arrivals—or rather what might be called *mistaken* arrivals:

> Among the objects in the scene, they soon discovered an animated one; it was a man on horseback riding towards them. In a few minutes they could distinguish him to be a gentleman; and in a moment afterwards Marianne rapturously exclaimed,
>
> 'It is he; it is indeed; —I know it is!' —And was hastening to meet him, when Elinor cried out,
>
> 'Indeed, Marianne, I think you are mistaken. It is not Willoughby. The person is not tall enough for him, and has not his air.'
>
> 'He has, he has,' cried Marianne, 'I am sure he has. His air, his coat, his horse. I knew how soon he would come.'
>
> She walked eagerly on as she spoke; and Elinor, to screen Marianne from particularity, as she felt almost certain of its not being Willoughby, quickened her pace and kept up with her. They were soon within thirty yards of the gentleman. Marianne looked again; her heart sunk within her; and abruptly turning round, she was hurrying back, when the voices

---

[1] Later he feels 'shut out for ever' from the Dashwoods (III.8.329).

of both her sisters were raised to detain her, a third, almost as well known as Willoughby's, joined them in begging her to stop, and she turned round with surprise to see and welcome Edward Ferrars. (I.16.86)

This is the first occasion in the novel when one character is expected, and another arrives. But only the first; there are five:
2. Mrs Jennings recounts (I.19.106) the sudden arrival of the Palmers:

'I thought I heard a carriage last night, while we were drinking our tea, but it never entered my head that it could be them. I thought of nothing but whether it might not be Colonel Brandon come back again..'

3. London (II.3.161): the Dashwood sisters hear a knock at the door:

Marianne starting up moved towards the door . . . in the extasy [sic] of her feelings at that instant she could not help exclaiming, 'Oh! Elinor, it is Willoughby, indeed it is!' and seemed almost ready to throw herself into his arms, when Colonel Brandon appeared..

4. Cleveland (III.7.316): Elinor expecting her mother and Col. Brandon:

The bustle in the vestibule, as she passed along an inner lobby, assured her that they were already in the house. She rushed forwards towards the drawing-room, —she entered it, —and saw only Willoughby.

5. Barton again (III.12.358):

..the figure of a man on horseback drew her eyes to the window. He stopt at their gate. It was a gentleman, it was Colonel Brandon himself. Now she should hear more; and she trembled in expectation of it. But—it was *not* Colonel Brandon—neither his air—nor his height. Were it possible, she should say it must be Edward. She looked again. He had just dismounted; —she could not be mistaken; —it *was* Edward..

The final example of a series of episodes, common elements in which show that they belong to the same preoccupation, returns us to the 'Prelude': in the novel's first five chapters, Norland is imagined as housing seven Dashwoods; yet if we consider this in the context of the way our novelist typically brings characters before us—by dialogue—it must be noted that not only is the first conversation (John and Fanny planning the dispossession) private— it is imagined taking place at Norland, but away from those it most concerns —but that the first five conversations of the book are all private duologues:
2. (I.3.16) Elinor and Mrs Henry Dashwood (about Edward);
3. (I.3.17/18) Mrs Henry Dashwood and Marianne (about Edward);
4. (I.4.19-22) between Marianne and Elinor[2] (about Edward);
5. (I.4.23) related as taking place between Mrs John and Mrs Henry

[2] Elinor refers here to other private conversations with Edward, ' "while you have been wholly engrossed on the most affectionate principle by my mother" ', i.e. Marianne has been prevented from playing gooseberry.

Dashwood (about Edward): the latter lady, we are told, could not 'pretend to be unconscious', so she 'gave her an answer which marked her contempt, and instantly left the room'.

When for the first time (I.5.25) we find assembled a large group of characters in conversation, the impression of sudden openness is considerable: it is then that Mrs Dashwood announces her forthcoming removal, and 'The family of Dashwood', with which we began, is fractured.

What does all this mean?

It means, first of all, that before we even start to look at what is commonly thought to make up the 'contents' of a Jane Austen novel—behaviour/emotions of characters/their interactions with each other and with objects in the 'world' imagined as housing them (the usual approach to 'what happens' in her books)—we might profitably reflect upon the way characters are brought into and taken out of the small lighted area of our conscious attention. We may if we wish say that an event happens to a character; but character and event, both made of words, are not of such different logical status as are people and their experience in real life: in the last analysis, a character—indeed the whole text of which this character is only a part—'happens' *to us*.

The second observation is that the various sets of what may be called *recurrences* have something in common: they throw into doubt principles on which, like the characters in the episodes related, we thought we could depend: through the *ostinato* effect of the mistaken arrivals, Jane Austen may be seen to be playing with us—playing in the very texture of prose with our expectation that events in novels can possibly be as realistic as they are (by definition) in reality. It is in the syntax that even we almost see the character who is *not* arriving: Mrs Jennings ' "**thought of nothing** but whether **it might not be**" ' Col. Brandon; Marianne cries ' "**It is he; it is** indeed—I know **it is!**"—And was hastening to meet **him**...'; Elinor hears a bustle: it 'assured her that **they were** in the house'; in the final example quoted this pounding of the verb 'to be' eloquently hammers out the ontological mockery.

Thirdly we should also be awake to what this demonstration reveals about the characters themselves: in that short space of three weeks it is the main male characters—the Dashwood girls' possible and impossible husbands, heroes and anti-heroes—who vanish; the private conversations each exclude a close member of the family; and the expulsions are all effected by relatives: the Steeles by their cousins the John Dashwoods, the four Dashwood women by Mrs Henry Dashwood's stepson and -daughter, Willoughby by the aged relative on whom he depends, Col. Brandon by his brother, Edward by his mother. Furthermore, these three observations are themselves interrelated:

'Of John **I know** very little, though we have lived together for years; but of Willoughby my judgment has long been formed...'   (I.12.59)

When Marianne tells Elinor this, the verb in bold type serves an irony (about which she knows best, brother or suitor) present elsewhere: in Edward's farewell, ' "..there was no distinction between Elinor and me: it was the good wishes of an affectionate **brother** to both" ' (I.9.39): the figure may go unnoticed if we do not recall that the unfraternal John Dashwood later declares: ' "I confess, it would give me great pleasure **to call** Colonel Brandon **brother**. His property here, his place, his house.." ' (III.14.375); similarly (with vicious intention) Lucy tells Elinor: ' "Mr. Ferrars . . . **looks upon** yourself and the other Miss Dashwoods, **quite as** his own **sisters**.." ' (I.22.130).

Elinor's surprise at Lucy's 'familiarity' (I.21.123) is often put down to an undigested attitude of her author's; but the word contains what has been called that author's god-term (sc., an entity never questioned): *family*. This alerts us to its significance in a more far-reaching preoccupation in this work (and others by Jane Austen) with false intimacy.

For a striking characteristic of the world into which the Dashwood women are thrust is the contingency governing relationships there: the Palmers raise Elinor's wonder at the 'strange unsuitableness which often existed between husband and wife' (I.21.118), the Colonel is 'no more adapted to be [Sir John's] friend than Lady Middleton was to be his wife, or Mrs. Jennings to be Lady Middleton's mother' (I.7.34); Sir John and his wife are 'dissimilar in temperament and outward behaviour' (32). At the other end of the scale, between the latter and Fanny Dashwood,

> ..a kind of cold hearted selfishness on both sides . . . mutually attracted them; and they sympathised with each other in an insipid propriety of demeanour, and a general want of understanding.   (II.12.229)

Most important, the spatial/material dispositions to which attention has been drawn, overlap with the moral: the Middletons resemble each other in a 'total want of talent and taste which **confined** their employments . . . within a very narrow compass' (I.7.32); at the Dashwoods' in London, 'no poverty of any kind, except of conversation, appeared' (II.12.233). Similarly whilst Sir John, 'whose prevailing anxiety was the dread of being alone' (II.3.157), 'delighted in **collecting about him** more young people than his house would hold' (I.7.32), Marianne has a cocooning technique—by remaining

> **unconscious** of it all; for she was as well able to **collect her thoughts within herself,** and be as ignorant of what was passing around her, in Mr. Gray's shop, as in her own bed-room.   (II.11.221)

With these considerations in mind, to close this section and prepare the next, a tiny detail may be quoted, relating perhaps to another sort of exclusion: Elinor has just informed Edward of the living in the gift of Col. Brandon; Edward leaves to go and thank the latter, and ' "When I see him again," said

Elinor to herself, as the door shut him out, "I shall see him the husband of Lucy" ' (III.4.291).

Given the care with which we are *not* told either: that it was Elinor who shut him out; or, according to his brother's financial/worldly statement later, ' "Poor Edward!—he has . . . shut himself out for ever from all decent society!" ' (5.299); given the preoccupations we have been examining, perhaps to ask the question, *Out of what, exactly is he shut?* will appear less supererogatory than when this inquiry was started.

- 2 -

To benefit from the above demonstration about series of episodes (which if they draw attention to themselves at all do so only by concatenation), we may now examine a single passage, what Empson calls 'a particularly dramatic point where the meaning needs to be concentrated'; and by exploring ramifications of meaning elsewhere in the text, we shall hope to justify the application to Jane Austen of what he calls characteristic of Shakespeare: '..one is helped by the rest of his work to put a great deal into any part of it'.[3]

Immediately after the last of the 'mistaken arrivals', Edward enters Barton cottage; and after some embarrassed weather talk we find this:

> 'Is Mrs. Ferrars at Longstaple?'
> 'At Longstaple!' he replied, with an air of surprise—'No, my mother is in town.'
> 'I meant,' said Elinor, taking up some work from the table, 'to inquire after Mrs. *Edward* Ferrars.'
> She dared not look up;—but her mother and Marianne both turned their eyes on him. He coloured, seemed perplexed, looked doubtingly, and after some hesitation, said,
> 'Perhaps you mean—my brother—you mean Mrs.—Mrs. *Robert* Ferrars.'
> 'Mrs. Robert Ferrars!' —was repeated by Marianne and her mother, in an accent of the utmost amazement;—and though Elinor could not speak, even *her* eyes were fixed on him with the same impatient wonder. He rose from his seat and walked to the window, apparently from not knowing what to do; took up a pair of scissars [sic] that lay there, and while spoiling both them and their sheath by cutting the latter to pieces as he spoke, said, in a hurried voice... [etc.]   (III.12.359/60)

The only critic to have noticed this episode in print (to my knowledge) is Tanner, who comments that Edward reveals '..his nervousness and resolution by an unconscious act which makes one begin to think that Jane Austen would not perhaps have been so very surprised by Freud's formulations as

---

[3] Op. cit., pp. 85 and 38.

we may at first suppose'; and he adds, a little later, an even more interesting observation: 'There are times when the scissors will destroy the sheath just as there are times when the sheath will contain the scissors.'[4]

We may perhaps go further than this: nay, rather we *must*. Indeed, if to use a figurative expression further comment can be said to be 'called for' by the episode, this seems to be almost literally true: surely the passage stands out and 'speaks' to us in a way others do not; surely some movement of thought is required of us, to correspond to or complete that movement of thought which produced it in 1811?

Since this is the first occasion in the present study on which psychoanalytic interpretation will be applied to an episode from a Jane Austen novel, the general credibility of such interpretation might be said to be somewhat critically at stake. The reader is therefore asked to try and abstain from reserves about the concepts themselves, which will only become interesting when it is seen how they offer a way of understanding and of grouping together a range of phenomena that illustrate Jane Austen's language in action.

It is particularly important to stress this since, although what we have to do with here—centrally, the passage with the scissors and sheath—is an act, at the risk of enraging the reader with an obvious remark it must be repeated that it is an act represented in words.

Moreover Edward is not a person, who might obligingly reply to our questions from the divan, but part of a text: it is only from the text that we can glean the associations needed for the better understanding of the passage.[5]

We may first observe that as a piece of behaviour the act diverges dramatically from what we have seen of Edward up to this point in the novel: indeed, it has some title to being described as the most violent act in the Jane Austen canon.[6]

We did not need Freud to tell us that people are capable of sudden acts of violence; but it is the very absence of what may, still in the lightest sense of the word, be called *manifest* meaning—that is, Edward can hardly be supposed to have a particular hatred of scissors or sheaths—that leads pre- or un- or anti-psychoanalytic perception to dismiss such an act as arbitrary, and which will most interest us. Faced with this scene in *Sense and Sensibility*, we may recall Freud's position with a hardly less well-known work (Michelangelo's 'Moses'): '..there are certain details which have hitherto not only escaped notice, but, in fact, have not even been properly described' (14.265).

---

[4] Tanner, op. cit., p. 87.

[5] Psychoanalysis presupposes consent of the person being analysed (15.109); so since 'we cannot question Hanold [a fictional character], we shall have to content ourselves with referring to his impressions' (14.97).

[6] Where no one strikes anyone (except in fun: Mrs Weston, teasing Emma about Jane Fairfax, exclaims ' "Do not beat me" ', *E* II.15.289); in *S & S*, Willoughby and Brandon fight their duel 'offstage'; the latter tells Elinor: ' "we returned unwounded" ' (II.9.211).

Freud was not unaware that his habit of invariably pouncing on details, in art or life, can be exasperating; it is a risk worth taking, however: the following analysis of the apparently insignificant may therefore be prefaced with the words he uses before trying properly to describe them: 'let us proceed on the assumption that even these details have significance.'

To begin with, though we may if we wish be content to say Edward's act has the effect (latish in the novel, according to realist decorum) of revealing something of his bottled-up state just before proposing to Elinor, it is well-known that when people start cutting things, psychoanalysts look up sharply, then gently inquire about those precious associations. Here they come:

1a) Three hundred pages earlier, Margaret Dashwood tells Elinor that she now has proof that Marianne and Willoughby are surely engaged. Elinor scorns this: after all, Margaret had been ' "..certain that Marianne wore his picture round her neck; but it turned out to be only the miniature of our great uncle." ' Margaret then recounts her presence at a scene between the lovers, at which Willoughby had asked for a lock of Marianne's hair:

> '..I saw him cut it off . . . he seemed to be begging something of her and presently he took up her scissars and cut off a long lock of her hair, for it was all tumbled down her back.' (I.12.60)

1b) Six chapters later (Marianne's suitor has vanished and Elinor's appeared) Marianne spies a plait of hair in a ring on one of Edward's fingers, and asks him if it is Fanny's hair; he, blushing

> ..and giving a momentary glance at Elinor, replied, 'Yes; it is my sister's hair. The setting always casts a different shade on it you know.'
> Elinor had met his eye, and looked **conscious** likewise. That the hair was her own, she instantaneously felt as well satisfied as Marianne; the only difference in their conclusions was, that what Marianne considered as a free gift from her sister, Elinor was **conscious** must have been procured by some theft or contrivance **unknown to herself**. (I.18.98)

Elinor learns later (I.22) that Lucy has a miniature of Edward, and Edward a lock of Lucy's hair in a ring; and still later (II.7) that Willoughby did have a lock of Marianne's; however, when she reads in Lucy's letter to Edward, ' "I . . . will return your picture the first opportunity . . . the ring with my hair you are very welcome to keep" ', her only reaction is to return the letter 'without any comment' (III.13.365).

This is one of the passages (Introduction, p. xvi, n. 10) where Jane Austen appears to be playing a language-game both extremely sophisticated in itself and also full of consequences for this study's main contention: Elinor's (erroneous) *certainty* is highlighted by the word 'conscious'—twice, and in its two different senses, the second juxtaposed with 'unknown to herself'.

55

2a) That semantic observation leads us to the second series of associations this novel affords us to understand what is going on in the final scissors-and-sheath scene; for when Elinor, intending to make clear she is referring, not to Edward's mother, but to Edward's wife, says ' "I meant . . . to inquire after Mrs. *Edward* Ferrars.." ', Edward replies ' "Perhaps you mean—my brother—you mean Mrs.—Mrs. *Robert* Ferrars." ' In other words, he thinks Elinor has made a slip, and corrects her.

This exchange, too, is adumbrated by another, two hundred and fifty pages before (I.22.129): Lucy, having asked Elinor whether she knows Mrs Ferrars —whom Lucy refers to, aloud, as ' "your sister-in-law's mother" ', and Elinor, to herself, as 'Edward's mother' (I.22.128)—explains that one day she and Mrs Ferrars will be ' "intimately acquainted" ':

> 'Good heavens!' cried Elinor, 'what do you mean? Are you acquainted with Mr. Robert Ferrars? Can you be—?' And she did not feel much delighted with the idea of such a sister-in-law.
>
> 'No;' replied Lucy, 'not to Mr. *Robert* Ferrars—I never saw him in my life; but,' fixing her eyes upon Elinor, 'to his elder brother.'

2b) Lucy later (I.22.130) turns the knife in the wound she has gouged:

> '..Though you do not know him so well as me, Miss Dashwood, you must have seen enough of him to be **sensible** he is very capable of making a woman sincerely attached to him.'
>
> 'Certainly,' answered Elinor, **without knowing what she said**.

We have come full circle.

Of the whole range of psychoanalytic concepts, the 'Freudian' slip is doubtless the one that has gained most currency, maybe in part owing to literary examples like this:[7] for neither Jane Austen nor her reader need have read Freud to sense it is somehow 'true' that Elinor should betray what she 'Certainly' feels for Edward—all the more so in otiose reply to what is after all merely a rhetorical question. Nevertheless, the unassuming expression 'without knowing what she said' may suggest to us that at some level Jane Austen knew what she was doing.

Associations in the text were first sought the better to grasp resonances for Edward's act; the upshot has been to multiply implications for understanding Elinor. And if one result of the demonstration with which this chapter opened was to indicate that at a key moment the very texture of the prose in *Sense and Sensibility* materialises Elinor's erroneous perception that Col. Brandon *is* the gentleman coming to Barton Cottage, so the whole web of her

---

[7] Otto Rank appears to have been the first to notice in print a Freudian slip in Shakespeare (Portia, to Bassano: 'One half of me is yours, the other half yours,—/Mine own, I would say': *The Merchant of Venice* III.iii) *Zeitblatt für Psychoanalyse* I.109, 1910, recounted with other examples by Freud (5.144).

relationships, illuminated by the most recent demonstration (with Lucy, with Marianne, and through them with Mrs Ferrars and Willoughby) has equally shown her in a new light: *pace* the traditional account, the light of irony—the irony of the unconscious.

One indication of this, in two stages, must suffice: given her (as it turns out justified) certainty that Willoughby has a lock of Marianne's hair, Elinor's (as it turns out unjustified) certainty that the hair in Edward's ring is her own, may not unreasonably be inferred to betoken a *wish* that it be so; although, when Edward later walks in, she 'knows' he is married, nevertheless she unconsciously refers to her own future self when she ' **"meant"** . . . **taking up** some work . . . "Mrs. *Edward* Ferrars" '; so when Edward too, 'not knowing what to do . . . **took up**' the scissors, it is *her* wish that he is fulfilling.

Conclusions of the utmost importance, both for the significance of the scissors scene in this novel, and through that for our understanding of Jane Austen's whole oeuvre, follow from that fact, and we shall return to them.

For the moment, from Edward's point of view, his act might be said to 'mean' *I cut it now*. By saying his act 'means' that, we say it comes from some other register of communication; furthermore that act, and the translation of it into the words *I cut it now*, are in the present tense, whereas the scenes to which the act refers are in the past.

Psychoanalysis distinguishes two ways of bringing past into present: by remembering, in words, and by *acting out* (which may include words in so far as they belong to the register of gesture). Acting out is further distinguished from *parapraxis* by its repetitive character; the reading proposed here draws together episodes in which the least that may be said is that *the text* is repeating a preoccupation.

Furthermore, this act is a highly *condensed* one: all over in a moment, for the reader as for Edward. Given that it is the last in the chain (powerful *ex*-pression of what has been *sup*-pressed), unsurprisingly it exhausts Edward: after a few words he falls 'into a reverie' and walks out to the village. For those who like concise technical vocabulary, Edward's act is *an adequate abreaction of the quota of affect*: in other words, as indeed we are told in the next chapter, 'Edward was free' (361).

Finally, his freedom has a verbal character, for the moment he utters the words ' "Mrs. *Robert* Ferrars" ', signifying that he is free, reverses the moment when Elinor's pains began: when Lucy revealed that ' "Mr. Edward Ferrars, the eldest son of [etc.] is the person I mean" ' (I.22).

If these suggestions are drawn together in terms of the conceptual scheme of psychoanalysis (italicised), we shall be able to go further.

Condensation has been mentioned; related to it, as a determinant of a *symptomatic act* which is a *derivative of the unconscious* through the *return of the repressed*, is another term: *displacement*. If Edward's act 'stands for' an unconscious content, it is a *substitute formation*; and we may now ask the question: how near is it to some other act the agent would like to be doing? What, in other words, does Edward *wish* to cut?

The first, perhaps most obvious answer might plausibly be: his brother Robert; and its plausibility would be fuelled not only by the fact that the immediate catalyst for the act is the *name* of his brother, but also (if such an entity may unoutrageously be mentioned in this context) by *the plot*..: Edward himself tells Elinor in II.13.366 that, relative to his mother, ' "Robert always was her favourite." '8

We know that being the firstborn has not given Edward freedom to marry whom he chooses. So this first reading has again the effect of linking the relation between the Ferrars brothers with the one between the Dashwood sisters. It is clear early on which of her daughters Mrs Dashwood feels closest to, and Elinor's resentment of the fact emerges with particular clarity when her mother arrives at Cleveland: 'to see Marianne was her first desire; and in two minutes she was with her beloved child' (III.9.334). This reunion makes her declare herself 'one of the happiest women in the world', but 'Elinor could not hear the declaration, nor witness its proofs without sometimes wondering whether her mother ever recollected Edward..'

We come now to the significant fact that the scissors suffer as much, in Edward's act, as the sheath does; it might legitimately be asked why Jane Austen should bother with such a detail.

Any reticence which might have been proper in asseverating this study's main contention on the grounds of its *prima facie* implausibility must in the present instance yield before the peculiar accuracy of the novelist's presentation. For apart from the aspects of Edward's act that fulfil the definition of any substitute formation (see above: *condensation* and *displacement*), a further key characteristic of any unconscious structure is that the repressed invariably returns in the form of 'a *compromise* between the repressed ideas and the repressing ones' (*SE* III.170). Indeed, it is thus that psychoanalysis justifies its view that the symptomatic act is always the *representation of a defensive conflict*.

The next question—as to between what and what any psychical conflict may be waged—is arguably the most fundamental which Freud attempts to answer; before we can apply to the particular conflict here represented what Freud calls 'metapsychology', more of the text of *Sense and Sensibility* needs to be explored. For the moment, this part of the discussion may be concluded with the following observation: the very fact that it has been found possible

---

8 Edward being the firstborn, this must mean since Robert's birth. Cf. '..many children who believed themselves securely enthroned in the unshakeable affection of their parents have by a single blow been cast down from all the heavens of their imaginary omnipotence' (10.172). Another suggestive overlap in the mothers-and-daughters/sons preoccupation is given when, after a period of resentment from Mrs Ferrars, Lucy is 'in every thing considered, and always openly acknowledged, to be a favourite child' (III.14.377).

to make *various* suggestions concerning the meaning of Edward's act, confirms its labelling as a formation of the unconscious. Contrary to the widespread supposition that Freud says x invariably means y, the very nature of the relationship between symptom and meaning is such, he often declares (e.g. 1.101) that any particular symptom may well express a number of meanings. And in dream interpretation he is quite 'prepared to find that the piece of content may conceal a different meaning when it occurs in various people or in various contexts' (4.179).

As at the end of section 1, it will be opportune now to pursue further implications of what has been presented. First, Jane Austen's recourse to the word 'unconscious' should be understood in the wider context of other expressions in the same preoccupation: we have seen Elinor's 'without knowing what she said' (133); two other examples must suffice: in London, we find her walking thoughtfully between the fire and the window '**without knowing** that she received warmth from one, or discerning **objects** through the other' (II.7. 190); earlier, following her husband's death, Mrs Dashwood was 'in such affliction as rendered her **careless of surrounding objects**' (I.3.16).

It is important that at moments of intense emotion characters' relations to *objects* should be suspended. In reviving an obsolescent sense of the word 'object', Freud was stressing the contingent character of what, in phantasy or reality, a *subject* may relate to. It is therefore not without interest, to begin with, that Jane Austen's work appears to be at the watershed between the two meanings:[9] the objects, in the last two passages quoted, could well include human ones (indeed, the last includes Edward); furthermore, both objects of the Dashwood sisters' preoccupations are thus evoked: in a passage already given above (p. 49): 'Amongst the **objects** in the scene, they soon discovered an **animated** one' (it turns out to be Edward); and when the sisters go to London (II.4), Elinor meditates on the blankness of

> ..her own **prospect** . . . how gladly she would engage in the solicitude of Marianne's situation to have the same **animating object** in view..

Between these two passages, another, comparing the sisters' situations, glances at other words we have noted: thus at II.1.141 no one would have supposed from their appearance that Elinor was mourning

> ..in secret over obstacles which must divide her for ever from **the object of her love**, and that Marianne was **internally dwelling** on the perfections of a man, of whose whole heart she felt thoroughly **possessed**.

The effect of these echoes is again to bring home to the reader the text's density; so that when, in what must be regarded as one of the novel's key

---

[9] Anne Elliott excuses herself for using the word ambiguously: ' "I believe you equal . . . to every domestic forbearance, so long as–if I may be allowed the expression, so long as you have an object" ' (*P* II.11.235).

sentences, we find Elinor attenuating her own emotions before Marianne—
'She was very far from wishing to **dwell** on her own feelings, or to **represent
herself** as suffering much' (III.1.261)—it should now be impossible to regard
as gratuitous in this sentence the *condensation of verbal fields*. Feelings, like
characters, are 'in need of a dwelling': how are they to be 'accommodated'
(I.4.23)? *Sense and Sensibility* is preoccupied with the representation of this
problem; but equally with the problem of its representation.

' "..what I felt is—in the common phrase, not to be expressed" .'

Phrases like this, of Willoughby's (III.8.325) are often quoted in the service of
what—buttressed e.g. by the I.18 debate on the picturesque—is inferred to be
a comic/satiric intention on the part of 'sensible' Jane Austen. Placing them
in the wider context of the book should enable us to see them, on the
contrary, as part of a very serious preoccupation indeed, and (again) one significant for the main contention of this study.

Tanner is no doubt right, noting Marianne's scream is 'at the heart of the
novel (almost literally at the centre, in the twenty-ninth of fifty chapters)'[10] to
draw attention to a formal characteristic of this work: screaming is the most
inarticulate but eloquent human expressive medium. But it might be added
that two chapters later we find Brandon's long ' "account of my family afflic-
tions" ', which he prefaces by telling Elinor ' "On such a subject . . . I can
have little temptation to be diffuse" ', and warns her that she will find him
' "a very awkward narrator" ' in his ' "short account of myself" ' (204 f.) The
materiality of 'account' contrasts with Brandon's reluctance to 'materialise'
his feelings in words, and the same distinction is to be found in a notation
following Elinor's resentment of her mother's preferential consideration for
Marianne. Mrs Dashwood had been '..trusting to the temperate **account** of
her own disappointment which Elinor had sent her' (II.9.335).

This detail adumbrates Mrs Dashwood's reaction to the revelation, by the
servant, of Edward's marriage: she is 'shocked to perceive by Elinor's countenance how much she really suffered', and realises that

> **..she had erred in relying on Elinor's representation of herself**
> . . . She found that she had been misled by the careful, the considerate
> attention of her daughter, to think the attachment . . . much slighter in
> reality, than . . . it was now proved to be.   (III.11.355/6)

We must not allow the word 'reality', here, to get away: where then, if not 'in
reality'—by which, even all these years after Freud's death, we still tend to
mean 'physical reality'—*is* it? It is to this question that we now address ourselves.

---

[10] Tanner, op. cit., p. 75.

Section 2 aimed to sharpen awareness of how a striking scene (scissors-and-sheath) late in the work, retroactively fills earlier episodes with meaning. In this section we shall examine an effect similar in implications but producing a longer-drawn-out presence in the novel. The effect is signalled by less ostentatious means: the mere tense of a verb, namely that pluperfect in Mrs Dashwood's 'she had erred', with which we now associate the notation that Elinor '**had always admitted a hope**, while Edward remained single, that something would occur to prevent his marrying Lucy' (III.12.357).

Mrs Dashwood's error, shared by almost all the critics, will interest us less than Elinor's hope, and its representation. In the most economical manner, that pluperfect invites us to review under its light the whole course of what has been presented to us about Elinor. Irony is present in some of her statements: little untruths such as ' "I have known myself to be divided from Edward for ever" ' (III.1.264) are extenuated by her self-imposed obligation to keep Lucy's secret (' "I have had her **hopes** and exultations to listen to again and again.." ') But far more important is the disjunction between such spoken statements and the narrative presentation of Elinor, where we may perceive the dimensions of what will now be denominated a *structural irony*. Use of this term requires some preliminary explanation.

Of this novel's formal characteristics, the most salient are: (a) it appears to have two heroines (we shall come to Marianne in due course) who are almost constantly together; and (b) there is a strict alternation between the physical presences of the two young heroes, who never meet, which may be represented schematically, thus:

	Vol.I			Vol.II			Vol.III	
	EDWARD	WILLOUGHBY	EDWARD	WILLOUGHBY	EDWARD		WILLOUGHBY	EDWARD
pp.	15-27	42-76	85-104	176/7	230		317-32	359-80
				+ 183 (letter)	240-4			
number of pages:	12	34	19	3	5		17	21

The most remarkable aspect of these presences is their brevity: the young men are physically present—i.e. quite near one of the sisters, and so within what may be called earshot of the narrative presence—for altogether just over fifty pages, or about one seventh of the novel, each.[11]

From Willoughby's entrance, Marianne's attention is almost entirely concentrated on him; this cannot be said of Elinor's thought, as it is manifest on the page, about Edward. Just before his final return to Barton, after an 'absence' of no less than one hundred and fifteen pages, we are told 'Elinor

---

[11] Manifestations of presence are to be interpreted broadly: Willoughby spends all his last presence (III.8. 317-32) talking (about himself); the only utterance Edward makes during his first presence (a comparable no. of pp.) is ' "Devonshire! Are you, indeed, going there? So far from hence! And to what part of it?" ' (I.5.25).

grew impatient for some tidings of Edward' (352); and the reader may share the feeling. On a first reading of the work we were perhaps impatient with what may seem awkwardness; the two-heroine model has been described as beginner's clumsiness in transforming to narrative form what is surmised to have been an earlier (?epistolary) novel entitled 'Elinor and Marianne'.

If we are to understand Jane Austen's status in the history of the European novel, we must resolve from the outset, in our reading of this first-published and undervalued work, not to attribute less sophistication to its author than we believe ourselves to possess.

To return to those pluperfects: we saw (p. 56) that a verbal echo links the moment when Lucy tells Elinor she is engaged to Edward, and the moment when Edward tells her he is no longer engaged to Lucy;[12] we may also note that the moments when Elinor hears of Edward's marriage and of his engagement are linked too, again by a pluperfect: whilst hearing of his marriage provokes the revelation that '**she had always admitted a hope**...' etc., the news of his engagement leads to 'an emotion and distress beyond anything **she had ever felt before**. She was mortified, shocked, confounded.'

The importance of this is marked by vol.I ending a paragraph later, with an ironic adumbration of Edward's freedom in the third: 'Elinor was then at liberty to think and be wretched' (I.22.135). Almost nothing we have so far been told about Elinor has prepared us for her emotion here.

To illustrate the strange truth of this statement, we shall now go through vol.I of the novel, staking out all the references to Edward, and dividing it for this purpose into five movements.

The first movement takes us from when Elinor is introduced to us, up to Willoughby's entrance in I.9. As Marianne has no attachment yet, all the sentimental interest is concentrated on Elinor. However, passages devoted to treatment of her feelings take up altogether about ten lines. A brief presentation in chapter 1 tells us that she 'had an excellent heart;—her disposition was affectionate, and her feelings were strong; but she knew how to govern them' (I.1.6), and in chapter 3, she is encountered in the same sentence as Edward, for the circumstance deciding Mrs Dashwood to remain at Norland is the growing 'attachment between her eldest girl and the brother of Mrs. John Dashwood' (I.3.15). In the following paragraph, about Mrs Dashwood's attitude to this attachment, all we learn is 'It was enough for her that [Edward] loved her daughter, and that Elinor returned the partiality' (15)—and it has to be enough for us, too. We may deduce, from Elinor telling her mother ' "I think you will like him . . . when you know more of him" ' (16) that a person who did not already feel something of this sort herself would

---

[12] A further neat irony: in her first lie she makes her intimacy with him less than it is: ' "..it is rather too much to pretend to know him very well" ' (I.21) and in her last, a 'flourish of malice' from the carriage (III.13), more.

hardly suppose it in someone else; similarly her defence of Edward's aesthetic sense—or sensibility—(I.4) would hardly be expressed, we may infer, in the absence of a certain affection. But when Marianne betrays her supposition that Edward and her sister are engaged (I.3.21), Elinor starts back in surprise: she felt 'that Edward stood very high in her opinion. She believed the regard to be mutual; but she required greater certainty of it..' She then explains 'the real state of the case' to her sister: ' "I do not attempt to deny . . . that I think very highly of him—that I greatly esteem, that I like him" ' and significantly enough—out of consideration for Marianne's sensibility—she gives her the following permission concerning her feelings:

> 'Believe them to be stronger than I have declared; believe them, in short, to be such as his merit, and the suspicion—**the hope of his affection** for me may warrant, without imprudence or folly..'

'the hope of his affection for me': that is the problem; that doubt characterises Elinor's feelings; and ' "till his feelings are known" ', she tells her sister, Marianne cannot ' "..wonder at my wishing to avoid any encouragement of my own partiality, by **believing or calling it** more than it is" ': 'believing or calling': this indication of the gap in Elinor between feeling and its expression recalls a preoccupation we have already examined.

On the next page we are given a narrative paragraph on Elinor's thoughts; however, we draw from it but few conclusions as to *her* emotion for we learn:

> She could not consider **her partiality for Edward** in so prosperous a state as Marianne had believed it. . . . A doubt of **her regard**, supposing him to feel it, need not give him more than inquietude.

In the next chapter, refusing to expose Elinor to Fanny's insinuations, her mother decides to leave Norland. For Elinor this is 'not a plan which brought any charm to her fancy . . . it was a removal . . . beyond her wishes' (I.4.24). But 'she made no attempt to dissuade her mother', and from I.5.25 on we find no further allusion to Edward or to Elinor's feelings about him until I.8, where we hear of her doubts as to his soon visiting them—and even these are based only on a deduction of her mother's (the spare-bedroom grate).

Willoughby's arrival in the novel (I.9) opens a second movement, radically changing the atmosphere; when the narrative tells us he 'read with all the sensibility and spirit which Edward had unfortunately wanted' (I.10. 48), we infer the thought to be Marianne's; the notation also reminds us of Elinor's suitor; the same effect is obtained by the intimacy of Marianne and Willoughby leading Mrs Dashwood 'secretly to congratulate herself on having gained two such sons-in-law as Edward and Willoughby' (I.10.49) Willoughby's presence makes 'the season of happiness to Marianne', but at I.11.54 we learn that Elinor's happiness was not so great.

> Her heart was not so much at ease, nor her satisfaction in their amuse-
> ments so pure. They afforded her no companion that could make amends
> for what she had left behind, nor that could teach her to think of Norland
> with less regret than ever. Neither Lady Middleton nor Mrs. Jennings
> could supply to her the conversation she missed.

Critical opinion has been divided on 'no companion', here; some suppose it
another relic of the perhaps epistolary original: a correspondent who should
have been ditched in revision.

  Another view might be that on the contrary the novelist achieves here an
effect of extreme and original subtlety: the narrative plunges into Elinor's
thoughts—and Edward's name does not figure there. This interpretation is
corroborated in the next allusion the novel makes to Edward—aptly enough,
to his name: Mrs Jennings asks Margaret one evening to give the name of

> ..the young man who was Elinor's particular favourite . . . Margaret ans-
> wered by looking at her sister, and saying, 'I must not tell, may I, Elinor?'
>   This of course made every body laugh; and Elinor tried to laugh too. But
> the effort was painful. She was convinced that Margaret had fixed on a
> person, whose name she could not bear with composure to become a
> standing joke.. [etc.]   (I.12.61)

When the subject of the conversation changes ('much was said on the subject
of rain') the reader cannot but be surprised, as Mrs Dashwood is in III.11, by
the force of the effect this conversation has on Elinor—

> ..amidst the various endeavours of different people to quit the topic, it fell
> to the ground. But not so easily did Elinor recover from the alarm into
> which it had thrown her..   (62)

—since nothing has prepared us for so strong an impression.

  However, if in the chapters which follow we expected to be admitted to Elinor's thoughts, we are disappointed: there is no further allusion to Edward,
or to her feelings for him, for twenty-four pages; instead, her mental energy is
entirely taken up with observing Marianne..

Edward's visit (I.16) opens a third movement; but it hardly advances our
knowledge of Elinor's feelings for him: indeed, 'Marianne . . . shewed more
warmth of regard in her reception of him than even Elinor herself' (16.87).
Only in retrospect do we make the inferences from the hair-in-the-ring scene
(I.18) indicated in section 1 of this chapter. We may infer from the remark
'His visit afforded her but a very partial satisfaction, while his own enjoyment in it appeared so imperfect' (96) that essentially Elinor's pleasures
depend on others'; but it is Edward's emotions which are then explored: it is
clear to Elinor that he is unhappy; '..she wished it were equally evident that

he still distinguished her by the same affection which once she had felt no doubt of inspiring..' [etc.].

In the following chapter (I.19.101) a parallel is drawn between him and Willoughby: she is

..very well disposed on the whole to regard his actions with all the candid allowances and generous qualifications, which had been rather more painfully extorted from her, for Willoughby's service, by her mother.

but no account of her feelings is given; Edward leaves (104) and she finds every day affords her leisure to think of him, and of his behaviour '..in every possible variety which the different state of her spirits at different times could produce;—with tenderness, pity, approbation, censure, and doubt..'— formulas so various as to be completely unenlightening.

The Palmers' arrival opens a fourth movement, lasting thirteen pages (105-118) during which not one allusion to Edward is found; so when in the fifth (starting with the Steele sisters' arrival) his name, preceded this time by its initial letter: 'The letter F—' (21.125) is pronounced, its effect, and the emotion we have seen the Steeles' reference to him cause in Elinor, are explosive.

There will be no need to go through volumes II and III in detail:[13] effects identified in vol.I are there multiplied, for further—and increasingly lengthy—stretches of text follow, empty of allusions to Edward:[14]

II.7.186 to II.8.198:   twelve pages;
II.8.198 to II.10.214:   sixteen pages;[15]
III.6.305 to III.9.335:   thirty pages.

This section hardly requires elaborate analysis of the effect evoked: though Edward rarely comes flush with the text's surface—seeming held just beneath that fine integument between writer and reader—his absence, and Elinor's silence on his account, are by no means narratologically empty, but constitute a masterly structural irony. If the reader is not 'allowed' to know much about Elinor's feelings, this is because she does not allow *herself* to think about them.

---

[13] The first longish period without any allusion to Edward is staked out by the recurrence of another significant word, for when the sisters leave for London, Elinor resolves 'to avoid every selfish **comparison**, and banish every regret which might lessen her satisfaction in the happiness of Marianne' (II.4.159); by Edward's next appearance on the text's surface, Willoughby has shown what he really is, and 'Her own situation gained in the **comparison**; for while she could *esteem* Edward as much as ever, however they might be divided in future, her mind might be always supported' (II.6.179).

[14] And not always by his name when they do: Elinor thinks (184) of 'the contents of [Willoughby's] letter, on the depravity of that mind which could dictate it, and, probably, on the very different mind of a very different person, who had no other connection whatever with the affair than what her heart gave him with every thing that passed'; when the name appears, it is often hidden in the middle of a paragraph of other thoughts: 'it was a matter of great consolation to [Marianne], that what brought evil to herself would bring good to her sister; and Elinor, on the one hand, suspecting that it would not be in her power to avoid Edward entirely, comforted herself by thinking, that though their longer stay would therefore militate against her own happiness, it would be better for Marianne than an immediate return into Devonshire. . .[etc., etc.]' (II.10.214).

[15] When Edward appears in person (II.13.240) he has been physically absent for one hundred and forty pages.

65

Chapter I's review of objections to Freud made no allusion to *metapsychology*, since its sheer unfamiliarity as a concept has protected it from opprobrium. It is, however, central to the whole contention of this study. This section therefore begins with some theoretical remarks.

The term (invented by Freud) occurs first in a letter (February 13 1896[16]), in 1901 makes a first appearance in print (5.322), and its second only in 1915 (11.184), by which time Eugen Bleuler's term 'depth psychology'[17] had gained some currency (which it has never lost) as is clear from Freud's wartime allusion: 'the psychoanalytic method of investigation, the only one which reaches to such depths' (12.85); by the 'thirties he was speaking of psychoanalysis as 'depth psychology or psychology of the unconscious' (2.193).

Metapsychology is arguably the core of psychoanalysis—Jones goes so far as to say Freud's ambition was to set up 'a new science' with this name[18]— for it attempts to answer the question, *Why is the human psyche not at ease with itself?* by exploring the dynamics between different parts of a personality which are at variance.

This is certainly the most radically original part of Freud's thought;[19] also the most speculative: the term recalls meta*phor*[20]—a figure bearing meaning from elsewhere—and it might almost be said that Freud's whole life (after an initial, and unfruitful, endeavour to formulate his psychology in neurological terms[21]) was devoted to attempts at 'picturing the unknown' (6.200). To this end he resorts throughout his work to a very wide range of imagery indeed.

Just one example: in 1899 we are told that 'The unconscious is the larger sphere, which includes within it the smaller sphere of the conscious' (4.773); twenty-six years later Freud asks us 'to picture the ego as a sort of façade of the id, as a frontage..' (15.295).[22] Having adjusted to the new figure (helped or hindered by knowing that the entities are in any case not quite identical in what is called his second topography) we may then read a paper of 1905 where Freud tells us that unconscious processes of thought are 'twined round a pre-existing structure of organic connections, much as festoons of flowers are twined around a wire' (8.122).

By now the reader may be pardoned for feeling a little confused. One can learn to make the imaginative effort required by each of the figures, as they

---

[16] 'I am continually occupied with psychology–really *meta*psychology..' (F/F 172).

[17] In *Die Kritiken der Schizophrenien*, 1914; he directed a Swiss psychiatric hospital.

[18] Jones (1964), p. 296: metapsychology represents the furthest goal psychology could attain (15.243).

[19] Herbart had envisaged a 'mechanics of ideas' (*Vorstellungsmechanik*); see Ola Andersson: *Studies in the Prehistory of Psychoanalysis*, Humanities Press N.Y., 1962.

[20] Cf. *Metaphysics*: Aristotle's so named by ancient commentators to designate the works after the *Physics*.

[21] The 'Project for a Scientific Psychology'. He sent it to Fliess in 1895 then never asked for it back or as far as is known expressed any further interest in it. Found amongst Fliess' papers at his death, first pub. in 1950.

[22] On one occasion (comic effect unconscious) he speaks of the id 'upon which my ego is seated' (*SE* XIX.133).

are encountered individually, but it must be admitted that, collectively, they constitute the most gigantic *mixed metaphor*.[23]

Freud was not unaware of the pitfalls inherent in metapsychology: as early as 1895 (3.377) he goes out of his way to emphasise the mutual incompatibility of his similes; forty years later he avers that 'analogies, it is true, decide nothing, but they can make one feel more at home' (2.105). His critics, by contrast, display varying degrees of willingness to picture the unknown: of Freud's metaphor for regression, Rycroft says 'I must confess I find myself floored by the idea of a distinction between backward and forward movements of the imagination.'[24] On the other hand, if no effort is made there can be no excuse for crudifying his thought: e.g. 'Freud is seeing the mental processes as static, while I speak of dynamics and relationship'.[25]

Nevertheless, if it is the *sub*concious which has caught the vulgar ear, Freud himself cannot be entirely exculpated from contributing to its currency: he asks Fliess in a letter 'whether I may use the name metapsychology for my psychology that leads *behind* consciousness' (F/F 301/2, my italics); it hardly helps the denial of anatomical intention to write of 'wishful impulses *lurking* in the mind' (4.331, do.), or of 'the psychical *underworld*' (2.89, do.). The evolution of Freud's thought is often ascribed to his gradual refining of the initial models;[26] his increasingly adjectival use of the term 'unconscious' may, also, have been a response to objections to his tendency to reify.

Applying Freud's metapsychological models to Jane Austen's work should help elucidate the nature of her art according to three closely interrelated interpretative principles, of which at this point it will be enough to indicate the headings.

The first is that a word Freud often uses in the metapsychological chapter (VII) of *The Interpretation of Dreams*, inevitably recalls our novelist's chosen form: he acknowledges that since as far as we know 'no psychical apparatus exists which possesses a primary process only', then such an apparatus 'is to that extent a theoretical *fiction*' (4.763, my italics).

---

23 *L & P* say Freud's metapsychological models are 'of various kinds, and of various degrees of assimilability to empirical neurology' (248). An understatement. Freud never lost sight of the hope his 'Project' had encapsulated, as may be seen from his italics in a remark of 1915: 'Our psychical topography has *for the moment* nothing to do with anatomy' (11.177).

24 Rycroft: *The Innocence of Dreams*, O.U.P. 1981, p. 25.

25 C.G.Jung: *Analytical Psychology: Its Theory and Practice*, R.K.P. 1976, p. 69. The reader is warned against those parts of Jung's work in which he either (a) represents Freud as a fool (for who but a fool would be capable of calling a process, static?) so as to gain kudos from the contrast, or (b) simply—and it must be said very dashingly—misrepresents Freud: what conceivable textual justification could be found for declaring that Freud 'derives the unconscious from the conscious', for example (ibid., p. 8)?

26 Already at the end of the Schreber study (1911) we read repression 'emanates from the more highly developed system of the ego—systems which are *capable of being* conscious' (9.205: 'systems', in the plural, is a significant adumbration); 'the laws of unconscious *activity* differ widely from those of the conscious' (1912, 11. 56); 'consciousness may be, not the most universal attribute of mental processes, but *only a particular function of them*' (1920, 11.295); 'the character of being unconscious begins to lose significance for us' (1923, 11.356); and finally 'when the unconscious material makes its way into the ego, it brings its own *modes of working* along with it' (1938, 15.399) (italics added throughout this note).

The second principle concerns the manner in which this 'apparatus' functions, particularly in its relation to language—its function being intimately bound up with how it is formed.

And the third principle has to do with the way Freud ends up describing the parts of that apparatus. The workings of his final metapsychological model—*id*, *ego*, *superego*—are evoked in anthropomorphic terms; by the same token, Jane Austen's deployment of *her* anthropomorphic entities—characters—is perhaps no less metaphorical than Freud's.

For all this to appear less abstract, it will be useful forthwith to relate these interpretative principles to concrete details from the novel in hand. Thus:

1) The encapsulating fiction is *Sense and Sensibility*, in which events happen first and foremost to the reader. Associations amplifying the dimensions of any detail are found staked out over the whole course of the text. Within that framework we have already glanced at other modes of representation (the miniature of Edward; the picturesque): verbal overlappings indicate further links in the chains of association with other areas of this preoccupation:

a) Just before Edward's last arrival at Barton, and his figurative act, with its telescoping of miniature/ring/hair, we are told

> In Edward—she **knew not what she saw**, nor what she **wished to see**;—happy or unhappy,—nothing pleased her; she **turned away her head** from every **sketch of him**.   (III.12.357/8)
> [seeing and knowing/wish/head (hair)/sketch (picture)]

cf. [Elinor] ..**pictured to herself** her suffering mother **arriving too late** to see this **darling child**.   (III.7.312)

cf. [Mrs Dashwood's] ..**wish** of bringing Marianne and Colonel Brandon together ... now her **darling object**   (III.14.378)
[picture/mother and darling child/death/seeing/wish]

b) We have seen 'how blank was [Elinor's] **prospect**' without an '**animating object in view**'; she later refers to Lucy as the person 'whose prior engagement **ruined all my prospects**' (III.1.263); when Edward first comes to Barton, Marianne says to him ' "Now, Edward," ... calling attention to the **prospect**..' (I.16.88).
[animating (hope)/object (future)/prospect (visual/imaginary)]

Both these clusters are moral/visual (pointing, as it happens, to dominant metaphorical presences in *Pride and Prejudice* and *Mansfield Park* respectively). With the reminder that what is seen in a novel must first be read, attention may now be drawn to occasions on which it is words themselves that bear this preoccupation with representation:

a) Sir John describes the Steeles as 'the sweetest girls in the world'; but Elinor knows that such are 'to be met with in every part of England, under every possible variation of form, face, temper, and understanding' (I.21.119).

b) Because the Dashwoods like reading, Lady Middleton fancies them 'satirical: perhaps without exactly knowing what it was to be satirical; but *that* did not signify. It was censure in common use, and easily given' (II.14.246).

In these passages the reader feels inverted commas, as it were, round the expressions 'sweetest girls in the world' and 'satirical'.

From sisters we may pass again to brothers and how they are represented: when Edward is cut off, John Dashwood declares that Robert ' "..will now to all intents and purposes **be considered as** the eldest son... **I do not know** that one is **superior** to the other" ' (III.5.297); Elinor's view is different:

> ..while she wondered at the **difference** of the two young men, she did not find that the **emptiness** and conceit of the one, put her at all out of charity with the modesty and **worth** of the other.   (II.14.250)

This whole demonstration—the upshot of which is that the world is being depicted as in large part a verbal construct—has important implications. That Elinor knows 'the sweetest girls in the world' spend their lives squeezed in between inverted commas tells us the interesting general fact that Jane Austen herself knows this is what language does—'makes' the world.

More specifically, a word in bold type ('emptiness', here at p.250) may be borne in mind as we set these passages alongside one of the novel's most remarkable symbolic juxtapositions, about a third young man: on the Palmers first appearance, Charlotte is pregnant. It is her mother who brings this up:

> '..I can't help wishing they had not travelled quite so fast, nor made such a long journey of it, for they came all round by London . . . for you know (nodding significantly and pointing to her daughter) it was wrong in her situation.. . . She expects to be confined in February.' . . . Lady Middleton could no longer endure such a conversation, and therefore exerted herself to ask Mr. Palmer if there was any news in the paper.
>
> 'No, none at all,' he replied, and read on.   (I.19.107)

One hundred and forty pages later (II.14.246), we find:

> ..**the newspapers** announced to the world, that the Lady of Thomas Palmer, Esq. was safely **delivered** of a **son and heir**; a very interesting and satisfactory paragraph, at least to all those intimate connections **who knew it** before.

cf., when Marianne learns of Willoughby's marriage, it is from Elinor, anxious that her sister should not receive notice of it from

> ..**the public papers**, which she saw her eagerly examining every morning. [She] at first shed no tears; but after a short time they would **burst out**.   (II.10.217)

cf. Edward had no idea of what Robert and Lucy had been up to; when '..it

burst on him . . . he had been for some time . . . half stupified [sic] between the wonder, the horror, and the joy of such a **deliverance**' (365).

We are thus returned to Edward's visit to Barton Cottage in III.12.

(Readers beginning to realise something of the verbal *density* attributed to Jane Austen's text from section 1 on will understood that to do justice to the complexity of associative echoes, even in this first-published of her novels, would make for a considerably longer study than this.)

The I.19 newspaper scene gives concrete expression to the two related preoccupations we have been exploring: Palmer's retort is, on the face of it, just a jest; but since five pages later he asks his wife not to ' "palm all your abuses of language upon me" ' (113), the retort may be read as an eloquent satire on the emptiness of Charlotte's usual language: truism (e.g. ' "we should have seen a great deal of him in Somersetshire, if it had not happened . . . that we should never have been in the country together" ' I.20.114, etc.)

But further than this, perhaps the cue Palmer receives from Lady Middleton for his jest itself indicates that more is at stake than the emptiness of language: to venture hypotheses about the psychical economy of so minor a character may seem bold, but as in dream interpretation it is fruitful to see 'propinquity in time as representing connection in subject matter' (4.346— another abrogation of the accusation that psychoanalysis is 'content bound'; cf. also 8.71) might not his remark be regarded as a *displacement* of his anxiety lest Charlotte be more than intellectually empty—lest, that is, there be no 'son and heir'?

2. These considerations lead us on to the second principle outlined above (p. 68) governing interpretation of Jane Austen's work by means of metapsychology: namely, the form and function of language.

Freud's work—which can be seen as a first grammar of the unconscious— makes frequent recourse to linguistic metaphor; the following examples are chosen to give an idea of its range.

'The unconscious speaks more than one dialect' (15.42/3) is an early perception; in 1899 he mentions 'a subordinate clause in the dream material' (4. 450); in 1905 we learn this material can take a 'step from the optative to the present indicative' (6.219); in the Schreber case 'Delusions of jealousy contradict the subject, delusions of persecution contradict the verb, and erotomania contradicts the object' (9.203); and most important for the dynamics of sexual identification, in obsessional neurosis 'the active voice is changed, not into the passive, but into the reflexive, middle voice' (11.125), etc., etc.

Thus if, looking back in 1914 to the dream-book he was able to recall: 'I now understood how to translate dreams' (15.76), this became part of his general outlook; for of the unconscious itself he says we know it only 'after it has undergone transformation or translation' (11.167).

We may return now to a detail in the rich texture of *Sense and Sensibility*, for questions Freud asks about how memory is formed, and how it functions, consciously and unconsciously, can throw light on the particular problem of why sheath suffers as much as scissors in Edward's symptomatic act. It may also enable us to understand something about the psychology of reading books—perhaps even, indeed, that of writing them—which the analyses of this inquiry suppose.

For while Freud's use of *Niederschriften* in a letter (F/F 207) must presumably be metaphorical (and it is apparently still impossible to say in what form a word, its sound or look, may be 'inscribed' in the brain[27]), obviously for memory to function at all there must be some organisation. Freud's way of picturing this is to compare memory to archives: a classification system arranged according to chronological order, associativity, and 'depth': that is, a measure of the accessibility to consciousness of a given detail.[28]

English 'sheath' derives from Germanic 'skaithjo', probably cognate with Greek σκιζω that also gives us 'scissors': so what encloses and what rives apart are, linguistically speaking, two aspects of a single event.[29] One has to consult a modern dictionary to discover this; what is most interesting about psychoanalytic linguistic theory is that we need neither attribute Jane Austen's antithetical juxtaposition to any extraordinary degree of philological erudition on her part—or, conversely, what is more, our sense that something is 'happening' in Edward's act, to any conscious knowledge on our part.

A final remark (to round off what, it may be repeated, is intended as only an initial glimpse of how the second principle will be made to work for us): this new philologically-coloured datum fuels the present reading's ascription of the act to a compromise formation, by means of a further essential characteristic. In the light of the foregoing, we may reasonably class the act, and whatever forces are 'behind' it, as *ambivalent*—under the consideration that 'what is pleasurable for one agency is unpleasurable for another' (*L & P* 28).[30] We shall have occasion to return to the concept of ambivalence.

---

[27] 'It should be made quite clear . . . that we are far from having any plausible neural mechanism that could account for human speech' (Erich Harth: *Windows on the Mind*, Pelican 1982, p. 67).

[28] Lacan suggests these categories include or presuppose structures of language itself; following hints in Freud's work about the infant's evolving sense of itself and language learnt, he has been thought to refine Freud's model: thus 'The unconscious is structured like a language' (op. cit. [1973], p. 23), or 'All truth has a structure of fiction' (op. cit. [1986], p. 21). Some would say 'refine' is too weak a term.

[29] Freud was struck by the fact that 'words with opposite meanings are . . . often interchanged; they are already associated in our linguistic consciousness, they lie very close to each other' (5.101). An English example is the verb 'to wear': if you go into a carpet-shop and ask for 'a carpet *that won't wear*', it is the same as if you insist on 'a carpet *that will wear*'. Discussion of how this comes about is beyond the scope of the present study, but it may just be noted that Freud's much-ridiculed theory of a phylogenetic factor in inheritance of, in the present instance, linguistic functions, has received some independent support from the work of Noam Chomsky: among the distinctions between humans and other animals is language, a symbolic structure for the learning of which the human brain may be uniquely adapted.

[30] *L & P* advise caution in use of the term, but consider recourse to it appropriate in 'analysis of specific conflicts in which the positive and negative components of the emotional attitude are simultaneously in evidence and inseparable, and where they constitute a non-dialectical opposition which the subject, saying "yes" and "no" at the same time, is incapable of transcending' (28).

3. This allusion to *agencies* brings us to the third general interpretative principle of psychoanalysis to be applied to our reading of Jane Austen.

We might say *borrowed from* psychoanalysis; but perhaps the ways the material we are dealing with responds to this approach, are beginning to suggest some profounder kinship with the material encountered in psychoanalytic praxis: first (to resume) *fictions*, closely related, second, to *language*.

These might be decribed as the *frame* and the *matter*, respectively, of Jane Austen's art. We come now to the *forms* taken by that matter in that frame.

The critical literature has so far regarded the basic formal entities in her work as being the characters; foregoing demonstrations of verbal overlappings have aimed to indicate that the characters must be seen as bearers of preoccupations in a very much wider context.

Henry James is puzzled to hear people speak of the 'ingredients' of novels— description, narrative, incident, dialogue, etc.—as if these things had

> ..a kind of internecine distinctness, intead of melting into each other at every breath, and being intimately associated parts of one general effort of expression. I cannot imagine composition existing in a series of blocks, nor conceive, in any novel worth discussing at all, of a passage of description that is not in its intention narrative, a passage of dialogue that is not . . . descriptive, a touch of truth of any sort that does not partake of the character of incident. . . . A novel is a living thing, all one and continuous, like any other organism, and in proportion as it lives will it be found, that in each of the parts there is something of each of the other parts.[31]

This paragraph was written at almost exactly the same time as Freud had his first inklings into the nature of hysteria: he was told of the patient known as 'Anna O.' in November 1882, shortly before his departure for Paris to work under Charcot. It was Anna O. who, referring to her mental state as her 'private theatre', described herself as split into two personalities: 'a clearsighted and calm observer sat, as she put it, in a corner of her brain, and looked on at all the mad business' (3.101). Freud found Bleuler's term *schizophrenia* (etymologically = split mind) misleading, because it identifies one mental disease with a characteristic of mind in general (as is clear from the simple reflexive expression 'I said to myself') and whilst Freud's recourse to figurative language in metapsychology is no doubt in part attributable to its facilitating his task of picturing the unknown, it became clear that if we think of ourselves as 'peopled', this must be because our inner world is—perhaps indeed cannot but be—structured from our experience of the outer.[32]

---

31 'The Art of Fiction', in *Selected Literary Criticism*, Peregrine 1968, pp. 87/8.

32 The ego is formed from an organism's developing sense of its surroundings and itself: 'The ego is first and foremost a bodily ego; it is not merely a surface entity, but is itself the projection of a surface' (11.364), and is 'a kind of actualised metaphor for the organism' (*L & P* 135), Lacan comments how strange it is we should say a person *has* a body (op. cit. [1973], p. 93). Cf. 'I do not know how the sentence "I have a body" is to be used' (Wittgenstein, op. cit. [1969], § 258) and 'The human body is the best picture of the human soul' (*P.I.* II.iv).

Our first experiences form (or suppose) a grammatical substratum: awareness of interesting objects' presence or absence leads to capacity to imagine them when they go away; rudimentary muscular control may give a glimpse of distinctions between notions of active and passive (voices of a verb, etc.); finally, these coalesce in the peculiarly human sense of oneself; indeed, in that sense it is only then that 'I', the First Person of our world, is born.

Freud's work concerns itself increasingly with the structure of the ego: partly because he thought at least something could be known about it, and something cogent said at least about its most conscious aspects, in contrast with the unconscious, of which he tirelessly reminds us:

> ..the unconscious is something which we really do not know, but which we are obliged by compelling inferences to supply.   (6.218)

Since his death, interest has continued unabated, to the point of spawning a whole school of 'ego-psychology', and of provoking *L & P*'s view (139) that it is difficult 'to integrate all the psychoanalytic contributions to the concept of the ego into a unified line of thought'. However, one of the few incontrovertible formulations which must, in view of a common misapprehension, be borne in mind as we move now towards a possible metapsychological reading of *Sense and Sensibility*, is that the ego should not be confused with consciousness, which is merely its 'nucleus' (11.362). As for its relationship to the id, Freud is quite clear: 'The ego is not sharply separated from the id; its lower portion merges into it' (ibid.); elsewhere he underlines indeed 'There is no natural opposition between ego and id: they belong together' (15.301); in the *Outline*, having evoked the ego, he then speaks of 'Its own id' (15.435).

In assimilating Jane Austen's configuration Elinor/Marianne to Freud's ego/id, various perspectives may be taken of the relationship depicted. The simplest is in terms of desire/defence: Marianne 'was . . . eager in everything; her sorrows, her joys could have no moderation'; whilst Elinor possessed coolness of judgement which '..enabled her frequently to counteract . . . that eagerness of mind . . . which must generally have led to imprudence' (I.1.6).

We see this dynamic often: e.g. she sees Willoughby at the London party, and 'her whole countenance glowing with sudden delight, she would have moved towards him instantly, had not her sister caught hold of her' (II.6. 176). Marianne's emotions are all extreme (' "those beautiful lines which have frequently almost driven me wild.." ' I.3.18); what is outside her is unselfconsciously assimilated to her inner nature: in London she imagines frosts setting in ' "with severity. In another day or two perhaps; this extreme mildness can hardly last longer—nay, perhaps it may freeze to-night!" ' (II.5. 167). There are signs, that is, of defective reality-testing:[33] when Willoughby

---

[33] 'The formation of the ego offsets the subject's initial failure to distinguish between hallucination and perception' (*L & P* 156).

offers her a horse, Elinor chides her for 'want of thought'; Marianne is '..un-willing . . . to awaken from such a dream of felicity, to comprehend all the unhappy truths which attended the affair' (I.12.58).

Nothing so far gleaned from the novel is incompatible with portrayal of a relationship in 'realistic' terms current in 1811 (siblings in particular often adopt complementary rôles in a family economy). Freud's view that the ego 'represents what may be called reason and common sense, in contrast to the id, which contains the passions' (11.364; cf. also 2.109) might indeed be said to play into the hands of anyone wishing so to read *Sense and Sensibility*. He was also aware of how 'the psychological novel' in general owes its nature

> ..to the inclination of the modern writer to split up his ego, by self-observation, into many part-egos, and, in consequence, to personify the conflicting currents of his own mental life in several heroes.   (14.138)

However, the implications of that view would lure us back to Janeism. More interesting for our present discussion is Ludwig Jekels' view that we some-times sense Shakespeare splits a character into two: parts 'which, taken separately, are not completely understandable and do not become so until they are brought together once more into a unity' (quoted 14.307); for the dynamic so far described belongs to the text's *manifest* content: Elinor and Marianne represent a clash between two 'groups of ideas' (*SE* XI.213).

But it is indications in the figurative underswell, *latent* content, that will interest us, showing kinship to Freud's radical metapsychological inquiry: namely: (1) behaviour of the agencies party to the dynamic, and (2) the nature of the instincts ultimately sustaining the conflict.

In approaching these fundamental matters it may be as well, in continua-tion of Chapter I's review of objections, to draw attention to the plural in the term 'groups of ideas'. Freud is accused of 'obstinate dualism' (Jones [1964] p. 475); but it is not clear whether, at this late stage in proceedings, 'two' is really something a thinker may reasonably be accused of *imposing on* the cosmos: to fault Freud for dualism is hardly more to the point than to criticise cricket for involving two teams, or to damn God for making two sexes: we all have two parents—only two—and must come to terms with that (Freud's critics' problems with dualism might be explained by reluctance to accept that fact.) But in any case the accusation is belied by several consider-ations: first by his demonstration that an individual's sexuality is an entirely synthetic phenomenon, a contingent and highly precarious mixture of diverse elements—it is 'the sexual *instincts*'. Of these component instincts making up adult sexuality, some are more regularly drawn than others into the service of the 'final genital organization of libido' (15.143).[34]

---

[34] Kissing (let alone holding hands) is not strictly required for procreation. But holding hands, then kissing, and finally making babies, are activities sometimes found in an associative series, and they may be said to make up one group of ideas: a first pole, therefore, in possible conflict with a second pole similarly constituted.

Second, the ego itself is not a single thing but a compound 'made up variously at different times' (10.110). So far we have seen the ego as the defensive pole in the composite structure Elinor/Marianne; but Freud had still to explain where the ego obtains the energy with which to repress the id's strivings, and it gradually became clear that (to simplify) defence mechanisms are only *more or less integrated into* the ego, which is merely the *agent* of the defensive operation (*L & P* 104). The 'conditioning factor for repression' is 'formation of an ideal' (11.88): the infant is said to abandon its illusory feeling of omnipotence in the face of parental criticism, which is then internalised as 'a self-observing function' that 'constantly watches the actual ego and measures it by the ideal' (ibid.). Repression, then, 'is the work of this *super*-ego and . . . is carried out either by itself or by the ego in obedience to its orders' (2.101, my italics); the ego 'comprises a part that observes and a part that is observed' (*L & P* 428), indeed on one occasion Freud declares: 'So long as the ego works in full harmony with the super-ego it is not easy to distinguish between their manifestations' (15.442).

It will hardly be necessary to illustrate at length the rôle of critical observer that Elinor adopts with regard to Marianne: she 'overhears' her sister's conversations with Willoughby (I.12.59, I.13.64/5, etc.); she later resolves upon 'watching his behaviour to her sister with . . . zealous attention' (II.4.159); in London she 'thought she could distinguish a large W.' on the first note dispatched to him (161); another is sent off 'with a privacy which eluded all her watchfulness' (167)—and so on.

More interesting are indications that Jane Austen senses the ego must work hard (e.g. 'Elinor, pleased to have her **governed** for a moment . . . adjusting her dress for her' II.8.193; Marianne is 'secured by the **exertions** of Elinor', '**prevailed upon** to join her sisters' I.16.85, etc.), and to don as it were an official uniform: we learn that on Elinor 'the whole **task** of telling lies when politeness required it, always **fell**' (I.21.122)—cf. the ego 'is the psychical agency to which the **task** of preserving the individual **falls**' (*L & P* 147); 'Elinor took possession of the **post** of civility which she had assigned herself' (I.16.86)—cf. 'the super-ego takes up a kind of intermediate **position** between the id and the external world' (15.443), and many Freudian figures such as *cathexis* ('Besetzung', military occupation of a territory); 'Elinor, to **screen** Marianne from particularity . . . quickened her pace and kept up with her' (I.16.86)—cf. 'The critical agency . . . stands like a **screen** between [the agency criticised] and consciousness' (4.690); 'Elinor saw nothing to **censure** in him but..' (I.10.48)—cf. '**censorship** . . . and reality-testing, among the major institutions of the ego' (11.256), etc., etc.

Present among these figurative expressions is a fourth party to the conflict —' "a better acquaintance with **the world** is what I look forward to as her greatest . . . advantage" ' (I.11.56)—a sizeable entity, occasionally evoked by

Freud: the ego is 'the portion of the id which is directed towards **the external world**' (15.300), and tries to mediate between the world and the id,

> ..to make the id pliable to the world and, by means of its muscular activity, to make the world fall in with the wishes of the id. (11.398)

This complexity of the ego's task applied to Elinor is seen in her behaviour at the mid-novel crisis: while constantly 'wishing to prevent Mrs. Jennings from seeing her sister's thoughts as clearly as she did' (II.5.167), later she has to give her attention to Marianne—'..could with difficulty keep her on the bed at all, and for some time was fearful of being constrained to call for assistance' (II.6.191); she has on further occasions to caution her hostess against mentioning Willoughby (195), to defend the latter (196), to explain things to Col. Brandon (199), she 'forced herself to welcome' Edward (241) and so on.

One remarkable aspect of the dynamic so far evoked (supported moreover by the non-equivalence between ego and consciousness), is Elinor's vigilance in maintaining her arduous rôle (cf. 'the numerous dependent relationships of the ego . . . and its efforts to humour all its masters at once' 10.213). As early as 1895, Freud was aware of 'the complexity of the relations between defence and the ego which is *made responsible for it* ' (*L & P* 104, my italics); again the full significance of this fact only emerged gradually:

> ..we find ourselves in an unforeseen situation. We have come upon something in the ego which is also unconscious. (11.355/6)

If the ego takes sides with the super-ego, it relinquishes itself to a power over which it has no control, comes under the sway of the (primary) process governing the unconscious, and thus establishes defences which are as compulsive as the forces they are fighting (*L & P* 134, 139 & 340). Indeed in 1895 Freud had written that the ego 'is *eager* for defence' (3.363, my italics): a word which, although we have seen it applied in the first instance to Marianne ('She was eager in everything' I.1.6), is significantly enough used of Elinor too: 'she was eager to gain from any one . . . confirmation of [Willoughby's] merits' (I.20.114); 'eager at all events to know what Willoughby had written' (II.7.182); 'by an eager sign, engaged [her mother's] silence' (III.11.350) as Marianne at last speaks of him, etc., etc.

These considerations bring us to the limit of the first of Freud's metapsychological approaches (p. 73, describing the dynamic in terms of the agencies party to it), and lead us to his second, more far-reaching inquiry: namely, the nature of the instincts underpinning the conflict.

- 5 -

Readers who know *Sense and Sensibility* well, may in the course of the foregoing have felt the text was being misrepresented so as to sustain an over-systematic interpretation. To keep their confidence, it will be opportune now to note details incompatible with a metapsychological reading.

First, Freud declares that the id 'has no direct communication with the external world' (15.433); but Marianne sometimes shows herself quite equal to parleying with that world, in order to achieve her ends:

> 'I thank you, ma'am, sincerely thank you . . . your invitation has insured my gratitude for ever, and it would give me such happiness, yes almost the greatest happiness I am capable of, to be able to accept it. But my mother, my dearest, kindest mother..' [etc., etc.]   (II.3.154)

Then (second) the id is 'totally non-moral' (11.395), whereas Marianne, on occasion, is 'afraid of offending' Elinor (e.g. I.4.19).

Sometimes, as here (third), we even see the elements of an internal conflict: Marianne 'would not wound the feelings of her sister on any account, and yet to say what she did not believe was impossible'. Occasionally indeed, the very vocabulary is borrowed from the critical register: 'Marianne severely **censured** herself for what she had said' (I.18.99)—and so on.

However, these are merely beginnings to a portrayal of human complexity; and although *Sense and Sensibility* belongs to the genre *novel*, not *allegory* (not even metapsychological allegory), it will perhaps be acknowledged that the reading presented in the present chapter does less violence to the representation of Marianne than to that of Elinor.

Marianne's fictional dimensions are palpably of less extent than Elinor's; though she plays a major *rôle* in this novel, Marianne is an unremittingly minor character. On that note, a short digression is in order.

It would be unreasonable in this chapter, on only the first-published novel, to hope support could be easily elicited for a contention announced from the outset as being sure to wound cherished prejudices, particularly as it affects certain much-'loved' characters; the reader is therefore requested to accept for the moment that Marianne's metapsychological significance will not be fully grasped till we have fully unrolled the carpet on which she constitutes only one motif. But perhaps we may avoid the necessity of returning to the whole storm she has brewed, of confusion between aesthetic and moral questions in art, by briefly pointing out the logical incoherence in the disappointed expectations of critics from 1952 (Mudrick) to 1986 (Tanner).[35]

The best reply to the particular complaint about Jane Austen's 'treatment' of Marianne (in a word, bourgeois authorial incorporation of radical heroine) is Wright's 'If only Prof. Mudrick could discourage the economic tail from wagging the psychological dog';[36] the most succinct general anwer is Booth's 'The novelist who chooses to tell *this* story cannot at the same time tell *that*

---

[35] 'Marianne, the life and center of the novel has been betrayed; and not by Willoughby' (Mudrick, op. cit., p 90); 'her creator... is certainly fond of Marianne, but is she also a bit frightened of her?' (Tanner, op. cit., p.100).
[36] Wright, op. cit., p. vii.

story';[37] and behind both is James' classic statement: 'We must grant the artist his subject, his idea, his *donnée*: our criticism is applied only to what he makes of it.'[38] (There is no logical reason, that is, why Jane Austen should not pursue the existential anguish of Sir John Middleton—or that of one of Willoughby's favourite pointers, for that matter—but ..she does not.)

If even conditional agreement of interest is granted to a metapsychological interpretation of how the composite structure Elinor/Marianne is presented, more than mere play on words may now be perceived in the application to this structure of *L & P*'s definition of psychical conflict: 'when contradictory internal requirements are opposed to each other *in the subject* ' (359). So: we shall say the 'subject' of *Sense and Sensibility* is 'Elinor-*and*-Marianne'.

From a metapsychological perspective, Elinor and Marianne are in entirely separate registers: this chapter's previous sections (especially no. 3) will warn us against coarse narratological descriptions, but we may perhaps metaphorically say Elinor's thoughts are *nearer* earshot of the narrative presence; Marianne's are invariably out of that earshot. Moreover, the fugitive glimpses of her mental world—e.g., that she 'would have thought herself very inexcusable had she been able to sleep at all the first night after parting from Willoughby..' [etc.] (I.16.83), and the few scenes in which we see her without her sister (e.g. I.3.17/8, I.8.38/9)—present nothing it would be impossible for Elinor to know.

Most important, all we know about Marianne is learnt through Elinor—which fits our metapsychological model well: the id 'is accessible even to our knowledge only through the medium of another agency' (15.433).

Having underlined the difference of register between Elinor and Marianne, it should be recalled that they do belong together, as a dynamic structure.[39] This highlights a further application of our model, for—to give it now its proper name—the *instinctual* pressure exerted is not from the outside world[40] but from within the structure. And indeed Elinor cannot escape from Marianne: 'flight is of no avail, for the ego cannot escape from itself' (11.145).[41]

The question, *Why should it wish to?* naturally arises here; and the answers Freud gives are also adumbrated in Jane Austen's work.

Defence is 'linked to the most fundamental conditions of the psychical mechanism (the law of constancy)' (F/F 163): it denotes protecting *something* and defending *oneself*; *L & P* speak of the ego as a 'space' in the personality (104/107). An earlier point about the ego as the projection of a surface (n. 32)

---

[37] Booth, op. cit., p. 78.

[38] James, op. cit., p. 89.

[39] Jane Austen did not repeat this configuration; the Marianne 'motif' is henceforth more diffusely presented.

[40] Already in the 'Project' Freud had said of the major needs—hunger, respiration, sexuality—'From these the organism cannot withdraw as it does from external stimuli' (*SE* I.297).

[41] Removal is 'against her wishes'; refusing the London invitation there is a rare lapse: it is 'without observing the varying complexion of her sister, and the animated look which spoke no indifference to the plan' (II.3. 153). She ends up going; the running joke about getting her to Delaford may be included in this schema.

is relevant here, as Freud 'assimilates the ego's functions to the perceptual and protective equipment of the organism' (*L & P* 141).[42] In his first instinct theory, the constancy maintained is said to serve instincts of *self-preservation*, whereas what disrupts that regulation are *sexual* instincts: 'the ego has set itself the task of self-preservation, which the id appears to neglect' (15.434).

In spite of perhaps appearing intolerably abstract, or distant from the Dashwood sisters, actually this contrast corresponds well to their behaviour —for example, on the departure of their suitors: when Edward leaves (I.19. 104), Elinor, ever vigilant against any modification in her outward behaviour, sits down to her work 'as soon as he was out of the house, busily employed herself the whole day, neither sought nor avoided the mention of his name'. That is, the reality-principle continues to function; by contrast, when Willoughby leaves, Marianne is 'without any power, because she was without any desire of command over herself . . . indulging the recollection of past enjoyment . . . she courted the misery', etc. (I.15.82 & 16.83).[43]

Moreover the text's *figurations* support the interpretation that Marianne continues to function according to the pleasure principle: for whilst Elinor 'did not seek to augment and fix her sorrow' (104), the satisfaction Marianne derives from her emotion is described in specifically oral terms: 'that violent sorrow which Marianne was. . . not merely giving way to as a relief, but **feeding** and encouraging as a duty' (77); whereas real food is indifferent to her— she 'could neither **eat** nor speak' (82), she is 'unable to talk, and unwilling to take any **nourishment**'—it is the '**nourishment of grief**' she seeks (83). The same imagery is found after the crisis: 'She neither ate, nor attempted to eat any thing' (II.7.181), but she 'might still **feed her wishes**' (178).

Finally, if Mrs Jennings is from this point of view the most motherly of the mothers in this novel (associated with food and drink: from salmon, cod, boiled fowls and veal cutlets in II.4.160,to the mulberry tree at Delaford: ' "Lord! How Charlotte and I did stuff.." ' [197], the ' "One shoulder of mutton . . . drives another down" ' [ibid.], 'sweetmeats and olives' [193] 'dried cherries' and wine [194] etc. etc.) it can hardly be insignificant that the 'Constantia wine' she brings Marianne is drunk by Elinor, who reflects that 'its healing **powers** on a disappointed heart might be as reasonably tried on herself as on her sister' (198). This recalls an earlier episode where infantile demands— Annamaria Middleton's—are met in similar terms: her mother

..remembering that in a scene of similar distress . . . some apricot marmalade had been successfully **applied** for a bruised temple, the same remedy was eagerly proposed for this unfortunate scratch.   (I.21.121)

for if in Marianne's case nourishment of grief 'was every day **applied**', we

---

[42] E.g. physical pain is 'a breach of the confines of the body . . . as a model of that internal aggression which the instinct constitutes for the ego' (*L & P* 107).

[43] Repeating thus, incidentally, emotions felt on her father's death, when both she and her mother 'gave themselves up wholly to their sorrow' (I.1.7).

are also told 'her sensibility was **potent** enough' (83); the fact is, as Margaret puts it—with more precision than she knows—*Willoughby* is 'Marianne's **preserver**' (I.10.46).

Self-preservative instincts are said to be easy to frustrate, for what satisfies them must be real (viz., food); sexual instincts, by contrast (and for various reasons) *can* only be fully satisfied by some participation of the mind, and often *are* so satisfied. Indeed, since it is their nature to be 'unrealistic', the unrealistic mode of satisfaction (phantasy) is their proper realm.

That Marianne's mode of satisfaction is essentially phantasy may be inferred from her object-choices, one of the earliest of which we saw to be based on sympathetic identification: trees, and what they shed.

The next is Willoughby. Wherever does he come from? Had we not a disadvantage of hindsight (Emma's and Anne Elliot's friends), 'Mrs. Smith' might be a joke. His most immediate source is literature: ' "Is he not a *man of* [honour and] *feeling*?" ' asks Mrs Dashwood (I.15.81,[44] my brackets and italics); for Marianne, 'His person and air' are 'what her fancy had ever drawn for the hero of a favourite story . . . all that her fancy had delineated' (43 and 49).

In the lightest sense then he fulfils a wish, unlike Edward who ' "..is not the kind of young man—there is a something wanting—his figure is not striking . . . His eyes want all that . . .**fire** which I should expect" ' (I.3.17).

The detail of the fire again brings us back to Elinor: what indeed would be the use of that grate (I.8) without something to put into it? But also, through the common image, it brings us further back, to a more elemental force.

One apparent insufficiency of our metapsychological model turns out here to have the virtues of its defects: whilst Georg Groddeck saw Nietzsche's 'das Es' (it) as 'whatever in our nature is impersonal and, so to speak, subject to natural law' (11.362 n.), Freud adopted the term to designate the mind's most archaic realm. Marianne is in this sense much older than Elinor, for the evocation of Willoughby corresponds to symbolic notations whose presence in myth, art, and 'texts' psychoanalysis deals with (dreams) led Freud to think that they must belong to some inherited register of primal phantasies.

In future Jane Austen novels the figurations in Willoughby's hunting, dancing and riding are extended; meanwhile, we have seen Marianne 'unwilling to awaken' from a 'dream of felicity' (galloping on the downs); here on High Church Down (I.9.41) she asks Margaret ' "Is there a felicity in the world . . . superior to this?" ' However, she is caught by the elements—and by something else, as she runs 'with all possible speed down the steep side of the hill which led immediately to their garden gate.' Let us read on: Marianne

> ..had at first the advantage, but a false step brought her suddenly to the ground, and Margaret, unable to stop herself to assist her, was involuntarily hurried along, and reached the bottom in safety.

---

[44] *The Man of Feeling* (Henry Mackenzie, 1771) a novel partly responsible for the 'sentimental' craze.

A gentleman carrying a gun, with two pointers playing round him, was passing up the hill and within a few yards of Marianne, when her accident happened. He put down his gun and ran to her assistance. She had raised herself from the ground, but her foot had been twisted in the fall, and she was scarcely able to stand. The gentleman offered his services, and perceiving that her modesty declined what her situation rendered necessary, took her up in in his arms without farther delay, and carried her down the hill. Then passing through the garden, the gate of which had been left open by Margaret, he bore her directly into the house, whither Margaret was just arrived, and quitted not his hold till he had seated her in a chair in the parlour.

*

One must never be in a hurry to 'define' symbols, for . . . symbols are not pat equivalents but areas of meaning.[45]
No art of interpretation would be feasible if there were no resemblances from one case to the next, and if it were not possible in these resemblances to discern types.[46]

The commentary which follows, on this episode of Marianne's fall, may be situated somewhere between these two hints.

On the one hand, though some details here find particular associations elsewhere in *Sense and Sensibility*, others belong rather to what psychoanalysis regards as a more universal register.[47] And indicating these (for reasons, themselves interesting, to be explored in due course) invariably appears not merely tendentious, but—to return to a prediction made in the Introduction—preposterous. As Freud says, 'in attempting to explain dreams it is not easy to avoid being fantastic..'; but then, he adds (drawing together old surprises from his physiological days and new ones from his psychology, in a way that we shall also find significant), '..Ganglion cells can be fantastic, too..' (4.159).

On the other hand, the passage recounts what is certainly the closest physical encounter between two characters in Jane Austen's oeuvre; furthermore the nub of what is happening in it is central to our present concerns.

The nub is the garden gate: in a perceptualist simulacrum, its being left open may hasten Willoughby's access to the house; but for us its being the subject of apparently gratuitous repetition has the contrary effect of arresting our reading the fraction of a second needed to tell us something is happening.

---

45 John Ciardi: 'A Burble through the Tulgey Wood', in *Aspects of Alice*, Penguin 1974, p. 308.

46 Ricoeur, op. cit., p. 365.

47 Exploring this register involves 'what is, strictly speaking, a second and auxiliary method of dream-interpretation' (4.339, n. added in 1925 ed.).

(To distinguish between particular and general registers, the following commentary is restricted to just a few of the details with specific textual echoes; psychoanalytic and other resonances are relegated to footnotes.)

It is again concatenation of detail which is remarkable: we might imagine a girl walking calmly along a flat surface; but no, she is **running with all possible speed down**;[48] she might pass the man and run on, but **a false step**[49] brings her down. **A gentleman carrying a gun**: Willoughby makes his first entrance as a sportsman, preparing Elinor's judgment that he was 'so unprincipled as to have been sporting with the affections of her sister from the first' (II.6.179), and fills with sinister meaning the final allusion to 'his breed of horses and dogs, and in sporting of every kind' (III.14.379); **with two pointers**:[50] no other notation in the novel more clearly recalls the scissors (III.12); **was passing up the hill**;[51] **her foot had been twisted in the fall**:[52] ' "can we wonder that . . . without a friend to advise or restrain her . . . she should fall?" ' (thus Col. Brandon, speaking of Eliza, 206).[53]

The more obvious notations may be passed over (e.g. the fact that the gentleman offered his **services**, that before **passing through the garden**[54] he **took her up** and **carried her down**: Middleton's earthy expression is ' "all this tumbling down hills" ' [I.9.44], echoing the first scissors-scene,

---

[48] Freud admits that 'we are not in possession of any generally recognized criterion of the sexual nature of a process' (1.362); nevertheless, analysis of e.g. adult precoital foreplay shows kinship with childhood pleasures (conversely, any physical or even intellectual activity may produce sexual excitement). Of many appropriate quotations from Freud, the closest to the above seems to be the passage where he recounts that 'A young medical colleague. . .quite free from any kind of nervous trouble, has given me the following information . . .: "I know from my own experience that in my childhood I had a peculiar sensation in my genitals when I was on a swing and especially when the downward motion reached its greatest momentum. And though I cannot say I really enjoyed this sensation I must describe it as a pleasurable one" ' (4.375/6 n.).

[49] An expression so apt for figuration that we have put it into French. When Freud was trying to grasp a hysterical symptom (sc. one with no identifiable physical basis) in Dora–she was dragging a foot–it comes to him that 'That is how people walk when they have twisted a foot. So she had made a "false step" ' (8.143); cf. ' "There. . . on that projecting mound,–there I fell; and there I first saw Willoughby" ' (344). A good example of 'symbolisation by means of a verbal expression' involving feet, is that of 'Frau Cäcilie', who had a pain in her right heel: 'she had been afraid . . . she might not find herself "on a right footing" ' with strangers' 3.252).

[50] 'Dreams very often represent castration by the presence of two penis symbols as the defiant expression of an antithetical wish' (4.539).

[51] 'The unconscious has a natural "upward drive" ' (15.413): keeping *down* = subjugate is built into our culture.

[52] (a) Feet and shoes are the most popular *fetish* (an object without which sexual excitement is impossible) because–depending how you think of it–one goes into the other, or the other fits snugly round the one.
(b) 'Dreams of falling . . . are more often characterised by anxiety. Their interpretation offers no difficulty in the case of women, who almost always accept the symbolic use of falling as a way of describing a surrender to an erotic temptation' (4.518). Some interesting research by Alice Chandler tells us that the name of the horse Willoughby wishes to give Marianne ('Queen Mab', I.12.59) may contain an implied sexual invitation: 'This is the hag, when maids lie on their backs,/That presses them and learns them first to bear' ('A Pair of Fine Eyes', *Studies in the Novel* 7, 1975, p. 90). Freud drew attention to the cynical expression 'When a girl fall she falls on her back' in order to indicate that his 'discovery' of parapraxes corresponded to the intuitions embedded in ordinary language: 'falling, stumbling and slipping need not always be interpreted as purely accidental miscarriages of motor actions. The double meanings that language attaches to these expressions are enough to indicate the kind of phantasies involved' (5.229).

[53] The Colonel seems to be involved in some kind of *repetition compulsion* with regard to his girl-friends.

[54] Gardens have long possessed sexual resonance: 'A garden inclosed is my sister, my spouse; a spring shut up, a fountain sealed' (*Song of Songs,* 4.12); as for the meteorology of the episode (leaving 'in the midst of a heavy rain' makes Willoughby 'still more interesting') as Freud says, drily: 'Love . . . makes things wet' (8.108).

where Marianne's hair ' "was all tumbled down her back" ' I.12.60);[55] and we may return to the gate.

When the Palmers arrive it is 'The closing of the little gate, at the entrance of the green court in front of the house' (I.19.105) which draws Elinor's attention, if not ours; their arrival at Barton Park is perhaps in more than one way 'mistaken', for Elinor is foiled of further information about Willoughby by the emptiness of Charlotte's replies. The important prop was however placed at the very beginning (I.6.28), when the Dashwood women arrive at what is now to become 'their own house. A small green court was the whole of its demesne in front; and a neat wicket gate admitted them into it.'

Before we pursue Marianne further, it is worth saying that the exploit of juxtaposing suitors belonging to such very different registers as Willoughby and Edward evinces a certain temerity on the novelist's part; furthermore, what can an ordinary Oxonian of twenty-four hope, when opposed to a mythical creature from millennia of dream-time? Edward must appear excessively ordinary in contrast.[56]

That Willoughby proving unsatisfactory leads to Marianne's disappointment, and to desire for a known source of comfort, is 'only natural':

..her impatience to be at home again now returned; her mother was dearer to her than ever; dearer through the very excess of her mistaken confidence..   (III.9.203)

However, interestingly enough her mother's reaction is negative: returning to Barton, she writes, 'would be bringing back the past'; remaining where she is will, Mrs Dashwood hopes, 'cheat Marianne at times, into some interest beyond herself' (II.10.213). In order to get her mother to come to her, Marianne must therefore regress to the position of infantile helplessness; and she does this by falling again: by falling ill, which always (8.75) involves a saving of psychical effort.

---

[55] Though today's Jane Austen reader can become conscious of more of her meaning than the 1811 reader, it is pointless to deny that some meanings in art become lost; in 'the confusion which crimsoned over her face, on his lifting her up' (43, underlined in I.10 with 'the embarrassment which the remembrance of his assistance created') one dimension of perceptualist suggestiveness has been lost in the passage of time, for undergarments were still 'undivided' at that period. This gives added meaning to Erich Auerbach's remark that 'All through the [18th] century we find motifs of this kind in literature (and not only in erotic literature in the strict sense): a disturbed idyll, a gust of wind, a fall, a jump, through which normally covered parts of the female body are revealed or which produce a generally "charming disorder" ' (*Mimesis*, Princeton 1953, pp. 398/9). Freud's early writing is at the temporal limit of such possibilities ('rational' dress for women as for men dating from the Great War): in 1899 he recounts a woman's dream of climbing over a fence which 'was not intended for climbing over [shades of Sotherton]; she had trouble in finding a place to put her feet in and felt glad that her dress had not been caught anywhere, so that she had stayed respectable..' (4.464).

[56] Perhaps for this reason Jane Austen makes his very existence somewhat precarious: in vol.I his rendering of Cowper (by whom he is ' "not to be animated" ') is ' "spiritless" ' (17/8); if Marianne attributes his not visiting them at Barton to illness (38), Margaret entertains us by supposing ' "he is lately dead" ' (61); at the cottage he is 'particularly grave' (99); in vol.II as we have seen he has to be given a 'living', since ' "The interest of two thousand pounds–how can a man live on it!" ' (268), and only at the end, after his 'annihilation' (373) by his mother, does he undergo a 'resuscitation'. Even then, 'In spite of his being allowed once more to live, however, he did not feel the continuance of his existence secure': announcing his engagement, he fears, might 'carry him off as rapidly as before', etc., etc.

..it emerges as being economically the most convenient solution where there is a mental conflict (we speak of a 'flight into illness') . . . The motive for being ill is . . . invariably the intention of securing some gain.

It would be out of character for her not to overdo this: she almost dies.

Freud's theory of 'death instincts' is no doubt among the most contested parts of his work, and to trace in detail the various avenues of his thought which together led to its formulation in *Beyond the Pleasure Principle* (1920), beyond this study's scope. Apart from the biologist's desire to explain death itself, there was the psychologist's need to understand the dynamics of excessive self-love, and the complementary and still more remarkable phenomenon of *masochism*: on the one hand, a centuries'-old association between sexual pleasure and annihilation[57] led him to ask whether the pleasure-principle were not in the service of the death-instincts (11.388). On the other, though as we have seen the super-ego is an explanatory anthropomorphised model for the human tendency to punish itself, in one of Freud's last papers he has come to the conclusion that this institution cannot by itself account for that need, and that elements of the death-instinct 'may be at work in other, unspecified places' (*SE* XXIII.242/3); these certainly include the id, which 'cannot say what it wants; it has achieved no unified will. Eros and the death-instinct struggle within it' (11.401).

And all that—death instinct, gain from illness, deeply regressive tendencies in both—is, *pace* the received account of Jane Austen as an 'entertaining' writer, to be found in this novel.

First, if Marianne is 'punished' it is, as she herself acknowledges, by herself: ' "Had I died, —it would have been self-destruction" ' (III.10.345); Elinor had earlier foreseen this danger: ' "Exert yourself, dear Marianne . . . if you would not kill yourself and all who love you" ' (II.7.185).

Second, whilst previous events which brought Marianne down (death of father; departure of Willoughby) are the occasion for her deriving satisfaction from the symptom of grief (what Freud calls *primary gain*), the *secondary gain* (entailing redistribution of psychic energy: 'painful and feverish illnesses exercise a powerful effect . . . on the distribution of libido', 11.305) is to the self-preservative rather than to the sexual instincts: it is the ego which now, faced with the symptom, resolves to 'draw as much advantage from it as possible' (10.251). That Jane Austen grasped at least the *mechanism* of this is clear from an episode already quoted: Annamaria gets 'her mouth stuffed with sugar plums [what Freud calls a 'disablement pension' 1.432] With such a reward for her tears, the child was too wise to cease crying' (I.21.121). But again—and the reader will by now have realised this is the tendency of

---

57 *La petite mort*, familiar French for orgasm: a spirited success entailing a more breathless *failure of desire—* which is what *Nirvana* means in Sanskrit.

everything that happens in this work—we are returned to Elinor: for just as she had intercepted the Constantia wine in chapter 8 of vol.II, so now in chapter 8 of vol.III (as 'The clock struck eight'!) the climax of the scenario that Marianne's 'imagination placed before her'—

> a letter from Willoughby, full of tenderness and contrition, explanatory of all that had passed, satisfactory, convincing; and instantly followed by Willoughby himself rushing eagerly into the room to inforce..   [etc., II.9]

—occurs (his III.9 nocturnal visit), but it is Elinor who reaps the benefit.

And that not only Marianne, but other characters, may be read as bearers of a central preoccupation transcending their individual significance, can be seen from other notations at Cleveland. Two examples realist decorum cannot accommodate: first, the sudden revelation of a callous side to Charlotte—

> ..listening to the gardener's lamentations upon blights . . . through the green-house, where the loss of her favourite plants, unwarily exposed, and nipped by the lingering frost, raised [her] laughter—and in visiting her poultry-yard, where, in the disappointed hopes of her dairy-maid, by hens forsaking their nests, or being stolen by a fox, or in the rapid decease of a promising young brood, she found fresh sources of merriment.   (III.6.303)

—in which the reader should now need no help in spotting ripples of the great parent/child groundswell of the work.

Second example: in the next paragraph, Marianne having 'depended on a twilight walk to the Grecian temple', takes us on to Barton, where this figurative tributary of her regression is repeated, in her plan to ' "..go to the old ruins of the Priory, and try to trace in its foundations as far as we are told they once reached" ' (III.10.343).

When Marianne is reunited with her mother, this movement is confirmed. The unconscious has no temporal order (9.237 n.), and Marianne's resolution of self-discipline, apparently antagonistic to previous drives, is in fact charged with the same excess: she resolves never to be later in rising ' "than six, and from that time until dinner I shall divide every moment between music and reading . . . By reading only six hours a-day.." ' [etc.].

She further resolves: ' "From you, from my home, I shall never again have the smallest inclination to move" ' (347): 'you', here, is Elinor, which suggests that the regression is to *primary narcissism*: 'total absence of any relationship to the outside world, and . . . a lack of differentiation between ego and id' (*L & P* 256)—a state, in fact, similar to that of sleep.[58]

---

[58] Perhaps indeed Marianne dreams Willoughby's night visit. A quite egregiously extravagant statement, this will appear; however at the end of this visit there are suggestions that they are in a sense all three of them asleep: towards the end of a long paragraph of Elinor's silent thoughts we are told: 'From a reverie of this kind she was recalled at the end of some minutes by Willoughby, who, rousing himself from a reverie at least equally painful, started up..' etc.; and at the beginning of the next chapter, our key word is again played on: 'When at last she returned to **the unconscious Marianne**, she found her just awaking, refreshed by so long and sweet a sleep to the extent of her hopes..' (III.10.331 f).

The 'first and second attachments' topic is part of this book's manifest content; here too, Jane Austen's prescience is uncanny, for whilst Freud gave new colouring to 'First Loves' ('The finding of an object is in fact a re-finding of it' 7.145), it will be recalled that whereas Elinor declares at the beginning that ' " thirty-five and seventeen had better not have anything to do with matrimony together" ' (I.8.37) (and this was commensurate with her rôle as critical agency for 'the ego ideal had the task of repressing the Oedipus complex' 11.374) the novel ends with Marianne's other first object-choice being offered her on a plate.

The juxtaposition of dreary Edward and dishy Willoughby thus corresponds to that of the maturest heroine (Elinor,arguably the most adult of the Jane Austen oeuvre) with the most infantile. And in terms of the metapsychological logic of this work, Marianne's marriage to Col. Brandon (who, it will not have been forgotten, she once said ' "is old enough to be *my* father" ' I.8.37) turns out to be extraordinarily *fitting*: for apart from his paternal behaviour ('patron' of the living) to Edward (who has also lost his father), he replaces the Dashwood sisters' father, but without taking their mother away from them. He is thus quite as much of a psychical, ideal reality as Willoughby, and thus also (since our first emotional ties are identifications, *L & P* 336) Marianne is authorised to return to the mother in a quite literal way: i.e. by *becoming* her—even down to two telling details: first, as her father ' "had himself two wives" ' (I.11.56), so naturally her spouse, too, must have had a previous love. Second, with that Father-figure in mind, it can hardly be accidental that when Marianne, excoriating herself for her former conduct (destructive of herself, but also, she now sees, of others: ' "Everybody seemed injured by me" '), asks Elinor's forgiveness, invokes religion—specifically using the word 'atonement'—wonders at her own recovery, and at the fact ' "that the very eagerness of my desire to live, to have time for atonement to my God,[59] and to you all, did not kill me at once." '

To 'atone', etymologically, is to be 'at one' with; and as Marianne's guilt and contrition bring her to compare her behaviour ' "with what it ought to have been; I compare it with yours" ' (viz. Elinor's, III.10.346), so Freud says of the ego ideal: 'As a substitute for a longing for the father, it contains the germ from which all religions have evolved.' (11.376).

We may now return to the rich interpretative possibilities of Edward's act in III.12, discussion of which in section 2 was suspended on the recognition

---

[59] The word appears three hundred pages earlier in the same sentence as 'enthusiasm': Elinor, judging her sister, tells Edward that there are ' "inconveniences attending such feelings as Marianne's, which all the charms of enthusiasm and ignorance of the world cannot atone for" ' (I.11.56). Might Jane Austen have known that the word 'enthusiasm' (a term applied in the 18th century to ecstatic behaviour, forerunner of the sensibility movement) contains *deus*? If she did, does it matter whether her knowledge was conscious or not?

The fact that it is Marianne who brings up father-religion—not Elinor, and not the narration—will have important consequences for us in Chapter IV.

that the spoiling of the scissors as well as the sheath, complicated an ascription of the act merely to symbolic violence against Robert Ferrars. Recourse in section 4 to the linguistic datum that the two components of the act are linked—the act itself therefore *ambivalent*—related, as the reader will have understood, to other occasions on which passages apparently about various 'minor' characters have driven us back to the two central ones.

The act has been called *violent*; it may now be given the psychoanalytic name *aggressive*. Freud thought that as all instinct was pushy by nature it was misleading to isolate an 'aggressive instinct'. Moreover as a key characteristic of aggression is that it tends 'to undo connections' (*L & P* 181), its outward tendencies are, he thought, merely a derivative of an essentially inward-tending, self-destructive death-instinct. This account has been simplified, but a final key point is that, with the exception of the melancholic (or depressive), whose super-ego is what Freud calls 'a pure culture of the death-instinct' (11.394), all manifestations of aggression have something sexual in them.

In trying to understand Edward's act, it will be seen that there is no question of its aggressiveness resulting from 'frustration caused by the object' (*L & P* 101).[60] On the other hand, though a specific 'instinct to master' is a post-Freudian theorisation, he did use the term *urge for mastery*[61]: an urge, that is, in which 'injury or annihilation of the object is a matter of indifference' (11.137): e.g. he thought so-called infantile cruelty could not properly be called *sadistic*, being no more than the exercise of new-found muscular power.

We might ascribe the word 'sheath' its most obvious (contraceptive) sense, and by slight figurative extension a hymeneal one: indeed it may have been that sort of 'interpretation' the reader first expected of the present study. However, apart from the poverty of its obviousness, such a reading would make Edward's act a mere pantomime of coarse male sexual aggressiveness.

Moreover, as we have seen from the associations, one of the objects spoiled (the pair of scissors) is very far from indifferent: in that perspective—Edward's scissors in chapter 12 of vol.III related to Willoughby's in chapter 12 of vol.I—a final interpretative possibility has in a sense already been given.

But to say Edward wishes to cut off a lock of Elinor's hair raises a logically prior question: why anyway should men wish to cut off bits of women's hair?

Whilst it is not unknown for women to possess keepsakes of this kind, the act of cutting them off (which is what we have to do with here) does seem characteristically male. And the trait most nearly related to it is the—again almost invariably masculine (15.438)—phenomenon of *fetishism* (mentioned

---

[60] Commentators who, for whatever reason, find the death-instinct unacceptable, have sometimes posited aggression as a *secondary* formation, resultant on such frustration.

[61] As (a) among compensations for the initial expulsion, when Fanny installed herself **mistress** of Norland', we are told that Marianne eventually becomes '**mistress** of a family', and 'patroness of a village' (III.14.379); and (b) that the second before Edward enters Barton cottage, Elinor resolves ' "I *will* be **mistress** of myself" ' (in contrast with Edward's act, in which he is clearly *mastered by* something beyond his conscious control), there appear grounds for seeing here an adumbration of an associative chain to be explored in *P & P*.

above, p. 82, n. 52), in which something is substituted '..for the sexual object . . . some part of the body (such as the foot or the hair) which is in general very inappropriate for sexual purposes.'[62]

We now return to a concept introduced on p. 71: *ambivalence*, now seen to be germane in so far as it is related to a mechanism involving a *splitting of the ego* as 'a means of having two procedures of defence exist side by side', of which one is directed towards the instinct and the other towards reality itself (*L & P* 429): the piece of reality in question is then said to be *disavowed*.

The prototypical form of disavowal is the male infant's refusal to 'see' that women do not possess a penis: by continuing to believe they do, he wards off the possibility of being deprived of his own.[63] In this sense, it must again be remembered that an infant's first emotional ties are identifications: it can only love what resembles itself; in other words, what is homogeneous; settling for the heterogeneous other sex—if that happens—being a much later formation, consequent on the dissolution of the Oedipus complex.

*

..ask an analyst what his experience has shown to be the mental structures least accessible to influence in his patients, the answer will be: in a woman her wish for a penis, in a man his feminine attitude towards his own sex, a precondition of which would, of course, be the loss of his penis.

Thus Freud in his last work (15.429, after half a century's analytic experience). A last remark—for the reader who is in any sense still with me—will return us to the hint (p. 57) to which all the analyses in this chapter tend, and thus to its Prelude; for if the whole text of *Sense and Sensibility* is seen as bearing the preoccupations of its central character, it must indeed be Elinor's wish that Edward is fulfilling: that is, she wishes she had something to cut off.

If this seem decidedly the last straw in *over*-interpretation, and the reader be driven by exasperation to quote against me my warning that the interpretative model advanced would be at least as preposterous as the reigning one, perhaps that reader may be reminded that, with the Bennet girls and the entailed Longbourn estate, the theme of the dispossession of women is to reappear in the next novel published by Jane Austen, to which we now turn.

*

---

[62] '..or some inanimate object which bears an assignable relation to the person whom it replaces and preferably to that person's sexuality (e.g. a piece of clothing)' (7.65/6): the quotation needs completing, as fetishism differs from 'psychologially essential overvaluation of the sexual object, which inevitably extends to everything that is associated with it' (7.66); that phenomenon, not limited to typical behaviour of either sex, is represented by Marianne's view after I.9: 'of all manly dresses a shooting-jacket was the most becoming' (43).

[63] It cannot be overlooked that by proposing to Elinor he is 'dishing' himself by cutting himself off from his mother—one (absent) woman—and that his act is committed in the presence of no less than four women.

NOTE

Paintings and buildings can be cleaned; musical compositions may be re-orchestrated; in both music and drama everything has constantly to be 'interpreted' afresh in performance. But apart from reversion to original typography, or publication in alluring new bindings, our material apprehension of novels cannot itself be renewed: they must simply be re-read.

Freud opens *Notes on a Case of Paranoia* (the psychoanalysis of a book) by asking his readers 'to make themselves acquainted with the book by reading it through at least once beforehand' (9.140). As the *Notes...* were published in the 1911 Psychoanalytic Yearbook, Freud's first readers could no doubt be counted on to do their homework. In the present context anything in the way of complementary effort can scarcely be required of readers—though perhaps it might be requested[1]—who may at all events be reminded that this inquiry is in every sense a *re*-reading: the sooner they take into their own hands that part of the work which is an indispensable preliminary to any interpretation, the better.

In line with the promise made in the Preface to vary the reading-experience as much as possible, this chapter will be a little different in approach from the last: hoping to benefit from *Pride and Prejudice* being doubtless better-known than *Sense and Sensibility*, a slightly more allusive way will be taken with the text; also, the reader will from time to time be pointed (by means of footnotes) towards details in other novels.

The reason for these dispositions is mainly one of economy: interpretative principles that have given a favourable yield may henceforth be expected to be put to work for us; nevertheless, their application will still not be so far taken for granted as to exclude giving some room to discussion of them, and of larger questions arising out of what has so far been seen.

Not the least of these will centre on what will from now on be a key concern in this inquiry, as its overall plausibility depends on the degree to which it succeeds in establishing relationships between contexts: namely, the attempt to arrive at a better sense of Jane Austen's oeuvre as a whole, and indeed to think of that oeuvre as being itself a sort of inquiry.

---

[1] One scarcely dare mention a still more extravagant suggestion: '..it is hardly possible to persuade an adult who has very much enjoyed reading a book to re-read it immediately. Novelty is always the condition of enjoyment.' (11.307). Even for those who re-read in order to arrive at coherent thought about what they have read, many second and subsequent readings are entered into with the (understandable) aim of recapturing the pleasure of the first. One of this study's key formal aims is to bring home to compulsive Jane Austen re-readers the essential treacherousness of such behaviour, which resembles what we all do with favourite old recordings of music: the melancholy truth is, that listening-through stops one hearing.

CHAPTER III

Pride and Prejudice

' "I am only a poor girl and he is such a rich man of good family.." '
(Miss Lucy R., who eventually) 'resolved to drive this inclination out of her
mind because it seemed to her incompatible with her **pride**.'
(Freud, 3.182 & *SE* III.48)

'..repression is often achieved by means of an excessive reinforcement of
the thought contrary to the one which is to be repressed. This process I
call *reactive* reinforcement, and the thought which asserts itself with excessive intensity in consciousness and (in the same way as a **prejudice**)
cannot be removed, I call a *reactive thought*.' (do., 8.89)

'She read, with an eagerness which hardly left her power of comprehension, and from impatience of knowing what the next sentence might
bring, was incapable of attending to the sense of the one before her eyes.'
(Elizabeth Bennet, in *P & P* II.13.204)

' "At such a distance as *that*, you know, things are strangely
misrepresented" ' (do., in *P & P* III.10.327)

- 1 -

'Behind every discovery he showed us a long row of new question marks.'[1]

In this testimony to the undogmatic, interrogative character of Sigmund
Freud's thought, the word 'new' should be underlined. And readers who have
allowed themselves to be led into this third chapter may now understand
that the present study aims to show how new are the questions the work of
Jane Austen raises when placed under the hard light of psychoanalysis.[2]
From time to time in the course of this chapter it will be worth while articulating some of these questions, even if they cannot be fully answered.

---

[1] Sachs, op. cit., p. 60.

[2] Arguably, enabling new questions to be asked could be considered an indispensable criterion for the value of
openness to further research in any area of thought; fortunately, the pleasure principle also lends its aid here:
if Thomas Hobbes was right in thinking a key factor separating man from beasts to be *curiosity*–which he
defined as 'care of knowing causes . . . a Lust of the mind [in] continual and indefatigable generation of
Knowledge'–then, as he said, in this area 'all delight is appetite' and 'there can be no contentment but in
proceeding..'(*Leviathan* I.6 and *Human Nature* VII.7).

90

One of the first which readers (even the least sceptical) may already be asking, is—supposing some of the dynamics in *Sense and Sensibility*, one Jane Austen novel to be placed under that light, have been clarified in the process —whether the same sort of analysis can necessarily be applied to another one. It is after all conceivable that the psychological structures in terms of which Freud came to understand his contemporary Viennese, might happen by some historical fluke to coincide with configurations of character and lexical field in just one work of English literature from a century before.

For readers responding to the hint in the p. 89 Note, at this watershed between examination of the two first-published Jane Austen novels, the question will be whether to go back to *Sense and Sensibility*, or on to *Pride and Prejudice*. Whichever option is embraced, a word of caution is in order.

One of Freud's expositional quandaries was how to describe, in readily comprehensible traditional terms, matters for which no tradition of representation existed. As early as 1892 he is troubled by 'the problem of how it will be possible to give a two-dimensional picture of anything that is so much of a solid as our theory of hysteria' (*SE* I.147).

He never satisfactorily resolved this difficulty: nearly half a century later we still find him lamenting that there is 'no way of conveying knowledge of a complicated set of simultaneous events except by describing them successively' (15.441).

The narrative techniques of which Chapter II tried to give an account— techniques serving evocation of a certain psychological structure in Jane Austen's first-published novel—constituted what were (as far as I know) wholly *original* exploitations of the genre's possibilities in 1811. Attempting to describe them entailed a correspondingly specific interpretative challenge, but also—here is the fact warranting a certain caution—although Jane Austen built on or refined some of those techniques (in ways we shall examine), in a sense she never repeated a trick.

Naturally, re-readings of *Pride and Prejudice*—perhaps at a slower pace— should not be discouraged; however, the present chapter will argue that the appearance in 1813 of this second novel constitutes, in its way, *another* revolution in the genre. A problem, then, for readers who think by revisiting this work to assess the degree of validity they feel intellectually comfortable in according to contentions made so far, is that although in the end some sort of re-reading experience is the decisive test, Chapter II may have been successful in its general aim of undermining the reader's sense of what kind of an object a novel by Jane Austen is, and thus of modifying the received account not merely of what *Sense and Sensibility* (say) is about, but moreover of how, as it were, it is about it.

How, then, should a Jane Austen novel be read?

The technique adopted in the last chapter was modelled on Freud's method of getting at the dream-thoughts by dividing the dream's manifest content into its component parts 'without considering any apparent meaning it may have [as a whole], and then by following the associative threads which start from each of what are now isolated elements' (6.216). The task of interpretation, then, is essentially 'restoration of the connections which the dream-work has destroyed' (4.422).

But how far can we take this? Can we disregard 'the apparent coherence between a dream's constituents' and 'trace back the origin of each of its elements on its own account' (4.581)?

The dream/novel parallel seems to pose some difficulties: that novels are much *longer* than any dream, for example, may appear seriously damaging to it; another problem concerns what is thought of as the essentially *private* character of dreams. We shall return to these difficulties; but for present purposes the only undeniable factor affecting interpretation is this: the nature of the difference between latent and manifest content in dreams is such that 'the essence of the dream-thoughts need not be represented in the dream at all' (4.414); in *Sense and Sensibility*, on the other hand, though the novel's core is a silence, that silence, it was argued in Chapter II, can be filled out and made to speak from what surrounds it.

This is a procedural point of some importance, since psychoanalytic interpretation often finds itself under attack for reading its meanings 'into' the world, for reading too much 'between the lines', claiming occult powers of vision into mazes of 'hidden' meanings, refusing to take things at their face value, perversely ignoring the obvious in favour of 'subtext', etc. etc.

As far as the present study goes, it is hoped such charges will now seem beside the point, since the discussions in Chapter II were resolutely of what was to be found *in* the lines, not between them. Indeed it is hard to know what 'between the lines', or the 'face value' of a work of art (or reading a book 'on its own terms', another ideal sometimes aired in critical theory) might mean; *an interpretation* may be more or less appropriate to its object, in ways that can be discussed; we shall return to this, too.

In fact, there is no such thing as the 'obvious' reading; and in the end, meanings are 'hidden' only when we stand something else in front of them.[3]

Let us now pursue the legitimate question of the *relation* between latent and manifest content: a dream is 'differently centred from the dream thoughts' (4.414); how far can we say something similar of a Jane Austen novel?

Part of the answer may be found if we put it thus: the manifest content of Jane Austen's writings is incomparably more organized than in dreams, which mostly seem nonsensical; to use the Freudian term in dream-analysis, *secondary revision*—the effort to make an intelligible whole—has been massive. Succumbing to a certain verisimilitude, we have been it seems under a

---

[3] Otiose tilting at long-extinct critical solecisms? As recently as 1993 we find it asserted in an essay on Jane Austen that 'fiction can be read in terms of the "hidden narrative" ' (M.Evans, op. cit., p. 33).

sort of spell (Freud speaks of a 'mild narcosis' induced by art, 12.269). For example, the sheer quality of story-telling in these novels is so compelling as to have perhaps concealed the art deployed in making them appear seamless sequences. At the risk of disenchanting the reader, some seams must nevertheless be pointed out. And it will be most opportune to focus now on *Pride and Prejudice*, since even in the manifest content of this novel the plausibility of stories plays a key rôle.

Readers may reflect, then: (1) that it is pure coincidence that Darcy has a friend who rents a house in the same village as the garrison Wickham chooses for his lieutenancy; (2) that it is pure coincidence that Darcy's aunt is Collins' patroness; and (3) pure coincidence that Elizabeth's aunt had spent a considerable time in the neighbourhood of Darcy's house. The convergence on a little Hertfordshire village of so many characters who have no reason but exigences of plot for being linked, might oblige us to recognize that Jane Austen had truly pulled the wool over our eyes ..were it not that in the last sentence of the novel, relating the Darcys' gratitude to the Gardiners, 'who by bringing [Elizabeth] into Derbyshire, had been the means of uniting them', the narrator just jiggles that wool a little.

This may be thought attributable to an established convention (sc., art concealing art). However, the principle governing the inclusion of such impurities in the realist mix is very closely related to the present study's central contention. For the questions which our consciousness of such art leads us to ask about the fundamental mechanism of events in the 'external' world ('Hertfordshire', 'Kent', 'Derbyshire') are empowered in this novel to spill over onto more pointed questionings about causality and the status of chance in *psychological* events.

To illustrate this, three examples—relating, first, to minor characters:

(1) a couple of days after learning Elizabeth has refused Collins, Charlotte Lucas perceived him '..from an upper window as he walked towards the house, and instantly set out to meet him accidentally in the lane' (I.22.121).

Just as, at novels' endings, sophisticated jokes which 'give the whole thing away' are sanctioned, so the sheer fun in this, at the expense of Charlotte— almost of the English language[4] —perhaps obscures a slily laid precedent.

(2) At Pemberley, Darcy is introduced to the Gardiners; the whole party moves off together, then we are told that after walking thus a while,

> ..the two ladies in front, the two gentlemen behind, on resuming their places, after descending to the brink of the river for the better inspection of some curious water-plant, there **chanced** to be a little alteration. It originated in Mrs. Gardiner, who, fatigued by the exercise of the morning, found Elizabeth's arm inadequate to her support, and consequently

---

[4] To spell it out: a semantic rupture (because one cannot 'set out' to do things 'accidentally') cleverly put to serve a focal rupture; for the space of the word 'accidentally', the focus changes to the point of view of someone ignorant of Charlotte's 'pure and disinterested desire of an establishment' (I.22.122).

preferred her husband's. Mr. Darcy took her place by her niece, and they walked on together.. (III.1.255/6)

In this passage (English prose is here at a supple height of suggestive possibilities) 'curious', it may be agreed, implies in the lightest way a word imagined as uttered; that prepares the explanation—a little too ample to be simply narrative—'fatigued. . .husband's', hardly imaginable unaccompanied by uttered words; then the very slight overformality of 'It originated in..' alerts us to the presence of a sort of intention on Mrs Gardiner's part, and a sort of intention on Jane Austen's part that her creature's intention should be just noticeable: the upshot of all this being to ensure the ironic resonance of the single word 'chanced'.

(3) Towards the end of the book Bingley returns to Longbourn, and at the critical moment when neighbours at table are in question, 'Jane **happened** to look round, and **happened** to smile: it was decided. He placed himself by her' (III.12.340).

Neither Charlotte's nor Mrs Gardiner's ploys are treated as rivettingly interesting, their designs coming only fleetingly within what in Chapter II was called 'earshot' of the narrative presence; Jane's rôle in the novel will engage us in due course. But now a passage relating to its heroine, ' "an excellent walker" ' (I.8.35): on more than one ramble at Rosings, we are told, did she

..**unexpectedly** meet Mr. Darcy.—She felt all the perverseness of the **mischance** that should bring him where no one else was brought; and to prevent its ever **happening** again, took care to inform him at first, that it was a favourite haunt of hers.—How it could **occur** a second time therefore was very odd!—Yet it did, and even a third.. (II.10.182)

How far is narrative 'lent' to Elizabeth's point of view here? Is *she* not quite straight with us (or with herself)?[5]—or should anything approaching guile perhaps (cf. the use of 'Edward' in the first novel) be imputed to the text?

However that turn out to be, the point of this first demonstration, apart from shining a hard light on 'chance' (and incidentally giving some first examples of what will be called *seepage* of irony from minor to central characters) is further to underscore the word of caution about re-readings voiced at the start of this chapter. Perhaps it goes without saying that this study will not wholly have failed of its object (in its author's eyes) if readers feel positively *driven* back to their Jane Austen, but it would be pointless to pretend to ignore that the closeness of reading being canvassed for—re-reading, slower reading, different way of reading—must encounter some resistance (of an entirely concious kind, naturally): a degree of attention which readers of long works such as novels are unused to being asked, and are perhaps unwilling,

---

[5] She is taxed with many things by her critics (in the novel and out of it) but not, as far as I recall, with *disingenuousness*; if more fuel for that charge could be found, it would support the view (p. 92) that manifest and latent content in this novel are 'differently centred'.

to bestow. That resistance may be stoked by a lingering scepticism as to whether it is plausible to posit of any novel what Freud (e.g. 9.274) claims for dreams: namely that *every* detail is significant.

At the present juncture, an answer can only be by appeal to pragma: if even a single detail in *Sense and Sensibility* to which readers hitherto assigned no special significance, or none other than what is attributable to a certain copiousness of material thought normal in the bourgeois genre of the novel,[6] or—the Janeite position—which they were pleased to identify as 'strays' (undigested items from Jane Austen's visual memory)—if Chapter II persuaded the reader that any one such detail had, in Freud's words, 'a place in an assignable mental context', and that it provided 'information, by a small indication, of a more important mental process' (1.286), then, so far, the main contention of this study may be allowed to stand.

This appeal granted should have repercussions on the most sceptical reader's openness to persuasion—might even retroactively lessen the outrage felt at the claim aired in the Introduction about the relation between application and confirmation of psychoanalysis. By 1908 Freud reported that 'those who know and practise the psychoanalytic technique *acquire* an extensive confidence in its findings' (7.187, my italics); even earlier (in 1901), discussing just such small 'chance' actions as those examined in Chapter II, he declared with still greater bravura that interpretations, and the evidence for them, emerge *together*, 'from the material which accompanies them' (5.251).

At this point the least sceptical reader might feel that if the psychoanalytic conceptual scheme turns out to account for so much in Jane Austen's work, this may itself be significant (of something about her intention..) One must put off as long as possible the alluring implications of this suggestion, because of its perfect logical circularity:[7] we need a better *a priori* reason for the correspondence mooted. There is such a reason, as it happens; but for the moment it will be preferable to build up from the examination of *Pride and Prejudice* better *a posteriori* support for Chapter II's contentions.

- 2 -

In III.17 Elizabeth reveals her engagement to Jane, who exclaims: ' "You are joking, Lizzy. This cannot be!—engaged to Mr. Darcy! No, no, you shall not deceive me. I know it to be impossible" '; it is unlikely that, on first reading this, one remembers Elizabeth's almost identical cry, 250 pages earlier: ' "Engaged to Mr. Collins! My dear Charlotte,—impossible!" ' (I.22.124).

Of the three sorts of close attention to text recommended, we saw the most elementary (re-reading) invited by certain techniques in *Sense and Sensibility*.

---

[6] What is the significance, for the novel's thematic centre, of *P & P* II.16.221, where a man (Chamberlayne) is described as dressed up in woman's clothes?

[7] Though this would not prevent the fact, if it is a fact, from being true.

In the novel now before us that invitation, together with its ironic implications for the portrayal of the heroine, is made in a more thoroughgoing way.

Moreover, support of a peculiar kind for the re-reading principle is found in the novel itself: the literal centre of *Pride and Prejudice*, too (cf. Chapter II, p. 60) is emblematic: the moment when the heroine starts to re-read Darcy's letter. Later, with a first reading behind her, 'the letter was unfolded again' (II.13.205), and at this second reading she 'commanded herself so far as to examine the meaning of every sentence.' (Razor-sharp writer's-irony, this, since such a degree of attention might seem the very least to be expected of any reader.[8]) This symbolic centre will also afford a vantage-point from which to observe some associative chains in *Pride and Prejudice*: signs of the text's promise to repay with interest any outlay vouchsafed in the form of extremely close attention.

When Elizabeth tells herself (II.13.208) she has been 'blind, partial, prejudiced, absurd . . . "I, who have prided myself..." ' etc., obvious echoes are set up with the words on the cover of the book. Without undervaluing those words, if what is really going on in Jane Austen's work may instead be found amongst 'the dregs, as it were, of the world of phenomena', and if 'everything is related to everything, including small things to great' (1.53), then we might again pounce on an unassuming detail: the letter was *unfolded* again.

The verb is used in its literal meaning (and positive form) on only one other occasion in the work: Mr Bennet 'folded up' Collins' first letter (I.13.63); all its other occurrences are metaphorical. In the proximity of p. 205 there are two more of them, forming together a significant cluster: thus just before Darcy's letter (191) Elizabeth tells him ' "Your **character** was **unfolded**" ' (in what Wickham had told her of him), and *in* the letter (200) Darcy tells her that whatever sentiments Wickham has created in her 'a suspicion of their nature shall not prevent me from **unfolding** his real **character**.' In this characteristically unostentatious way, at a key moment, a tiny physical act preparatory to Elizabeth's mental act of reassessing Darcy's representation of himself is brought into connection with one of the most important words in the novel's manifest content.[9]

From this central rib, various metaphorical *liernes* may be traced. First, another cluster of notations links 'character', in its turn, to a metaphor of representation—of a kind seen to be significant in the first novel: while Elizabeth is dancing with Darcy (having thought she could safely promise her mother never to) she describes their common disposition, to which he replies: ' "This is no very striking **resemblance** of your own **character** . . . *You*

---

[8] Moreover this local irony 'rhymes' with one of the large *structural* ironies of the book: what Elizabeth denies to Collins, turns out after all to be true: she *is* ' "one of those young ladies . . . who are so daring as to risk their happiness on the chance of being asked a second time" ' by first rejecting what he calls ' "the addresses of the man whom they secretly mean to accept" ' (I.19.107).

[9] The word 'character' occurs ca. 54 times in *P & P*; to forestall suspicion that the word's banality makes its frequency of appearance unsurprising, n.b. that in *S & S* the word occurs less than half as often, ca. 26 times.)

think it a **faithful portrait** undoubtedly" ' (I.18.91); later he asks her to what a series of her questions tends; she says it is ' "to the **illustration** of *your* **character**" '; he replies he would prefer her ' "not to **sketch my character**" ' at that moment; but she wants, she says, to seize the present opportunity to ' "**take your likeness** now" ' (93/4).

In any but first-readings these notations adumbrate, consciously or not, the scene before the portrait at Pemberley;[10] meanwhile, another ramification of this theme may be noted: whilst (to complete two already-quoted notations, she tells him on p. 191 his character was unfolded 'in the **recital**' she had had from Wickham, on p. 94 he asks her not to sketch his character since he fears that ' "the **performance** would reflect no credit on either" '. In a psychoanalytic light, such notations from the performing arts will naturally interest us. Further demonstration of textual density in this context—characteristic examples in two other areas of the same preoccupation, furnishing a transition to section 3—may be sent to a note, where literal/metaphorical possibilities associated with acts of reading are illustrated.[11]

Before we go further, to touch on the question predicted in Chapter I as likely to be a regular bother, about the consciousness of Jane Austen's processes (enough occupied our attention in Chapter II to keep it at bay, but it may be resurfacing in readers' minds): it will be desirable and should be possible to keep questions of consciousness distinct from questions of intention. Clusters of the kind so far illustrated constitute evidence for the attribution ('merely') of an intention.

Two further general considerations: regarding metaphors associated with books/reading etc., a whole set of notations (a small selection only has been quoted), that could be called 'dead' metaphors in the novel as we have it, may be 'revived' when it is recalled that an *Ur-Pride and Prejudice* is thought to have existed under the title 'First Impressions'. The other consideration will have more far-reaching repercussions.

- 3 -

On the evening of the day Elizabeth comes to Netherfield (to care for her sister), having picked up a book, she is the witness of a conversation about Pemberley; after a few paragraphs, we are told she 'was so much caught by

---

10 Where *tiercerons* may be seen: e.g. Elizabeth tells Darcy ' "Implacable resentment *is* a **shade** in a character" ' (58); at III.1.249 she thinks 'In what an amiable **light**' Mrs Reynolds' testimony places him.

11 1) Mr Bennet gets Elizabeth to read Mr Gardiner's letter aloud: ' "I hardly know myself what it is about" ' (302); Jane writes to Elizabeth 'I am afraid you will not be able to make it out, but I hardly know what I have written' (274); and Lydia's letters to Kitty 'were much too full of lines under the words to be made public' (238; there is an uncannily Freudian feeling to this: cf. for example 4.224/5 n.).

2) We are also invited to relate the key question of resemblance of an account to the truth (an ostinato theme in manifest content) to *visual* representation, and thus again to the Pemberley portrait-scene: Elizabeth is described as '**reading in her neighbours' looks**' (90) their amazement at her dancing with Darcy; to the reasons she gives Jane a few pp. before for believing Wickham's ' "**history** of himself" ', she adds ' "Besides, there was **truth** in his **looks**" ' (86); a few pp. after, she 'instantly **read** her [sister's] **feelings**', etc.

what passed, as to leave her very little attention for her book; and soon laying it wholly aside..' (I.8.38); three chapters later, Miss Bingley invites her to
take a turn about the room; she agrees to it; Darcy looks up, and we are told
'He was as much awake to the novelty of attention in that quarter as Elizabeth herself could be, and **unconsciously** closed his book..' (I.11.56).

One interesting question raised by this novel (to return to terms this chapter
began by tendering) will be how it is we can confidently say we *know*—from
early on, even at a first reading—that Elizabeth will marry Darcy at its close.

Various answers may be made, according to various levels in the question's
meaning. At one level we might say these characters get married because of
a Jane Austen wish; perhaps *Pride and Prejudice* exists expressly for them to
get married at the end of it: we shall return to that in a moment. A second
level, reached by subtracting from consciousness such utter determination of
characters by their author, resembles Borges' language-game (Chapter I, p.
39, n. 88) where we play at taking actors for real, free people like ourselves.

At a third level, to which only a psychoanalytically-based aesthetic can do
justice, we suppose fictional characters to be as much motivated by unconscious forces as we ourselves are—with the corollary that our own faculty for
understanding them may also be partly unconscious.

The brace of quotations from I.8 and I.11 heading this section intimates,
in one of the subtlest ways imaginable, that Elizabeth and Darcy are in unconscious unison advancing from very early on through their book: that they
are, as it were, in the same fate.[12]

It will thus be seen (with amusement, perhaps) that all the ado hitherto
made about more careful, or slower (re-)reading, is paradoxically in one sense
beside the point; and to pick up the 'other' consideration left suspended in
section 2, Jane Austen's showing such communication in operation has no
tendency to entail that she 'knew' she had done so.[13]

Without prejudice to the success or failure of ways readers may devise for
settling questions of consciousness in this novel—or elsewhere—we may now
relate it to what we saw in *Sense and Sensibility*. The text, of apparently
homogeneous surface, is again used in the most varied ways to represent
preoccupations of a mind; what we require in order to understand that mind

---

[12] As common purposes among insects are decided without words, Freud speculated that some form of
telepathy may have been 'the original, archaic method of communication between individuals' (2.86).

[13] More paradoxically still, it perhaps fuels the view that she did *not* know. Another example from material
recently examined: apart from (a) two uses of 'to unfold' in its literal meaning (Darcy's letter to Elizabeth,
Collins' to Mr Bennet); and (b) a cluster around p. 205 (Darcy's and Wickham's character) something
remarkable may be noted concerning the three other metaphorical recourses to the verb: after mentioning
Bingley's and Jane's common liking for certain card-games, Charlotte says ' "with respect to any other leading
characteristic, I do not imagine that much has been unfolded" ' (I.6.23), Sir William Lucas 'unfolded the matter'
(Charlotte's engagement, I.23.126), and at II.1.133 we learn Miss Bingley's 'wishes' (for her brother's
engagement to Miss Darcy) had been 'unfolded in her former letter'. In the matter of unfoldings, *P & P*
displays a sort of perfectly equitable distributism; the question this raises is whether such patterning
necessarily betokens conscious authorial tinkling of a little bell.

is there, but not invariably where we expect it to be—which is as much as to say we may attribute to it as a whole, if not disingenuousness or dishonesty, certainly a sort of guile..

The vagueness of the term 'a mind' must, given Chapter II's metapsychological complexities, be found inadequate. It will gain in precision if we now look closer at the character-configurations of this novel.

To start with Jane Bennet affords the beginnings of an answer to the question how it is we know Elizabeth will marry Darcy, for one reason why the heroine must marry Darcy is because the heroine's sister must marry Darcy's friend: all these characters are prisoners of tacit conventions; it is impossible under these conventions either to cheat the reader of at least one marriage at the end of the book, or to count on readers' 'belief' in marriage between characters making too late an appearance in it. A Jane Bennet disappointed of a Charles Bingley, at the close, would suit an odd and unacceptable sort of farce (of the sort we find, incidentally, in Jane Austen's *Juvenilia*, where she was trying out registers) rather than a comedy; and though we must eventually ask how far a psychoanalytic interpretation of these works suits with their categorisation as comedies, that shadow can wait.

Features already in place in the first-published work, remain (two heroines again, it seems, thus in a sense two plots: the possibility or otherwise of double-marriages hangs over this novel[14]); the first work's fictive composite is not repeated, though, and Jane is even more minor a character than Marianne. Jane is merely the heroine of Longbourn House; Elizabeth, that of *Pride and Prejudice*: these two heroineships are fictive entities even more worlds apart than that of the Dashwood sisters.[15] The importance of this modification may be highlighted if we place it in the context of Jane Austen's inquiry as presented in this study: it is once more by structural means that she communicates her proto-psychoanalytic vision.

To begin with, Elizabeth is not *Miss Bennet* : placing *not* the principal sister at the centre of the novel's interest (she is 'next to [sc. just *after*] Jane in birth and beauty' (I.15.71) makes the point with still greater economy than in the first, that it is what is *below* that is the level of greatest significance.

Next: Elinor's interest in Marianne's affairs was 'covered' by her elder sister rôle (good *mimetic alibi*, a structuralist might put it); Elizabeth, not being elder, is neither protector nor conscience: ' "I will have no reserves from *you*" '

---

14 E.g. ' "when there has been *one* intermarriage, she may have less trouble in achieving a second [Miss Bingley/Darcy]" ' (119); 'expectation of one wedding [Bingley's], made every body eager for another [Darcy/Elizabeth]' (360); a negative example: 'An union of a different tendency [Wickham/Lydia], and precluding the possibility of the other [Elizabeth's] was soon to be formed' (312), etc.

15 There is a playful allusion to the attention fallacy: on the single occasion narrative is 'lent' to Jane, it tells us nothing is going to be told: when Bingley returns Jane is 'anxious that no difference should be perceived in her at all, and was really persuaded that she talked as much as ever. But her mind was so busily engaged, that she did not always know when she was silent' (III.11.337/8).

says Jane (118); and there is indeed nothing important Elizabeth does not know about Jane and Bingley.

Finally, heroine's relation to sister's suitor is simpler than in the first book; this is obviously made up for by far greater complexity in relation to her own.

Complementary to streamlining effects in the female centre of the novel, is treatment of the suitors: Darcy[16] is more developed than Edward (not saying much, the latter's rôle being practically restricted to generating emotion in Elinor); more is made of hero/heroine compatibility than in the first novel, but again it is merely a question of degree.[17] The main modification of the second in this area is the presence in (only in) vol.I of passages[18] from which the heroine is physically excluded, in some of which (unlike what was said of *Sense and Sensibility*) we learn things the heroine is at least not represented as knowing—the most important being that Darcy is attracted to her.

The upshot of these modifications will emerge in what follows.

- **4** -

One characteristic first ploy to which a human psyche has recourse confronted with a idea incompatible with smooth running of its *internal* economy, is to pretend to itself that the idea is not really part of itself at all, but *external*. And most often, the idea is doubly misplaced: first in the act of projecting it on the outer world, and second in the spot it finds, out there.

The way this works in *Pride and Prejudice* is as follows: Elizabeth's drama (at least as far as it is represented in the present of the novel) begins when she hears Darcy, '**looking** at the eldest Miss Bennet', say the words, ' "the only handsome girl in the room" ' (I.3.11). Attracted by Darcy at first sight (this is what will be argued, *pace* the received account) Elizabeth is all the more offended therefore by seeing him look at *her* disparagingly, and by hearing him describe her as merely ' "..tolerable; but not handsome enough to tempt *me*.." ' (12).

Her amatory affairs are thus inseparably linked with her sister's. This allows the central 'error' of the book to acquire some plausibility: for when a reason has to be found for the Netherfield party's staying on in London, it is the degradation of *Bingley's* connecting himself with the shameful Longbourn family that, in the course of long talks between Elizabeth and Jane in vol.II about Bingley (also therefore inseparably about Darcy) is allowed to establish itself as an explanation.

However, since, as we shall see, it is able to do so only at the cost of contradicting the evidence, we must again ask whether it is a text that does not

---

[16] Bingley, absent for roughly two hundred and twenty pages from the space seen or heard by the narrative presence, need hardly concern us at all.

[17] Critic seeks disappointment: 'We're not allowed to know as much about [Darcy's] inner workings [as Elizabeth's]' (P.M.Spacks: *The Female Imagination*, Allen & Unwin 1976, p. 118). The question of the author's artistic investment in male characters is postponed till we find a hero whose fictive dimensions call for it.

[18] There are ten: pp. 15-17; pp. 23/4; p. 27; pp. 35-7; p. 40; p. 46; pp. 52/3; p. 58; pp. 59/60; & p. 94.

play fair with us, or a character: not only, at the end of a first reading of the novel, are Elizabeth's explanations seen to have been erroneous—for we then learn that it was supposing Jane indifferent that led Bingley to accept staying away—but, further, if that fact is kept in mind on a re-reading, the suppositions are seen to have been invalidated by contrary evidence available *at the time*.

The reader may be inclined to attribute all this to those passages from which Elizabeth is excluded (where we learn what Darcy later writes in his letter: 'want of connection could not be so great an evil to my friend as to me' II.12. 198). But this will not do, since it is from Elizabeth's point of view that we learn Bingley's 'feelings were not of a sort to be much distressed by the folly which he must have witnessed' (I.18.102).

Our clarity of recollection is it appears constantly *blurred*, by two specific, even peculiar, circumstances: (1) Bingley's reactions are invariably juxtaposed to Darcy's; (2) Jane's reactions are all seen from Elizabeth's viewpoint: hence by II.1 Bingley is being described as 'the slave of his designing friends' (133), in spite not only, a few pages before, of Elizabeth's representing him as 'a young man so totally independent of every one' (120), but also despite Jane herself, still earlier, affirming the categorical opposite of the p. 133 notation: ' "He is his own master" ' (117).

The key point, to spell it out now, is this: Jane's shameful family (which, Elizabeth supposes, contributes to dissuading Bingley) is the same entity as Elizabeth's shameful family (indeed the main factor in dissuading Darcy).

In other words, Elizabeth's involvement in Jane's affairs is a case of *projection*—of, it should be specified, a psychological, not metapsychological sort.

Now: whilst this becomes abundantly clear at the end of the novel,[19] one clue at least is laid far earlier, in the same textually dense ball-scene: Elizabeth tries to dissuade Collins from introducing himself to Darcy ('it must belong to Mr. Darcy, the superior in consequence, to begin the acquaintance' 97); Collins demurs, and we learn that it vexes Elizabeth 'to see him **expose himself** to such a man'.

Why, we may pertinently ask, should she care?

Because of 'foreground privilege', the question is not raised; instead, 'As Elizabeth had no longer **any interest of her own** to pursue, she turned her attention **almost** entirely on her sister and Mr. Bingley.'; the 'interest of her own' remains unexplained; when her mother voices the question we have just asked, Elizabeth's reply is a *non sequitur*:

'What advantage can it be to you to offend Mr. Darcy?—You will never recommend yourself to his friend by so doing.' (99)

---

19 ' "..why should you wish to persuade me that I feel more than I acknowledge?" ' asks Jane (III.12.343) when Elizabeth intimates disbelief in her affective serenity. An awkward question: Elizabeth can only reply ' "That is a question which I hardly know how to answer." ' She passes to a series of *general* remarks (another species of projection) and the chapter ends, significantly, on this tardy evidence of sororal tension.

Whilst Chapter II aimed at overall revision of the received account as to what *Sense and Sensibility* is about, its specific upshot—intimately bound up with that revision, as readers will have understood—was a reassessment of how Jane Austen's heroines are presented to us. In the present chapter, the most recent analyses have aimed further to strengthen conviction that the 'identification' theory drastically simplifies things: 'foreground privilege' turns out to be untrustworthy.

Pride and Prejudice constantly invites us to reinterpret earlier in the light of later scenes: techniques of the first novel are, in this area too, refined and extended: the modifying power of retrospection is, we have seen at the work's emblematic centre. Just one telling example in the second novel of the use of the pluperfect (cf. Chapter II, p. 61) may be quoted as a further contribution to the case the reader will by now see is being made for the text's guile, and all that implies. Wickham is introduced to the reader and to Elizabeth in Meryton High Street one morning in I.15. The next three pages are full of movement and impressions: awkward meeting with Darcy, visit to the Philipses, Collins' reactions on the walk home, etc. At the Philipses next day,

> ..the interval of waiting appeared very long. It was over at last however ... and when Mr. Wickham walked into the room, Elizabeth felt that she had neither been seeing him before, nor thinking of him since, with the smallest degree of unreasonable admiration. (I.16.76)

Yet in the period mentioned there had been no textual indication—save Elizabeth's brief report to Jane of 'what she had seen pass between the two gentlemen'—that the heroine had been thinking of Wickham.

Elizabeth's attraction to Wickham is no surprise; more surprising is her reply to Jane's question, late on, as to how long she has loved Darcy: ' "It has been coming on so gradually, that I hardly know when it began.." ' (III.17. 373). Such is her first reply; much critical ink has been spilt over her next sentence: ' "But I believe I must date it from my first seeing his beautiful grounds at Pemberley" '. This flatly contradicts the first, but the more serious truth of the first shortly finds support in another telling echo: she in turn asks Darcy how long he has loved her; he replies ' "I cannot fix on the hour, or the spot, or the look, or the words, which laid the foundation. It is too long ago. I was in the middle before I knew that I *had* begun" ' (380).

More evidence for retrospectively placing the critical moment for Elizabeth as early as I.3 (with important implications this has for defining the structure of her feelings) is found in what she replies to that—' "My beauty you had early withstood" '—and in the fact that, reading backwards from there, similar remarks give the measure of how deep the first impression (a look, and the words with it) had been. After the letter's second reading she analyses herself as having been 'Pleased with the preference of one, and offended by the neglect of the other, on the very beginning of our acquaintance.' (II.3. 208). Before that, she told Col. Fitzwilliam of when she first saw Darcy:

> '..at this ball, what do you think he did? He danced only four dances! I am sorry to pain you—but so it was. He danced only four dances, though gentlemen were scarce; and, to my certain knowledge, more than one young lady was sitting down in want of a partner.'   (II.8.175)

As in the shorter Wickham example, such notations show that the trust which on one level we are invited to enjoy is treacherous: we heard nothing at the time about her being offended by his neglect, etc.; so here we discover we had not been told everything; in other words, as in *Sense and Sensibility*, a long silence is not narratologically empty.

This will be brought out if we return now to the ball-scene. The paragraph following Darcy's slight begins 'The evening altogether passed off pleasantly to the whole family' (12): the pleasure of each female member of the Bennet family is detailed in a series of long sentences; of the heroine, the text restricts itself to four words: 'Elizabeth felt Jane's pleasure'. Chapter 3 concludes with Mrs Bennet telling her husband of the slight; Elizabeth is silent on the subject.

This silence lasts through chapter 4 (Elizabeth's talk with Jane) and almost all chapter 5, with the result that the heroine's first words about Darcy —the promise never to dance with him, and ' "I could easily forgive *his* pride, if he had not mortified *mine*" ' (20)—are forceful; her silence is the more remarkable given that though at the time the slight occurred she 'remained with no very cordial feelings towards him', she '..told the story however with great spirit among her friends; for she had a lively, playful disposition, which delighted in any thing ridiculous.'

Of this passage, we may first note that 'story' links this notation with more of the metaphors of representation mentioned earlier.[20]

Second, the incident is made to appear the subject of Elizabeth's 'great spirit': the essence of rendering a sting innocuous is *humour*, the *grandeur* of which, declares Freud, 'clearly lies in the triumph of narcissism, the victorious assertion of the ego's invulnerability' (14.428/9).

With this first allusion to the ego in the present chapter, readers who found favourable the interpretative yield from metapsychology in Chapter II may be ready to believe it will help us understand *Pride and Prejudice*. For given that narratological gap or division between Elizabeth's joke and Elizabeth's silence just referred to in the I.3 ball-scene, then if this study's overall

---

20 ' "Good Lord! Sir William, how can you tell such a story!" ' exclaims Lydia (126) when Lucas announces Charlotte's engagement; a neat irony at Elizabeth's expense is found when she tells Jane that Bingley ' "is unacquainted with several parts of the story" ' (96), etc.

contentions about the nature of the Jane Austen text be accepted, we must conclude the division to be in Elizabeth.

To continue: it becomes clear that Elizabeth removed the sting by quoting Darcy's very words: in her account to her husband Mrs Bennet exclaims ' "Not handsome enough to dance with!" ' (13); next day Charlotte picks up another key word: ' "Poor Eliza!—to be only just *tolerable*" ' (19). More interestingly still, these words have lodged themselves in the heroine's mental flesh. The paragraph opening with the first plunge into Darcy's thoughts, concludes with Elizabeth's thought: to her 'he was only the man who made himself agreeable no where, and who had not thought her handsome enough to dance with' (23).

Furthermore—and decisively—Elizabeth's silence nothwithstanding, *the text* continues to chatter away about the slight: passages already quoted from the novel's last third to illustrate the ostinato of sore reminder would in themselves make it plausible to interpret as textual guile in the first third e.g. 'the mother was found to be **intolerable** and the younger sisters not **worth** speaking to' (21), and 'in Darcy's breast there was a **tolerable powerful** feeling towards her' (94). These notations link our sensitive word, respectively, to the shameful-family theme and the question of *worth*, and to another key word which will engage us later: *power*.

With the second of those notations (and the important positive transformation for Darcy which it contains) in mind, the importance of the two main characters meeting at a ball may next be touched on, for the symbolic significance of dancing—not invented by Jane Austen—is considerably exploited in her works from *Pride and Prejudice* on. If to the celebrated comparison with marriage in *Northanger Abbey* (' "in both, man has the advantage of choice, woman only the **power** of refusal" ':[21] an intimation of subsequent rôle-polarisation) we add the suggestiveness of partners moving rhythmically together before marriage,[22] then as a final example of what is going on in vol.I of *Pride and Prejudice* it will be germane to note the way the text plays with the word 'man'.

We should first recall that in the proposal scene Elizabeth taxes Darcy with not behaving ' "in a more **gentleman**-like manner" ', adding ' "You could not have made me the offer of your **hand** in any possible way that would have **tempted** me to accept it" ' (II.11.192). The reader will note that (a) the verb 'tempt' here is the one element missing in the near-verbatim quotations of the initial slight; (b) offer/acceptance-of-a-hand is revealingly ambiguous between dance and marriage; and (c) whilst Darcy's first appearance in the text is as 'another young **man**' (10), and that all allusions to him over the next sixteen pages (other than by his name or as 'Bingley's friend')

---

[21] *NA* I.10.77. N.B. Darcy has ' "great pleasure in the **power of choice**" ' (183).

[22] 'To be fond of dancing was a certain step towards falling in love' (9).

repeat that word, yet when at the Netherfield ball he 'with grave **propriety** requested to be allowed the honour of her hand' (I.7.26) Sir William says Elizabeth and Darcy should dance, ' "though this **gentleman** dislikes the amusement." '

One might almost say the text itself awaits Darcy's propriety: when we learn Elizabeth's 'resistance had not injured her with the **gentleman**' (27), the title sticks—even Mrs Bennet uses it: ' "that **gentleman** . . . seemed to think the country was nothing at all" ' (43)—till Elizabeth herself uses the old word, but with a new adjective which (like *powerful*, with *tolerable*) changes everything: 'She hardly knew how to suppose that she could be an object of admiration to so **great** a **man**.' (51).

- 6 -

From examining techniques deployed to portray Elizabeth Bennet, we can now move the interpretative process further: apply psychoanalytic criteria of meaning, seek the origins of conflicts represented in terms of the metapsychology outlined in Chapter II, and introduce further conceptual terminology.

Attention has been drawn to a gap between Elizabeth's silence and textual 'chatter': between (to adopt the simplest bi-partite descriptive psychology) Elizabeth's *public* and *private* self. The defence mechanism of *projection* explains her involvement in Jane's amatory affairs—a handy site (because of the 'coincidence' mentioned, the common shameful-family factor) into which the unacceptable idea can be thrust, and where an attitude to it can continue safely to be expressed.

Freud stresses this need for an idea somehow to find expression: ideas imbued with emotional charge mostly succumb to a 'normal' process—*wearing away*; on the other hand a *supervalent* train of thought shows its pathological character by '..the single peculiarity that no amount of conscious and voluntary effort of thought . . . is able to dissipate or remove it' (8.88).

Another way unavowable feelings may find expression is by *becoming their opposite*. Of this mechanism the concisest evocation comes (not an isolated case, and this fact will interest us) from the heroine of *Pride and Prejudice* herself: analysing—analysing *out*, one might say—any lack of deep feeling for Wickham on her part by candidly disclaiming its continuance in another form, she tells her aunt she has ' "never been very much in love" ' with Wickham: ' "had I really experienced that pure and elevating passion, I should at present detest his very name, and wish him all manner of evil" ' (II.3.150).

Reaction formation[23] (negative version) is a defence mechanism represented in this novel with casebook-worthy clarity: Elizabeth having accepted Darcy's invitation to dance, Charlotte suggests she may find him agreeable; her friend cries:' "Heaven forbid!—*That* would be the greatest misfortune of all!—

---

[23] Viz. 'an unacceptable impulse mastered by exaggeration of opposing tendency' (Charles Rycroft: *Critical Dictionary of Psychoanalysis*, Penguin 1972, p. 136).

To find a man agreeable whom one is determined to hate!—Do not wish me such an evil" ' (I.18.90).[24]

Moreover—and what proto-psychoanalytic acumen has sensed this?—the phenomena (projection and reaction formation) are related: Elizabeth's *own* negative emotions are extravagantly *projected* onto Darcy as she introduces him to the Gardiners: 'as she named their relationship to herself, she stole a sly look at him . . . and was not without the expectation of his decamping as fast as he could from such disgraceful companions' (III.1.255).

This relatedness finds its most grotesque form of exaggeration (and in revealing imagery) when Mrs Gardiner suggests Jane return to London with her: meeting Bingley is unlikely unless he comes to see her. Elizabeth cries:

> '..in such a part of London! My dear aunt, how could you think of it? Mr. Darcy may perhaps have *heard* of such a place as Gracechurch Street, but he would hardly think a month's ablution enough to cleanse him from its impurities, were he once to enter it..'
> (II.2.141)

We are driven to conclude that '*this excessively intense train of thought must owe its reinforcement to the unconscious*' (8.88/9: italics original). *Super*valence brings us to the most important of the concepts recourse to which will help us grasp Elizabeth's psychology: touched on in Chapter II, it is *ambivalence*.

The relation between love and hate started to assume critical importance for Freud from about 1915, under pressure from a combination of theoretical and empirical considerations the details of which have great intrinsic interest that would unfortunately take us too far from our present concern. Briefly, he came to see that the key question raised in 1915 ('how it is that love so frequently manifests itself as "ambivalent"—i.e. as accompanied by impulses of hate' 11.137) could only be answered by working out detailed histories of both emotions. Earlier he had wrestled with the strange fact that 'incipient love is often perceived as hatred' (9.118) and with the still more remarkable hint from Wilhelm Stekel[25] that 'hate and not love is the primary emotional relation' (10.144).

But the roots of the problem lie further back, in Freud's very point of departure as scientist and thinker: in a sense the whole of his work is an attempt to work out a psychology which would conform to the materialist medical 'philosophy' of Hermann Helmholtz (1821-94) in which the only forces one might legitimately posit had to be somehow reducible to the fundamental governing physical forces of attraction and repulsion.[26]

---

[24] One can only determine to hate someone whom it is a struggle to; *determining* to *hate* involves a category mistake, cf. *setting out* to meet him *accidentally*; more fabricated emotion is found when Elizabeth re-reads Jane's depressed letters 'as if **intending to exasperate herself** as much as possible against Mr. Darcy' (188).

[25] Already in the 'Project', though, we find the seminal hypothesis: a fellow human being is 'simultaneously [the subject's] first satisfying object and further his first hostile object' (*SE* I.331).

[26] This has been argued by e.g. Jones (1964), p. 63 f.

In 1913 Freud suggested: 'One possible assumption is that [ambivalence] is a fundamental phenomenon of our emotional life' (13.219): in other words, what are experienced as feelings (and the instincts which underpin them) are perhaps never simple and straightforward, but invariably come 'bound together in pairs' (9.117).

Suspicion of the implications behind these recent psychoanalytic excursi (more of Freud's unpleasing discoveries?—something fundamentally ambivalent in women's sexuality?) may make some readers dig their heels in unyieldingly here. As a last heuristic gesture in their direction, a rhetorical question: if the first impression Darcy makes on Elizabeth is entirely negative, why does she subsequently expend a sizeable proportion of her energies pursuing him through the novel?[27]

More interesting even than the sheer handiness of Jane's illness (did not Marianne's illness bring Willoughby to her—or at least to Elinor?) and of Charlotte's invitation (are Elizabeth's reasons for taking it up, at II.4.151, candid?) are further indications, in the detail of the pattern, that there is a contrary force running under the surface of events.

The real nature of an action can sometimes be divined by its effects: so at least we may judge from Darcy's reaction to Elizabeth's I.7 walk: he is 'divided between admiration of the brilliancy which exercise had given to her complexion, and doubt as to the occasion's justifying her coming so far alone..' When Miss Bingley invites her to walk, Elizabeth is 'surprised, but agreed to it **immediately**' (the result, we know, is Darcy **unconsciously** closing his book, 56). In I.18 she is '**suddenly** addressed' by Darcy, who

> ..took her so much by surprise in his application for her hand, that, **without knowing what she did**, she accepted him. He walked away again **immediately**, and she was left to fret over her own **want of presence of mind**. (90)

At Hunsford in II.12, yet again on a walk, the day after the proposal,

> ..on hearing herself called, though in a voice which proved it to be Mr. Darcy, **she moved again** towards the gate. He had by that time reached it also, and holding out a letter, which she **instinctively** took,.. (195)

Could the cumulative suggestion of these notations—*want of presence of mind*, *immediate* response, *not knowing* what is done—justify the hypothesis that Jane Austen associated the other two notations, and somehow 'knew' that what is done *unconsciously* is done *instinctively*?

---

[27] And some way through England: first she follows Jane to Netherfield where (as she knows) Darcy is; she then follows Charlotte to Kent where (as she knows) Darcy's aunt's house is; finally she follows the Gardiners into Derbyshire and as far as Pemberley House, Darcy's county and home (as she knows).

The reader should need no further illustration of the presence of strongly opposed forces in Elizabeth's attitude to Darcy; what remains is the possibility of identifying the *determining causes* of the state of affairs represented.

The general principle at stake is so well known that to state it explicitly in Chapter II appeared unnecessary: at its most straightforward, it involves Freud's progressive realisation 'that psychoanalysis could explain nothing belonging to the present without referring back to something past' (15.67).

We can now articulate that general principle a little: given (1) that 'the structure of the Oedipus complex [is] the central problem of psychoanalysis';[28] (2) that our first loves invariably fail, because such 'early blossoming is nipped by the frost' of impossibility; and (3) that therefore 'none. . . can avoid the fate of repression' (10.173/4)—then (4) there is no adult state of being in love 'which does not reproduce infantile prototypes' (*SE* XII.168); and specifically (5) that an adult's ambivalent attitude to a love-partner is likely to have its roots in, be traceable back to, some infantile ambivalence.

Even readers hostile to this study's exploration can hardly disaffirm that in the evocation of the Bennet family there is at least material open to some interpretation. However, whilst reference to difficult parent/child relations in Jane Austen is a commonplace of the critical literature, so is strenuous avoidance of any psychoanalytic implications they might have, no doubt motivated by lingering reluctance to lose a Jane Austen to whom tribute is paid as chronicler of the essentially *normal*, in the context of '18th century realism'. We gaze with complacency on divergences from 'the normal' in the physical near-monstrosities who people Hogarth's paintings, and shun the psychical oddities which it was one of Freud's lessons to insist were just as 'normal'.[29]

- 7 -

..do not the facts argue in favour of the. . .view that there are transitions and degrees in nervous disposition . . . no family escapes it altogether?[30]

So: what is the problem with the Bennet family?

---

[28] Ernst Kris: *The Origins of Psychoanalysis*, Imago London, 1954, p. 30.

[29] What is (as far as I know) the only study of the novelist in an official psychoanalytic journal begins by stating that Jane Austen is 'particularly attractive for' such a study 'because she is one of the most beloved and apparently "normal" of novelists'. The promise in 'apparently' is not developed, though, for we soon get 'all of her work is singularly lacking in passion'; the rest is just psychoanalytic Janeism (Clarissa Rinaker: 'A Psycho-analytical Note on Jane Austen', in *The Psychoanalytic Quarterly* vol.V (1936), pp. 108 & 111.)
  When Freud refers to 'normal mental events which are so well concealed' (1.338), this may be Gibbonian irony (sc., *they don't exist*..) Comparing communal and individual neurosis, in the latter 'we take as our starting point the contrast that distinguishes the patient from his environment, which is assumed to be "normal" ' (12.338). The difficulty in postulating neurosis of a whole civilization is that we have no norm to measure it by; as more of the psychical topography became unconscious in his thinking, 'controlling' ego more servant than master, so 'the normal' (the socially 'well-adjusted') came to seem rarer and rarer; eventually it devolved into a merely theoretical construct. But he foresaw the possibility of a 'pathology of cultural communities' (12.339).

[30] March 1896 issue of *La Revue Neurologique*, where the term psychoanalysis (in French) appears for the first time (reprinted *SE* III.144). It is commonly (sc. erroneously) thought that among early theories Freud ditched—he being charged with blithe high-handedness for this—was any notion of the aetiological rôle of here-

Our best guide (to the parents, first) is again Elizabeth herself: for sheer, cruel objectivity of analysis—by a daughter, be it noted—there is perhaps nothing in European literature before 1813[31] like the two long opening paragraphs of II.19. Let the reader turn them up and judge from their poised understatements, whether the conditions evoked do not plausibly correspond to Freud's description of 'powerful infantile [viz., *first*] impressions' of just the sort to engender an ambivalence: bad relations between a child's parents 'excite its emotional life and cause it to feel love and hatred to an intense degree while it is still at a very tender age' (12.53).

Whatever else Elizabeth closes her eyes to, she 'had never been blind', II.19 tells us, to the cracks in the Bennet family foundations: it is she who 'felt so strongly . . . the disadvantages which must attend the children of so unsuitable a marriage'; she who has perceived that her father (to start with him) '..had married a woman whose weak understanding and illiberal mind, had very early in their marriage put an end to all real affection for her'; she who has tried 'to banish from her thoughts that continual breach of conjugal obligation and decorum' which we witness from Bennet elsewhere in the book: exercises 'in **exposing** his wife to the contempt of her own children'.

All this, Elizabeth 'had always seen . . . with pain'. And she only 'endeavoured to forget' this because, as we also see, if Bennet is, like Palmer in the first novel, 'soured by finding . . . that through some unaccountable bias in favour of beauty, he was the husband of a very silly woman' (*S & S* II.20. 112), and can only function by shutting himself away with his books, emerging to spatter his family with sarcastic remarks, he yet makes a sort of exception for his daughter Elizabeth, and she is '**grateful** for his affectionate treatment of herself'.

Contrary to Lady Catherine's supposition,[32] Elizabeth is close to her father; the novel subtly underlines this: returning home from a first absence she is linked with Jane: 'their father . . . was really glad to see them' (their mother merely 'wondered at their coming' I.12.60); on her second the sentiment is particularised: 'The only pain was in leaving her father, who would certainly miss her' (II.4.151); and when she returns with Jane, 'more than once. . .did Mr. Bennet say voluntarily to Elizabeth, "I am glad you are come back, Lizzy." ' (II.16.222); unsurprisingly, in her final, permanent absence, he 'missed his second daughter exceedingly.'

Father/daughter ties are several times touched on in the same pointed but unobtrusive way: for example, implicit in much of her behaviour is his 'love of

---

dity in the neuroses: the upshot would be to deprive him of any part in foreseeing the present view, i.e. the growing evidence for hereditary factors in all disease; as usual, the truth is near enough to this vulgar falsehood for the latter to have passed for the former: a valuable summary of the progression in Freud's thought from *aetiological equations* to *complemental series* may be found in the ed. intro. to *SE* III.121 f.

[31] And not much like it, *after* that date, until the early years of the 20th century, in the scalpel-brandishing Edwardian sons, dismembering their scarce-cold Victorian fathers.

[32] ' "Oh! your father of course may spare you, if your mother can.–Daughters are never of so much consequence to a father" ' (II.14.211). Cf. ' "I am sure your mother can spare you very well" ' (*S & S* II.3.153).

independence' (III.8.308);[33] another link, love of absurdities (II.4.152) often seems, as his, essentially unshared (maybe indeed the more intense for being so, e.g. II.10 passim);[34] perhaps interestingly related to that, they share a taste for surprising people;[35] finally, if we agree with Freud that 'laughing at the same jokes is evidence of far-reaching psychical conformity' (6.203/4), then we shall find point in the specific character of their humour: namely the pleasure of seeing their disenchanted view of the world confirmed;[36] his tribute to her 'greatness of mind' (III.6.299; recalling Freud's 'grandeur . . . in the triumph of narcissism') is ushered in by characteristic irony: ' "I bear you no ill-will for being justified in your advice to me" ', inescapably suggesting what we already knew: Elizabeth is a better counsellor of her father than is Mrs Bennet.

Before we move on to the last-named character, it will be useful again to relate what has been said most recently to part of the inquiry in Chapter II.

The least question-beggingly evolutionary account of Jane Austen's work has to note the *fatherless* condition of the heroines (indeed, of all the young people) in *Sense and Sensibility*. Not only was this a schema she never repeated, but—without being too oppressively teleological at this stage—it may be observed that mothers, after *Pride and Prejudice*, yield presence to fathers; in *Emma* and *Persuasion*, indeed, the mother is dead.. But in the second-published novel, the presence of both parents is necessary because the relation between them is as important as the child's relation to them.[37]

Elizabeth's ambivalence may become clearer, then, if we recall Freud's theory about first emotional ties being identifications. *Pride and Prejudice* II.19, earlier discussed, begins thus: 'Had Elizabeth's opinion been all drawn from her own family, she could not have formed a very pleasing picture of conjugal felicity or domestic comfort.'

This sentence (containing the significant picture metaphor) sends us in two directions: it recalls the shameful-family theme of manifest content (the species of pride Elizabeth most lacks occasion to enjoy are just those Wickham imputes to Darcy: ' "Family pride, and *filial* pride" ' I.16.81); and it prepares the moment when she realises that 'no such happy marriage could now teach

---

[33] This receives an authorial fillip from the picture metaphor when she escapes a walk:

' "No, no; stay where you are.–You are charmingly group'd, and appear to uncommon advantage. The picturesque would be spoilt by admitting a fourth. Good bye."

She then ran gaily off, rejoicing as she rambled about..' (etc., I.10.53).

[34] In Collins' presence he keeps 'the most resolute composure of countenance, and except in an occasional glance at Elizabeth, requiring no partner in his pleasure' (I.14.68).

[35] E.g. I.2: 'The astonishment of the ladies was just what he wished', cf. 'the **power** of revealing what would so exceedingly astonish Jane' (II.15.217), etc.

[36] ' "For what do we live, but to make sport for our neighbours.." ' (III.15.364); cf. ' "..one's neighbours. . . Let them triumph over us at a distance" ' (III.6.293).

[37] A solution to an enigma evoked in Chapter II's Prelude? Was *S & S* perhaps finished or submitted first because a sort of urgency in Jane Austen's prescient analytic vision attached to the fundamental metapsychological division which, it was argued, dominates that work?

the admiring multitude what connubial felicity really was' (III.8. 312). So: two factors are present here: a wish to go one better than the mother; and, since it is a 'union of a different tendency' (the Lydia/Wickham marriage) with which her own imagined match is contrasted, also the wish to do better than the first sibling married.

Thus far, the *general conditions* for Elizabeth's ambivalence correspond well to Freud's description (put in rather stronger terms) from a 1919 essay, on the affections of a little girl that are fixed on her father, '..who has probably done all he could to win her love, and in this way has sown the seeds of an attitude of hatred and rivalry towards her mother' (10.172).

Since with regard to the daughter/mother relation this novel is no innovation on the first—what we inferred of Elinor is merely made quite explicit here: 'Elizabeth was the least dear to [Mrs Bennet] of all her children' (I.18. 103)—our first temptation may be to suppose that, in terms of Jane Austen's inquiry, what is being proposed might be called a sort of corrective by addition. Viz., *Why* is a heroine least dear to her mother? Obviously, it seems, *because* she is her father's favourite. However a reminder that this, though perhaps a necessary, may not be a sufficient, aetiological factor, is given by the presence in *Pride and Prejudice* of the other factor (relating to sibling rivalry with Lydia): jealousy of another child, on the grounds '..that her mother is fonder of it than of her . . . serves as a reason for her giving up her attachment to her mother' (7.338).

We shall not be able at present to take this any further without understanding the mother; but a superabundance of aetiological data—the phenomenon known as *overdetermination*—is (naturally) quite normal..

Mrs Bennet, now. Jane Austen may be usually associated with—liked indeed for portraying—the unpathologically normal; nevertheless even the least psychoanalytically-minded reader recognises Mrs Bennet to be patently, in some sense of an overused word, *neurotic*.

An interesting issue concerns what extension, in space or time, Freud's concepts possess. In the spatial dimension, could the American lady of 1909 be justified, for example, when she stoutly protested to Jones that Viennese dreams might be egocentric, but American ones were always altruistic?[38]

The temporal dimension extends in two directions: as an example of the way forward, the question arises whether dissemination of psychoanalytic ideas has now rendered e.g. hysteria extinct as a disease.[39]

As for backwards in time, since we are at present concerned with asking whether the word 'neurotic' may unproblematically be used of a character in a novel of 1813, two facts will engage us: the first is that when Charcot made a study of the symptoms of hysteria, he 'drew copiously upon the sur-

38 The story (Jones [1964], p. 348) clearly tickled Freud, who repeated it in 4.374 and 12.74.

39 Analysts in private practice are 'quite familiar with hysterical phenomena' (Rycroft, op. cit., p. 65).

viving reports of witch trials and of possession' in the European Middle Ages, and concluded 'that the manifestations of the neurosis were the same in those days as they are now' (*SE* III.20).[40]

The second fact is that the year *Pride and Prejudice* was published saw the conversion of what had been Louis XIII's arsenal into the Salpêtrière hospice where Charcot was a houseman in the year of Freud's birth (1856), eventually holding the chair in neuropathology when Freud studied there under him.

In his obituary of Charcot, Freud recalls that the professor had 'a great number' of patients at his disposal (*SE* III.12). Something of an understatement, this: we learn elsewhere that the hospice was a refuge for no less than *five thousand women*. As Freud laconically comments, from the extraordinary nature of conditions there, it followed that 'chronic nervous diseases were bound to figure in this clinical material with particular frequency' (*SE* I.7).

So: Mrs Bennet blaming her problems on her *nerves* (' "People who suffer as I do from nervous complaints can have no great inclination for talking" ' I.20. 113) might be seen to have a certain interesting *topicality*. The question is: how seriously can we apply any of the detailed nosological categories to Mrs Bennet's symptoms?

Some may naturally retort that she is *merely* 'a "nerve case", as the awkward phrase goes' (14.224), but has 'nothing wrong with her', and that her noisy complainings, like Mrs Palmer's physical pregnancy and mental emptiness, ironically highlight the heroine's fullness of emotion. On this view, Mrs Bennet is not 'really' ill, for the ill person 'gives up his interest in the things of the external world, in so far as they do not concern his suffering' (11.75).

If we diagnose thus, Freud lived in vain. Mrs Bennet's ailments are *real to her*, whereas (even) the typical doctor, as Freud lamented in 1909 (*SE* X.6) does not take the hysterical patient seriously. Mrs Bennet may well cry ' "Nobody can tell what I suffer! . . . nobody is on my side, nobody takes part with me, I am cruelly used, nobody feels for my poor nerves!" ' (113).

A key concept in Freud's work is the *need to be ill*: this arises from 'the patient's desire to convince herself and other people of the reality of her illness' (3.324). But whereas *need* to be ill is pathognomonic of hysteria, *fear of being* ill is pathognomonic of hypochondria; Mrs Bennet's own account of her symptoms—' "tremblings. . .flutterings, all over me. . . spasms in my side. . . pains in my head, and . . . beatings at heart" ' (III.5.288)—rather suggest hypochondria; then if we recall that certain hypochondriacal phobias are 'common enough in women who are not satisfied by their husbands' (*SE* III.78), this might return us to Mr Bennet.. were we not specifically told her nerves are

---

[40] From the datum that nuns during medieval epidemics became victims of hysterical deliria which 'took the form of violent blasphemies and unbridled erotic language', Freud boldly inferred that this was owing to no chance coincidence: indeed the connection 'was a more intimate one'–viz., 'the hysterical condition may perhaps be *produced* by the laborious suppression' (*SE* I.126); cf. 'the "discharge" is the more powerful, the higher was the preceding damming-up' (6.208).

his ' "..old friends. I have heard you mention them with consideration these twenty years at least" ' (I.1.5).

A final question: are Mrs Bennet's symptoms 'entirely *somatic* processes, [viz.] in the generating of which all the complicated *mental* mechanisms we have come to know are absent' (1.435, my italics)? Hypochondria is one of the so-called 'actual' neuroses, sc. having a purely physical aetiology in the present (not in an infantile conflict). Its symptoms, therefore, in a sense, have no *meaning*. Mrs Bennet may be regarded as a 'real' neurotic only if it can be proved hers have: can she be shown to think those around her are doing something to her deliberately (which might suggest paranoia); or can her ailments rather (11.257) be regarded as *self-reproaches*..?[41]

It seems we are like those, discouraged at one of Charcot's Tuesdays, when the great man 'allowed some of these cases, to use his own expression, to sink back "into the chaos of a still unrevealed nosography" ' (*SE* I.9).

Let us change tack, then: and to enable us to do so, two details may help us: first, let us take for example 'Frau X', in 1911—

> ..of a good middle-class family . . . married with three children. She suffers from her nerves, it is true, but has never needed any energetic treatment as she is sufficiently able to cope with life.   (5.238/9)

But how on earth, the reader may be asking, are Mrs Bennet's marriage projects for her daughters, and the relation suggested here between nervous illness and *class* considerations, to advance this discussion?

In a word, because the poles between which psychoanalytic concerns move are on the one hand requirements from within the individual (instinctual drives) and on the other, requirements imposed on the individual from without: a social construction. Class, in its rôle in present control of property, and marriage, in its monogamous form, concerned with preventing fornication, arrival of illegitimate children and uncertainties about future disposal of property, are the two supporting pillars of that construction. That Jane Austen was cognizant of all this we glimpsed in the first novel; exploring how it moves to the foreground of her attention in the second, will now engage us.

- 8 -

Perhaps the most fundamental question raised by Freud's thought[42] is whether 'discovering the unconscious' changes anything, in philosophy. Leonard Woolf went so far as to describe Freud's work as 'the second eating of the

---

[41] Neuroses occur only rarely in isolation; more often they are intermixed with each other: it is salutary to recall Freud's word of caution (1.438) to that effect, however far into our analytical cheek our critical tongue may be allowed to have strayed in these remarks.

[42] Not raised by Freud himself in his writings, though he was aware of having caused a revolution in sharpened vision, as witness a remark on a passage in Goethe which has, since psychoanalysis, become very arresting: 'In pre-analytic days it was possible to read this without finding occasion to pause..' etc. (14.324).

apple on the tree of knowledge';[43] without wishing to diminish the power of that remarkable phrase, one may say that it begs, or perhaps merely puts off answering, the question as to the substantive status of such knowledge, and its relation to consciousness.[44]

A certain curiosity about Jane Austen's text has led us to inquire into the consciousness of her characters, that of her own artistic process, and that of her readers. The exaggerated consciousness of the critical enterprise leads to such inquiries: the sort of reading in which we are engaged is as different from 'ordinary' reading as psychoanalysis is different from vague rumination on one's past. The process of becoming conscious perhaps itself constitutes therapy: we shed our Janeite illusions, which betoken a kind of innocence.

But: 'no one wants to get to know his unconscious'; do we wish to lose our unconsciousness, our innocence?

The possibility of psychoanalysis illuminating our reading of Jane Austen depends on supposing that, since her time at least, something in human nature has not fundamentally changed. Indeed, such a supposition is presumably extendable much further back in time, otherwise we should not find far older literature (*Isaiah, Oresteia, Gilgamesh...*) comprehensible, or even respond to it at all. And comprehension no doubt entails a greater degree of consciousness than response: when Freud wrote of 'the deepest and eternal nature of man, upon whose *evocation* in his hearers the poet is accustomed to rely' (4.346, my italics), 'evocation' is quite non-committal as to the degree of consciousness involved.

In that case, perhaps even a process as closely tied to the conscious as *recognition* appears to be—Freud quoted with approval Aristotle's view that 'joy in recognition' is 'the basis of the enjoyment of art' (6.170)—may operate without conscious participation.[45]

From Aristotle to Lydia Wickham may seem a long step; yet it is this dictum of the Stagirite's which will show us how we understand, long after responding to it, the scene where Lydia returns to Longbourn, and

> ..when at length they all sat down, looked eagerly round the room, took notice of some little alteration in it, and observed, with a laugh, that it was a great while since she had been there. (III.9.315)

A common objection to psychoanalysis is that it (too cavalierly) assigns meanings from a (too pocket-size) dictionary of symbols; but what might have at least the appearance of a good case is commonly spoiled by the defensive

---

[43] *Beginning Again: Autobiography of the Years 1911-18*, Hogarth 1964, p. 73.

[44] If we endorse the position aired in Chapter I (p. 8) that by affording a new unifying approach to areas of subject-matter not themselves new, psychoanalysis best described as a branch of philosophy, then we may recall the view that philosophy 'leaves everything as it is' (*P.I.* ¶ 124).

[45] Freud touches on the possibility that a 'state of intellectual bewilderment' may be 'a necessary condition when a work of art is to achieve its greatest effects' (14.254); if such a state could be seen to involve a lack of completely conscious understanding, the remark might be allowed retrospectively against the limitations in the view quoted in Chapter I. Naturally, Freud did not go out of his way to *court* intellectual bewilderment.

dash to the other extreme (of the why-do-things-*always*-have-to-stand-for-other-things? variety) where behaviour is *never* acknowledged to be metaphorical. Freud invariably sets his interpretations firmly in the context of everyday psychology, making sense out of the inherently associative character of the human mind: things do make us think of other things—and not just any old other things.[46] Readers who found the spare bedroom grate example (Chapter II, p. 80) far-fetched (but would the notation have the same effect if it were a matter of replacing, say, a washstand?) may encounter more difficulty with a similar notation in the second novel: Collins, being told Jane is not available, 'had only to change from Jane to Elizabeth—and it was soon done—done while Mrs. Bennet was stirring the fire..' (I.15.71).

Why is this so effective? Why is there a 'knowing' character to our chuckle? The fact that one does not necessarily explain to oneself why, suggests another possibility: perhaps one cannot; maybe certain symbols are irreducible to terms more elementary—or elemental, as fire[47] is elemental. And perhaps that is why dictionaries of symbols cannot help being pocket-size.

We may now return to Mrs Bennet's favourite, via her mother:

> 'When you have killed all your own birds, Mr. Bingley . . . I beg you will come here, and shoot as many as you please, on Mr. Bennet's manor. I am sure he will be vastly happy to oblige you, and will save all the best of the covies for you.'   (III.11.337)

Knowing what is really on Mrs Bennet's mind fills not only this invitation with erotic innuendo, but retrospectively Lydia's sexual pride in her 'dear Wickham' (III.9.318), with whom 'no one else was to be put into competition', and who did everything 'best in the world; and she was sure he would kill more birds on the first of September, than any body else in the country..'

Nothing as delicate as innuendo, however, colours the notation in the III.5 letter Lydia, living with Wickham, sends Kitty—a notation which clinches that it is 'some little alteration' in *herself* that is projected outwards onto the room, and whose anatomical crudity can still shock:

> 'I shall send for my clothes when I get to Longbourn; but I wish you would tell Sally to mend a great slit in my worked muslin gown..'   (292)

Readers may be, or fancy themselves, or wish they (still) were, more innocent than texts;[48] if so, the desentimentalizing approach, here vindicated in unexampled unreticence, may be distasteful. If not, our shock, it must be recog-

---

[46] 'Compulsion to associate' appears in the 'Project' (*SE* I.338; cf. 3.126 n. and 4.124).

[47] 'Kindling fire, and everything to do with it, is intimately interwoven with sexual symbolism' (1.196); the 'little alteration': cf. ' "[Isabella] will have her own room, of course; the room she always has; –and there is the nursery for the children,–just as usual, you know. Why should there be any change?" ' (*E* I.9.79); as for fire, what of Fanny Price's, in the East Room (*MP* III.1)?

[48] E.g. Duckworth (op. cit., p. 138), who says there is 'Popean, if not Freudian, skill' in this–and says no more.

nised, is hypocritical. Turning it instead against ourselves we might again take a leaf out of Elizabeth's book: hearing Lydia speak slightingly of Miss King ('the most remarkable charm' of whom, to Wickham, had been 'the sudden acquisition of ten thousand pounds', 149) she is

> ..shocked to think that, however incapable of such coarseness of *expression* herself, the coarseness of the *sentiment* was little other than her own breast had formerly harboured..   (II.16.220)

*

> ..everyone hides the truth in matters of sex.. (10.71); It would seem that the information received by our consciousness about our erotic life is especially liable to be incomplete, full of gaps, or falsified. (9.394); In matters of sexuality we are at present, every one of us, ill or well, nothing but hypocrites.   (*SE* III.266)

Such charges ring with growing harshness through Freud's early writings, blame usually being laid at the door of *civilization*: appearing as early as in letters to Fliess,[49] the specific theory of an 'inverse relationship between civilization and the free development of sexuality' is discussed in the 1905 *Three Essays* (7.168), and by 1908 an overall theory of the 'cultural requirement' is in place: 'Generally speaking, our civilization is *built up on* the suppression of instincts' (12.38, my italics). Effects of this state of affairs are also divisible into general and specific: generally, society has allowed itself to be misled into the greatest tightening of moral standards and 'has thus forced its members into a yet greater estrangement from their instinctual disposition. (12.71); specifically, 'society *pays* for obedience to its far-reaching regulations' (12.54, my italics), payment made in the form of 'the increase of . . . nervous illness . . . rapidly spreading in our present-day society' (12.34).

Concluding that the Bennet family ills (and we have not done with them yet) are symptoms of the discontents in civilization of which Freud wrote, resolves not only the question asked on behalf of lingering scepticism at the start of this chapter (could the contentions of Chapter II be 'applied' to another Jane Austen novel?) but also the more far-reaching question asked in the Introduction, and which this whole study aims to answer: under what circumstances is the 'application' to an oeuvre of an 'external' interpretative system appropriate?

Confirmation of psychoanalytic contentions was to be regarded as specially triumphant if such confirmation emerged from material that at first sight seemed least favourable to such 'application'. And that appeared to be the

---

[49] Freud might have appreciated (had it been pointed out to him) the irony of his juxtaposing, in a letter (31 May 1897, F/F 249) reflections on 'the source of morality' and the account of a dream in which, 'with very few clothes on', and mounting a staircase, he noticed a woman follow him up; this paralysed him ('the fulfilment of an exhibitionistic wish'); a catalyst for the dream had been that before he went to bed 'I had in fact gone up the stairs from our ground-floor apartment–*without a collar...*'

case, since it appeared so well established—this was *the initial assumption*—that there was 'no sex in Jane Austen'.

In this chapter, accumulation of further evidence to support Chapter II's contentions were entered upon with a view to avoiding what was thought of as a suspicious circularity in the circumstance that Jane Austen's work 'responds' to psychoanalytic interpretation.[50]

However, if it be now acknowledged that the initial assumption has been adequately contradicted by accumulated evidence, then the reader is at present in a position to see that the *a priori* there mentioned as being sought, has been found.

The whole enterprise embarked on in the present study, it now surprisingly transpires, *was to be expected*, for when allowance is made for obvious differences (country vs. urban, settled vs. cosmopolitan, English vs. Austrian, etc.) basic attitudes to marriage, property, sex, self-control, etc., are the common 'background' of the two oeuvres this book brings together. In other words, it is of 'Jane Austen's World' that Freud is the implacable analyst.

This conclusion will be seen to have far-reaching explanatory power over enigmas present since this book's opening pages: the reason Jane Austen is liked turns out to be *the same* as the reason Freud is disliked; if they have not appeared in company together, this is because they are simply never invited to the same parties.

The civilization that they share requires for its upkeep constant expenditure of energy; but Jane Austen readers (the *epitome* of the civilized[51]) have become so used to this outlay that great effort is now required in order to realise that fact. In Jane Austen's work we glimpse a world where civilization is quite effortless[52] (just think: a world in which you never need to blow

---

[50] Stepping for a moment as far back as possible from our concerns in this inquiry, it should be mentioned that some circularity perhaps cannot be avoided in any system of propositions. Without embarking on the question (Introduction, p. xxiii, n. 37) of how anyone finds what is not being looked for, the following rider is perhaps in order: the fact that Jane Austen and Sigmund Freud turn out to share certain preoccupations does not prove that what either of them says about human nature is *true*–or even that that is an adequate description of what they are doing–merely that they are cultural cousins.

[51] Freud imagines an experiment in which a church is treated as a place 'where no arrests might be made'; if we then wanted to catch a particular criminal, we 'could be quite sure of finding him in the sanctuary' (1.329).

[52] In occasional signs of consciousness that the whole set-up is oppressively *over*-civilized, the time between Jane Austen and Freud's may be collapsed:

'..[Elizabeth] opening the [Longbourn drawing-room] door, perceived her sister and Bingley standing together over the hearth, as if engaged in earnest conversation; and had this led to no suspicion, the faces of both as they hastily turned round, and moved away from each other, would have told it all.' (III.13.346)

'[Aunt Maud] found them standing together near the fire . . . Kate and he, no doubt, at the opening of the door, had fallen apart with a certain suddenness, so that she had turned her hard fine eyes from one to the other..' (*The Wings of the Dove* [1902], X.2, Penguin ed., p. 463).

That for James at least, this situation suggests a further intimacy, is clear from what precedes: '[Kate] was once more close to [Merton], close as she had been the day she came to him in Venice. . . He was to remain for several days under the deep impression of this inclusive passage, so luckily prolonged from moment to moment, but interrupted at its climax, as may be said, by the entrance of Aunt Maud, who found them standing together near the fire. . .[etc.]'

your nose[53]) and this gratifies one agency within us. But since it is implausible to explain the success of e.g. *Pride and Prejudice* (probably the most popular Eng. lit. classic) merely in terms of a boost to the reader's super-ego, an equally important factor in that success may be supposed to be the presence within the text of that subversive *bribe of pleasure* (to another agency: the id) which Freud thought so key a component in the mechanics of a successful joke.

So Jane Austen's text can be seen as itself a metapsychologically-structured object, corresponding to the reader's own metapsychological structure: this explains the 'uncanny feeling of reality' in her work; it may also make us wonder if, after all, our dreams *are* essentially private.

Naturally, to say the unreticence in Lydia's letter belongs to the text's latent content, also holds only in an analogical sense: it is latent only if, and in the sense that, it is not consciously noticed. Lydia's letter is as much part of the text as Darcy's; so if it goes unnoticed, the reason for that, too, is now clear: it is not because of some typographical contrast which would hide it, but rather by virtue of what Freud, speaking of sexual life, says is the 'very great contrast it presents to the rest *of the personality*' (*SE* I.150, my italics).

In Chapter IV we shall see how very far Jane Austen took exploitation of this characteristic of her chosen genre: poetry has the grace to signal some of the designs it has on us (emphasising certain words by place in the metre, etc.); prose—a more recent and sophisticated medium—lumbers so good-naturedly along to the end of the line, turning there so regularly back, it seems treacheries would have nowhere to hide. But it is just this apparent surface evenness, seen from the distance at which most observation of her work has been carried out, that is suspect; secondary revision in dreams likewise produces 'a smooth façade that cannot fit its true content' (2.50).

In the received account what may be called a massive scotoma is thus the result of a negative wish: the manifest content has been taken for the meaning in order not to see the rest.

- 9 -

Freud's view at seventy was that resistances to psychoanalysis were a reaction to the 'assault upon the dignity of the human race' (15.269) of which he stood accused;[54] his theoretical positions in the years up to the Great War

---

[53] Freud associates rise of civilization with decline of olfactory stimuli in human sexual response, giving way to the increased rôle of visual excitation (12.288 & 9.127). The possibilities for continuous effect in the latter fit in well with the disappearance of oestrus and the negative effect of menstrual smells. The compensatory importance of hearing and especially of looking, in Jane Austen's work, can hardly be exaggerated.

[54] History has been kind to Freud here, for the collective lesson of the 20th century's structural anthropology, linguistics etc. contributed to the plausibility of his particular thesis: our ancestors had things the wrong way up: 'primitive' forms—savages, languages, societies—do not reveal less complexity than ours. 'As regards the primitive peoples who exist today, careful researches have shown that their instinctual life is by no means to be envied for its freedom. It is subject to restrictions of a different kind but perhaps of greater severity than those attaching to modern civilized man' (12.306).

had been characterised as an 'assault upon the innocence of childhood';[55] and his demythologizing project with regard to women is also essentially an assault—this time on an *idea* entertained about one half of humanity.[56]

To the first of these three assaults we shall return at the end of this chapter; concerning the second, the reader may already be thinking about *Northanger Abbey* in terms of hints given in Chapter II that Jane Austen's proto-analytic vision extended to an understanding of infantile desire.

As for the third area, now: if Freud's demythologization is of the childlike state or appearance of innocence in which civilized men have had their reasons for wishing to see and keep women, Jane Austen's vision could be similarly described: just as her wool-jiggling at the end of *Pride and Prejudice* pokes fun at the naivety of our belief that fictional characters can be united without considerable help from their creator, so Lydia's letter makes a mockery of young women's innocence.

We may now place 'the Lydia Bennet Problem' within the context of Freud's early contentions on the civilization/instinct opposition. Without distinction of sex, '*the majority of people* who make up our society are constitutionally unfit to face the task of abstinence' (12.45, my italics): the task, that is, 'of **mastering** such a powerful impulse as that of the sexual instinct by any other means than satisfying it' (ibid.).[57]

At the same time the 'high psychical significance of this function *especially in the female sex*' (*SE* I.51, my italics) was never doubted. As (to return to a link aired in Chapter I, p. 17) we have no reason to suppose girls less inquisitive than boys, the result is that women labour in life under the harshness of 'an early prohibition against turning their thoughts to what would most have interested them—namely the problems of sexual life' (12.231).

A perhaps even more fundamental reason for this state of affairs will emerge in a moment; at any rate its key symptom is that 'education in the better classes of society . . . strives towards the refinement of feeling and of

---

[55] J.A.C.Brown: *Freud and the Post-Freudians*, Penguin 1961, p. 26. In view of attacks on Freud following the most recent rearguard attempt to re-sentimentalize children, it should be better known that far from abandoning another early theory—seduction of children—Freud in fact returned to it again and again, indicating complexities in the subject and refining it: in 1905 he points out that the mother's behaviour with her baby derives 'from her own sexual life: she strokes him, kisses him, rocks him' (7.145); active/passive rôles in adult/child relations play an important part in 'Little Hans' (1909), in 1917 we read 'parents themselves often exercise a determining influence on the awakening of a child's Oedipus attitude by themselves obeying the pull of sexual attraction' (1.376), in a later lecture 'Most analysts will have treated cases in which such events were real and could be unimpeachably established', adding that these often 'related to the later years of childhood and had been transposed into earlier times' (1.417); in 1932 (2.154) he discusses fantasies behind seduction by fathers or mothers and in his last work he declares of the mother 'By her care of the child's body she becomes its first seducer' (15.423). All this was perfectly compatible with his epoch-making find that 'sexual impulses operated normally in the youngest children without any need for outside stimulation' (PFL ed., 7.36).

[56] As Freud recalled, ten years after the Paris period: 'I had come fresh from the school of Charcot, and I regarded the linking of hysteria with the topic of sexuality as a sort of insult—just as the women patients themselves do' (3.342).

[57] Freud notes a causal relationship here, which perhaps we take for granted: it is not an accident, in other words, that 'There is no more personal claim than that for sexual freedom and at no point has civilization tried to exercise severer suppression than in the sphere of sexuality' (6.155/6).

sensibility' (*SE* I.54); and its result is that, in 'good' society at least, 'women are high-minded and *over*-refined' (12.44, my italics). In so far as they have to 'go through life concealing their sexual feelings' (*SE* III.265), then, women are *forced* to be dishonest.

Readers of a century after the programme Freud announced in 1898 (quoted at the head of the Preface: *SE* III.278) will judge for themselves whether the situation has fundamentally changed. At all events, with this allusion to dishonesty, hints made in foregoing pages about Elizabeth and Lydia may now be synthesised. For, while Lydia is a quite 'credible' minor character (as far as she goes: cf. Chapter II, p. 77), a plethora of notations about her, and about Elizabeth's attitude to her[58] suggest that what is going on, albeit less systematically than in the first novel's fictive composite, is an ironical evocation of Elizabeth's attitude to inadmissible parts of herself..

Suggestive ironies are in the area of vanity—naturally, for Elizabeth's fear for the ill-effects of her shameful family centres on Lydia, who ' "will never be easy till she has **exposed** herself" ' (230); Elizabeth's own behaviour in I.8 is described as ' "an **exhibition**" ' (36); is that 'admiring multitude' which she imagines (312) so different from Lydia's when, 'with the creative eye of fancy', she imagines 'herself the object of attention, to tens and to scores..' (232)? Planning to tell Jane of Darcy's proposal, Elizabeth foresees gratifying 'whatever of vanity she had not yet been able to reason away' (II.15); this receives ironic charge by juxtaposition:[59] at the start of II.16, the vanity of Lydia's purchasing a hat, meaning to ' "trim it with fresh" ' satin; it may be remembered that Mr Bennet's first words in the book to Elizabeth (about her next ball, I.2.6) are uttered while she is 'trimming a hat'.

The psychoanalytic upshot of all this for understanding Elizabeth will be clear if we recall her relationship with her father. Not only is Lydia preferred by her mother; not only does she skip past her elder sisters by virtue of her

[58] (a) Lexical overlap: Lydia has 'high animal spirits' (45), is 'untamed [and] wild' (315); she is accused (by Elizabeth) of ' "wild admiration" ' for Wickham (285); she is 'always unguarded and often uncivil' (126), 'ignorant . . . and vain' (213). Cf. Elizabeth, dancing with Wickham, her 'spirits were . . . high' (87), she is told not to ' "run on in the wild manner" ' they are used to at Longbourn (42); where Lydia characteristically 'ran into the room' 315, two pages later Elizabeth 'ran out of the room'; after her first run to Netherfield ' "she really looked almost wild" ' (35); later, conjectures about Darcy 'rapid and wild, hurried into her brain' (320); at 190 she is ' "uncivil" ' to Darcy, and we learn she had ' "courted . . . ignorance . . . vanity . . . has been my folly" ' (208) etc.

(b) Seepage is also handled by other means: the description of Lydia as having 'a sort of natural self-consequence' (45) could equally serve for Elizabeth, as is underlined when Miss Darcy's being 'exceedingly shy' (261) contrasts with Elizabeth's exceeding lack of it; whereas Lydia never listens (213, 223, 235 etc.), the metaphor of blindness characterises Elizabeth, whose ears are unusually sharp, etc.

(c) Ironic strands from her attitude to Lydia in areas seen: when she exclaims that Lydia ' "has no money, no connections, nothing that can tempt him.." ' (277) it is not just the word still resonating from the slight which tells us that her own plight is being described. Hints arise from the fact that although Wickham eventually marries Lydia, Elizabeth was his first choice: e.g. in a fine condescension towards her own past: ' "Every girl in, or near Meryton was out of her senses about him for the first two months" ' (285). Elizabeth is not only economical with the truth *about* her father (she tells her aunt he is ' "partial to Mr. Wickham" ' [144]–we know why [138]) but also *to* him: when he asks who has been ' "kept aloof by Lydia's folly" ' Elizabeth replies she has ' "no such inquiries to resent. It is not of peculiar, but of general evils, which I am now complaining" ' (231), etc.

[59] Propinquity in time suggesting connection in subject-matter, again (4.346, cf. Palmer's newspaper, Chapter II, p. 70). Perhaps both girls could be described (*S & S* 45) as 'setting their cap' at men.

status (' "Jane, I **take your place** now, and you must go **lower..**" ' III.9. 317), but Bennet bears responsibility for this situation: ' "It has been my own doing" ' he admits (III.6.299). In other words Lydia ' "fell" through her father's fault': this expression occurs in a case-history featuring a 'real' fall, which Freud interprets as a metaphorically telling expression of 'the wish to have a child by her father' (9.389) to be found in the female unconscious.

Keeping in mind that particular interpretations are from now on to be placed in the wider perspective of Jane Austen's work as a developing inquiry,[60] the moment has come to recall that the problem posed by the sex of the Bennet offspring in the second novel continues the preoccupation begun in the first:

> Mr. Bennet's property . . . unfortunately for his daughters, was entailed in default of heirs male, on a distant relation..   (I.7.28)
> When first Mr. Bennet had married, economy was held to be perfectly useless; for, of course, they were to have a son. This son was to join in cutting off the entail, as soon as he should be of age . . . Five daughters successively entered the world..   (III.8.308)

- 10 -

> The individual himself regards sexuality as one of his own ends; whereas from another point of view he is an appendage to his germ-plasm, at whose disposal he puts his energies in return for a bonus of pleasure. He is the mortal vehicle of a (possibly) immortal substance—like the inheritor of an entailed property.   (11.70/1)

One way of gauging the gap between 'Jane Austen's [over-civilized] World' and ours would be to ask how soon (already, perhaps) readers of *Pride and Prejudice* will require a note explaining the almighty fuss made about getting Lydia married as soon as possible.[61]

The reason is that 'Society believes that no greater threat to its civilization could arise than if the sexual instincts were to be liberated..' (1.48); and instincts being 'hard to educate' (11.278), the only answer must be: 'marriage, which civilized sexual morality thinks should be the sole heir to the sexual impulsions' (12.52).

And this is especially to be enforced for women: society does not tolerate 'any impulse of love *in her* which cannot lead to marriage' (12.49, my italics); the reason for the social requirements on the individual being the patriarchal

---

[60] Thus readers may be sent in two directions by these demonstrations: notations about Lydia's fall ('this false step' 297; ' "one false step involves her in endless ruin" ' 289; ' "such a step" ' 283/290; 'her sister's ruin' 295, etc.) recall *S & S*; those relating to Wickham (Mr Bennet defies Lucas ' "to produce a more valuable son-in-law" ' 330, and even refers with his wife to Wickham and Lydia as ' "your son and daughter" ' 310) look forward to *MP*, where ambiguities–in more than mere terminology–about conjugal and sibling ties, are exploited: 'Fanny was indeed the daughter that [Sir Thomas] wanted' (472), etc.

[61] ' "..they *must* marry! Yet he is *such* a man!"
"Yes, yes, they must marry. There is nothing else to be done." ' (III.7.304)

121

principle ' "*pater semper incertus est*", while the mother is "*certissima*" ' (7.223) —in other words 'Female chastity alone protects social relations from complete disorder'.[62]

From another point of view, that of biology in the quotation heading this section, the purposes of sexuality 'go beyond the individual' (11.121). Lady Catherine de *Bourgh*'s syntactical solecism—' "While in their cradles, we planned the union" ' (355)—shows the pretensions to verbal sophistication of a *boor*. It is also evidence that Jane Austen understood the pendant to Lydia must be found in Darcy's aristocratic aunt's views (III.14) on the *irrelevance* of the individual.[63]

But to return now to the entail: just as the crude realities of an individual's sex-drive are instanced by Lydia's letter, so in this 'entail' the text reaches equivalent unreticence: it stands for the patriarchal force *controlling* the individual. The entail governs the destinies of all the Bennet family; it constitutes the main dynamic of plot in *Pride and Prejudice*. That the vulgar word[64] for the object the Bennet girls lack is contained in the forensic term denominating the whole situation must, then, at the very least be considered a most remarkable coincidence.

Independent of the issue of author's consciousness,[65] the degree to which the present reader accepts the phallic resonance in 'entail' depends on that reader—female or male—endorsing certain psychoanalytic contentions: (a) the distinction between the sexes being one of the child's first[66] pressing problems, (b) discovering that girls have no penis is the most important event in the (female or male) child's young life (2.146); (c) 'there is no stronger uncon-

---

[62] Eduard von Hartmann, in *Philosophy of the Unconscious* (1868), quoted by Whyte, op. cit., p. 165. A point is specifically made of what came to be seen as a double standard in *MP*: 'That punishment, the public punishment of disgrace, should in a just measure attend *his* [Henry Crawford's] share of the offence, is, we know, not one of the barriers, which society gives to virtue. In this world, the penalty is less equal than could be wished..' (III.17.468); cf. Freud's summary of von Ehrenfels' view that 'consideration of the natural differences between the sexes makes it necessary to visit men's lapses with less severity'—this view being an eloquent indication, Freud comments, of society's application of 'a *double* morality' (12.34). As for adultery, 'the more strictly a woman has been brought up and the more sternly she has submitted to the demands of civilization, the more she is afraid of taking this way out' (12.47). Mrs Bennet is not afraid to admit, in front of her husband, that she still likes a red coat (I.7.29); interestingly enough, the possibility is mentioned that *he* might have indulged, but was 'not of a disposition to seek comfort . . . in any of those pleasures which too often console the unfortunate' (II.19 again: 236).

[63] If we remember Elizabeth's admiration for the balance of nature and 'taste' at Pemberley, surely the terms of her contempt at Hunsford are not accidental: ' "..is this all? I expected at least that the **pigs** were got into the garden, and here is nothing but Lady Catherine and her daughter!" ' (II.5.158). A final irony, given the antipodean distance between Lydia and Lady Catherine, is that the part of Longbourn garden the latter selects (III.14) for her attempt to frighten off Elizabeth, is *the wilderness*..

[64] '..tail . . . one of the most familiar symbols and substitutive expressions for the male organ' (14.176).

[65] It is impossible to know with what degree of guile Jane Austen uses the expression *cut off* the entail, and therefore how disingenuous is her, or her text's, apparent ignorance of the word's etymology (*Entail*, 'estate limited to a person and heirs of his body' comes from *tailler*, French for 'to cut' [O.E.D.]). Unless a coarse private joke with one or more of her earliest readers is to be surmised (not impossible), broadly speaking one could say that the lesser the degree of unconsciousness in her intention, the greater the likelihood of that ignorance; otherwise, the (internal) censor would hardly have let it past.

[66] The first use to which scopophilia (pursuit of knowledge by *looking*, 7.112) finds itself put, is the question of the distinction between the sexes (7.336, n.2).

scious root for the sense of [a man's] superiority over women' than his possession of a penis (8.198 n.), conversely of a woman's sense of inferiority to men,
than her non-possession of one; and (d) the girl 'extends her judgment of
inferiority from her stunted penis to her whole self' (15.428; cf. the principle
[Chapter I, p. 17] of things sexual being a pattern for the rest).

Perhaps the nearest one can ever get to proof is explanatory power. Each of
the Bennet offspring has, and with increasing fervour, been hoped to be a
son. Mrs Bennet's complaint,[67] then, is a real one: why should the accident of
being female un-house her and her children, and instate a male?[68] The answer is that the male ideal of female chastity protects the male ideal of male
property. Whilst Mrs Bennet's grudge against another propertied male issues
on one occasion in her cry ' "I am sick of Mr. Bingley!" ' (I.2.7), Elizabeth goes
further, lumping together Derbyshire and Hertfordshire males in the exclamation ' "I am sick of them all!" ' (II.4.154). Ironically enough, Rieff, in a
magisterially succinct phrase, summarises Freud's principal lesson thus: 'We
are sick', he says, 'of our ideals'.[69]

Elizabeth's ambivalence, it can be argued, is a response to this sickness. On
the one hand, like all Jane Austen heroines she is self-possessed,[70] in word
and deed:[71] as an example of the latter, one might almost regard as emblematic the fact that (unlike Maria Lucas, after Lady Catherine's advice, II.214)
s*he* feels no need to repack her trunk.. In word proverbially self-possessed,
her most pointed question in all her bouts of verbal fencing with Darcy,[72] is
to ask him: ' "I wonder how long you *would* have gone on, if you had been left
to yourself. I wonder when you *would* have spoken, if I had not asked you!" '

---

[67] Her hypochondria (repressed vindication against entourage) expresses the reproach that none of her girls
is a boy (obviously, next best to being a man is: produce one); moreover in the chaos of pre-Mendelian
genetics a Mrs Bennet (n.b. indefinite article) might–hysterically, as it were–think it the fault of her υστερα/
uterus. Perhaps that is why she fights shy of understanding the entail–because she feels guilty herself? Similar
terms, interestingly enough, serve her almost Charlotte-inspired near-reproach of Jane for not helping
Bingley on–' "if I was her, I would not have put up with it" ' (II.17.228)–and of her husband about the entail–
' "I am sure if I had been you, I should have tried long ago to do something or other about it" ' (I.13.62).

[68] A self-commending male who has by 'fortunate chance . . . early and unexpected prosperity' (70). Mrs
Bennet's view about what he deserves are expressed in another chapter-enjambing (I.12/I.13) unreticence:
before he is mentioned, 'a private had been flogged'..

[69] Rieff, op. cit., p. 320.

[70] Lascelles, op. cit., p. 126. The term 'self-possession' is used only of Elizabeth *Elliot* (*P* I.1.6). The word
'mirror' appears only in *P* (and not Anne Elliot's but her father's..); before Fanny Price's ball we learn 'she did
not dislike her own looks' (*MP* 270). Why do Jane Austen heroines not need mirrors?

[71] Her walking we have noted: in I.7 'at a quick pace' she covers three miles of fields; in I.10 she 'ran gaily off'
in the garden; in I.11 she runs upstairs to Jane; in III.9 she runs away from Lydia, and in II.10 walks fast to
get rid of Wickham. Her physical vigour is thrice compared with other women's: the long walk to Oakham
Mount is ' "too much for Kitty" ' (III.17.375); 'Jane . . . not so light, nor so much in the habit of running as
Elizabeth, soon lagged behind' (III.7.301); and Mrs Gardiner (III.1) is 'fatigued by the exercise of the morning',
but Elizabeth shows no sign of it. Movingly, on her last walk in the book, she and Darcy 'wandered about, till
she was beyond her own knowledge' (III.17.372).

[72] One example from each vol.: ' "Did you not think, Mr. Darcy, that I expressed myself uncommonly well just
now . . .?" ' (I.6.24); ' "How very suddenly you all quitted Netherfield last November, Mr. Darcy!" ' (II.9.177);
' "Is your sister at Pemberley still?" ' (III.12.341).

(III.18.381); we too may wonder, for the novel leaves suspended the issue raised in I.6: how active a rôle a woman needs to play in 'helping a man on'.

> '..I meant to be uncommonly **clever** in taking so decided a dislike to him, without any reason. It is such a **spur** to one's genius, such an opening for wit to have a dislike of that kind.' (II.17.225/6)

In this self-analysis the resonance of 'spur' (and the fact that the adjective is used of Darcy, I.4) suggests that psychoanalytic implications of her verbal vigour have been overlooked: 'The motive force for the production of innocent jokes is not infrequently an ambitious urge to show one's cleverness..' (6. 194). This link with *showing* enables us to understand the other half of Elizabeth's ambivalence. Freud continues thus: '..to show one's cleverness, to display oneself—an instinct that may be equated with exhibitionism in the sexual field'; he further speaks of sensing the presence 'of numerous inhibited instincts whose suppression has retained a certain degree of instability'.

Exhibitionism is almost exclusively, like fetishism, a *male* perversion, associated, that is, with activity (its female counterpart being *voyeurism*). Passive (sc. female) exhibitionism is indeed practically a contradiction in terms (since the compulsion to exhibit is dependent on the castration complex[73]) any inclination to it being 'almost invariably buried under the imposing reactive function of sexual modesty' 6.142); 'allowable' against that, for women, is showing off of figure, clothes, etc.

Readers will now see the significance of the performing arts metaphors, and of the shameful family factor: parading themselves, they merely exhibit inferiority:[74] one series of notations, with more or less reticent overtones, relates to Elizabeth's 'low connections' (36);[75] another, complementary to that series, plays with the Bennet girls not being 'brought up high' (106)[76] and since the

---

[73] '..a means of constantly insisting upon the integrity of the subject's own (male) genitals. . . it reiterates his infantile satisfaction at the absence of a penis in those of women' (7.70).

[74] Elizabeth fears 'lest her mother should be exposing herself again' (45), Mary seizes 'an opportunity of exhibiting', though her 'powers were by no means fitted for such a display' (100), and it seems the whole family had 'made an agreement to expose themselves' (101).

[75] Darcy's 'sense of her inferiority', evinced even as he proposes (189); cf. Collins', as he does: ' "Your portion is unhappily so small" ' 108); we hear of the 'mediocrity of her fortune' (207) and the 'inferiority of her connections' (52, 192); Lady Catherine's imagery of disgrace when she calls Elizabeth a ' "woman of inferior birth" ' (355) is echoed when Mr Bennet says Darcy ' "never looks at any woman but to see a blemish" ' (363); Miss de Bourgh, by contrast, is 'dignity unblemished' (361), etc. Of Elizabeth's keyboard playing, we learn 'her performance was. . .by no means capital' (25); given the reinterpretation being argued for Jane Austen's figurations, and of the fact that her medium is language, the rarity of deliberate puns in her characters' dialogue calls for comment. Punning is typically a male form of humour (perhaps related to exhibitionism, since both involve uncovering something?) Miss Bingley's pun (Elizabeth's uncle ' "lives somewhere near Cheapside." "That is capital". . .they both laughed heartily' I 8.37) is in Freud's terms (e.g. 6.132) tendentious: she refers to something Elizabeth has not. Miss Jane Austen knew 'money is dirt' (*L* 361), so maybe this should be related to Lady Catherine's remark about pollution (357)–especially since she says *her own* ' "instrument is a capital one, probably superior to–" ' (164), and indeed to Elizabeth's, about ablutions (see above, p. 106).

[76] Charlotte is not surprised Darcy thinks ' **"highly** of himself" ' (20); Mrs Bennet makes a connection by exclaiming ' "So **high** . . . so very **great!"** ' (13); we constantly hear of '**high** rank' (e.g. 70); and the Bennet girls are not ' **"grand** enough for" ' the Bingleys (119), etc.

psychological and physiological resonances of greatness[77] are thus with characteristic deftness associated, the remarkable cumulative suggestion of this novel seems to be a kind of figuration of sexual difference itself.

- 11 -

..As a brother, a landlord, a master, she considered how many people's happiness were in his guardianship!—How much of pleasure or pain it was in his power to bestow!—How much of good or evil must be done by him! Every idea that had been brought forward by the housekeeper was favourable to his character, and as she stood before the canvas, on which he was represented, and fixed his eyes upon herself, she thought of his regard with a deeper sentiment of gratitude than it had ever raised before; she remembered its warmth, and softened its impropriety of expression.   (III.1.250/1)

This scene provides a nodal point for several preoccupations: it is the culmination of our metaphors of representation; it furnishes another play on the physical and moral meanings of a word ('regard'); and—fittingly for a novel centring on *ambivalence*—it contains a striking *ambiguity*: what is the subject of the verb 'fixed'? Is it he—in the portrait—who looks at her, or she who obliges the portrait to do so?[78]

On the one hand, in reply to many passages where Darcy does the looking, by outstaring him Elizabeth claims the right to look actively. This interpretation is buttressed by various notations: 'she felt, that to be **mistress** of Pemberley might be something! . . . "of this place . . . I might have been **mistress!**" ' (245/6); in the next chapter she wonders whether to 'employ the **power**, which her fancy told her she still possessed, of bringing on the renewal of his addresses' (266), and the word (its appearances elsewhere are invariably revealing) has been prepared by Charlotte's view (what testimony, we might ask, is more valuable than that of an intimate friend?) that Elizabeth's dislike of Darcy 'would vanish, if she could suppose him to be in her **power**' (181).

On the other hand we must reckon with notations, in the Pemberley chapter and elsewhere, suggestive of the opposite drive: if looking is active, the 'imposing *re*active function of modesty' seems at the second proposal scene to resurface: '*Had* Elizabeth been able to encounter his eye, she *might* have seen..' etc. (366, my italics). Then, we may say Elizabeth is proudly deter-

---

[77] Mrs Bennet links **high** and **great**; but Bingley's deference to Darcy owing to his being ' "such a **great tall** fellow" ' (50) takes us back to his first entrance as a 'fine, **tall** person' (10); this first impression seems indelible: even 'The gentlemen pronounced him to be a fine figure of a man' (ibid.) and it is the first thing the Gardiners remark on: they 'expressed their admiration of his figure' (252); cf. Kitty's ' "That **tall**, proud man" ' (334); and finally, amongst Mrs Bennet's eighteen exclamations on p. 378 are ' "how rich and how **great** you will be! . . . such a charming man!—so handsome! so **tall!**" '

[78] Penguin's 1969 Introduction (and not checked since, it seems) corrects Jane Austen, ironing out the ambiguity of 'and', by printing 'she'.

mined not to be bested; yet we also hear that at Lambton she is 'more than commonly anxious to please', and fears 'every power of pleasing would fail her' (260); Lydia's flight convinces her that 'Her power was sinking' (278) etc.

Given Elizabeth's magnificent cheek to social superiors—not only not punished, but rewarded (probably a key factor in the book's popular appeal)—when at Lambton she is herself 'quite amazed at her own discomposure', we may be too; before meeting Miss Darcy 'she dreaded lest the partiality of the brother should have said too much in her favour' (260); this self-doubt resurfaces several times: when Darcy returns to Longbourn, she is delighted at the thought 'that his affection and wishes must still be unshaken. But..' adds the text, '..she would not be secure' (334); even on the eve of the second proposal, she fears 'that perhaps, instead of [her father's] seeing too *little*, she might have fancied too *much*' (364)—and so on.

At Pemberley, she is 'overpowered by shame' (252): it will be worth examining what exactly this emotion involves.

For Freud, shame is 'a feminine characteristic *par excellence*', its purpose 'concealment of genital deficiency' (2.166).[79] Rycroft dubs it 'the Cinderella of the emotions':[80] opportunely for us, but the relation between Jane Austen's novels and centuries'-old stories was bound sooner or later to arise.[81] Elizabeth does not quite begin in rags, but the contrast with Darcy's riches is sensational enough to suggest the story of Cinderella, who might be grateful to escape constraints of an entail, as well as horrible sisters.[82] Since Darcy's 'regard', reversing the I.3 slight, excites her gratitude, it may be noted that the gratitude theme long pre-dates his self-abnegating service to Lydia, and that Charlotte's association of it with another theme we have explored (" "..so much of gratitude or vanity in almost every attachment" ' I.6.21) follows hard on Mary's famous distinction: ' "Pride relates more to our opinion of ourselves, vanity to what we would have others think of us" ' (I.5.20).

---

[79] Its difference from *guilt* is important: women know from archaic times they have done nothing wrong, and also have nothing (beyond constant mortification, that is) to fear, but by the same token no strong super-ego spur. Shame 'occurs if we fail to achieve an ideal behaviour we have set ourselves'; guilt 'if we transgress an injunction derived from outside ourselves but represented in the super-ego' (Rycroft, op. cit., p. 40).

[80] Cf. 'experiences which call into question our preconceptions of ourselves, and compel us to see ourselves through the eyes of others' (op. cit., ibid.).

[81] 'The need to interpret such productions has long been felt; some "secret meaning" has been suspected to lie behind them' (15.50/1); Bruno Bettelheim rose to this challenge; Cinderella's humility is 'the conviction of her superiority to mother and sisters' (*The Uses of Enchantment*, Peregrine 1978, p. 241).

[82] Between (A) Elizabeth's reactions to Darcy's proposal at II.11.189, (B) the account she gives straight after it (190), and (C) another movement after the second reading of the letter (212), there are telling differences, which it is worth taking some space to illustrate.

Schematically, (A) runs thus: 1. 'astonishment . . . beyond expression'; 2. 'could not be insensible to the compliment of such a man's affection'; 3. 'at first sorry for the pain he was to receive'; 4. 'roused to resentment by his . . . language . . . lost all compassion in anger'.

In (B), (A1) is skipped entirely; (A2) elaborately disclaimed (' "In such cases as these, it is, I believe, the established mode to express a sense of obligation for the sentiments avowed, however unequally they may be returned. It is natural that obligation should be felt, and if I could *feel* gratitude, I would now thank you. But I cannot.." ' etc.); (B3) is the same as (A3); (A4) evident through the sequence. But once Darcy leaves, (A) is returned to, and (A2) reinstated: '..it was gratifying to have inspired **unconsciously** so strong an affection'.

These elements are shaken to a third order (C) after the re reading: (A1) has worn off; (A 2, 3, 4) become (C 4, 3, 2), so we now conclude 'His attachment excited gratitude'.

In this four-part conceptual jig, pride seems to pair off with shame, guilt with vanity; might we not infer indeed that the *sociological* message of the Cinderella story conceals a profounder, indeed radical, *sexological* subversiveness? And might the need to continue to hear *that* story (women forging their mode of communication with men) contribute to the continuing sales of *Pride and Prejudice*?

How then shall we interpret the datum that those two appearances of 'mistress' in III.1 are outbalanced by a plethora of fifteen, in the chapter's twelve pages, of the word's masculine counterpart? On a first level inescapably an expression of the hero's power (line 3 in the passage quoted above); but in the context of the mode of reading Jane Austen's work which this study is arguing for, must not that plethora also be read as betokening a preoccupation in the heroine's mind?

Can we commit ourselves further? Well, half a dozen pages before the end of this chapter, we might allow ourselves a flourish: we could say Elizabeth remains mistress—of herself[83]—by conquering a master.

On the other hand, there is evidence that Elizabeth is quite as 'activated'— Freud will also shortly help us to grasp the paradox—by *passive* aims: from the relative closest to her comes another testimony: her father says she would not be happy with a husband ' "unless you looked up to him as a **superior**" ' (III.17). This seems also to be the tenor of what might be called two conclusions of the semantic journey travelled by the first word in the novel's title: Darcy, she tells her father, ' "has **no improper pride**" ' (ibid.); as for herself, 'she was humbled; but she was **proud of him**' (III.10.327).[84]

On that view, it is by *identification* with what a man (Darcy as 'master' of sexual power) has, that woman finds satisfaction. The I.3 ball-scene, with its supposition that a man interests a woman by being and showing himself interested in her, could then be regarded as a social figure for the biological datum that the male must be excited for intercourse (and thus impregnation, which is all that 'nature' is interested in) to take place; hence it is that, for women, 'to *be* loved is a stronger need. . .than to *love*' (2.166, my italics).

It should particularly interest us, then, (1) that *Elizabeth* concludes that the Lydia/Wickham elopement was 'brought on by the strength of her love, rather than by his' (III.9.318); (2) that *Elizabeth* at Hunsford *defends* Lydia's drive: ' "The last born has as good a right to the pleasures of youth, as the first" ' (II.6.165); and (3) that two otherwise gratuitous notations suggest the

---

[83] The expression is used of Mary Bennet (289) with uncanny appropriateness: she is a bookworm: a sublimator; Lydia by contrast 'extorts a real satisfaction' (10.120) from the world; both confront 'the same tasks of **mastering** their libido' (10.126; 'to master' in German is *Herr*werden). Mary also bears the text's last tilt at Elizabeth's slight: her siblings all married, Mary is 'no longer mortified by comparisons between her sisters' beauty and her own' (III.19.386).

[84] Cf. 'in the state of love. . .the subject seems to give up his own personality' (11.68); 'a person in love is humble' (11.93); 'love puts a check upon narcissism' (12.156); 'the state of being in love . . . involving a sacrifice of the self' (15.240): no sex-distinction here, it seems. On the other hand has Elizabeth's pride not itself changed, but the object of it (13.364); is she not proud of herself for not having, for seeing through, Wickham?

heroine's ambivalence towards the 'captivating softness' (180) and 'gentle . . . gallantry' (79) of Lydia's partner: the heroine's insistence on *Darcy* being a **gentle**man came up before; it is revealing, then, that she comes to find, 'in the very **gentle**ness which had first delighted her [in *Wickham*] an affectation and a sameness to disgust and weary' (233).[85]

If the reader has not been carried along in these demonstrations of Elizabeth's ambivalence, that may be because, as at the end of Chapter II, we again encounter here what Freud thought the greatest stumbling-block to understanding in psychoanalysis: reluctance to see *masculine / active* and *feminine / passive*[86] as characteristics not of people, but of drives; in other words refusal to acknowledge the implications of our inherent bisexuality.[87]

Freud said he had never 'come through a single psychoanalysis of a man or a woman without having to take into account a very considerable current of homosexuality' (8.95). So strong is outward polarization in this area that, sophisticated Western vanguard notwithstanding, his famous dictum—'When you meet a human being, the first distinction you make is "male or female?" ' (2.146)—has arguably lost none of its force. Hence the 'exercise' set (n. 6, p. 95): in the light of that dictum, readers may now consider whether, in a novel that contains so much psycho-sexual ambivalence, the notation ' "We dressed up Chamberlayne in woman's clothes" ' (II.16.221: a man, sartorially at least, emasculated—by Lydia and her girlfriends, what is more) can possibly be put down to gratuitous detail or 'local colour'.

- 12 -

In this final section we shall go further, and explore the most important general upshot of the line of thought followed so far.

But first, those reluctant to perceive implications section 11 might hold for the fact that this novel is most civilized *male* readers' favourite, may employ in their service the reassuring datum that Freud himself had difficulty accep-

---

[85] That the text suggests a complementary ambivalence in the novel's hero need no longer surprise us: at the first proposal Darcy accuses Elizabeth of lacking 'civility' (190); *her* retrospective view is on the contrary that ' "..you were **sick** of civility . . . You were **disgusted** with the women who were always speaking and looking, and thinking for *your* approbation alone. I roused, and interested you, because I was so unlike *them*" ' (380). This highly interesting analysis—which Darcy does not contradict—suggests that he is attracted to her not in spite of but because of the 'degradation' involved; and that Elizabeth appears to have been cognizant of this, retrospectively illuminates the Netherfield breakfast-room scene, I.7: having been 'springing over puddles', she arrives with ' "her ancles [sic] in dirt" ', ' "her petticoat, six inches deep in mud" ', 'dirty stockings and a face glowing with the warmth of exercise' (32 & 36). Perhaps then there is something in Miss Bingley's estimate of Elizabeth that she is ' "one of those young ladies who seek to recommend themselves to the other sex by undervaluing their own" ' (I.8.40); in view of her final assessment of Wickham, it is interesting that in *his* honour, by contrast, she 'dressed with more than usual care' for the Netherfield Ball (I.18.89).

[86] If this be thought an unwarranted extension of Bleuler's term ('opposing pairs of instincts are developed to an approximately equal extent, a state of affairs described by Bleuler's happily chosen term "ambivalence" ' 7.118), on at least three occasions (9.256, 9.362 and 11.128 n.) Freud uses the word to decribe a conflict, not between love and hate, but between activity and passivity.

[87] Despite 'obvious' facts: 'no individual is limited to the modes of reaction of a single sex but always finds some room for those of the opposite one, just as his body bears, alongside of the fully developed organs of one sex, atrophied and often useless rudiments of the other' (15.422).

ting bisexuality.[88] There are regular reminders in his work of the force of women's libido, sometimes expressed with wry amusement: e.g. 'It is clear that education is far from *under*estimating the task of suppressing a girl's sexuality till her marriage, for it makes use of the most drastic measures..' (12.49, my italics).

Strange, then, that women tend to 'yield' (in Freud's writings, that is: e.g. 8.123).[89] Should we weigh personal factors here: the unscientific and distorting circumstance that he was *gallant* (he once refers to 'the service of women and military service' 5.206[90])?

Before we run to the nearest exculpating conclusion—that ambivalence was the 'something-not-analysed' in Freud—it will be salutary, first, to heed the reminder that it was Freud who 'invented the tools that have enabled his biographers to explain his insights and limitations'.[91]

More specifically, we all come to psychoanalysis along different paths. For readers of such a study as this it may be most natural to draw *historical* factors (the vote, the dishwasher, the pill..) into arguments about sexual politics;[92] but Freud himself came to psychoanalysis from *biology*: indeed his perspective is often *palaeo*biological, as when he approves Ferenczi's speculation (e.g. 7.279) that female resentment of men might date as far back as the differentiation between the sexes.[93]

---

[88] In letters to Fliess we find frequent acknowledgement of his own: from anodyne general statement ('No one can replace for me the relationship with the friend which a special—possibly feminine—side demands', F/F 412) to unreticent particular (to their forthcoming meeting he will 'bring nothing but two open ears and one temporal lobe lubricated for reception', F/F 193; there is nothing comparable to that in his published works).
Cf. ' "I do *not* like to be the mother in transference—it always surprises and shocks me a little. I feel so very masculine." I asked him if others had what he called this mother-transference on him. He said ironically and I thought a little wistfully, "O, *very* many" ' (H.D.: *Tribute to Freud*, Carcanet, p. 146).
Jones glosses the first 'screen memory' analysed by Freud (*SE* III.316), in which a male cousin and he 'deflower' a girl, with the remark that 'Freud's sexual constitution was not exclusively masculine'; he elsewhere notes that Freud had the desire to be loved 'more strongly than is customary with men', and writes that he himself sensed 'some slightly feminine aspect in [Freud's] manner' (Jones [1964], pp. 40, 126 & 333); others have underlined a passivity *necessary* in a job which involves listening all day.

[89] We would not now, of lovers, say 'she granted him her favours' (2.75); imagining the prohibitions of civilized life lifted, he says: 'if, then, one may take any woman one pleases as a sexual object' (12.194); he tells dreams of adult males in which they 'throw a woman down, strip her and prepare for intercourse' (7.194), and although there are occasional allusions to 'the relative positions of the two people' (e.g. 7.198), he seems to suppose children invariably interpret sights and sounds of parental coition as acts of violence committed by the father on the mother. 'On' the mother in all senses—though might not the puzzle over the verb 'draufsetzen' (8.202) be elucidated by supposing 'Little Hans' witnessed a scene in which his mother was 'on top'?

[90] The word is still used for both; whether you regard this as attractive mode of foreplay or subtly belittling depends on considerations too fascinating to be dealt with briefly.

[91] H.Stuart Hughes: *Consciousness and Society*, Paladin 1974, p. 126.

[92] Freud himself makes sociological observations such as (since in his day a far larger number of sexual acts ended in pregnancy) that 'In many marriages the wife does in fact recoil from her husband's embraces' (7.199).

[93] Or further: males being bigger than females may derive from males' need to overpower females sexually. The Chapter II formula—always something sexual in the aggressive (p. 87)—might be reversed: 'The accomplishment of the aim of biology has been entrusted to the aggressiveness of men and has been made to some extent independent of women's consent' (2.166; pithily, 'a woman is not asked' F/F 101). Most human conceptions take place without what in Western society we should call full female consent. If men had waited for that, would you, dear reader, be here? At all events, 'The coupling of activity with masculinity and of passivity with femininity meets us . . . as a biological fact' (11.132); to extend the biological necessity mentioned above (p. 127), 'behaviour of the elementary sexual organisms is . . . a model for the conduct of sexual individuals during intercourse . . . the male sex-cell is actively mobile and searches out the female one, and the latter, the ovum, is immobile and waits passively' (2.148).

Male/female difference may be the first distinction men and women make; but in a psychoanalytic light it is a very *coarse* distinction, obscuring what at a deeper level of identity are different distributions.

Strictly speaking, Freud seems to tell us, there is no such thing as men and women; rather there are impulses, bundled together more or less contingently. In so far as they do get polarized, this is only partly owing to the character of the two somatic envelopes;[94] it is also partly owing to the more or less precarious settlements individuals make with themselves over their parents, who are—a familiar fact, perhaps too often taken for granted— invariably of different sexes.

> ..the chief **part** in the mental lives of all children who later become psychoneurotics is **played** by their parents. (4.362)

Readers who have responded to the implications of arguments presented in the present chapter for understanding other works by Jane Austen, may in this matter of ambivalence to parents or parental figures think forward to the theatre metaphor in *Mansfield Park*; those acquainted with the *Juvenilia* may recall the numerous death and abandonment jokes there, by the conversation that closes vol.I of *Pride and Prejudice*. Mrs Bennet imagines Charlotte 'resolving to turn herself and her daughters out of the house, as soon as Mr. Bennet were dead'; he replies with characteristic irony that she might ' "..hope for better things. Let us flatter ourselves that *I* may be the survivor" ' (I.22.130). The alternative set up here was adumbrated by the 'unhappy alternative' he lays before Elizabeth:

> 'From this day you must be a stranger to one of your parents.—Your mother will never see you again if you do *not* marry Mr. Collins, and I will never see you again if you *do*.' (I.20.112)[95]

It may be said that this is *a joke*, and that not to treat it so is tendentiously to solemnify a *comedy*, the genre-category in terms of which all Jane Austen's work is usually discussed. But if light has been thrown on this novel by uncovering the unhilarious nature of what is at stake in the drama of Elizabeth's ambivalence, we may return now to the shadow cast on p. 99, and reply that the categorisation 'comedy' puts the cart before the horse. With *Mansfield Park* we are going into a world where that categorisation is strained about as far as can well be; but it is already pretty strained in the second novel, by

---

94 'The way the subject situates himself vis-à-vis his biological sex is the variable outcome of a process of conflict' (*L & P* 243).

95 More interesting still are the terms of Mrs Bennet's fears: she constantly supposes Charlotte 'to be anticipating **the hour of possession**'; it is intolerable to think that she will be ' "..**mistress** of this house, that *I* should be forced to make way for *her*, and live to see her **take my place** in it!" '—which suggestively links Lydia's phrase (*take your place*, quoted above, p. 121) and an expression (*hour of possession*) usually bearing *male* sexual connotations, with the *mistress* notation discussed earlier. Readers may wish to think about what this implies for *Emma*, the first of Jane Austen's novels at the end of which it is the male who ostensibly enters the female space.

being required to contain an extraordinary set of responses to Lydia's elopement.[96]

The first Jane Austen works to come down to us are extended jokes,[97] and it is more than a coincidence that Freud's first published application of 'the analytic mode of thought' (15.96) to an aesthetic question, was his 'Joke-book', since on one occasion in that book he makes a tantalising surmise about the psychical state or condition prerequisite for joking: 'I suspect', he writes, 'that this is *in general* the condition that governs all aesthetic ideation..' (6.139).[98]

A famous formula—'If it was not for death and marriage I do not know how the average novelist would conclude'[99]—might suggest the nature of the distinction between, at the least, some tragic potential in what Elizabeth, like all the heroines, *has to go through* to get to Pemberley, and the 'comic' ending: the comparative perfunctoriness of marriage could be regarded as belonging to an entirely conventional change of register: like the jingle of a rhyming couplet at the close of a tragic scene.[100]

One conclusion appears inescapable: in so far as Jane Austen's work can be shown to have anticipated Freud's thought, it must in some sense share the tragic implications of that thought.

For Freud's is a tragic philosophy. He tells us we do not know what we want, because we want impossibly contradictory things; psychoanalysis is a tragic genre because it treats, not of marriage (marriage is a comic solution) but of desire (inherently tragic), and offers no solutions to human conflict.[101]

If we say there is indeed something *comical* about supposing that the contradictory drives we have uncovered could possibly all be accommodated at Pemberley, we are using the word in an older and darker sense—that of the *human comedy*, which psychoanalysis dissects.

From one point of view, it might be said that by allowing Elizabeth to become mistress of Pemberley Jane Austen goes some way towards fulfilling

---

[96] Her mother is utterly delighted, her father only just persuaded not to behave as Sir Thomas Bertram does with Maria, the neighbourhood would have preferred Lydia to have 'come upon the town' (309), and Collins' view is that ' "The death of your daughter would have been a blessing in comparison of this" ' (296). It may be objected that Collins' remark, too, is a joke; readers ready with that retort will have to explain why a still more exaggerated reaction in the face of a similar event in *MP* (Fanny's view that 'the greatest blessing to every one' in the family would be 'instant annihilation' 442) is to be treated differently; perhaps a gap between the two works, artificially widened by the traditional account, may already thus be partially bridged.

[97] In spite of the archaeological interest, to read the *Juvenilia* after one of the mature works is an unnerving experience: so much that is at least 'serious' in the latter is in the former *purely*, albeit often savagely, comic.

[98] My italics; characteristically, Freud at once closes the perspective: '..but I understand too little of aesthetics to try and enlarge upon this statement.'

[99] E.M.Forster: *Aspects of the Novel*, Pelican 1962, p. 102.

[100] This may also throw light on the question raised at the start of this chapter about the relation of latent to manifest contents. In one example Freud analyses, the core of the dream-thoughts is 'loosely connected with [the dream] by an antithesis' (4.414): the *tonal* distinction between tragic and comic might fulfil the conditions necessary for the dream being 'differently centred' from the dream-thoughts.

[101] None at least beyond Freud's famous definition of mental 'health': 'a sufficient amount of capacity for enjoyment and of efficiency' (1.510).

the aim Freud attributes to psychoanalysis: that of reconciling us to civilization (12.228). But from another (to conclude with a final pair of 'coincidental' allusions to the title of the work discussed in this chapter) when Freud makes excursi into anthropology, he is, says Rieff, on the contrary 'intent on *questioning* the **pride** of civilization';[102] Freud's own view was that psychoanalysis '*wounded* the **prejudices** of civilized humanity at some specially sensitive spots' (15.172, my italics). This second novel ends with Elizabeth mistress of Pemberley; in the first, it may be recalled, Elinor Dashwood girds her loins before the scissors-and-sheath scene with the stern resolution: ' "I *will* be mistress of myself" '.

To be mistress *of oneself..*

Since one upshot of this study should be to offer for thoroughgoing reassessment Jane Austen's place in relation to the 'classical' post-Cartesian surge in self-confident philosophical individualism which launched the Enlightenment—a movement into the coffin of which Freud may be said with his psychology to have bashed a sizeable nail—Elinor's resolution recalls Freud's own famous definition of his place in intellectual history, after Copernicus' and Darwin's displacement of man from the magisterial place he had occupied at the centre of the universe and of animate creation: although 'thus **humbled** in his external relations', he has nevertheless felt himself still 'supreme within his own mind' (*SE* XVII.141), but now the '*naive* self-love' of man's ego has had to submit to 'its third and most wounding blow', since it is forced to admit it has only 'scanty information of what is going on unconsciously in its mind' and is therefore 'not even **master in its own house**' (1.326).

Since this final expression, too—like the theatre-metaphor and the responses to Lydia's elopement, mentioned above (p. 131, n. 96)—will probably bring to the seasoned Jane Austen reader's mind the world of Sir Thomas Bertram, it leads us to the next-published work, *Mansfield Park*, where the novelist takes her inquiry further, and into other problems.

But before we follow her there, it is worth anticipating a little, and observing that the reappearance of the dispossession of women in a still later-published work (*Persuasion*) shows that the problem set in *Sense and Sensibility* seems not to have been discharged—and certainly not, in spite of all the laughter in *Pride and Prejudice*, laughed off.

---

[102] Rieff, op. cit., p. 198 (my italics).

FOREWORD

Interpretation of this novel is at the heart of Jane Austen Studies, bearing a symbolic status: as in works taken individually up to now, we have seen, details may be identified, from words to whole episodes, that the traditional account can make nothing of, so here an entire book—a sizeable element in her oeuvre—has been singularised, or marginalised, as her 'Problem'-novel.

The specific Problem this novel has posed for criticism is thus merely the aggregate of the common problems of the traditional account, writ large. And as the corrective model proposed in this study aims to make sense of a mass of details—to show, indeed, that they are part of the novelist's sense—so the justification for the whole interpretation may not unreasonably be assessed by the degree of success with which this chapter re-integrates this novel within the Austen oeuvre.

The real problem, it will here be contended, is that *Mansfield Park*, no less in its way than *Pride and Prejudice*, is a subversive work, and raises far-reaching questions about the fundamental nature of Jane Austen's writing.

The habit this inquiry early established—anticipating and replying to imagined objections—will be even more called for, and assume a formal character in this chapter: the reader will here find both a coming-together of strands from the foregoing, and the elaboration of interpretative principles retroactively applicable to the whole. The most important of these concern the limits of the critical, and the terms on which *the world* is brought into discussion of Jane Austen's art.

Philosophical questions; and in so far as critical theory is philosophically based we have indeed been applying the view that 'The philosopher's treatment of a question is like the treatment of an illness'[1]—though the most relevant part of Wittgenstein's thought to our concerns in this chapter is where he foresaw the possibility of dissolving (false) problems.[2]

Let us for the moment say that the critical task is to find coherence. On this view, criticism uncovers the internal logic of a writer's inquiry, trying to find a point from which the interrelations between its constituent parts become clear. And the need to find a way of talking about the whole Austen oeuvre—in particular to make this novel comprehensible in terms of the same

---

[1] (*P.I.* ¶ 255)—with the difference that in most psychoanalytically-inspired criticism the author is put on the couch; in this study it is a certain critical position that constitutes the suitable case for treatment.

[2] E.g., ibid., ¶ 133.

criteria as the others—these are, as it happens, the central efficient causes for the existence of this study.

If, as Jane Austen's near-exact contemporary G.W.F.Hegel thought, 'The truth is the whole', the only complete truth would be: everything—so the only complete criticism would be to quote the whole novel.. But partly because of its length (almost a quarter as long again as its predecessors) even what has escaped the attention of criticism cannot be dealt with all at once. *Mansfield Park* contains even more hitherto unquoted material than the two discussed in Chapters II and III. This material must at least first be quoted, and then, because 'new' material calls for new descriptions (which in turn set new problems), put into the context of what we have seen so far.

To give a preliminary idea of this, three examples. When Mary tells Fanny she regrets leaving Mansfield because ' "You have all so much more *heart* among you, than one finds in the world at large" ' (359), this is almost 'literally' true: instances of the word 'heart' increase over the three volumes (in vol.I there are 26 occurrences; in vol.II, 38; and in vol.III, 56—more than twice the figure for vol.I; instances of the word 'mind' increase at an even greater rate: in vol.I 17 occurrences, in vol.II, 23, and in vol.III, 51—three times the vol.I total).[3] This could be called a small example—though perhaps it will be agreed, a striking one—yet it can hardly be introduced and illustrated in less than a paragraph.

Other lexical dispositions would take far longer to illustrate appropriately: the key word 'absence', for instance, occurs ca. sixty times.

At the other end of the scale there is Tom imagining himself nailed to a card table (I.12.119): a single short phrase with extraordinary resonances seeming to cry out for comment, and which I have never seen quoted.

So much by way of preparing readers for increased demands to be made on their attention in the following pages. Freud opted in one of his books to exclude theory almost entirely, in favour of sheer 'accumulation of examples' which could only be explained on 'the assumption of *unconscious yet operative* mental processes' (5.336 n.). This chapter proceeds by alternating doses of theory and practice. An initial survey examines upshots of the foregoing and sketches the directions interpretation will take in succeeding sections, some of which merely accumulate examples (counting on operation of the principle *verbum sapiendi sat est*: a way of responding in kind to the novelist's own requirement of attention) and which may be regarded as affording various ways into this work's metaphorical economy, denser and more complex than in the previous novels. Frequent recourse to bold type will help readers to see cross-references between the work's various lexical fields.

---

[3] All such figures in this book are preceded by an implicit 'circa': they have been arrived at by one sort of process; wordcrunching Jane Austen (which would almost certainly reveal errors in the totals) is a different sort: not equivalent, and maybe—this is said at the risk of being charged with Luddism—even incongruent.

CHAPTER IV

Mansfield Park

' "..where is Fanny?—Is she gone to bed?" '   (I.7.71)
' "..where is Fanny?—Why do I not see my little Fanny?" '   (II.1.177)
' "where is Fanny?" became no uncommon question, even without her
being wanted for any one's convenience.'   (II.4.205)

' "..You have a very smiling scene before you."
"Do you mean literally or figuratively?.." '   (I.10.99)

'..though it told her no more than what she had long perceived, it was
a stab;—for it told of his own convictions and views. They were decided. He would marry Miss Crawford. It was a stab..'   (II.9.264)

- 1 -

After an initial period of fascination with the sheer expressive extravagance
of the unconscious, in the form of the symptom, by ca.1908 Freud's interest
was turning (e.g. 10.86 f.) from symptoms to the fantasy-structures whence
they proceed. Something similar in the present exposition may now be taken
for granted: discussions of the two first-published novels should have prepared some of the work of interpretation on the third.

For example, *Mansfield Park*'s configuration of characters (to be explored in
sections 2 to 5)—their number, rôle and energy troublingly disproportionate,
for the traditional account, to that of the heroine—will be less problematic in
the light of foregoing readings of character in terms of metapsychology.

Similarly, related to that, the centrality of figuration in Jane Austen's art
(sections 6 and 7). This is the single most important upshot of Chapters II
and III; moreover, it is in discussing *Mansfield Park* that the link between
the two parts of Chapter I—the impossibility of realism (as Janeism means
it) and the necessity of figuration, in language—should be vindicated.

More specifically, metaphors of representation examined in the foregoing
will have paved the way for understanding the theatricals: the episode, and
the metaphorical presence of the theatre throughout the novel (section 8).

The theatre is close to the nub of—almost the guarantor for—metapsychological interpretation of Jane Austen's work as a whole, underwriting this

study's contention about the essential kinship of her preoccupations with Freud's, for a number of reasons, some of which may be sketched here.[1]

While *pro*-jection concerns how self is (re)presented outside self, with the appearance in this novel among those energetic characters of other-than-ineffectual parental figures, together with high instances of conduct, authority and responsibility, we are also confronted here with the related phenomenon of *intro*-jection: how, from childhood (*passim*, but especially section 9), one comes to be 'peopled'.

In the century of psychoanalysis, the distinction between inner and outer drama came to seem arbitrary. Maybe that is why, of all literary media, theatre has become for us the most live metaphor for the psyche. On the one hand, many passages from Freud assume uncanny relevance for *Mansfield Park*: for example, he observes that patients do not express their fantasies 'in the form of symptoms, but as conscious realisations, and in that way . . . *stage* assaults, attacks, or acts of sexual aggression' (10.90); elsewhere he notes: 'identification' enables them 'to suffer on behalf of a whole crowd of people and to *act all the parts in a play single-handed* . .' (4.232); Anna O., it may be remembered, 'indulged in systematic day-dreaming, which she described as her *"private theatre"* ' (3.74); Freud called off a lecture on realising that he 'would have to present all sorts of intimate and sexual matters . . . quite unsuitable for *a mixed audience of people who were strangers* to me' (F/F 437); and in a bridge between theatre and First Loves highly suggestive for Jane Austen readers, the difficulty in transference is described as being that of persuading patients that they are 'not in love, but only obliged to *stage a revival of an old piece*' (15.328, my italics throughout this paragraph).

Conversely, notations in *Mansfield Park* have acquired a strikingly 'modern' feeling:[2] e.g. Tom's 'sense of the insignificance of all his parts together' (I.18).

The nub of the Problem is how its elements relate to each other in the novel, and to its central figure Fanny Price; to the uncharacteristic absence of irony thought to separate her (and her creator) from these characters, an absence of irony said in turn to bear strongly on her future husband's reaction to the theatricals and on his future profession ('the ordination theme', on which section 12 aims to shed fresh light); as the symptomatology of the Problem is so complex, it might be rash to overestimate the substantive results of foregoing chapters: partly because, as must be again underlined in approaching *Mansfield Park*, each of Jane Austen's works sets its own interpretative challenge, but also for another reason.

---

[1] The significance of the theatricals for this study is neatly symbolised in the fact that the sole occasion on which, in the collected works of one of the authors whose name figures on the cover of this book, we find a work by the other referred to, is when Freud evokes one of Kotzebue's plays, and an editorial note reminds the reader that another (*Lovers' Vows*) 'was *not* performed at *Mansfield Park*' (5.305 n.).

[2] An editorial comment in the key PFL volume, *On Metapsychology*, glimpses (11.342) the question whether it was not a 'historical accident' that psychoanalysis had its origin in study of hysteria, the prototypical 'malady through representation'. Depending what force we give 'accident', perhaps we have the germ here of an explanation (cf. Introduction, p. xxiii, n. 37) of how Freud found what he was not seeking.

This is arguably its author's only work which can sustain comparison with the highest achievements of the European Novel. A masterpiece, in fact: just the sort of thing no single interpretative approach can 'explain'. Something of its originality has been recognised—e.g. the sustained brilliance of the last third of vol.I and the proto-'naturalist' Portsmouth chapters in vol.III—nevertheless its chief claim on our attention (prime gauge of its symbolic relation to the whole oeuvre) seems to have been fundamentally misunderstood.

Powerful interests have been at work misreading this novel: interests arising from reluctance to accept the hard implications[3] of the light psycho-analysis shines on basic components of our humanity: the nature of childhood, of religious morality, the relation between those two, and most important the relation of all of that to sexuality: most important since (again the symbolic relation) *this* novel's heroine is doubtless the paradigm for the view that there is no sex in Jane Austen.

Readers acquainted with the history of psychoanalysis may at this point recognise something oddly familiar in the *Mansfield Park* Problem: in 1914 (15.118) we find Freud writing of human beings—

> ..weighed down by the burden of their sexual needs, . . . ready to accept anything if only the 'overcoming of sexuality' is offered them as a bait.

—foreseeing perhaps already the massive resistance to the emphasis psycho-analysis places on sexuality, and the relatively greater acceptance in our time of various mysticised, *de*-sexualized derivatives. It was obvious to Freud that the more the hard (and hard-won) truths of psychoanalysis were sacrificed, the more resistances would vanish. The key term emerges from the metaphor he then uses to explain the remarkable success with which e.g. Jung or Adler manage to 'court a favourable opinion': it is, he says, by their putting forward '.. *lofty* ideas.'

There is nothing lofty about the unconscious. Indeed, a key 'characteristic of unconscious thinking' is that there, 'in all probability no process that resembles "judging" occurs' (6.233); the form judgement takes in the unconscious is: repression.

It is therefore germane to note that Freud thought 'civilization *and higher education* have a large influence in the development of repression' (6.145 my italics) since in a strikingly similar development the received account of Jane Austen, anchored in the anglo-saxon university world, with its Johnson/Arnold/Leavis moralistic tone, has used criticism to promulgate *lofty* ideas about female education. Still more disastrous than the mirror-of-nature model for Jane Austen, is the one according to which her novels are boxes in which girls are taught lessons.

---

3 Russell wrote of J.M.Keynes: 'like most people, [he] will accept a view without accepting its consequences, which is what makes me call him soft' (quoted in Brian McGuinness, *Wittgenstein, A Life*, Penguin 1990, p. 138).

Doubts as to whether (1) specific lessons (2) and if so, which, (3) can be, or (4) ever actually are, drawn from these works—let alone whether Jane Austen herself (5a) consciously or (5b) unconsciously 'put' them there—were aired in Chapter I. These doubts must now be given a broader base, for seeing the originality of what Jane Austen was doing in this novel depends on grasping the nature of the illness of which the *Mansfield Park* Problem is a symptom.

Freud could be said to have restated the facts of life; misunderstanding the relation of literature to morals is the expression of reluctance to countenance the (different) facts of art; what we find in books resembles the contents of minds rather than of the world. If the reason for that is partly that books issue *from* minds, it is also because they are directed *to* minds: their effect then takes place in minds, not directly in action;[4] a critical tradition which supposes art has an effect in the world is in the end a not very distant cousin to the inappropriate action of the yokel who in the last scene of *Othello* leaps on stage to defend Desdemona from her assailant.

Freud, unconfident of the mere possibility of any such thing as girls learning lessons, and with no educational axe to grind, is sceptical about our capacity to change the world; to understand it would already be quite an achievement.[5]

In his seventieth year he is still lamenting that though a relation between the sexual activities of children and of 'perverts' had been recognised, it was invariably with moral indignation, and *without understanding*. He goes on to explain (not for the first time) that 'The most important of these perversions, homosexuality, scarcely deserves the name', defends his earlier description of children as 'polymorphously perverse' (not yet over, the trouble that term got him into) by declaring that for him 'no moral judgement was implied by the phrase', and concludes (15.222) with the unequivocal statement 'Psychoanalysis has no concern whatever with such judgements of value'.

For readers who found an echo to their own response in the observation that Lydia's 'slit' can *shock*, it is worth making clear that scientific detachment did not come automatically to Freud, himself often *shocked* by his own discoveries (a fact in itself guarantor that he did not, in the sense in which he is often accused, project his own 'lurid' sexual imaginings onto patients).

Indeed one occasionally gets a fugitive glimpse of the Victorian gentleman in him: Jones tells the story of a compound slip committed by Jung (notification of a meeting it would have suited Jung for Jones to miss, sent to a

---

[4] This study hopes to bring Jane Austen's work nearer to fictional worlds with which hers has been too absolutely contrasted: even to e.g. Emily Brontë's, in so far as that is a world 'shaped by kinetic rather than ethical forces'(Dorothy van Ghent, *The English Novel, Form and Function*, Harper & Row 1967, p. 210).

[5] As Elizabeth Bennet's lexical journeys constitute an achievement more like an analysis than like an education: from the time when she 'only wanted to know how far she wished' to the time when reflection comes 'to make her understand her own wishes' (*P & P* 266 & 278). Freud described the action of the Sophocles play from which he took his most famous formula, Oedipus' increasing (self-)understanding, as a 'process of revealing . . . that can be likened to the work of a psychoanalysis' (4.363).

wrong address, wrongly dated); when Freud learnt of this his reaction was 'A gentleman should not do such things..'—but even so 'moral' a remark was touched by humour, for the retort concludes:—'..even unconsciously.'[6]

'Gentleman' is often thought a specifically English concept, and *Mansfield Park*, we shall see, makes considerable play with birth and breeding; so to pursue the 'pathology of cultural communities', it will be instructive to quote an obituary notice of Freud, towards the end of which its author relates a conversation he had with its subject about nations' attitudes to one another:

> ..I remarked on the common Continental condemnation of English 'hypocrisy' and wondered if it had not some justification. Freud looked at me in surprise. 'But surely' he said, 'you cannot doubt that England is rightly held to be morally pre-eminent.'[7]

It appears not to have occurred to the writer that there may have been just a dash of irony in Freud's words.

Previous chapters have aimed to demonstrate that Jane Austen's ironies are psychological rather than moral, that her concern was with exploring problems of perception rather than with reaffirming readers in existing moral positions. So for us, one great interest of *Mansfield Park*, where the irony has been overlooked as in Freud's remark, will be that in this work questions of consciousness and questions of judgement are, so to speak, constantly jammed up against each other.

'The everlasting difficulty of Shakespeare criticism is that the critics are so much more moral than Shakespeare himself';[8] to say the same of Jane Austen critics would be an understatement. Another element of the Problem, then, may be illuminated by extending discussion about a text as a complex metapsychological object: if books survive by communicating to various psychical agencies in us, we can ask which parts of the mind are gratified by which parts of the text.[9]

Freud, we recall, regarded a collective mind as the basis of his whole position; the traditional account of Jane Austen might well be described as an

---

6 Jones (1955), p. 145.

7 A.G.Tansley: Obituary Notices of Fellows of the Royal Society, vol.3, p. 274.

8 Walter Raleigh (quoted in A.P.Rossiter: *Angel With Horns*, Longman 1970, p. 54). Moralistic attitudes to literature are obviously not an English monopoly; nevertheless a complex set of factors–survival of the didactic rôle of writing from a time when all writing was didactic; special situation of the church (decline of the confessional) and of church 'literature'; odd status of e.g. Bunyan in histories of prose fiction; the immense status of Johnson–'it is always a writer's duty to make the world better' (*Preface to Shakespeare*: G.Watson says Johnson 'took it for granted that everyone is more or less agreed about the difference between right and wrong' [*The Literary Critics*, Penguin 1962, p. 217]) etc.,–such combined factors seem to make it a peculiarity that something in the English, even while making this a subject for humour, likes to be told, as the preacher in *Cold Comfort Farm* roars at his congregation: 'Ye're all damned!' (Stella Gibbons, Longman 1932, chap. 8).

9 Freud's view that writers project disguised 'personal day-dreams' in their work needs nuancing–openings for psychoanalytic Janeism, were there any material to hand–but his view of the reader's side of things need not be quarrelled with: our engagement with a work, he says, 'proceeds from a liberation of tensions in our own minds. It may even be that not a little of this effect is due to the writer's enabling us thenceforward to enjoy our own day-dreams without self-reproach or shame' (14.141).

exercise in collective narcissism. He further speaks of the super-ego boost which the individual draws from works of art that 'picture the achievements of his particular culture and bring to his mind its ideals in an impressive manner' (12.193). On a simple level (where we need not long remain) the evocation of Pemberley is like a tour round a stately home, the pleasant self-congratulatory illusion boosted by our being acquainted with its owner. However, one of the instructive treacheries of film adaptations of Jane Austen's work (discussed in section 4) is that they invariably extend a minor feature to the whole. For 'the Pemberley effect' is not transferable within Jane Austen's oeuvre: in *Mansfield Park*, Sotherton contains 'more rooms than could be supposed to be of any other use than to contribute to the window-tax' (85) —that alone would be enough to show up its moral emptiness.

Our dream/novel parallel is to receive further extension in this chapter: one draw that dreams had for Freud was that they are a *field-day of ruses*: indeed 'the essential characteristic and most important part' of the dream-theory was 'the derivation of dream distortion from an internal conflict, a kind of inner dishonesty' (15.77). If text is to be regarded as an emblem of a mind (another key upshot from the foregoing) questions about text's guile cannot be kept separate from questions about the consciousness, 'innocence' and honesty of that mind.

Again, Fanny Price cannot be excluded from such inquiries. Edmund cries:

'Thank God! . . . it seems to have been the merciful appointment of Providence that the heart which knew no guile, should not suffer..' (455)

and *we* know, with Fanny, that there is something excessive in this.

A link between fascination with the unconscious and with dishonesty was to be expected in any forerunner of Freud: arguably, writers are in any case concerned with just those parts of ourselves we feel most uncomfortable with; since theatre is one of the most persuasive forms of what the Houyhnhnms call *the thing which is not*, so by virtue of the psychodrama, that 'release from internal conflict by means of play-acting' (*L & P* 61), the Mansfield theatricals—a field-day for various forms of dishonesty—may be seen as an emblem of the whole novel.

For, it will be contended, *Mansfield Park* is *about* dishonesty.

Any attempt to correct the picture of this novel as devoid of the usual Austen irony faces a difficulty: humour is a delicate matter. Notoriously, nothing is as unfunny as an explained joke: that subversive 'bribe of pleasure' has to catch us unawares.

Regrettably then, one is driven to a rhetorical 'surely': *surely*, with or without religious convictions of the sort this novel itself dramatises—that is, even with them—we must see textual guile in, for example, Mr Yates' fantasy

(121) of the 'long paragraph' by which, with the other actors at Ecclesford, he would be '**immortalized** . . . for at least a twelvemonth..'

To respond to that is to understand the nub of the novel's irony: our being invited to distance ourselves so far from the values represented by Edmund and Fanny, that we savour what they disapprove.[10]

And surely then, that long paragaraph in mind, we can savour the irony of the débâcle too, 300 pp. later, announced in another paragraph—a short one —the scandal-column tattle about 'matrimonial *fracas*', 'the beautiful Mrs. R whose name had not long been enrolled in the lists of hymen', who has 'quitted her husband's roof' with 'the well known and captivating Mr. C.' (440).

Not to respond to such invitations is to confuse meaning and matter. This may seem *cussedly* querulous about the received account, but some self-deception seems to have played a part in maintaining a view of Jane Austen's girls in terms of self-deception: an approach which takes no cognizance of sorts and degrees of knowledge and self-knowledge, present in her work.

Of self-knowledge, or indeed of consciousness: passages in the second novel told the reader things which the heroine is at least not represented as knowing, and obviously Elizabeth is 'wrong' about many things; ignorance about others is a backdrop throughout Jane Austen's work to not-knowing about oneself (for the reader, too: wondering whether to believe Darcy or Wickham is a context for wondering whether we should believe manifest or latent content). But as we also saw, it is plausible that, bursting in on the Netherfield breakfast-room spattered with mud, Elizabeth on one level very well 'knows what she is doing'—just as well as her friend Charlotte, whose eventual marital condition has the effect in retrospect of giving her views on marriage in I.6 the chilly status of accurate foreknowledge; similarly, if Mrs Gardiner's injunction to the heroine herself not to ' "let your fancy run away with you" ' (144) is used to fuel a lofty theory of a girl learning a lesson, it must be pointed out that when later 'her fancy told her she still possessed' power over Darcy's heart (266), the deceiving elf tells her right..

The example is chosen designedly: it is with the same faculty that Fanny Price conjures up Edmund Bertram's presence for a second evening running:

> As she walked slowly up stairs she thought of yesterday; it had been about the same hour that she had returned from the Parsonage, and found Edmund in the east room.—'Suppose I were to find him there again to-day!' said she to herself in a fond indulgence of fancy.
>
> 'Fanny,' said a voice at that moment near her. Starting and looking up

---

[10] Representation of sentiments independent of morals has been dated not much earlier in the European novel than Stendhal; that dating might have to be revised. Outside the novel, and earlier, a writer (perhaps for this reason always a difficult possession for the English, and an important presence in *MP*) Shakespeare is 'in one sense the least moral of writers' since 'morality (commonly so called) is made up of antipathies; and his talent consisted in sympathy with human nature in all its shapes' (William Hazlitt, quoted in Rossiter, op. cit., p. 62): Iago may shock us, but he *interests* Shakespeare: while Emilia is hurling abuse at her husband, 'Shakespeare' is standing quietly down at prompt corner, observing it all.

> she saw across the lobby she had just reached Edmund himself, standing
> at the head of a different staircase.'   (II.9.267)

This remarkable scene might be described in terms not of meta- but almost of *para*-psychology; and since three pages later it leaves Fanny with 'very precious sensations', and the lyrical expression 'Now, every thing was smiling', readers need only be reminded that this is itself the second encounter with Edmund on a staircase (cf. I.2.15) to see how very far *Mansfield Park* extends ironical questions the previous novel asks, about the fundamental mechanism of events.

In Fanny's case there is no irony of unawareness (so it cannot operate as it did against Elizabeth in being 'unacquainted with several parts of the story', *Pride and Prejudice* I.18.96); indeed maybe her bad press in the received account is partly owing to having no more to learn, for she is thus in the manifest content *contrasted* with the other characters. To deny this is to join their ranks: defective themselves in self-knowledge, they are constantly wounding Fanny—thoughtlessly, unconsciously.[11]

On that view, among highlights of the Portsmouth episode, we must place the uncompromising reference to Fanny's **'perfect consciousness'** (388).

However, one must be allowed to feel a little uncomfortable with the expression, to feel a number of reserves—here too, perfection should not have come quite so soon, perhaps?—and (as a general preparation for what is to come in the present chapter) even begin, now, to express a selection of these.

For a start, are we told what this perfect consciousness is *of* ? As with Elizabeth, there may be matters about Fanny of which we are told nothing, but which we can—and for a coherent picture of the novel must—infer from the latent content.

No problem of self-knowledge; very well, but what is her self-knowledge *of*? We learn in III.5 'Her secret was still her own'; yes but *what* secret is that?

---

[11] Prominent even in manifest content: the Bertram girls are 'entirely deficient in . . . self-knowledge' (19): Maria 'did not want to see or understand' (44) and of Julia we read 'the want of . . . that knowledge of her own heart' (91); from the understatement that Mrs Norris 'perhaps . . . might so little know herself..' (8) to the doubt of Dr Grant's 'knowledge of himself' (112), to Rushworth's opinions being unfixed, 'without seeming much aware of it himself' (200), to Mary, 'a mind led astray and bewildered, and without any suspicion of being so' (367), and the general assessment: ' "the most valuable knowledge we could any of us acquire—the knowledge of ourselves" ' (459), etc.

The error is also compounded: Sir Thomas, despite 'all his knowledge of human nature' is 'little aware of what was passing in his niece's mind' yet inclined to think ' "you do not quite know your own feelings" ' (316); this could stand for all the characters: Edmund's supposition that Mary ' "certainly understands *you* better than you are understood by the greater part of those who have known you so long" ' (198), and Henry who, though himself not 'in the habit of examining his own notions' (114) is 'not at all aware of [Fanny's] feelings' (225): 'vanity . . . inclined him . . . to think she did love him, though she might not know it herself' (326); Mrs Grant 'could by the easiest self-deceit persuade herself that she was doing the kindest thing by Fanny' (205), etc.

Finally, it leads to numerous unconscious woundings: Sir Thomas' ' "As to Edmund, we must learn to do without him.." ' (284) is emblematic; also to fantastic hypocrisy: e.g. Edmund, who has not 'suffered from being torn from' *his* 'earliest pleasures' (370) telling Fanny she is ' "of all human creatures the one, over whom habit had most power, and novelty least . . . you could tolerate nothing that you were not used to.." ' etc. (354). William is the only exception: on the way to Portsmouth, in spite of his admiration for Henry, 'knowing her wish on the subject, he would not distress her by the slightest allusion' (375).

Similarly, she 'knew her own meaning' (327); what meaning *is* it? The novel is packed full of people meaning something or other:[12] we may well react as poor Mr Rushworth does (186), and hardly know what to do with so much.

She is 'always more inclined to silence when feeling most strongly' (369): do we always know what is *in* her silence? The question may be asked, since sometimes—as when the text asks 'And Fanny, what was *she* . . . thinking?' etc. (48), then tells us—the book is sufficiently advanced here for us to know we are not being told all.

Irony may be pictured as the relation of something to a frame: the hen comes to expect her daily dinner from her friend the farmer, till the day he takes her away and wrings her neck: no joke, for her.[13] The question then becomes: where is the frame? The reason why the *Mansfield Park* irony has been overlooked might be that the frame is further out than has been thought.

And indeed, this chapter will show, the irony goes far deeper in this novel than anywhere else in Jane Austen's work.

In order to avoid seeing it, in order (to put a high court card on the table now) not to see subversion of a high civilized ideal, criticism has had to turn round and pretend to entertain *less* lofty ideals than Fanny, finding a convenient handle for this contortion in the theatricals and 'ordination theme'.

Critically an extreme and illogical ploy, psychologically this is highly revealing, for it displays the 'grain of truth' which even a psychosis contains, thus responding in kind to something in the work itself.

In other words if criticism has gone too far that is because the novel which is the cause of all the fuss, itself goes too far.

For *Mansfield Park* is a work of extremes—although all are logical developments within Jane Austen's inquiry. Certain elements of foregoing novels are extended further than others: for the moment, it will be enough to give the headings.

To begin with, then: in our inventory of structural modifications the second-published novel makes on the first, the chief significance of the heroine not being *Miss Bennet*, it was argued, is a *metapsychological* disposition. In the novel now before us the significance of what is 'below' is pursued still further: Fanny's patron makes clear from the start that ' "she is not a *Miss Bertram*" ' (10)—not *even*, that is: not even a younger sister. When Edmund asks her what is to prevent her being important to anyone, she replies ' "Every thing—

---

[12] Henry banters 'with a look of meaning' (88); Edmund tells Fanny that to return the necklace would have ' "the *air* of ingratitude, though I know it could never have the *meaning*" ' (263); Fanny 'knew her own meaning, but was no judge of her own manner' (327); she says she had no idea Henry's ' "behaviour to me before had any meaning" ' (353); Sir Thomas, 'sitting down again' when Fanny tells him she cannot marry Henry, says to her ' "I do not catch your meaning" ' (315) –and so on.

[13] Russell's witty parable on the problem of induction, in *The Problems of Philosophy*, Butterworth 1912, p. 98. Naturally, it may be that we too are in a joke: as C.S.Lewis puts it, 'for the symbolist it is we who are the allegory' (*The Allegory of Love*, Galaxy 1958, p. 45).

my **situation..**" ' (26); this last, we shall see, is a key word in the novel (Maria's ' "situation is a very delicate one" ' counts among Edmund's first objections to the theatricals, for example); and Fanny's situation is that of the extreme lowest limit, perhaps, that Jane Austen could place at the centre of a work: a poor, dependent cousin[14]—and a child..

One large structural irony of the book that begins with Sir Thomas' problem of how to preserve in his daughters' minds ' "the **consciousness of what they are**" ' (10), is that it ends with his own awareness that Fanny is 'indeed the daughter that he wanted' (472). If Elizabeth is the heroine of *Pride and Prejudice*, and Jane merely that of Longbourn, the novelist goes still further than in that work, for the heroine of *Mansfield Park,* from the heroine of Mansfield Park; indeed the latter (Maria) must be eliminated for the former (Fanny) to take her place.

Given influential billing of the novel genre as essential social history, this downwards-trend of the heroine might in the 20th century have led to a Marxian reading of *Mansfield Park*. But by virtue of asserting that humanity can be master in its own house—that the enemy (poverty, injustice, etc.) is without—Marxism is broadly an optimistic theory; psychoanalysis, though issuing from the same scientific positivism as Marx's, is by the same token pessimistic:[15] Freud tells us the hardest thing: that the enemy is within.

For the reader of *Mansfield Park*, this contains a wealth of meanings, among which we may place first Freud's Wordsworthian conviction: 'the child is psychologically father to the adult' (15.421); in one obvious sense, then, this novel represents an entirely logical development of Jane Austen's inquiry—since for Freud (e.g. 1.247) the unconscious *is* the infantile.

Given that a frightened child is near the centre of Freud' s work, too, further features of the *Mansfield Park* Problem are illuminated. For the novel's main preoccupation, it will be contended in this chapter—another (extreme) extension of a heroine having to go through something—is exploration of the structure, the meaning, the *economics* of Fanny's pain.

> The grandeur of the house astonished, but could not console her. The rooms were too large for her to move in with ease; whatever she touched she expected to injure, and she crept about in constant terror of something or other; often retreating towards her own chamber to cry..   (14/5)

Passages like this give Jane Austen historical priority over Charles Dickens' (more extended) exploitation of the most obvious difference between adults

---

[14] No one at Mansfield ever lets her forget this, not excluding Edmund: for example, by telling her Mary's ' "attentions to you have been—not more than you were justly entitled to—I am the **last** person to think that *could be..*" ' (263), he unthinkingly betrays the presence of that very thought in his mind.

[15] The best gauge of this regards the two thinkers' views of the probable fate of their own work: Marx seems to have believed the truth must prevail because it is the truth (Isaiah Berlin: *Karl Marx*, Gallimard 1962, p. 70); Freud almost thought the opposite. One factor in the 20th century's resistance to psychoanalysis was perhaps its temporal coincidence with Marxism; though in the sense that we desire long before we work, psychoanalysis may turn out to be regarded as the more radical philosophy.

and children—that is, the most obvious one to children themselves, and the one adults most willingly forget. Adults may escape childhood impotence and passions; 'none escapes the repressions to which they give rise' (15.419).[16] We shall be returning in what follows to the Aristotelian insight (Chapter III, p. 114) about art working by recognition—and not just in the domain of what Freud calls 'ego smallness' (F/F 168).

To understand the child in us is perhaps a sort of cure:[17] as we grow up, our ideas about how some people are 'bad' begins to diminish:

> This frightful evil is simply the initial, primitive, infantile part of mental life, which we can find in actual operation in children, but which, in part, we overlook in them on account of their small size. (1.247)

Aunt Norris being condemned—herself uncondemning Maria—is a shocking feature of this novel's ending; but in other senses Fanny does not 'grow up'.[18]

Another measure of this novel's extremes may be taken by seeing that all the characters are teetering on the edge of something: Henry, whose philosophy of love is an amusement for ' "days that I do not hunt" ' (229) almost becomes an honest man; Edmund almost yields to Mary—perhaps Fanny, almost, to Henry. And whether it be the wealth and inanity of Rushworth (' "..better employed, sitting comfortably here . . . doing nothing" ', 186), the idleness of Lady Bertram ('sunk back in one corner of the sofa, the picture of health, wealth, ease, and tranquillity', 126), the prodigality of Tom (who has ' "robbed Edmund for ten, twenty, thirty years, perhaps for life, of more than half the income which ought to be his" ', 23) or the gluttony of Dr Grant (who actually dies of overeating, like something out of the violent world of Jane Austen's own *Juvenilia*), it is through the exaggerating, magnifying lens derived from the vision of the child that these are seen.

The most obviously proto-Dickensian *moral* exaggeration in the book is thus given a context: Mrs Norris' almost preposterous degree of nastiness is coherent with an essentially childhood-derived extremism.

More generally, the way the cards seem so very decidedly *stacked against* certain of the novel's characters, also finds an explanation in remarks Freud

---

[16] One Freudian idea concerning the nature of the comic was that 'everything comic is based fundamentally on degradation to being a child'; in support of that hypothesis he adduced 'The fact that comic pleasure has its source in the "quantitative contrast" of a comparison between small and large, which after all also expresses *the essential relation between a child and an adult*' (6.292 n., my italics).

[17] 'Psychoanalysis has relieved me from the grip of my childhood' (Lomas, op. cit, p. 4).

[18] In one sense Fanny grows—physically (it is vital that she 'improve' in this way)—yet there is considerable metaphorical fallout from early insistence on her *literal* smallness on pp. 12, 13, 14 & 15: Edmund refers to her ' "constant little heart" ' (27); ' "Have you any reason, child, to think ill of Mr. Crawford's temper?" ' It may be natural for Sir Thomas (317) to address Fanny so, but since it is underlined (13) that Julia is only two years Fanny's senior, there is less reason for ' "Why, child, I have but this moment escaped from his horrible mother" ' (100); similarly Tom's word 'creepmouse' (145) is a reminder of when Fanny 'crept about'; given that we are specifically told Mary is 'rather small' (66), her thinking of Fanny as ' "dear little soul" ' and ' "as good a little creature" ' (231), ' "a sweet little wife" ' (292), 'giving her little heart a happy flutter' (277), ' "my dear little creature" ' (416) etc., is ironical. Cf. also ' "lowest and last" ' (221).

makes on the essentially childish moral simplism of pulp fiction, in which characters 'are sharply divided into good and bad, in defiance of the variety of human characters that are to be observed in real life' (14.138).

It is in this focus, finally, that the reprobatory tone and judgements at the close of the novel may be illuminated. And to prepare the way for that—most important, for examination of its terminology, and the relation of that terminology to Fanny Price (section 12)—a final extension of psychoanalytic understanding of the infantile may be mentioned here, since it is furnishes the key index of exaggeration.

If Freud was right that psychoanalysis 'deserves a place in the interest of every educated person' because of 'the profundity of its hypotheses and the comprehensiveness of its connections', one of its most far-reaching connections bears on this relation of archaic and infantile, and thus on the element of the *Mansfield Park* Problem we shall consider last: 'the ordination theme'.

In the absence of clear indications to the contrary, religion cannot reasonably be exempted from classification amongst essentially human activities;[19] for psychoanalysis, it is an essentially childish one.

Assertions about a Jane Austen novel must always be supported by its linguistic dispositions: *Mansfield Park* is a field-day of verbal extremes.

As a first set, we read of Admiral Crawford's 'mistress' (41) whom he had brought to live with him; of Henry being 'so well made, that one soon forgot he was plain' (44); of Edmund's 'gratification', when Mary takes his arm, 'of feeling such a connection for the first time' (94), of her seeing Henry and Maria rehearse ' "exactly at one of the times when they were trying *not* to embrace" ' (169); or such dialogues as II.7: ' "I cannot be satisfied without. . . making a small hole in Fanny Price's heart" . . . "I will not have you plunge her deep" ' (229, 231), etc., etc.

Such notations—of a 'frankness' unique to this novel—are one direction taken by its extremes in register: the newspaper tattle of III.15 (redolent of Joyce's Gerty MacDowell) is another, and the (proto-Zola) 'naturalist' passage at Portsmouth is famous, but these have perhaps obscured the constant teetering on a register seemingly antipodal to the modern novel: that of allegory. In another genre, a character named 'Rushworth' would inescapably suggest a person not worth a rush:[20] since Rushworth is twice

---

[19] For Werner Heisenberg, the most pressing problem to occupy human thought in the two thousand years after Plato was the inescapably awkward datum that 'The immediate connection with God happens within the human soul, not in the world' (*Physics and Philosophy*, Penguin 1990, p. 65). Cf. 'We have to remember that science is a human activity' (Anthony O'Hear: *What Philosophy Is*, Penguin 1988, p. 38); even time and space are of 'earthly lineage . . . concepts . . . free creations of the human intelligence' (Albert Einstein: *Relativity, a popular exposition*, Methuen 1960, p. 141); cf. also 'mathematics is after all an anthropological phenomenon' (Wittgenstein: *Remarks on the Foundations of Mathematics*, Macmillan 1956, V.26.) A.J.Ayer comments that the paradox lies 'in reconciling the view that mathematics is a human invention with its seeming to compel us to accept certain conclusions, which in many cases we have to labour to discover' (*Wittgenstein*, Penguin 1986, p. 64); the question may be asked: do the pronouncements of theology compel us in any comparable way?

[20] 'Not worth a rush(-candle)': a now obsolescent term for a person of feeble intelligence.

described as not 'a shining character' (190 & 201) what it comes down to is that this character may be seen as a sort of walking pun; and since punning is in the common or garden sense a rarity in Jane Austen, we must regard this ostentatious case as a signal that something more serious is going on.

(The p. 133 Foreword made clear that objections will by the nature of the Problem assume an extreme formal character: readers already feeling that in this case of Rushworth's name too much is being made of too little may be assured: the objection relating to it will receive a formal answer, in section 5).

For the moment the following example may be considered: Mary's comment to Henry in vol.II on Fanny, ' "Her eyes should be darker" ' (230), may at first sight be thought classable with Miss Bingley's bitchy ' "Her nose wants character" ' (*P & P* 271). But if we go forward to Edmund's vol.III judgement, Mary's mind is 'darkened, yet fancying itself light' (367), does that not slightly alter the force of the vol.II remark?—and that in turn affect our reading of a vol.I notation, where Mary's flirting with Tom includes the disingenuous ' "I do not know who or what you **mean**. I am quite **in the dark**.." ' (49)?

And further—without driving too hard an interpretative bargain at this stage—will not this in all conscience affect our reading of the very details in the terms by which the two girls are on a key early occasion contrasted—we are told of Mary's 'talents for the **light** and lively' (81)—and make us wonder who 'owns' the observation that Edmund is in 'an ecstacy [sic] of admiration' of Mary's qualities, including 'her **light** and graceful tread' (112), or whether there is not something more serious than appears, in the estimation that compared with the weight of his fellow Oxonians Mary is ' "only a fly in the comparison" ' (94)?

Perhaps, finally, it is unfair to ask Edmund, admiring Fanny's dress in his infatuated state, not to make his disobliging comparison with Mary's: it is after all, as he says himself, only ' "as well as I can judge **by this light**" ' (II.17.222).

This is not a one-off case. Together with the widespread phenomenon of the plethora of registers, it contributes to evidence for the thoroughgoing presence in *Mansfield Park* of 'serious' word-play. The nub of Jane Austen's art.

For complementary to the 'frank' register illustrated, is the (equally extreme) euphemistic delicacy of language used on the last page of the novel for what readers of this study will see to be a key teleological fact: Grant dies just after Edmund and his wife 'had been married long enough to begin to want an increase of income'—which very round-about expression means that Fanny has borne a child.

We can now waken the metaphor in an earlier allusion to birth and breeding, for the backdrop to that key fact is a *play* the text makes (a *flirt*, almost) with a word too coarse for Fanny, but present in a passage from the *Juvenilia* that readers of this study will find equally revealing: Lady Polly tells her husband Sir George Harcourt the daughter they have adopted is ' "our real

Child" ' whom Polly had abandoned, ' "dreading your just resentment at her not proving the Boy you wished" '; when Sir George declares his ignorance of her ever having been pregnant, she explains ' "You must remember Sir George, that when you sailed for America, you left me **breeding**.." ' (*MW* 38).

In *Mansfield Park*, Edmund is for Mary 'a **well bred** man' (56); on his return from America Sir Thomas walks from his study into the next room, where we are present at 'the metamorphosis of the impassioned Baron Wildenhaim into the **well-bred** and easy Mr. Yates' (182); Fanny finds 'every body **under-bred**' (395) at Portsmouth; something of the text's density will be seen if we note that not only the improvement theme—' "Ay—you have been **brought up to** it" ', Mary tells Fanny (57, a notation whose meaning is otherwise unclear)—but also the theatricals, belong to the same preoccupation: Edmund says he ' "would hardly walk from this room to the next to look at the raw efforts of those who have not been **bred to the trade**" ' (124); later we learn 'Miss Price had not been **brought up to the trade** of *coming out*' (267, italics original); Mrs Norris, in answer to Sir Thomas' concerns about 'cousins in love, & c.', replies that on the contrary to avoid mischief what must be done is to ' "**breed her up with** them" ' (7)—and so on.

Of the many ways in which Jane Austen's work, like Freud's, is about the instinct/civilization opposition, *Mansfield Park* further extends one aspect of the Bennet Family Problem: at the inn where the girls meet for lunch, Lydia starts to talk of Wickham, her elder sisters 'looked at each other, and the waiter was told he need not stay'; Lydia comments ' "Aye, that is just like your formality and discretion" ' (*P & P* 220): another case of her mother's influence, for no one opposes Mrs Bennet's staying in her room with her nerves when Lydia elopes, knowing 'she had not prudence enough to hold her tongue before the servants, at table'; Elizabeth later voices her concern that with the house in confusion there were not ' "a servant belonging to it, who did not know the whole story before the end of the day" ' (292).

At issue in all this, is what can or cannot be said or done in public or private (an important distinction: another of Edmund's objections to the theatre). The Miss Bertrams break out in vol.III because of their restraint in the two other volumes: in vol.I Julia has to 'restrain her impatient feet to [Mrs Rushworth's] slow pace . . . The politeness which she had been brought up to practise as a duty, made it impossible for her to escape' (91); in vol.II Maria has to 'bury the tumult of her feelings under the restraint of society' (193); when 'The maid-servant of Mrs. Rushworth, senior, threatened alarmingly' and 'had exposure in her power' (450/1), the débâcle comes.[21]

Again, most important, Fanny is not excluded from this preoccupation: the staircase-scene already partly quoted continues with their proceeding 'up

---

[21] Interestingly, though she knows ' "very little of the inferior ranks" ' in the navy (60), Mary imagines the servants' ordeal: the maids ' "starched up into seeming piety, but with heads **full** of something very different" ' (87). Edmund says she has given them ' "an amusing sketch, and human **nature** cannot say it was not so." '

stairs together' (since, we are then rather inconsequently told, their rooms are 'on the same floor above'), ending when they get to 'the second floor, and the appearance of a housemaid prevented any further conversation' (270).

So now: if all Jane Austen's work turns out to be, like Freud's, about the strain of civilization (built entirely on suppression of instincts, and the unconscious complement to that: repression—among other things, of childhood memories), and if *Mansfield Park* is a field-day of extremes, what is the extreme example of that strain?

- 2 -

Fanny Price is one of the most silent heroines in European literature: perhaps no other comparably central character is 'absent from the text', save for a brief allusion to her 18th birthday, for so long as the eleven pages ending 'And Fanny, what was *she* doing and thinking all this while?' (48). It is this work's aesthetic paradox: the active, vivid presence of other characters, and Fanny's notorious 'passivity'.[22]

The state of unawareness all those characters are in about her could be seen as emblematic of Freud's absence from Austen Studies: for even the least psychoanalytically-oriented person, unacquainted with *Mansfield Park*, and to whom the novel's plot is related, might ask how it is that a poor girl who becomes a loved 'daughter', refuses with daring individualism a 'good' match with a husband that she does not want, gets one that she does, secures the exile of her enemies, etc., etc.—how a girl who accomplishes all this can possibly be described as 'passive'.

A trenchant phrase may for now supply a sort of explanation: 'An act so often understands how to disguise itself as a passive experience' (1.86).

One might almost suppose **Lady Bertram**, the first character we are to consider, to have been 'planted' in the novel, with her sofa, so as to forestall such a misreading. Her characteristic prop could seem the emblem of a complete *contrast* between Fanny and her sedentary aunt—after all, ' "Fanny is as little upon the sofa as any body in the house" ' (71). However, this section will demonstrate that the narratological ploy we called 'ironic seepage' in discussing *Pride and Prejudice* is enormously extended in *Mansfield Park*; and we start with Lady Bertram because her importance is less to show what real passivity is, than to start, in the novel's first sentence, the cycles around which the novel turns: Miss Maria Ward, then, '..had the good luck to

---

[22] Fanny's isolation is, however, no more than another extreme extension of a ploy we have observed in the first two novels: in *S & S*, Marianne's tendency to escape into solitude is criticised by Elinor; in *P & P*, between the Jane/Bingley passage of intimacy and the return of Darcy, 'Elizabeth . . . was left by herself' (347) —a poignant anticlimax for her (in whom the signs of envy, so clear in Elinor, have to be guessed) which concretises earlier notations: 'in the solitude of her chamber' (157); 'shut into her own room' (186); 'solitary hours' (212); 'took refuge in her own room' (307, cf. her father, again), and so on.

captivate . . . and to be thereby raised to the rank . . . all the comforts and consequences . . . short of any equitable claim..'

All the terms here might be printed in bold, for all continue to resonate to the novel's last page. To take for the moment just a few: though about Fanny too there may not be 'much in her first appearance to **captivate**' (12), the novel ends with her married to Lady Bertram's son, a man to whom she is still shorter of any equitable claim. We often read she thinks 'lowly of her own **claims**' (20), her 'opinion of her **claims** on Sir Thomas's affection was much too humble to give her any idea of **classing** herself with his children' (176), she 'rated her own claims to **comfort** as **low** even as Mrs. Norris could' (221), 'fearful of appearing to **elevate** herself as a great **lady**' (396), etc.

In II.4 'Fanny's **consequence** increased on the departure of her cousins'; by III.6 'She had **tasted** of **consequence**' (366); for comforts, after the I.2 meeting, 'From this day Fanny grew more **comfortable**' (17); notations such as 'Edmund looked pleased, which must [= had to] be Fanny's **comfort**' (70) are a characteristic expression of present pain, corresponding to the economy of pain forecast for when Edmund, on whom '**comfort** and cheerfulness' depend (284) would be gone; a first reaction to the III.4 talk with Edmund is again 'Fanny had not felt so **comfortable** for days and days' (347).

Lady Bertram's 'good luck' points to other economies, to which we shall come later; now we just note that when Fanny arrives Mrs Norris has lectured her all the way from Northampton on 'her wonderful **good fortune**' (13).

The importance of such *profane* economies as luck/good fortune must be stressed, partly to correct an imbalance of emphasis the received account has placed on the *sacred*, but also to set in context the most important of these: pug's puppies (' "next time pug has a litter you shall have a puppy . . . more than I did for Maria" ', 333) belong to the same metaphor as the (four) pheasant's eggs Mrs Norris scrounges at Sotherton (106); Edmund tells Fanny that going to live with Mrs Norris would bring out her '**natural** powers' (27), but it turns out Fanny no more needs aunt Bertram's breeding nudge than she needs Mrs Chapman's help in dressing, to attract Henry (271); or dark eyes, for that matter, in spite of Edmund as late as p. 459 rhapsodising on 'how delightful **nature** had made her'—that is, Mary.

The go-better-than-mother theme (Chapter III, p. 110) is here enriched by a link between heroine-as-child and heroine-with-child;[23] Fanny as good-mother is early prepared by the notation about her rôle with siblings 'as playfellow, instructress and nurse' (14)—one sense in which she has, as Edmund says, ' "been given a **taste** for **nature** in early life" ' (113); in contrast to Mary, she observes from a carriage window '..the harvest, the cottages, the cattle, the children' (80).

---

[23] Without trumpeting teleologies we have not yet the evidence to underwrite, we may note that Marianne ends up 'mistress of a family' (*S & S* 379, a vague phrase); Elinor and Elizabeth are not imagined with child; indeed Elizabeth's rather brisk way with her nephews (*P & P* 286) is contrasted with Jane's (239).

At the risk of tiring readers' attention with accumulating examples, it must be mentioned that while 'nature' is a frequent index of the parallel we are exploring—Lady Bertram 'in her own good nature' will not prevent Julia going to town with Maria (284); agreeing to it is 'attributed to her nature' (285); persuading her later to part with Fanny, Sir Thomas similarly 'demanded it of her goodness' (371); likewise we hear of Edmund's 'fond dependence on [Fanny's] good nature' (172) at a critical moment—this parallel is also signalled by a characteristic ploy: the *rare* word: e.g. Lady Bertram listening to her husband on his return from Antigua has 'unbroken unalloyed enjoyment' (179), cf. Edmund says he has no pleasure ' "so complete, so unalloyed" ' as contributing to Fanny's (262).

Finally, the symbolic gauge of the principle this study is arguing for—*characters* not being 'where the action is', but rather in language by which they are made to bear wider resonances—their relation to the 'theatricals': these are, it will be seen, more than just an episode, more than a brilliant set of six chapters at the end of volume I (13—18); in each character's relation to them there is an especially acute ironic parallel with Fanny.

For Lady Bertram we take just three examples.

First: her relation to the theatre might seem entirely negative, given that when the topic is first canvassed in her presence she is asleep (126); on another, creaturely drives again dominate: she passes from a summary injunction not to act anything improper, to saying she must have her dinner (140/1); when on the last occasion her attention is drawn elsewhere (deliberately now, by Mrs Norris) even in the terms of the contrast—Lady Bertram is 'quite resigned to waiting'; Fanny was not: 'she thought of the morrow a great deal' (167)—there lurk ironies. We are not yet ready to explore these; it will suffice to ask: (a) is not Fanny herself, in a larger sense, 'resigned to waiting'? and (b) what are the resonances of 'thought of the morrow'?

Second: when Mrs Rushworth is 'pressing Lady Bertram' to come to Sotherton, the latter 'constantly declined it; but her placid manner of refusal made Mrs. Rushworth still think she wished to come' (76); the same division is seen when Fanny fails in discouraging Henry because she 'knew her own **meaning**, but was no **judge** of her own manner' (327): that division is just what acting turns on.

Finally, the theatre metaphor itself: no one will call Lady Bertram a hypocrite; but when Tom falls ill, is it not extremely interesting that it should be Fanny who perceives her aunt's emotion to be '..a sort of **playing at** being frightened' (427)?

Chapters II & III should have prepared the way for seeing the ironic relation between Fanny and **Mary Crawford**, since one of those 'contrasts which dominate the erotic life of women', so interesting to Freud—'the contrast between reserve and seduction' (14.200)—is clearly near the centre of this work.

The two girls are even in manifest content linked: as rivals. On the way to Sotherton, looking back 'a "there he is" broke at the same moment from them both', then 'they were united' (81; the formula reappears, slightly changed: ' "here he is" ' 211, with the witty narrative suggestion that one or both are thinking of Rushworth); when Edmund says it often happens that a man, ' "..before he has quite made up his mind, will distinguish the sister or intimate friend of the woman he is really thinking of, more than the woman herself.." ' (I.12. 116) we infer that speaking here of Henry/Julia/Maria he is with unconscious knowledge identifying his own psychological mechanism.

A subtler parallel:

> 'You were staying near there?'
> 'Very. I was most kindly pressed, and had nearly consented'. . .
> 'You spent your time pleasantly there.'
> 'Yes; that is, it was the fault of my own mind if I did not.' . . .
> 'The Miss Owens—you liked them, did not you?'
> 'Yes, very well.' (III.4.355)

This sends readers back to an earlier question and answer series:

> 'How many Miss Owens are there?'
> 'Three grown up.'
> 'Are they musical?'
> 'I do not at all know. I never heard.'
> 'That is the first question, you know,' said [Mary], trying to appear gay and unconcerned, 'which every woman who plays herself is sure to ask about another.' (II.2.288)

Were the received account right (Jane Austen's art serving morality) the creation of Mary would approach the core of the paradox of such art: seduction in representation itself. Indeed Fanny is herself seduced: she goes to Mary, and we are told 'it seemed a kind of fascination': she could not be easy not going,

> ..and yet it was without loving her, without ever thinking like her, without any sense of obligation for being sought after now when nobody else was to be had; and deriving no higher pleasure from her conversation than occasional amusement, and *that* often at the expense of her **judgment**, when it was raised by pleasantry on people or subjects which she wished to be respected. She went however.. (II.4.208)[24]

Mary does not through seductive art steal the show in the novel, for Fanny has an edge on her in a kind of knowledge: a subtle touch in Mary's portrayal

---

[24] Though this study is evaluative only by implication, one may venture to remark that refusal to be wiser than a character is the acme of Jane Austen's modernity. And this is not an isolated case: e.g. at II.10.281 we find the following undogmatic exploration of Sir Thomas' motives in sending Fanny to bed at 3 a.m.: he 'perhaps might not be thinking merely of her health. It might occur to him, that Mr. Crawford had been sitting by her long enough, or he might mean to recommend her as a wife by showing her persuadableness.'

is that despite no conceit of immediate understanding (' "I begin now to understand you all, except Miss Price" ' 48) and *pace* Edmund's tribute to ' "great discernment" ' (198), she is unaware of Fanny's secret: she asks her if she could ' "say such things" '[25] as Amelia does to Anhalt, then ' "But then he is your cousin, which makes all the **difference**" '. So the theatre is again the key: for (to spell it out) the point of the novel is that Fanny cannot say any 'such things' as 'a declaration of love . . . made by the lady' (167)—' "I can *say* very little of it" ', she declares; ' "*None* of it, I suppose" ', replies Mary.

Given the importance of each actor's 'object of interest, their part, their **dress**, their favourite scene' (159), it is revealing that when Fanny is caught in a shower Mary is given the rôle of 'providing her with dry clothes' (206).

At Portsmouth, a key question is to know 'How Miss Crawford really felt— how she **meant to act**, or might **act** without or against her **meaning**' (417), in which two key preoccupations overlap, echoing Edmund's first question about the theatricals: ' "You are not serious, Tom, in **meaning to act**?" said Edmund in a low voice, as his brother approached the fire' (I.13.125).

In manifest content, **The Miss Bertrams** are presented in contrast to their cousin (for whom, unlike for them, there is not ' "a great deal more . . . to learn" ' 19); latent content structure and imagery patterns indicate however that they constantly bear meaning about her. A first clue to the ironic relation between the heroine and **Maria** is their common designation by a rare word: Mary, writing of the Rushworths' London house tells Fanny that Henry

'..could not have afforded her such a house.[26] I hope she will recollect it, and be satisfied, as well she may, with moving the **queen** of a palace, though the king may appear best **in the back ground**..'   (III.9.394)

Edmund's attempt to stop the theatricals by telling Maria that ' "it is *you* that are to lead" ' almost works: 'This picture of her **consequence** had some effect, for no one loved better to **lead** than Maria' (140). At the vol.II ball given for Fanny, we learn she 'little understood her own **claims**' until it becomes clear 'that *she* was to **lead** the way and open the ball'; to the guests it has long been clear that since she 'was now to make **her first appearance** [she] must be regarded as the **Queen** of the evening' (267 & 275). The person she longs to be with at the ball, 'as he walked about at his ease **in**

---

[25] Among things none but Mary can say, there is a particular register: given the text's serious word-play, it is significant that Mary produces no less than four variants: her parody of Browne's 'Address to Tobacco', extemporised in anticipation of Sir Thomas' return (161); a deliberate pun in a letter to Fanny ('take away his rants, and the poor Baron has nothing. What a difference a vowel makes!–if his rents were but equal to his rants' 394); and earlier she disingenuously disclaims: ' "Of *Rears* and *Vices*, I saw enough. Now, do not be suspecting me of a pun.." ' (60); as, whatever one thinks it means, that is what the English call *risqué*; there seems to be a sort of *jeu de mots* when, playing with different titles for Edmund–' "Mr. Edmund is no more than Mr. John or Mr. Thomas" ' (211)–she lights on the rustic *sobriquet* for the male sex-organ: perhaps this might be called *unconscious* smut ('Smut is like an exposure of the sexually different person to whom it is directed', 6.141).

[26] The notation 'marriage with Mr. Rushworth would give her the enjoyment of a larger income than her father's' (38) is a variant of the going-better-than-parents theme in *P & P*.

the back ground of the scene' (273) is William, so this may in its turn be linked to the card-game in II.7, in which amidst other innuendo Henry advises Fanny ' "No, no, you must not part with the **queen**. You have bought her too dearly" '; he tells the other player that Fanny ' "..does not part with the queen. She is quite determined" '—again, the other player is William..

A third register of queens, in vol.III (336 f.), and yet another sort of play, the one Henry reads, further underlines the Fanny/Maria parallel: not only are both courted by him, but Maria marries Rushworth as a second choice, out of disappointment; if Fanny almost yields to Henry, perhaps it is for the same reason. Maria's thought when Henry goes—'He was gone . . . and so ended all the hopes..', etc. (194)—echoes Fanny's thought when Edmund goes: '..*he* was gone..', etc. (284).

Maria's quoting Sterne's starling (' "I cannot get out" ', 99) points up Rushworth's view that Sotherton is ' "a dismal old prison" ' (53); even before she enters it her father offers to 'release her' (200), but it is 'restraint which her father imposed' that 'She must escape'; 'hatred of home' (202); cf. notations for Fanny at Portsmouth, 'a sad place' where Fanny is 'very much confined' (401, cf. 'the confinement of Portsmouth', 410 & 432); even 'the barriers, which society gives to virtue' (468) in Maria's punishment, recall Fanny's joy when she 'passed the barriers of Portsmouth' (445); she has been 'debarred from her usual, regular exercise' (409), for 'they did not often get out' (401).

So: ' "is she out, or is she not?" ' (48): is Fanny free? In vol.II (near the novel's centre) we are told that Mary 'left Fanny to her **fate**' which might have been hard 'had not Fanny's heart been guarded in a way unsuspected by Miss Crawford' (231), and in vol.III she thinks Henry could not have succeeded even 'Had her own affections been as free—as perhaps they ought to have been..' (329). A moving irony, then, that it should be *she* who asks her uncle about the slave trade (198).

Maria is associated with a starling; in a related register (with implications to be seen later) she is 'the pride and delight of them all—perfectly faultless—an **angel**' (39); the same word is used (again by Crawford) of Fanny: ' "You have some touches of the **angel** in you" '(344); the deepest irony is in Mrs Norris' ' "suppose her even to have the beauty of an **angel**, and she will never be more to either than a sister" ' (7); Fanny sees those whom Henry has courted as 'infinitely her superiors' (306); later he tells her she is ' "infinitely my superior in merit" ' (343).

The theatre: Maria is always on show—she and Rushworth are 'the principals' (202); but later Fanny is 'principal lady' at the parsonage (223); Maria may be an angel, but Mr Price puts her among those ' "fine ladies [who] were going to the **devil**" ' (440), Mrs Norris sees Fanny as 'the **daemon** of the piece' (448); the Mansfield angel ends up banished to just such a 'spare-room for a friend' as Sir Thomas had been in vol.I misled 'to suppose . . . really intended for Fanny' (28).

The Miss Bertrams schema admits of a series of contrasts; within this series the ironic relation between **Julia** and Fanny is developed: Julia's temper is for example contrasted with Maria's as being '**naturally** the easiest of the two', and she had not such 'a **degree** of **self-consequence**' (466); her marriage to Yates is allowed because she is '**humble** and wishing to be forgiven' (462); cf. Fanny, who until the Miss Bertrams leave had been 'so **humble** a third' (205). Further implications in 'degree': Julia thinks herself 'a little **inferior**' to her sister (466) but 'not **superior** to the hope of some distressing end' to Henry's attentions, and 'punishment to Maria' (162). Related to that register (to which we return in section 12), is Julia's 'a **state of** complete **penance**', ' "Such a penance as I have been enduring" '—especially given that she adds ' "I am not obliged to punish myself for *her* sins" ' (91 & 100); Fanny's Portsmouth stay is described as 'a **state of penance**' (430).

Frederick retaining Agatha's hand (176) is told from Julia's point of view; the scene echoes Fanny seeing or imagining Edmund do the same, in the I.7 riding scene.

Further notations about Julia are assimilable to Fanny's own situation: indeed 'Julia could better bear a subordinate situation' (204); as the carriage nears Sotherton, Julia's 'happy star no longer prevailed' (90); cf. Fanny looking at the stars two chapters later (113); while Henry had 'trifled with her [Julia's] feelings' in vol.I (160), in vol.II Fanny considers Henry's proposal as 'mere trifling' (301), etc.

The ironic relation again centres in the theatricals: Julia and Fanny are the only two young people not to take parts: the theatre finds Julia 'sitting by disregarded' (161); cf. the east room reflection about Fanny: 'her feelings disregarded' (152) is her usual state; ' "Those who see quickly, will resolve quickly and **act** quickly" ' (61): thus Julia, attributing to Henry a celerity from which she hopes to benefit. Yet Julia—who is 'on the barouche box in a moment', the 'place of all places' (80), and the first of whose highly effective 'lines' (' "If Edmund were but in orders!" ') is cried *running* (89) in Sotherton chapel, and whose 'temper was hasty' (101)—is excluded from the rôle of rôles in the play within a play because 'she walks too quick and speaks too quick' (134); she is further the subject of one of the most telling recourses to theatrical language within the theatre-chapters: Crawford was 'at treacherous **play** with her' (135).

Innocent by accident, then, Julia is rewarded on her father's return: ' "*I* need not be afraid of **appearing** before him" ' (175), she is able to declare; Fanny by contrast is full of 'dread' (176): we shall need to ask why.

This section of ironic parallels may close with a key-word of this study. Julia twice defends Fanny: it is she who makes the remark about the sofa (71); and when Maria expresses surprise at Edmund's plan to stay at home that Fanny may go to Sotherton, Julia comments that Fanny ought to be obliged to him, but is partially exculpated by her **'consciousness** that she ought to offer to stay at home herself' (79). The word is echoed later: she had entertained 'a dear though irrational hope' of Henry, and felt 'a strong sense of ill-usage' (162; cf. ' "how ill you [Fanny] have been used by them!" ', 97); her jealousy 'escaped the notice of many' save Fanny who 'saw and pitied much of this in Julia' because it is her own situation. The passage concludes with a very striking expression:

> ..but there was no outward fellowship between them. Julia made no communication, and Fanny took no liberties. They were two solitary sufferers, or connected only by Fanny's **consciousness**.. (163)

- 3 -

While aesthetics develops general ways of talking about art (what it is for works to have a theme or subject, to be 'about' something) criticism involves understanding and saying what we feel a particular work is about: 'understanding is not one thing; it is as various as the language games themselves are'. What a work is about is a function of what it is made of; and the outcome of presenting something under a new light is new descriptions.

Of the sentence just quoted, we might first say that by a remarkable narrative disposition Fanny 'contains' Fanny; but as section 2 began to illustrate, and as the next will further illustrate, that description can stand for what this novel—indeed in a general sense the whole Jane Austen oeuvre, with increasing single-mindedness—presents.

And psychoanalysis provides terminology capable of making coherent sense of this: a psychoanalytic account of the dispositions so far evoked in this chapter would be that the effect is of a massive *projection*.

Not a new term in this study, projection; but the extent of the parallels so far illustrated will make us punctilious about identifying its exact nature: so (to return to a distinction which became necessary when we saw that something in *Pride and Prejudice* goes beyond conventional representations of inter-personal psychology): is it psychological or metapsychological? More pointedly: whose is it?

In both novels so far discussed, heroines' interest in their sisters' affairs is psychologically credible: a screen for their own affective problems, a representation of projection in the *story*; but sorority is also a fundamental part of the *structure* of the story: sisters are different entities and parts of the same entity. Serving the key theme of the secret, it is the most metaphorical relationship, an alibi for a felt *meta*psychological (almost *mythical*) structure: the secret kept from oneself.

' "Who says we shall not be sisters? I know we shall. I feel that we are **born** to be **connected**" ' (359): notations such as this show new extension

156

of sorority in *Mansfield Park*, and we shall take account of this progression in Jane Austen's inquiry; but the extension of parallels makes our present concern to ask if something is being said about a 'new' character (Fanny, i.e. *she* 'projects' more), or if 'Fanny' is a more complex portrait?

In other words, is wider extension being given to a technique used in previous works, or is the technique at the service of a new preoccupation?

To answer these questions, we may first separate normative from other explanations: setting these novels against the furniture of the genre as it stood in 1800, between Jane Austen and her heroines there is a relationship we need make no fuss in calling *economic*.

Bluntly, for there to be an interesting novel, someone has to see something; one solution is to make one or more characters observant.

The lexical overlaps in *Mansfield Park* illustrated so far, though they correspond to none of Fanny's desires as are represented in the novel's manifest content, are similarly credible in terms of her (psychological) projection: to elevate herself (Lady Bertram), to speak (Mary), to become a queen (Maria), and so on. However, something is going on in this novel which extends beyond depiction of Fanny's (more or less conscious—that is another question) female-rôle emulation.

To begin with, section 2 illustrated massive ironic seepage from female characters; yet the phenomenon is just as widespread from *male* characters. The following are again chosen to give an idea of this strategy's pervasiveness; and in each of them figurative preoccupations elsewhere are pointed to.

Towards the end of the novel **Dr Grant** is appointed to a post for which he 'had almost ceased to form hopes' (469). That the 'point' of this is to highlight Fanny's attitude to Edmund's love, two pp. later—'of which she has scarcely allowed herself to entertain a hope' (471)—can be confirmed by other echoes: Grant 'succeeded to a stall in Westminster' (469) and Fanny is 'a match which Sir Thomas's wishes had even forestalled' (471); Grant's 'permanent removal' is justified by 'increase of income' from the appointment; and it is because of Fanny's child (emphasised by the need for 'an increase of income') that they 'removed to Mansfield' (473).

From hopes to a stall, and from there tiercerons go in an unexpected direction: Henry is disappointed of what he had 'set his heart upon . . . a little home-stall at his command' (246); this is later described as a 'small hunting-box' (405). (Naturally, Fanny as horse must seem ludicrous at this stage in the demonstration.)

The web of association spreads still further, linking to others mentioned already or shortly to be mentioned: Edmund's predecessor may make us think of Grant's predecessor Norris, who as he ' "could hardly ever get out" ' (54, incidentally he 'could no more bear the noise of a child than he could fly', 9) limited his improvements in the parsonage garden;[27] ' "early tarts" ' into which Dr Grant's fruit goes (55) recall the first thing Fanny eats at Mansfield (13). (N.B. on the manifest level [e.g. 111], Fanny *disapproves* of Dr Grant, as, on the same level, she is antipodal to Mary Crawford.)

In the same way, when **Mr Rushworth** says to Fanny that in his opinion ' "these Crawfords are no addition at all. We did very well without them" ' (102), they are united in their opinion: the irony is, we may say, on the surface—in the sense that at least one of the characters (Fanny) is aware of the irony. But when Rushworth's future marital possibilities are described as a 'second spring of hope' (464), we cannot but be reminded of the importance for Fanny of the turning year (another aspect of the 'nature' theme) first presented in one carriage on the way to Sotherton, in vol.I (80), and given what we shall see to be metaphorical force in another carriage in vol.III, when she returns to Mansfield with Edmund (446).

Similarly when we read Rushworth 'was young enough to improve' (201), the notation is like a reappearance in one corner of a carpet of one of the major motifs near its centre: the improvement theme, and its relation to Fanny.

Henry says of Maria/Rushworth ' "She is too good for him—much too good" ' (224); cf., of Fanny/Edmund, 'She was of course only too good for him; but as nobody minds having what is too good for them..' (etc., 471).

Apart from such structural parallels, Rushworth-notations constantly return us to the heroine: a tiny example might be his failure to bring a key at a critical moment (98), recalling a similar oversight of Fanny's (73)—also in great heat; an example with deeper resonances, the reason for Rushworth's eligibility as a 'connection' to Sir Thomas—that he is 'in the same county, and the same interest' (40)—returns us to Fanny's talk of ' "the same soil and the same sun" ' (209).

As for the theatricals, Fanny's 'containing' Rushworth is the object of what seems almost an authorial wink when Henry reminds her of her efforts ' "to give him a brain which **nature** had denied—to mix up an understanding for him out of the superfluity of your own!" ' (224/5); Rushworth, more interested in his costume than the others, is to wear a ' "fine fancy suit by way of a shooting dress" ' (139), in Mary's view Fanny must congratulate herself for ' "the glory of fixing one who has been shot at by so many" ' (363); Rushworth does not ' "much like the idea of being so fine" '; at a key moment in a carriage, Fanny asks Edmund ' "I hope you do not think me too fine" ' (222).

Readers will have material to decide whether the novelist knows what she is up to here, when we return to the important fact that **Tom Bertram** falls ill while Fanny is at Portsmouth: his 'extreme impatience to be removed to Mansfield, and experience those **comforts of home**' (427) is echoed a few pages later: with what 'impatience . . . "she wants her home" ' etc.: some will

---

[27] And Fanny is Mrs Grant's successor in the parsonage, so in more than one sense it is her part she is to play; but she goes better than her predecessor, who merely fills the place with pretty furniture (41).

interpret as a wink the detail 'she could not suppose any school-boy's bosom to feel more keenly' this yearning (431); perhaps he recovers from his illness because 'she could not **spare** him' (428); this too can hardly be accepted now.

Other structural Tom/Fanny parallels—all the more interesting since between two characters who have so little to do with each other in the manifest content—are signalled by Tom's realisation at one party that Grant is near making 'a change of expression and subject necessary' (119) being echoed at another party where Fanny, seeing her uncle nearer than supposed, also 'found it necessary to talk of something else' with William (250): these notations furnish a figure for guilt—the feeling of being watched—and so lead into the theatre metaphor: whilst Tom speaks his lines 'so quick he would be unintelligible' (164), Fanny's note to Mary in III.13 is 'scarcely intelligible' because she sees Henry coming towards her for it (' "You cannot think I **mean** to hurry you" ', 307); and to the notation mentioned in section 1 about Tom—'the insignificance of all his parts together' (164)—there is an echo in Fanny feeling 'sad and insignificant' (159); on the same two pages he is 'unemployed' and 'all were finding employment' except she.

Sir Thomas Bertram and Fanny are linked in many ways: his 'own dear room' (181) echoes Fanny's: 'The room was most dear to her' (152); on his return he 'meant to try to . . . forget how much he had been forgotten himself' (187) echoes Fanny's feeling in the riding-scene ('if she were forgotten the poor mare should be remembered' 68), at Sotherton (her wishful 'it was impossible for Edmund to forget her so entirely', 100) etc. Uncle and niece are also linked by a rare word: Fanny sees he has the 'fagged, worn look of fatigue' (178); Edmund later notices Fanny looks ' "tired and fagged" ' (267).

As for the theatre, we may see a structural parallel in the novel's first drama (theatricals) occurring in Sir Thomas' absence, and the second (Wimpole St. débâcle) in Fanny's; he, on returning home, makes 'his first appearance on any stage' (182); we have seen that expression also used of Fanny.

Now: readers will easily accommodate extension of 'projection' beyond the psychological (heroine's projections on characters of her own sex): we used in Chapter III the relevant bit of psychoanalytic theory encountered early in this study: 'masculinity'/'femininity' are characteristics of drives, not of people.

But the term 'extension' begs the question: stretched beyond their explanatory power, terms outlive their usefulness: something is going on in *Mansfield Park* for which character-analysis breaks down completely, in spite of these characters' vividness and range. The question, what is the novel really about? will take the form: where is the frame (or, the Chapter II term, the 'encapsulating fiction')? And we must ask: what *exactly* is the relation of the characters to that frame?

Remaining for the last time within terms of character (a sort of tribute to an outmoded description) and repeating that what these novels are about is how they are about it, this is nowhere better exemplified than in how Fanny is presented with what we may still call the character **Mrs Norris**.

Five examples. First, *Mansfield Park* can be called a field-day of *exaggeration*: the very diction of the two characters links them in this area:

[Aunt:] ' "I should be the last person in the world to withhold my mite [6], of all things upon earth *that* is the least likely [ibid.], feel for this little girl the hundredth part of the regard I bear your own dear children [7], Fanny live with me! The last thing in the world for me to think of [28], ready to move heaven and earth to persuade my sister [189], [Rushworth] has a thousand good qualitites [190]" ', etc.
[Niece:] ' "I shall remember your goodness, to the last moment of my life [26], could not act any thing if you were to give me the world" [145], obliged her to bring down her mind from its heavenly flight [262], four words ... which she could have looked at for ever [265], "speakingly incomprehensible" [208] ', etc.

Second, in contrast to that pervasive effect, a one-off ironic link, in its way equally telling, between Mrs Norris' place ('the White house' 28) and Fanny's bed-room, 'the little white attic' (9)—which in the register of allegory seems emblematic of the skull, dwelling of the mind..

Third, what the aunt *says*: the exchange with Edmund which ends with her reflection on Fanny's dependent situation (146), starts by her exclaiming ' "What a piece of work here is about nothing" ': the formula appears anodyne until or unless we notice it is an almost exact replica of the (*first*) line in the part Fanny is asked to play in *Lovers' Vows*: ' "here's a piece of work indeed about nothing!" ' (Oxford ed. of *Mansfield Park*, Appendix, p. 490; as we shall see, this 'quotation' is not an isolated instance.)

Fourth, as after Fanny's III.1 'private walk' the formula is found summing up how Mrs Norris always addresses Fanny—'She was talking *at* Fanny'—it is as if we no longer need to hear her at all, for a page later not only does she make her final mistake—*What*, she asks should Sir Thomas want Fanny for?

'It is me, Baddeley, you mean; I am coming this moment. You mean me, Baddeley, I am sure; Sir Thomas wants me, not Miss Price.' (324)

—but this is the last word she speaks in the novel.

Fifth: characters can be made of the absence of words; silence, readers of this study need no longer be told, is never narratologically empty; in other words, a frame is also always a mask, excluding as much as containing. The Fanny/Norris relationship is arguably the closest in the novel, yet (or should it be 'therefore'?) in the whole course of the novel's four hundred and seventy pages Fanny is represented as addressing Mrs Norris ..*once*: aunt tells niece to follow Edmund if he wants to leave the parsonage in the evening, and niece replies ' "Yes, ma'am, I should not think of anything else" ' (II.5.221).

All these parallels, 'expressive' of Fanny's psyche, are at the same time quite 'unrealistic': it is obviously 'incredible', for example, that a girl should speak to her aunt only once in nine years.

Jane Austen's irony takes disturbing forms, then, in *Mansfield Park*: a meta-psychological reading in this instance—Fanny contains Mrs Norris, too—corresponds to the hard truth of psychoanalysis: we do not wish to know that not only instincts subserving self-preservation are endogenous, but also those of self-punishment, that a part of us wants to hurt ourselves. In other words, once again, that the enemy is within.

- 4 -

New descriptions raise new questions. One to be tackled straight away arises out of the fact that the whole foregoing part of this book has illustrated an artistic exploit that will almost certainly appear *original*; by the same token it may now seem (and maybe not for the first time in the inquiry) that altogether too particular, even *peculiar*, an interpretation of Jane Austen's work is being argued for; on this view, to put it bluntly, the whole thing is too odd to be likely.

A first general answer to this is to inquire why oddness is to be judged itself objectionable. It may be recalled (Chapter II, p. 81) that Freud related fantastic dream-interpretations to surprises in physiological research.[28]

The interpretation this study offers, it may be repeated, cannot hope to supersede the received account, aiming rather to make sense of it; so it is important to see that the language-game readers are being asked to believe Jane Austen was playing is no odder, no more artificial, than one which requires us to believe in a castful of noseless characters.[29]

And just as we conceded nothing gleaned of Elinor-&-Marianne is incompatible with the portrayal of a relationship in 'realistic' terms current in 1811, to say that *Mansfield Park* characters are participants, with their figurations, in something larger, is not to subtract from the credibility of those characters in what may be called another *mode* of reading. We can continue to 'believe in' characters whilst also reminding ourselves that it is, quite literally, a bit of a game to do so. We can become aware of what game is being played. If we say these novels are realistic in the sense of 'true to

---

28 Considerable thinkers have declared for the likeliness of unlikelihood: e.g. Russell says 'The truth about physical objects must be strange' (and Anthony Quinton calls this 'highly characteristic', Magee, ed. cit., p. 15); cf. 'Berkeley tells us [a table] is an idea in the mind of God; sober science, scarcely less wonderful, tells us it is a vast collection of electric charges in violent motion' (Russell, op. cit., p. 24); surprises in 20th century physics give retrospective force to Berkeley's own retort (in *Three Dialogues*..) when his conclusions are objected to on the grounds that their consequences will be too odd, 'I hope you will stick at nothing for its oddness..'

29 'Middle-class realism' was not the novel's pre-ordained programme; in some periods the metaphorical character of the encapsulating fiction signifies *deeper* realism: mediaeval artists were mostly concerned with picturing what they thought was invisible.

life',[30] it is worth drawing attention to what odd-shaped slices that life comes in. (Fancy never being able to see your interlocutor's nose..)

And that it is certainly a different game from seeing characters more literally, should transpire from a brief consideration of 'adaptations' of Jane Austen's novels, for the big or little screen.

A study of this kind could impunitively not notice such things, but to set her oeuvre in the perspective of a genre with quite other figurational criteria, by showing how such adaptations are *necessarily* 'untrue', will be unexpectedly instructive about the nature of that oeuvre.

To begin with, Jane Austen was not writing 'historical' novels. The question of who is her ideal reader is a not uninteresting one—a contemporary of hers, or one whose cultural baggage includes tools of conscious interpretation unavailable in her time?—but at least Chapman relegated his invented 'background' (which some readers of any period will clamour for) to back pages; film forces into the foreground of our attention everything the novelist specifically does not wish us to think about: every square inch of today's screen is filled with representation of costumes, furniture, houses, etc., claiming to represent the 18th century.

'Claiming' may sound petulant, yet even on its own terms 'authenticity' is misleading, film 1800 being as far from real 1800 as from Jane Austen; readers two centuries on, spirited back without the double-glazed protection of the screen, would find real Jane Austen's England unbearable for more than an hour or two; seeing Jane on the screen in order to get away from our own painful century is thus as misguided as reading Jane with the same motive;[31] adaptations are 'untrue', then, because the pastness they go into is itself an entirely fabricated one.

A graver charge would be that anchoring Jane Austen's work in the past, and in the world, obscures seeing that it is about the present, and the mind.

But the most basic reproach must be laid at the door of those who have forgotten, or betrayed, the principle that in works of art form and content are one. Not an 'academic' principle, this—any more than artistic value is a sort of beauty-spray—as should be clear if we recall, taking an example from Chapter III, that it is not the *thing seen* (Elizabeth unfolding a letter) which is important in Jane Austen's meaning, but the *word* 'unfold' *read* on the page. When everything which was narrative becomes visual (an invariable tendency of film) the distinction underlying that principle—a fundamental

---

[30] The two modes can be called psychological and metapsychological, and these terms applied to the Fanny/Norris relation: metapsychologically it corresponds to the principle that psychical tendencies are essentially complementary (cf. 'pairs of opposites', Chapter III, p. 107); psychologically, there is an inescapable link between victim and torturer, sadist and masochist: 'A sadist is always at the same time a masochist, although the active or the passive aspect of the perversion may be the more strongly developed in him, and may represent his predominant sexual activity' (7.73).

[31] Having done noses, we may now take mouths; in 1800 everyone's teeth were rotten, unlike the uniform BBC gleams resulting from modern dentistry.

distinction: words, and things—becomes lost. We are now to pursue further implications of that distinction.

- 5 -

If previous sections have succeeded in showing that the means by which Fanny Price's psyche is evoked, are independent both of division of text into characters, and division of the characters into two sexes, the claim (Introduction, p. xxix) that describing Jane Austen's novels in terms of her characters constitutes a radically inexact and misleading account of her art, may now be considered substantiated.

Characters—whatever their 'sex' in the perceptualist simulacrum—are only a special mould of language; they are the largest, most noticeable moving objects in that simulacrum, but it is a contingent fact that they correspond to the human reader's size and identity: 'focussing' on them as we read, our 'vision' of the rest is muddied. One answer to the question *whose projection is it?* then, would be: *ours.*

We cannot avoid referring to characters; Jane Austen's work pictures human experience—in a sense all art does. But the ways in which it does so are various, and in order to catch *Mansfield Park*'s way, we must move from the large building blocks to the material of which they are composed.[32] Looking at the same material at this more elemental level will enable us to see that this novel refines a preoccupation of *Pride and Prejudice*: the distinction now dramatised is one which—logically, perhaps temporally—is prior even to that 'first distinction' we make (same as me, or not?; male, or female?)—a more fundamental one: the distinction between me and the world.

To pursue that preoccupation the novelist plays with two registers: almost two realisms; we must understand the relation between them.

We might call it realism of inner and outer worlds, but then we have to remind ourselves, first, that in a novel there is no inner and outer (any more than in a picture there is foreground and background) only representations of such categories; and second, that we do not yet know where the frame is.

Another way of putting it would be to say that in this novel the figurative is constantly jammed up against the literal (a combination unusual in a novel but not in a dream, cf. Chapter I, p. 44). Just one example for the moment to indicate the sort of thing we shall be concerned with: in *Mansfield Park* III.15 we read the celebrated passage in the slanting late-afternoon light: the 'sickly glare' of the parlour, just before Mr Price holds out the newspaper to Fanny, 'ragged carpet', 'stains and dirt that might otherwise have slept', crockery 'wiped in streaks' (439), etc. But terms and their associations from the very height of this register ('Portsmouth naturalism') figure elsewhere, quite at home in another register. In the preceding chapter we read Mary's

---

[32] To the reader on the brink of refreshing acquaintance with a Jane Austen novel, perhaps the recommendation may be humorously ventured not to forget, while re-reading one, to read *the words.*

view of Edmund's precipitate ordination: 'the evil of a few days may be blotted out in part. Varnish and gilding hide many stains' (434); and in the next, we learn Lady Bertram's view of the débâcle: she 'could see it only in one light, as comprehending the loss of a daughter, and a disgrace never to be wiped off' (449). If the parlour-scene is proto-Zola, Mrs Price's reaction to the newspaper story is out of *The Waste Land*: ' "..I hope it is not true . . . it would be so very shocking!—If I have spoke once to Rebecca about that carpet, I am sure I have spoke at least a dozen times . . . And it would not be ten minutes work.." ' Of her sister, by contrast, while Sir Thomas was away 'her own time had been irreproachably spent during his absence; she had done a great deal of carpet work..' (179).

That last paragraph may raise an objection which must be dealt with at once: as in Chapter III, the occasion has arisen to make a point about matters present since the outset of the inquiry, and the reason for quoting certain material in sections 6 and 7 will be understood beforehand.

The objection would be to the following effect: is it not possible that what this study claims Jane Austen is doing is not peculiar or original, but on the contrary a quite ordinary characteristic of her chosen medium, language?

To answer this, we must look at Freud's view of the relation of language to the unconscious: noting clients recurrent use of words and expressions, he writes: 'the locality at which the repressed breaks through is the *word presentation* and not the concept attached to it' (F/F 287, Freud's italics).

The importance of this for the understanding of literature has not, it would seem, been recognised; it would be hard to exaggerate the significance of its implications.

Freud goes on: 'The tendency toward breaking through *makes use of* these ambiguous words' (my italics); obsessive ideas 'frequently are clothed in a characteristic *verbal vagueness* in order to permit such multiple deployment' (Freud's italics).

At the same period Breuer, seeking to grasp what seemed an '*irrational* "symbolic" relation between the precipitating cause and the pathological phenomenon', is struck by the fact that this relation 'is often based on the most *absurd* similarities of sound and verbal associations' (3.294, my italics).

In Chapter I (p. 5) the paradoxical character of psychoanalysis was evoked thus: a reasoned view of the irrational, *or what seems such*: but one of Freud's theoretical triumphs was to demonstrate that the unconscious has (as we call it in English) its own *rationale*.

Further, he found that its rationale has, in one sense, a *verbal* character: he observes that the person making use of ambiguities in the language is 'not taking liberties with words, but is simply reviving once more the sensations to which the verbal expression owes its justification' (3.254): in other words that person is in some sense 'right'.

Freud and Breuer make the further key point that this relation is 'such as healthy people form in dreams' (3.55), for dream-work prefers to use 'words the sound of which expresses different meanings' (6.220).[33]

Just as (Chapter I, p. 22) the psychoanalytic relation is a linguistic one, the dream is the account we give of it (do., p. 44); a ploy with the same aim as what has just been described is the dream-work's recourse to recent impressions, often from the preceding day; broadly, the shorter the period a memory has been in one's mind, the less the conscious realises its significance, and sleep is protected: 'By selecting these residues, the dream deceives the censorship. Under the cover of their insignificant aspect, repressed contents are able to find expression' (*L & P* 96). Repressed ideas, were they to become conscious, 'would be bound to stand out in the crudest contrast to the rest of the conscious processes' (11.174).

To apply this now: Jane Austen has similarly been 'protected' from psychoanalysis; the material brought to light in this study has remained unnoticed because each instance of it is furnished with a well-prepared alibi: crude 'tail' is hidden in anodyne 'entail', and everyone's unconscious is indemnified.

We hardly need telling that this associative impulse is how exploitation of linguistic density works,[34] but we do need reminding that it is a *peculiarity* of books to be totally composed of word-presentations, forgetting it because it is familiar, or because word-presentations so rapidly become thing-presentations in our mind. Incidentally, Jane Austen was aware of this mechanism: at the end of *Northanger Abbey* we are told Viscount X (General Tilney's son-in-law) is 'the most charming young man in the world', then: 'Any further definition of his merits must be unnecessary; the most charming young man in the world is instantly before the imagination of us all' (II.16.251).

In reply to the imagined objection, then: Jane Austen's contribution to the genre's possibilities was to seize on a characteristic of language itself, and to exploit a parallel between the main distinguishing characteristic of the genre, and of word-presentations in human psychology.[35]

(This further supports the paradigmatic status of dream interpretation, thus furnishing a reply to an imagined objection to the dream/novel parallel

---

[33] To an early reviewer of *The Interpretation of Deams*, the associations recorded seem either to be preposterously far-fetched, or else stale jokes (F/F 414).

[34] Cf. '..if one's mind does not in some way run through the various meanings of a word, how can it arrive at the right one?' (Empson, op. cit., p. 86).

[35] More artifice –at least on the supposition that the unconscious, wholly composed of thing-presentations, has no word-presentations in it. We are at the limits of critical relevance of such matters, behind which lurk (not new) questions as to which comes first, experience or organization of it. Kris' expression 'the "language" of the id' (op. cit., p. 116) is perhaps metaphorical; but Freud (who pursued few philosophical implications of his work) was undogmatic about this, as suggestive comparatives in the following, italicised, show: 'Thinking in pictures stands near*er* to unconscious processes than does thinking in words, and it is unquestionably old*er* than the latter both ontogenetically and phylogenetically' (11.359). Lacan's (revisionary) position is that the unconscious is not a repository for biological drives–but, well, is Lacan in a position to know? The unconscious is presumably only a construct when we name things in it, so one of his slogans ('the unconscious is structured like a language') might almost make better sense the other way round: could our language receive the imprint of instinct? Might not the very plurality of instincts suggest a first feeling of being 'peopled'?

at the start of Chapter III: the novel's length and evolution in time suit it to representing the psyche's multiple associations.)

With regard to *Mansfield Park*'s copious material, a proviso is to be made about this reply to the imagined objection: Jane Austen exploits a characteristic of *language*, but *the English* language is not centred round Fanny Price. As knowing the facts of art involves grasping the implications of books being configurations of words not of things, so there is a difference between finding a word ('wipe', for example) in *this* book (*Mansfield Park*) and finding it in other books—even in those whose peculiar pattern we yet take for granted (dictionaries).

The nature of artistic intention and originality has recently been clarified, in reaction to incoherences in Romantic theory of expression: it has come to be seen that art always develops within the context of a specific medium, that intention is not a private matter, and that no artist can be totally original. Indeed, the concept is empty: 'A work of complete originality—if it could even be thought of—would communicate as little as does a work of a completely expected nature'.[36]

Although in that sense art cannot do more than represent what everyone already knows, this study aims to increase consciousness of Jane Austen's specificity: what she *does with* the furniture of the genre, novel, as she found it. Understanding the implications of meaning being context-dependent[37] will help us identify the point at which the question of Jane Austen's originality becomes a *critical* one. For if the margin within which an artist works is narrow, the range of what has specifically critical interest is correspondingly narrow; it will be useful to put what we need now to pursue (section 6, *et seq.*) in the context of what we need not.

(1) Catherine Morland's father is 'a very respectable man, though his name was Richard' (*NA* I.1): unless no more is at stake than an allusion, from the viewpoint of a child discovering English history, to Richard III's wickedness, the meaning is now unretrievable. So: no critical upshot.

(2) Mr & Mrs Jones were both rather tall & very passionate, but

> were in other respects, good-tempered . . . both very tall, but seemed in other respects to have many good qualities. (*MW* 12/3; cf. also 98)

This is 'original', i.e. it perhaps originated in a private joke (cf. Henry Austen and a friend come to dinner, '—both tall, & well, & in their different degrees, agreeable', *L* 289): its lack of critical upshot is qualified by its *acquiring* 'public' meaning (the symbolic significance of tallness in *Pride and Prejudice*).

---

[36] Gombrich, op. cit., p. 97. Behind the aesthetic point there is the philosophical one: 'anything absolutely unique . . . would necessarily defy description—for we could not, *ex hypothesi*, say of what sort it was, what it was *like*' (G.J.Warnock: *Berkeley*, Blackwell 1982, p. 65.)

[37] The concisest example known to me is a *Private Eye* newspaper headline howler: *Shell Found On Beach*: a public joke, in the sense that it is comprehensible by anyone who understands English.

(3) A preoccupation present in successive novels: particular but not private or incomprehensible: that might have critical relevance in another study.[38]

(4) There are cases where the effect on the reader is of being present at a series of attempts of some metaphor, in the course of Jane Austen's oeuvre, to *wake up*. Such cases are obviously of interest for readers of this study, and we shall have occasion to refer back to the example chosen.[39]

(5) Finally, one sometimes sees an appropriate place being found for a notation which appears elsewhere in an essentially similar form but (so the critical judgement would be) with less perfect appropriateness.[40]

In what follows, we are to explore the critically relevant cases for this study: categories (4) and (5).

- 6 -

The rest of this chapter aims to point various ways into *Mansfield Park*'s dense lexical configuration, treating characters as large bits of pattern. This section and the next give a general illustration of the categories of time and

---

[38] The following are from pieces of writing stretched over perhaps thirty years: Charlotte is sad to leave her native town in a post-chaise, but 'little thought in what a strange & different manner she should return to it' (*MW* 8); two girls get to know each other while dressing for a ball, return to the parlour and 'entered it with much easier feelings . . . than they had taken away' (*MW* 323); 'What totally different feelings did Emma take back into the house from what she had brought out!' and next morning there is 'half an hour stolen . . . to go over the same ground again with him, literally and figuratively' (*E* 434/5); after Louisa's fall in *P*, the young people tread 'back with feelings unutterable, the ground which so lately, so very lately . . . they had passed along' (111), and after Mrs Smith's revelations, Anne decides to behave differently to Mr Elliot, and 'to retrace, as quietly as she could, the few steps of unnecessary intimacy she had been gradually led along' (214).

[39] Many interesting things happen in carriages in Jane Austen's work: Willoughby drives Marianne 'through the park very fast, and they were soon out of sight . . . both seemed delighted with their drive, but said only in general terms that they had kept in the lanes, while the others went on the downs..' (*S & S* 67). Forty years before, Johnson declared that if he had 'no reference to futurity', he would spend his life 'driving briskly in a post-chaise with a pretty woman' (Boswell, op. cit., II.120); forty years after, Emma Bovary is carried off in a Rouen fiacre (*Madame Bovary*, III.1). Readers who find the implication cynical may recall that Louisa Musgrove, speaking of Frederick, says she ' "would rather be overturned by him, than driven safely by anybody else" ' (*P* I.10.85): this age-old association may help us understand why Kitty is sick in the carriage on the outward journey which takes the younger Bennet girls to meet the elder (II.16: on the return journey the Chamberlayne escapade is related.)

The sexual act is not all the metaphor mutters of as it sleeps: when Elton enters Emma's carriage: 'the door was to be lawfully shut on them' (*E* I.15.129): the matter here is marriage, it seems; cf. Anne Elliot's comment on the Crofts' manner of driving: 'no bad representation of the general guidance of their affairs' (*P* I.10.92).

Elsewhere, the metaphor seems unsure of its meaning: Marianne in London, 'expected to see [Willoughby] in every carriage' (*S & S* 141), Fanny looks for 'the carriage which was to bring her a brother' (*MP* 233), Maria apprehends her father's return, 'for to her the father brought a husband' (ibid. 107), and the little Morlands 'expected a brother or sister in every carriage' (*NA* II.14.233).

This demonstration will only be persuasive for those unoutraged by a question-begging remark in Chapter II (p. 53) about episodes in *S & S* which, if they draw attention to themselves at all, do so only by concatenation.

[40] Henry's intention to woo Fanny on ' "days that I do not hunt" ' (*MP* 229) and the notation that he has 'shut himself out for ever from Fanny' (456) recall key moments in *S & S*. The theatre metaphor so prominent in *MP* is not absent from *S & S* or *P & P*, but the only recourse to it with any resonance is at the I.18 *P & P* ball, where it seems to Elizabeth that it would be impossible for her family 'to play their parts with more spirit' (101); Darcy's remark to her ' "We neither of us perform to strangers" ' (176) would have resonance in *MP*, and for something very like Elizabeth's observation that the time she had passed in Kent 'had made a great difference in the country, and every day was adding to the verdure of the early trees' (195) cf. *MP* III.15.446, which will engage us in due course.

Any account of how Jane Austen got to the point of being able to publish four novels in four years must be hypothetical, but her inquiry was ineluctably conducted in time: evidence of concurrent composition of the 'first' three novels (at least) may not be a critical fact, but would explain occurrence of phrases 'out of place'. A concise example of 'concurrence' is that at *S & S* II.13.238 we learn Elinor had seen enough of Mrs Ferrars' **pride**, her meanness, and her determined **prejudice** against herself'.

space, a particular space and time (theatre, and childhood) requiring closer attention (sections 8 and 9); we start with some general remarks about these two categories.

A key characteristic of the genre whose possibilities Jane Austen exploits, then, is its temporal extension; and this work uses formulaic repetition to evoke an economics of time. Time clearly has special significance for Fanny, which may be blandly summarised as covering what has grown from her past—' " You will take in the whole of the past.." ', her uncle charges her, ' "..you will consider times, persons, and probabilities" ' (313)—and what she expects for her future; more specifically, *hope* is an entity existing essentially in time: ' "the hope of creating that regard which had not been created before. This, we know, must be a work of time" ' (347: ironically, Edmund here, speaking of Henry). In a sense, Fanny spends the whole novel waiting: for Rushworth with his key, for Tom to ask her to dance, for her uncle and a kind word, for Mary to return from her ride, for Edmund to return from Mary. Everything happens in time (Mary imagines 'the Sir Thomas complete, which [Tom] was to be in time' 114; Fanny's uncle will see in her ' "as much beauty of mind in time" ' 197; Mrs Norris says the parsonage never bore 'a bad character in *her time*' 31), and time is everywhere, from its smallest divisions—'Fanny was up in a moment, expecting some errand' (145)—through clock-time (Edmund's watch in the wilderness, 95; Sir Thomas' inquiry if 4.20 will do, 221; William 'breakfasted and be gone by half past nine', 280) —to longer periods (' "that week, that acting week" ', 358), to the longest human stretches—'ages of doubt and anxiety' (176) Tom was 'the better for ever for his illness' (462)—and beyond: ' " that **situation** . . . which has the charge of all that is of the **first** importance to mankind . . . temporally and eternally" ' (92); 'In this world . . . hereafter..' (468), etc., etc.

So we are constantly reminded of time in this work; yet many of its time-effects are unobtrusive: a series of allusions prepare the fact that though, for example, the riding-scene ('he had hold of her hand; she saw it, or the imagination supplied what the eye could not reach', 67), or the Madeira-scene ('the tears which a variety of feelings created', 74) have sudden intensity, they do not strictly surprise us: we simply as it were back-date their application.[41]

Everything happens in space, too. Such a platitude might have been avoided were not *overlap* between time-expressions and the space they occur in (key-words pertain to both registers: 'absence', 'spare', 'old/new') central to what Jane Austen is doing: overlap often in the context of physical activities whose metaphorical suggestiveness we have seen before, lending puissance to the figuration. Just one example: 'her hand being so eagerly sought after, that her indefinite engagement with *him* was in continual perspective' (278):

---

[41] The only comparable effect known to me is the ageing of the narrator—whose age is yet never mentioned—in *A La Recherche du Temps Perdu*.

this recalls the dance/marriage ambiguity illustrated in Chapter III, but it also coincides with other important areas of imagery specific to this work: 'perspective' is part of the improvement theme.[42]

Similarly, the two scenes just referred to ('riding' and 'Madeira') for their time significance, also evoke spaces, of two very different sizes and types: the first with its 'cinematic' picture of 'the park, and . . . a view of the parsonage and all its demesnes, gently rising beyond the village road'; the second concluding with the remarkable expression 'the pain of her mind had been much beyond that in her head'.

Although, concerning Fanny, *second* readings irony does not function (again, the love concretised in the marriage at its end does not surprise us), one of this study's aims—to wean Jane Austen readers away from lines, towards structures, by *re*-reading—is almost more applicable to *Mansfield Park* than elsewhere, since the novelist's most specific extension of the possibilities offered by the time and space in which the heroine exists, is exploration of the cyclic, which may pass unnoticed unless one reading is quickly followed by another: plot sweeps us on, and by the time we reach the end of the novel we have forgotten the beginning. The cycle was introduced with relation to the start of the novel (it opens with a time-expression); but its most visible symptom relates to Fanny's surrogate at the end: Susan 'succeeded so **naturally**', 'it was possible to **part** with her, because Susan remained to supply her **place**.—Susan became the **stationary** niece . . . Susan could never be **spared** . . . she was **established** at Mansfield', etc. (472). 'Place' here is, as often, associated with rôle: e.g. in the key notation that Sir Thomas 'seemed to stand in the **place** of [Fanny's] parents' (314).

The importance of Fanny bearing a child at the novel's end may be gauged by its evocation in a space-time expression; here too there is a cycle: if one starts to reread the first page after reading the last, shocks start on the second page, when we momentarily share Sir Thomas' surprise '..that Mrs. Norris should ever have it in her power to tell them, as she now and then did in an angry voice, that Fanny had got another child.'

And if 'spare', like 'absence', is a key word with meaning in time and space for the Mansfield sisters (Mrs Norris' ostinato 'spare room for a friend', I.3, she is ' "not one of those that spare their own trouble" ' [9], the ' "spare hen" ' under which she will place her eggs; and Lady Bertram who ' "cannot very well spare time [to play cards] because of her fringe" ' [119], who 'would of

---

[42] Duckworth's ground-breaking book (op. cit., see References at the end of this volume) starts from the assumption that his material relates to something outside the novel; but this theme is, in it, only the tip of the metaphorical iceberg: an ostentatious topical pun (Capability Brown) shows one only has to juxtapose Henry on Sotherton's 'capabilities' (90) with his later feeling 'no longer in doubt of the capabilities of her heart' (235) to see that its centre is Fanny. For accumulated examples: 'the improvement of her mind' (22); 'improvement in Fanny's age' (24); the years spent not ' "entirely without improvement" ' (33); 'equal improvement in health and beauty' (178); ' "Your complexion is so improved" ' (198); ' "improvement that has taken place in her looks" ' (229); and the point of the whole thing, at the end: 'Her mind, disposition, opinions, and habits wanted . . . no reliance on future improvement' (471).

course be spared all thought and exertion' [253], and whose ability or other-wise to spare Fanny comes thrice: I.8, II.4 and III.17), it is also an index of a moral as well as temporal and spatial cycle. An index of forgiveness, indeed, for whereas Fanny cannot spare Tom, she can (in another sense) spare Mrs Norris, whose spare room is now Maria's: not only a but *the* Miss Bertram.

There are many other signs of this preoccupation; before we assess its col-lective significance two in particular must be mentioned, since they will have special resonances later. One is a plethora of time notations constituting an attaint to what is new rather than old: for Edmund, the theatricals are wrong as 'an innovation'; but even before his objections, Tom has 'so much leisure as to make almost any novelty a certain good' (123—he is not alone in this: Julia was 'as eager for novelty and pleasure as Maria', 204; it is Fan-ny's resistance which makes Henry's 'situation . . . new and animating', 327 etc.). The other is that Fanny is the only heroine to refer to the largest, oldest cycle known to humans: the stars.[43]

Playing against all these signs of what the text itself calls 'this world of changes' (374), is what may be called Fanny's evergreen rhapsody:

> '..how astonishing a variety of **nature**! . . .—that the **same** soil and the **same** sun should nurture plants **differing** in the **first** rule and law of their existence. You will think me rhapsodizing..'   (etc., II.4.209)

Readers were warned that some of this chapter's sections would proceed by accumulating examples; but this cannot be entirely at the expense of expla-natory comment. They will understand that the necessity of bringing onto a printed page a mass of unquoted material has throughout this study con-stantly warred with the uneasy awareness that a bore is a person who tells you everything. No systematic account of the novelist's lexical field is claimed; even the most pointed illustrations give only a sample of relevant data.

If works of art are the human products showing least imprint of an imper-fection characterising what issues from beings of imperfect coherence, and if classics are works where themes are developed with the most interestingly complex forms of coherence, in which the smallest number of ingredients could be changed without harm to the whole, then in describing such works, account must be taken of the largest number possible of these ingredients.[44]

On grounds of *coherence*, then, the question about what is inside/outside a frame is answered. Jane Austen anticipated a change of perspective in which psychoanalysis has taken part: the inner/outer (me/world) distinction coming to seem arbitrary; in *Mansfield Park* everything (the word-world) is Fanny. *Complex forms* of coherence, for the profusion of time expressions illustrated

---

[43] Freud remarks that 'observation of the great astronomical regularities' furnished man with a model for order: 'Order is a kind of compulsion to repeat..' (12.282).

[44] Naturally 'the largest number possible' is as near as we can get to Chapter I's fourth principle of dream interpretation (p. 45), though Freud was uncompromising: 'It is always a strict law of dream interpretation that an explanation must be found for every detail' (9.274).

furnishes a continuous effect of 'textual chatter' (a strategy we have seen employed in Jane Austen's previous work, extended much further here); their point, what they highlight or give meaning to, is the central drama.

Characters round or 'outside' Fanny in the perceptualist simulacrum are, we saw, a metaphor for this drama, representing what is behind her silence, tendencies she contains; it should now be clear that non-human things, too, also bearing resemblances to what is 'inside', participate in this drama.

Before the second half of this illustration (section 7, on the spatial existence of some of these things), an example from another of the 'economies' *Mansfield Park* dramatises: nature, because on the space/time borderline, will underline the importance of the evergreen.

One of the first Mary/Fanny contrasts is that Mary 'had none of Fanny's delicacy of taste, of mind, of feeling [for] **nature**' (81): a contrast returned to in this II.4 passage, for Fanny concludes ' "One cannot fix one's eyes on the commonest **natural** production without finding food for a rambling fancy" '. This in turn recalls ' "the **natural** taste of our apricot" ' (54) in the same garden; so when we later find another allusion to a living thing that has been moved from her native soil—Mrs Norris attributes all Fanny's 'personal beauty . . . to her **transplantation** to Mansfield' (276)—we should almost be unsurprised to find, on the next page, Mary's reflection (speaking of her experience of a sibling, deserted for a wife, n.b.): ' "All are **supplanted** sooner or later" '. The metaphor is so alive that Fanny's evergreen can hardly be regarded other than as a figure for her own unchanging love.

If the whole thing is about Fanny, who contains Mansfield Park, in a sense the whole novel takes place in her mind. Another answer to a question asked earlier, then, must be that it is Fanny's—massive—projection. So massive, indeed, that it could be described as *textual* projection.

One might ask how it comes about that we so easily take it as 'natural' that the text sees only what is in Fanny.

As a way of pointing up the ironic implications of this section's illustration, of sowing what the rest of the chapter will reap, and of involving readers in the interpretative process, some more material may now be put in question-form:

Given that another extension of what may be called *obsession* with the temporal, is 'firsts and lasts', can it be that, parting from Mary, whom she does not like, and who speaks of it as their last meeting ' "for I do not know how long" ', there are reasons why Fanny is affected other than as 'her feelings could seldom withstand the melancholy influence of the word "last" ' (359)?

What are they? What is all this about? What, more particularly, is the specific resonance of Mrs Norris' expression (joining one of these words to fallout from the novel's first sentence, illustrated section 2) that Fanny is

171

' "lowest and last" ' (221)?[45] Returning to 'old and new': what is the resonance in the theatricals starting from a desire for some ' "amusement among ourselves, just to vary the scene, and exercise our powers in something new" ' (125)?

Finally and most pointedly, given that there is another related plethora of notations about 'early and late':[46] what is the reason for Easter being 'particularly late this year' (430) the year Fanny goes to Postmouth?

- 7 -

In approaching space in *Mansfield Park* it may first be said that, bracketed with time though it be, there are asymmetries between the two categories: e.g. space has three dimensions and time one; similarly, there seems no equivalent in time to the gaps between things in space.

Metaphysical irrelevance, all this might seem,[47] were not 'gaps' this study has already identified—e.g. between what characters do and what they say, or between different accounts of them resulting from attention to manifest and latent content—*metaphorical* spaces, we must call them—very variously evoked by spaces—*literal*, in the simulacrum, where the characters evolve in *Mansfield Park*.

These spaces are also (*sc.*, as with Time) of very various dimensions: Sir Thomas' West Indies trip is balanced by Fanny ' "taking a trip into China" ' (156); within England, physical proximity—from Mansfield to Portsmouth, from the great house to the parsonage or the White House, ' "You speak as if you were going two hundred miles off, instead of only across the park" ' (26; cf. Yates on the 'death of one of the nearest connections' of the Ecclesford family concluding his theatrical hopes, ' "all happening two hundred miles off, I think there would have been no great harm" ', 122)—is dovetailed with

---

[45] Henry is 'the **first** of human characters' for William (375); Edmund tells Fanny that next to her happiness Henry's ' "has the **first** claim on me" ' (351); text's density can be shown here by altering bold type emphasis in notations already quoted: Mary's inquiry about the Owens' musicianship is 'the **first** question' which every woman who plays asks; her taking Edmund's arm gratifies his pleasure 'of feeling such a connection for the **first** time'; it is 'the **first** spare hen' Mrs Norris will use for her eggs; Henry, whose chair is the **first** to be given a direction, hopes to bring the '**first** tidings' of William's promotion'; it is Fanny's **first** appearance; the '**first** pleasures of Mr. Rushworth's wife' (210), etc.

Henry speaks of ' "heaven's *last* best gift" ' (43); he is told he will like Julia ' "best at **last**" '; William breakfasts with Fanny for ' "the **last** time, you know, the **last** morning" ' (280); Edmund is ' "the **last** person" ' to think Fanny unentitled to Mary's favour (262); Sir Thomas' ' "the **last** winter of [Edmund's] **belonging** to us" ' (284); Edmund presses Fanny to let Henry ' "succeed at **last**, Fanny, let him succeed at **last**" ' (347), etc.

[46] Mary had 'an **early** presentiment' that she would prefer the elder son (47), the cause of poor reading is 'want of **early** attention' (339), Henry was 'ruined by **early** independence' (467); a ' "very **late** hay harvest" ' (58) delays arrival of Mary's harp; ' "She will be **late**" ' says Sir Thomas before he grasps the parsonage invitation (218); Chapman arrives 'too **late** of course to be of any use' to Fanny in dressing for her ball (271), etc.

[47] In D.W.Hamlyn's careful formula, these '*seem* to constitute the two great continua which give form to the possible relations in which things and events in the world stand' (*Metaphysics*, C.U.P. 1984, p. 134). Without the italics (mine) we get a redolence of Jane Austen's near-contemporary Kant, for whom time and space were necessary conditions of thought; Einstein (op. cit., p. 142) gives priority in that to Hume, whose 'psychological empiricism' has been described as 'a Scottish version of Kant's Copernican Revolution' (H.H.Price, quoted in *A Critical History of Western Philosophy*, Free Press 1964, p. 256). The point of all this is to give a context to a question about Jane Austen which the Introduction predicted might arise: 'where did she get it from?' It can hardly be answered yet, but some readers will naturally ask it: had Jane Austen read any Hume?

affective proximity: ' "I may be discovered by those who want to see me" ', declares Mary, ' "I shall not be in any doubtful, or distant, or unapproachable region" ' (289), and so on. Vocabulary at the start (the breach between the Ward sisters), reappears in the II.6 conjugal/sibling comparison, and in the different formation within the family at the end: division, connection, intercourse, divorce, new attachments and ties, etc., etc.

As for smaller physical gaps, we may take the following example: William and Fanny sitting together at the deserted card table not thinking of the rest

..till some of the rest began to think of them. Henry Crawford's chair was the first to be given a direction towards them, and he sat silently observing them for a few minutes; himself in the meanwhile observed by Sir Thomas, who was standing in chat with Dr. Grant.   (II.7.249)[48]

This chair and table may make us think of others: Lady Bertram's sofa was described as emblematic; given that Grant dies from 'pleasures of the table', his own large round one could in another register be called the instrument of his martyrdom (a reading which will receive unexpected support later.)

But they also afford the occasion to return to the terms of this study's very first interpretative principle (Preface, p. xi): the furniture looks 'real', but like everything else in a book it is rather to be likened to the contents of a mind than to that of a drawing-room. We take for granted that in so far as Jane Austen's work pictures human experience, such experience is carried on in space, and that those humans may occasionally sit on chairs and at tables; but it is all *stage* furniture: every piece has been laboriously 'bought in' by stage management and placed on the set—even as the property-mistress must with studied care hand the least little playing-card to the actress as she goes on. That principle should be borne in mind through the following demonstration, as we move towards the lexical dispositions of a very specific space (in section 8): the theatre of Fanny Price's mind.

To say *Mansfield Park* extends the figurative rôle of space, then, is an understatement:[49] to begin with a manifest fact (apologies might be in order for this, but, we shall see in the next section, what is done with it may not be so obvious), the novel's very title designates a place full of spaces (rooms, shrubbery, plantations, etc.) to which attention is constantly drawn, with relation to Fanny. And even in manifest content her situation, her place, is central from start to finish: from ' "I love this house and every thing in it" ' (26), to 'She had tears for every room in the house, much more for every beloved inhabitant' (374; in both cases the order is significant: the priority, for her, belies

---

[48] There seems not to have been enough astonishment about passages such as this: for proto-'cinematic' subtlety, at least, I know of nothing similar in European literature before 1814–strikingly reminiscent, moreover, of the keyhole 'gaze' in *L'Etre et le Néant*, about which so much fuss has been made.

[49] After Chapter II, it was pointless systematically to point out all spatial/psychological overlaps in *P & P* except for particularly striking examples–e.g. 'beyond her own knowledge', 'hour of possession', 'taking place', etc.–and when specially germane, as where Elizabeth could be seen imagining herself in a picture-space.

'much more'[50]); from the moment when Mrs Norris designates her the little white attic—' "I do not see that you could possibly **place** her any where else" ' (10)—to when she is '**placed** above so many elegant young women' at her ball (II.10.275), and her thoughts fly to those

> ..**absent** cousins . . . not **at home to take their own place in the room** . . . she looked back to the **state** of things in the autumn, to what they had all been to each other when once dancing **in that house** before..

In this section we can benefit from the stand established with regard to Time (the whole thing is about Fanny) and also see many strands come together from foregoing works. This last passage adumbrates her more permanent *taking* of other girls' *place* at the end of the novel (cf. Chapter III, pp. 120, & 130 n. 95); it also sends us back to her first ball: asking herself what Maria looked like, we learn 'she had been dancing with Edmund herself, and had not thought about her..' (117)—and thence to a still earlier wish: she loved to hear about her cousins' dancing parties, especially 'whom Edmund had danced with; but thought too lowly of her own situation to imagine she should ever be admitted to the same..' (35).

Most important, we can now follow up the strong ironic implications of the stand established (with regard to Space, now): readers must decide for themselves whether resonances in dance/marriage ambiguities illustrated so far lend that particular wish-fulfilment specifically sexual suggestiveness; what we are to demonstrate is a general, cumulative, sexual charge in the evocation of Fanny Price, and thus thoroughly abrogate the received account's picture of her.

The axiomatic significance of spaces in psychology may not itself now be thought cavalier,[51] yet its application in what follows can hardly but seem so, for the good reason that, as was to be expected in a work of extremes, the mimetic alibis in this work are themselves *extremely* convincing. But we cannot for a coherent picture of the novel ignore the corroborative colour of a mass of data in which literal is jammed up against figurative: with that association between dancing with Edmund, and reversal of her lowliness, in mind, what we are to trace in the rest of this section are associations of ideas that, seen with the proper distance which ignores those local alibis, collectively evoke spaces occupied in the course of Fanny's progression from lowly situation at the start, to her elevation at the close.

---

[50] Prose enacting thought is also a narratological ploy (cf. 'foreground privilege', Chapter III, p. 101) that this novel extends: e.g. 'alas! it was not such a home, she had not such a welcome, as—she checked herself; she was unreasonable..' (etc., 382); 'For her own gratification she could have wished that something might be acted, for she had never seen even half a play, but every thing of consequence was against it' (131). In *MP* we are more than ever led to suppose we are being told all; but an example which graphically reveals that we are not, is when Fanny, entering the east room at II.9.261, sees Edmund 'with something in his hand'.

[51] Unexpected upshots follow from a view of the novel as Fanny's space: the formula about Mr Knightley (Chapter III, p. 130, n. 95) was over cautious: maybe he is *ostensibly* the first male to enter the female space.

As a first example: in vol.I Fanny was **stooping** (73) among flowers; later we learn that Mary resents Edmund 'fixing himself in a situation which he must know she would never **stoop** to' (228); it is possible not to see a dozing metaphor here, until we notice the terms in which Mary recalls how exquisite it was when Edmund took the rôle of Anhalt: ' "His sturdy spirit to **bend** as it did!" ' (358), and the metaphor bears a family-resemblance to others—almost ostentatious: e.g. though at Sotherton they start off down a '**straight** green walk' (96) returning to Fanny 'a few more **windings** brought them before her' (103).

Another 'detail': Fanny's stooping is done in great heat; Mary's response to Edmund's p. 228 attitude is 'she would now meet him with his own cool feelings': we must in this work often be aware of meteorology and temperature; otherwise when we read Maria's irritation (at missing a chance to be with Henry, Rushworth not turning up in I.7) described as: 'the happiness of one of the party was exceedingly clouded' (70) we shall not hear Jane Austen's chuckle two pages before, when clouds come up so handily in support of Edmund's sophistical exculpation of Mary, for appropriating Fanny's horse.

So from dancing strolling and stooping we return to sitting, which may be called an activity, for it is the spatial occupation of horses, carriages, chairs, etc., whose figurative possibilities Jane Austen exploits, and a few associative chains of which we are now to follow.

This I.7 incident, it will be recalled, is a replay of an earlier time when Fanny had not 'the power of riding' (74): already elements of the extravagant association aired in section 3 (p. 157) are given: when 'her valued friend the old grey poney' dies, we learn of her 'feeling the loss in her health as well as in her affections' (35), whereas Mrs Norris had consoled herself for loss of her husband 'by considering that she could do very well without him' (23; cf. ' "If you could do without her". . ."..but I *cannot* do without her" ', 78); Mary imagines brothers ' "when obliged to take up the pen to say that such a horse is ill, or such a relation dead, it is done in the fewest possible words" ' (59).

On the earlier occasion, with no horse to sit on, Fanny 'sat at home' till Edmund returns to find 'how Fanny was situated' (36): an emblematic case of the way 'situation', and the words it contains or implies, work together chapter after chapter: to such an extent that it is difficult to know whether the literal gives a sense to the figurative, or *vice versa*. Thus in I.5 Mary's image- and money-based criteria characterise her thought of a future husband's home figuring among 'engravings of gentlemen's seats': in other words, as we read on the same page (48), 'he [Tom] and his situation might do'; in I.6, with Tom gone, she 'retook her chosen place near the bottom of the table', and Rushworth talks of ' "Smith's place . . . little enough . . . a mere nothing before Repton took it in hand" ' (cf. ' "a child [Fanny] one had in a manner taken into one's own hands" ', 6); half a page later we find adumbrated another contrast which is to emerge when they all get to Sotherton, for Fanny 'was sitting on the other side of Edmund, exactly opposite Miss Crawford'; in the I.7 riding scene, 'to Fanny's timid nature it was most astonishing to see how well [Mary] sat' (67); coachman draws attention to the word in a rare active sense: ' "never see one sit a horse better" '; as if to point the moral ambiguity Maria says ' "good horsemanship has a great deal to do with the mind" ' (69); in I.8 Julia cries ' "I wish you had my seat" ', which a page before was described as 'The place of all places, the envied seat, the post of honour' (80), and so on.

As with Time, the advantage of a unifying interpretation is that it gives rich yields of ironic implication in notations otherwise attributable to no more than the copiousness of the novel genre in corroboration of character; because the projection is so substantially ours (p. 163, above), character is the 'local alibi' *par excellence.*

If we ask for example why Jane Austen has Mrs Norris, in the course of a long speech to Sir Thomas about going to Sotherton, tell how she got out of the carriage and walked up hill (' "I could not bear to sit at my ease" ', 189), an answer might relate to character, showy self-denial being typical of her. But the fact that it works in terms of the story—the 'irrelevance' is intended to distract him from her remissness over the theatricals; he 'gave up the point, foiled by her evasions'—may distract us from larger and profounder coherences: the only other occurrence in the novel of the rare word is figurative:

> '..I am aware, more aware than Crawford can be, that the man who means to make you love him (you having due notice of his intentions), must have very up-hill work, for there are all your early attachments, and habits, in battle array..'
>
> (III.4.347)

The irony which binds the text together in this coherence, then, is also complex, for the circumstance of which (with a synonym for 'conscious') Edmund boasts awareness, is nearer home than he knows: he himself does *not* have uphill work.[52]

Furthermore, as section 1's quotation was intended to hint, up*hill* sends us to up*stairs*: why, as 'They proceeded up stairs together', is the *trouble* taken to tell us Fanny's and Edmund's bedrooms are 'on the same floor above' (268, three pages later called 'the attic floor') unless to carry a suggestion? And why should Jane Austen bother to make Mrs Norris' economical rendezvous involve Nanny having ' "a bed at her cousin, the sadler's" ' (8)?

Fanny's room, we recall, is 'the little white attic'; in the reference to Croft's mistress, quoted in section 1 for its 'frankness', we may now notice a detail: he had brought her 'under his own roof' (41); Maria, in the newspaper tattle,

---

[52] Mrs Norris' explanation: ' "the poor horses . . . you know how I always feel for the horses" ', elsewhere ' "You should always remember the coachman and horses" ' (251); the dense I.7 riding-scene ends with: 'if she were forgotten the poor mare should be remembered'; 'Her feelings for one and the other' (68) drums it home.

'quitted her husband's roof' with Mr C. (440); and Fanny supposes Mary will have no motive for writing to her when she is 'no longer under the same roof with Edmund' (376).

In the light of all this, the resonance in Mrs Norris' resentment at Fanny's right to a horse ('no measures were taken for mounting her again', it is improper that she 'should have a regular lady's horse of her own in the style of her cousins', 35/6) or to a carriage (221)[53] is deepened; it then becomes equally significant that Edmund procures the one for her in vol.I, as that Sir Thomas orders the other for her in vol.II; and the short trip Edmund and she take to the parsonage which is to be her own final home adumbrates the long voyage home in vol.III.

To conclude this set of figurations, another detail linking the two journeys, a further literal/figurative cross-reference, a further step towards the child born of that rendezvous, and the nearest Fanny's genteel language gets to the coarseness of Lydia Bennet's muslin gown: if we do not read *Mansfield Park* as Fanny's novel, by the time Edmund, in II.5, admires her dress—she is ' "all in white" '—we may have forgotten his sisters' 'survey of . . . her frock' in I.2, holding her 'cheap on finding she had but two sashes', and 'the maid-servants sneered at her clothes' (14). From the carriage in III.15 bringing her not just to a home but to a husband, surely it is more than promise of the season's state of undress Fanny imagines or foresees, seeing that the trees,

> ..though not fully clothed, were in that delightful state, when farther beauty is known to be at hand, and when, while much is actually given to the sight, more yet remains for the imagination.   (446/7)[54]

The most important space at Mansfield Park for Fanny, those well acquainted with the novel may agree, is—even in sheer terms of plot or of character—the east room. And since its figurative significance, which is to concern us not merely in the present section, but through to the end of this chapter, will again be the occasion for drawing-together strands from the foregoing, maybe readers will not find too peremptory the request to turn up I.16, where that room is introduced; nor then consider it too oblique a form of critical short-hand if their attention is drawn to a paragraph (168) in the key final chapter of vol.I, last of the 'theatrical chapters', where Fanny's attempt to show herself '**mistress** of the room', to Mary, is hampered by a circumstance pre-

---

[53] A further association of ideas not without poignancy leads Mrs Norris from a carriage abandoned in II.2 to betrayal of what she would—naturally—have liked to happen: of forming 'the connection' with Rushworth ' "every body considers it as my doing" ', retailing Mrs Grant's remark that ' " 'if Mr. Rushworth were a son of your own he could not hold Sir Thomas in greater respect' " ' (190).

[54] Literal/figurative jam echoed elsewhere: Mary is glad to be seen with Edmund in society, as 'Luckily there is no distinction of dress now-a-days to tell tales' (416), yet learning he is to be a clergyman she apologises for earlier insolence by saying that had she known she ' "would have spoken of the cloth with more respect" ' (89).

sented in I.16: she 'looked at the bright bars of her **empty grate** with concern'; Mary replies ' "I am quite warm, very warm" '.

It is hard to know how readily (or how consciously) today's readers respond to the associations possessed by fire in the culture of *Mansfield Park*;[55] but even those sceptical of this study's interpretative approach can hardly avoid attributing a symbolic dimension to Fanny's east room fire when her uncle at last grants it to her.[56] We may believe him when he says to her ' "You cannot suppose me capable of trying to persuade you to marry against your **inclinations**" ' (330); nevertheless he has spoken to her 'with a good deal of cold sternness' (318), twitted her for supposedly regretting not feeling ' "what a young, heated fancy imagines to be necessary for happiness" ' (do.) and for refusing ' "a little more time for cool consideration" ' (319): when the fire is laid, is he not trying to heat her fancy?[57]

His accusations culminate in ' "But, Fanny, if your heart can acquit you of *ingratitude—*" ' (319), and the effect of this is: 'Her heart was almost broke by such a picture..'—to be thought 'ungrateful'; when he has gone down to Henry again, it is once more '..ungrateful! to have appeared so to him', and she imagines Edmund too thinking her '..ungrateful. She might have to endure the reproach again and again' (321); the result of her uncle engaging on his return for silence (thus she will be '**spared** from her aunt Norris's interminable reproaches!') is that he leaves her 'in a **glow** of gratitude' (322); when she finds the fire 'lighted and burning', 'to be giving her such an indulgence, was exciting even painful gratitude'; a few lines further ' "I must be a brute indeed, if I can be really ungrateful!" said she in soliloquy; "Heaven defend me from being ungrateful" '.

Altogether, the words gathered round a single idea occur no less than eight times in just over three pages. Such association of ideas could naturally be considered coincidental, did it not appear elsewhere in the text;[58] and did not interpretation of 'grateful' as including a 'full grate' likewise receive warrant from the presence in the text of other things that are filled or something-ful.

---

[55] It was still possible in 1942 to capitalise succinctly on these essentially binary associations: we are 'Consumed by either fire or fire', but equally we can be 'redeemed from fire by fire' (T.S.Eliot, 'Little Gidding', IV, *Collected Poems*, Faber and Faber 1963). One half of the charge is present in such notations as Mrs Norris' remark that lines which are ' "too warm" ' in *Lovers' Vows* ' "can be easily left out" ' (141), or in Edmund's act of 'pressing [Fanny's] hand to his lips, with almost as much warmth as if it had been Miss Crawford's' (269).

[56] As with the horse and the carriage, if we recall that in vol.I it is Mrs Norris who stipulates that Fanny must not have a fire, and that in vol.III Henry's proposal to Fanny is 'an injury' to Julia (332), we shall find telling the juxtaposition in vol.II: while her niece is 'practising her [dance] steps' before the ball, Mrs Norris is occupied with 'injuring the noble fire which the butler had prepared' (273).

[57] One way of preparing our return to the fire in a later section is to ask those familiar with the same books as Jane Austen: what are the 'book' associations of Sir Thomas' act?

[58] On at least three occasions: when Mrs Grant takes the part of Cottager's wife, Fanny finds Mary's 'kind exertions were to excite her gratitude, and whose merit in making them was spoken of with a glow of admiration' (159); during the east room rehearsal of Mary and Edmund '*She* could not equal them in their warmth. *Her* spirits sank under the glow of theirs', and when 'At last the scene was over . . . she was thanked and pitied' (170); later, Mary asks Fanny to imagine the ' "heart-burnings of dozens and dozens!" ' in town once her conquest of Henry is known; this last meeting between the two ends with Fanny again having to feel 'gratitude towards her' for not reproaching her more (365).

A brief illustration of the very various manifestations of this presence is the opportunity for a bridge to the next section—the theatre metaphor—as will be clear when we recall that the whole problem of the particular play chosen is contained in Edmund's reaction: ' "I should not have thought it the sort of play to be so easily **filled up**, with *us*" ' (139).

The improvements lexicon, turning on use/misuse of spaces, is constantly dovetailed with individuals' usefulness or otherwise.[59] Three examples: (a) the notation on the uselessness of most rooms at Sotherton leads directly to the chapel (where Mary imagines servants ' "with heads full" ' of something) once ' "in constant use" ', now empty most of the year (86-9); when the ordination theme, begun there, returns, Edmund asks ' "how the church is to be filled, if a man is neither to take orders with a living, nor without?" ' (109)—the church is metaphorical; (b) in a characteristic bridge to a register whose implications we shall explore later, Mary describes Maria's match as ' "a public blessing" ', since it will enable her to ' "fill her house, and give the best balls in the country" ' (210); (c) when the east room, since it had 'become useless, and for some time was quite deserted', becomes Fanny's, it is 'the use of what nobody else wanted' (151), which is the equivalent of her own consequence increasing 'now when nobody else was to be had' (208).

It is not just spaces that can be full or otherwise: at the key moment when Fanny joins the cross and the chain, 'those memorials of the two most beloved of her heart', we are told she 'felt how full of William and Edmund they were' (271). These notations send us back to an early chapter-ending when 'her heart was divided between the two' (22); but we also learn in II.10 that the cross and chain are 'dearest tokens so formed for each other by every thing real and imaginary'. We are not ready to ask exactly what this last clause means, but the literal division in the object is clearly intended to parallel a metaphorical division—or, in the terms this study handles, a metapsychological one.[60]

---

[59] Edmund's character ('bid most fairly for utility..' etc.) is early linked to 'He was to be a clergyman' (21); William's 'glory of heroism, of usefulness, of exertion, of endurance' is contrasted, near the centre of the novel, with Henry's selfish indulgence (236); Lady Bertram 'never thought of being useful' to anyone (219); 'how little useful'; Tom's life had been (428) is contrasted with what he eventually becomes—'what he ought to be, useful to his father' (462), and so on: notations forming a backdrop to the association of Fanny with usefulness: in I.4 she enjoys 'being avowedly useful as her aunt's companion' (35) to four hundred pp. later when she longs 'to be useful to those who were wanting her' (432), this almost obsessive association culminates in, and receives meaning from: 'She was returned to Mansfield Park, she was useful, she was beloved' (461).

[60] Further examples may be arranged, elliptically, in four categories: (a) Space as metaphor for mind: Lady Bertram likes having 'her ear amused and her whole comprehension filled' (179); Yates arrives 'with his head full of acting' (121); Julia's emotion being unnoticed is imputed to 'the fulness of their own minds . . . totally preoccupied' (163); Mary's 'mind was entirely self-engrossed' (358): the notation that Edmund, at the end, 'had not to wait and wish with vacant affections for an object worthy to succeed her in them' (470) is thus given particular eloquence. (b) Edmund in I.9 having said he may often ' "blunder on the borders of a repartee" ' we learn 'Each was thoughtful'; when Fanny confesses she is tired he says ' "how thoughtless I have been!" ' (94); in I.16 ' "my head has been full of this matter" ', then ' "empty your head of all this nonsense of acting" ' (156): before, we were told her possessions 'were all within her reach', now, regarding her cousins, 'She was beyond their reach'; (c) numerous divisions: 'Rushworth-feelings, and Crawford-feelings' (81); pain and pleasure; private and public (to be pursued in section 8); 'à la mortal, finely chequered' (274), etc.; (d) Sir Thomas going to solve problems in America, and the ones he should have tackled 'at home'.

And this is very far from being an isolated incidence—as, once more, three examples will show: (d) the work's original seating-arrangements are yet again seen when we learn that, sitting at the dinner-table with Henry (on the day he announces William's commission and proposes marriage), 'nothing could have tempted [Fanny] to turn her eyes to the right hand where he sat', then that she does not even join the conversation about William, 'for his commission came all from the right hand too, and there was pain in the connection' (304; cf. Edmund taking a girl on each arm at Sotherton, his gratification at 'feeling such a connection for the first time', 94); (e) Edmund's divided self, as he debates whether Mary will accept 'privacy and retirement': this question, 'though oftenest answered with a "Yes", had sometimes its "No" ' (255; cf. Fanny's answer to the leading question her uncle asks in II.1—whether her affections are engaged: 'her lips formed into a *no* . . . She would rather die than own the truth [sc. *yes*]', 316/7); (f) the Mansfield/Portsmouth contrast in Fanny's literal 'review of the two houses', compared to Dr Johnson's contrast between matrimony and celibacy' (392).

To conclude, a handful of representative incidences of a word recurrent in various contexts of this preoccupation, to take us to section 8.

When we read Fanny's vol.III reflections on Mary's friendship for herself being 'the most respectable **part** of her **character**', Mary's letter arrives, requesting confirmation of Tom's decline, supposing '**part** of the family . . . are aware of it', and that Fanny 'must be included in that **part**, that discerning **part**' (433; telling him of this later is 'adding to his knowledge of [Mary's] real character' 459), this recalls Edmund's vol.I conflict '**between his theatrical and his real part**' (163). To return to the first space-expressions quoted above—Fanny remembering 'dancing in that house before'—that notation is taken up again the day after the ball, when she thinks of 'the difference which twenty-four hours had made in that room, and all that **part** of the house' (283), which in turn recalls the 'unusual noise in the other **part** of the house' in vol.I (172) on the evening Sir Thomas returns.

Similar echoes are found between Fanny's learning on one page that she is 'one of [Edmund's] two dearest', and on the next, her locking up his interrupted note to her, 'with the chain, as the dearest **part** of the gift' (II.9.264/5); and most strikingly, between Edmund's lament for the Grants' relegation from the family evenings after that return, when he says to Fanny that he feels they ' "seem to be **part of ourselves**" ' (196), and, at the end of the novel, Sir Thomas' metapsychologically expressed relief at relegating Mrs Norris altogether from Mansfield: it is all the greater since he had felt her to be '**a part of himself**, that must be borne for ever' (465/6).

And so the word 'part' bring us to the theatricals, where, occurring ca. fifty times in the first two of the chapters I.13-18 alone, it bears a specific sense: 'each had . . . their part, their dress, their favourite scene'; this can be called 'an episode' with a proviso: its lexical dispositions, intimately related to what we have just seen, will take us another important step towards the metaphorical core of the novel.

On a bench at Sotherton (p. 99: some time before I.13, that is), Henry tells Maria ' "Your prospects . . . are too fair to justify want of spirits. You have a very smiling **scene** before you" ', and she asks whether he means this ' "literally or figuratively? Literally I conclude. Yes, certainly, the sun shines.." ', the complicity between the characters receives emphasis from the theatre metaphor here (cf. the picture metaphor in *P & P*). And long after I.18, textual guile plays on the literal situation of the bench: Edmund writes to Fanny ' "There is not a **shadow** of wavering. [Henry] thoroughly knows his own mind, and **acts** up to his resolutions" ' (423); meanwhile the possibility that if Henry's estate is not capable of improvement *he* may be, has been conveyed by the wry 'here' in 'It was pleasing to hear him speak so properly; **here**, he had been **acting** as he ought to do' (404).

Similarly, there is little surprise that the arch self-dramatiser of the novel— with her dialogues in which she casts herself the *beau rôle* (e.g. I.15.143; II.2.189), her 'affectionate preparatory speeches' (34) ready in the event of a fatal catastrophe, etc.—little surprise that, long before I.13, we hear of Mrs Norris' readiness to play Lady Bertram at Sotherton (desiring 'nothing better than a post of such honourable representation', 35). Indeed the very first occurrence of the key verb (accompanied by a telling preposition) marks out the hypocrite: in wishing for Fanny at the White House, Edmund says ' "My aunt is **acting like** a sensible woman" ' (26).

Since the cards are stacked against Henry and Mrs Norris from the start, such incidence of theatre terminology constitutes no further irony at their expense; what is ironical is again *seepage* onto characters in whom the thespian strain has gone unsuspected: Sir Thomas and, crucially, Fanny Price herself.

Sir Thomas first: (1) In the light of Maria's bird imagery (section 2), it is a fine irony that the notation about his readiness to free her from Rushworth is 'He would **act for her** and release her' (200), given that after the débâcle Edmund writes that his father 'is not overpowered . . . He is still able to think **and act**' (442).

(2) Mrs Norris' 'quotation' from *Lovers' Vows* (section 3, p. 160) is not an isolated instance: Sir Thomas is drawn into the theatricals—like Fanny, made to act, in spite of himself—by being associated with two lines from the play: a) We know that Edmund, having 'formed [Fanny's] mind and gained

her affections . . . had a good chance of her thinking like him' (*MP* 64); in the play, the Baron (Amelia's *father..*) has told her ' "..that he who forms my mind I should always consider as my greatest benefactor" ' (*LV*, pp. 503/4);
b) ' "Young as you are, . . .it is hardly possible that your affections—" ' (*Mansfield Park*, 316). In the play, Wildenhaim says ' "I would not thwart a first affection [of his daughter]. . . But that her affections are already bestowed, is not probable" ' (*LV*, pp. 499/500.) It seems (Introduction, p. xxii) we do need to have read Kotzebue..

(3) When Sir Thomas opens his study door, then, it is indeed only 'his *first* appearance on any stage' (my italics): 'Sir Thomas in **the house**!' (175), an entrance 'most **ill-timed**' is indeed a horrible irony for the actors: '**The house would close** with the greatest éclat' (183) echoes notations already illustrated: Maria's brief marital run starts when she 'will **open one of the best houses** in Wimpole Street'.

The upshot of this seepage onto the 'master of the house'[61] will be seen if we join the demonstration so far to the way Julia, who is '**a sufferer** too, though not quite so blamelessly' (160), innocent of even an entrance in the German play (though she has an 'exit' at Sotherton, 101), gets one of the best first-act curtain lines in the English novel: ' "My father is come—! He is in the hall at this moment." '

In other words the whole novel, under its title (the house), is a sort of massive pun. Certainly Fanny Price's pun, moreover, thus related to her massive projection. Two sorts of evidence must be martialled to make this clear.

First, Fanny is by no means excluded from theatre metaphor: indeed her relation to the theatricals is *fundamentally* ironic. Again, the words: chapter 2 opens 'The little girl **performed** her long journey in safety': the very first occurrence of the verb is hers (another ironic parallel between aunt and niece, incidentally.)

Then, a play is made of acts and scenes: the first (substantive) 'act' is the 'act of injustice' (I.3.23) to which Tom's spending drives his father—'different disposal' of the living meant for Edmund; the last, in vol./Act III is Fanny's 'act of kindness' to Susan (the knife) (another ironic parallel between uncle and niece.) The word 'scene' occurs (outside I.13-18) ca. eleven times in *Mansfield Park*: the first (65) shows Mary playing for Edmund;[62] the last refers to 'the scenes and people [Mrs Grant] had been used to' (469: a further ironic parallel, with Mrs Grant.)

Not only do *all* the novel's other instances of the word pertain to Fanny—which circumstance alone bears a strong ironic charge—but that irony is compounded by the fact that the first contrasts Mary's indifference to 'great

[61] Tom is described as being this temporarily (123), but his father on his return 'resumed his seat as master' (190), and this is again drummed home later: 'But he was master at Mansfield Park' (370).

[62] Given that the first 'play' is the Miss Bertrams' duet (14), the fact that Fanny does not play an instrument or speak French again gets in her way no more than not having dark eyes.

houses' with Fanny's capacity to 'warm her imagination with **scenes** of the past' (85), and the last contrasts Edmund's gloom with Fanny's delight on returning to 'the lovely **scenes** of home' (447). Between these two patterned instances we find '**scenes** of her infancy' (369); Fanny's fear on returning to the east room with Mary 'that she had a more distressing **scene** before her' (357) than any before; the 'happy **scene**' (281) she views on her way after the ball; her excitement at 'terrific **scenes**' at sea which William describes (235); and her pleasure in seeing Edmund's 'eyes soon turned like her's [sic] towards the **scene** without', preparatory to stargazing (113).

That scene contains further irony: quotations from *Lovers' Vows* having been noted, Fanny's rhapsody ' "on such a night as this" ' has special resonance for a novel in which no less than seven Shakespeare plays are alluded to (the first is *The Merchant of Venice*). For the moment we may call this a case of gross *textual* guile, judging Fanny herself technically innocent.

(Hard, too, to avoid seeing ironic resonance in the name 'Bertram' from *All's Well That Ends Well*,[63] since the situation there—the woman, Helen, empowered to choose her man [Bertram enjoying no power of refusal, incidentally]— is Amelia's in *Lovers' Vows*, and what is impossible for Fanny in *Mansfield Park*: things she cannot say [cf. p. 153, *supra*], a role she cannot play.[64])

Pending graver charges, *technical* innocence is also the most charitable description of what happens on (just as a sample, now) two other occasions: her uncle asks whether her affections are already bestowed, eyeing her fixedly:

> He saw her lips formed into a *no*, though the sound was inarticulate, but her face was like scarlet. That, however, in so modest a girl might be very compatible with innocence; and chusing at last to appear satisfied, he quickly added, 'No, no, I know *that* is quite out of the question—quite impossible.' (III.1.316)

The hedgings ('though', 'but', 'however', 'might appear') suggest he does not really want to hear; himself finally uttering the word 'No'—that the whole tale belies.

Our key verb reappears a few days after her interview with the uncle: she undergoes another, with the cousin, fears she has been 'saying too much, **overacting** the caution which she had been fancying necessary' (III.4.354); and when she tells him ' "In my **situation**, it would have been the extreme of vanity to be forming expectations on Mr. Crawford" ', and asks ' "How was

---

63 Edmund's remark: ' "we all talk Shakespeare" ' (III.3.338) is, we shall see, more than Jane Austen's theatrical wink, but there are other echoes of famous lines: Fanny is told ' "you do not quite know your own feelings" ' (316) cf. Polonius' 'I must tell you/You do not understand yourself so clearly' (*Hamlet* I.3; cf. also 'what a piece of work..' 58); *King Lear* seems to be glanced at in 'Poor Tom!' (427), in Edmund 'playing the fool' (350), in ' "Oh! Never, never, never; he never will succeed with me" . . . "Never, Fanny?" ' (347), in a nuncle (*passim*) and in the overall configuration of wicked-sisters-vs.-Cordelia (who cannot 'act', either); *The Tempest* in 'the book was closed, and the charm was broken' (337), etc.

64 The others solve the difficulties of restraint by lying under cover of 'rehearsal': by a fine irony, the application of more artifice (the play within the novel) frees Henry and Maria: they embrace, as it were, within quotation-marks, just as Mary uses them round 'Rears and Vices' as an alibi for her risqué pun.

I to have an attachment at his service, as soon as it was asked for?" ', we must find her at the very least disingenuous, since that is precisely her situation with regard to Edmund.

These cases of technical innocence in vols.I and III lend retrospective ironic colour to, and explain, what is at stake at the start of vol.II: though at first merely 'a quiet auditor' (136), Fanny is soon 'prompter' (165), has sewn Rushworth's cloak (166), and finally is drawn in to read a part—*almost*, for again we need to read Kotzbue to know that the moment of Julia's appearance with her curtain-line, 'Frederick was listening with looks of devotion to Agatha's narrative, and pressing her hand to his heart' (175, cf. ' "Don't look at me, dear Frederick" [Frederick . . . takes her hand, and puts it to his heart] ', *LV*, 487)—that is, just three pages before Cottager's Wife makes her first appearance. (A Chapman-type note on how the gentry behaved before the invention of latchkeys [cf. Gen. Tilney in *NA*, II.13.222] might lead us to say Fanny is here 'saved by the bell'—just as, in I.18, she is saved by the first knock on the east room door being Mary's, not Edmund's.)

Two sorts of evidence were mentioned above as needing to be martialled in support of reading the whole of Mansfield Park—the house, and its eponym the book—as a massive pun, centred on Fanny; we move now to the second.

There is more than one way of cutting up a cake: that the lexical dispositions of such large ingredients of a novel as characters, or such large features as a theme (improvements) or an episode (the theatricals) are metaphorical, suggests the possibility that even *tonal* dispositions may also be, and by that very fact perhaps bear an ironic relation to the theatricals.

Such is indeed the case: the moment has come to recall with what unconscious deftness the received account, harping on Edmund's objections to the theatricals—one constituent of the 'Problem'—has linked them to its final constituent: the so-called untypical and 'un-ironic' didactic tone, and its thematic warrant, ordination; both are parts of the ironic structure which is *Mansfield Park*.

1) 'In a *general* light, **private** theatricals are open to some objections';

2) '..injudicious, and more than injudicious . . . It would show great want of feeling on my father's account, absent as he is . . .It would be **taking liberties with my father's house in his absence** which could not be justified';

3) '..it would be imprudent, I think, with regard to Maria, whose **situation** is a very delicate one, considering every thing . . . I must now, my dear Maria, tell *you*, that I think it exceedingly unfit for private representation . . . it is your place to set them right, and shew them what true delicacy is' (140);

4) 'The innovation, if not wrong as an **innovation**, will be wrong as an expense.'

Such are, schematically, the ordinand's objections (I.13.125 f.), reference to which can now be made by number; pointing out all ironic resonances will be superfluous (e.g. regarding [3], we saw *space* connotations of 'Maria's situation' in section 7; the *time* before her marriage [ca. the novel's second fifth up to p. 203] corresponds to the time dominated by Fanny's equally 'delicate situation': suspense about Edmund until it is clear he 'must be for ever divided from Miss Crawford', 453); (4) will concern us last; some illustrations may now be made about (1) and (2).

(1) Tom assures Edmund ' "We want no audience, no publicity" ' but the latter knows inviting Maddox will be ' "the end of all the privacy and propriety" ' (153), and takes a part himself in order to restrain ' "the publicity of the business" ' (155); we subsequently learn that 'the privacy of the representation' has been abandoned, since Tom is 'giving an invitation to every family who came in his way' (164).

Objection (1) that Edmund makes *against the theatre*, then, 'rhymes' with his first objection *against Mary*: ' "I do not censure her *opinions*; but there certainly *is* impropriety in making them public" ' (63)[65]; her 'disinclination for privacy' (255) constitutes a serious obstacle to their future; and publicity is attainted elsewhere in the work: in vol.I Julia hopes Maria's flirtation will 'bring a public disturbance' (163); in vol.II breaking her engagement would be awkward because it has been 'long standing and public' (200), and the vol.III débâcle is deplorable because 'Everything was by that time public beyond a hope' (451), etc.

These all figure the work's central privacy: when Fanny goes to Mary in II. 8 'the privacy of such a discussion was a most important part of it to Fanny'; the requirement to act and allusion to 'the **dependence** of her situation' are specially horrible because of 'the shock of an attack . . . so **public**' (150); Mrs Norris gives Fanny's III.1 '**private** walk' first metaphorical then semantic extension Fanny does not like, she says,

> '..to be dictated to; she takes her own **independent** walk whenever she can; she certainly has a little spirit of **secrecy** . . . about her.'   (323)

(2) Any 'absence' (given ca. 60 instances in the novel) is clearly central: they are all about Fanny's recurring, painful thought; readers will now understand this to be Edmund's permanent future absence, poignantly formulated in vol. II: '*he* was gone . . . He would soon be always gone..' (284), prefigured in vol.I: 'Edmund was absent at this time, or the evil would have been earlier remedied' (36); and echoed in vol.III: 'She had no one to take her **part** . . . Her only friend was absent' (321). Her uncle says: ' "we must learn to do without him" '; it is a lesson Fanny, even after the age of seventeen, anticipates having to learn.

---

65 Edmund having formed Fanny's mind, etc., is enough to explain why her first reaction too, reading the play, is 'astonishment that it could be proposed and accepted in a private Theatre' (137); but the reader will not resent the reminder that in 'proposed and accepted' there is another marriage ambiguity; Henry's 'look of meaning' in Sotherton private *chapel* is a proposition: is he not accepted there?

With this section's illustration, then, we have taken a step closer to the core of the work's meaning according to this study's interpretation of Jane Austen's inquiry; for to go now to the second part of objection 2, despite 'her dread of taking a liberty with him' (436) Fanny has herself in fact been taking liberties with her father's house; moreover, to sum up the meaning of the other objections and relate them to no. 4, for Fanny there is no want of feeling, but it is private, involves no strangers, and its object is the opposite of new.

- 9 -

As we saw in Chapter II, Freud gave 'First Loves' fresh meaning; the biologist turned psychologist had by 1912 moved so far from a 'naturalistic' approach that he was able to say that, 'however strange it may sound' (and it does still sound strange), we must reckon

> ..with the possibility that something in the nature of the sexual instinct itself is unfavourable to the realization of complete satisfaction.   (7.258)

Nor was this bombshell tossed without covering fire; he goes on to explain: 'the final choice of the instinct is never any longer the original object, but only a surrogate for it', as a result of two factors: first, 'the diphasic onset of object choice' (i.e., a renewal at puberty of what had been left off during a period of latency); and second, 'the interposition of the barrier against incest'.

Incest (central to psychoanalysis: *vide* Chapter I, pp. 13/14) takes various forms;[66] most do not concern us, but if attention is now drawn to a tightly knit cluster of elements in *Mansfield Park* which, it will be clear, a psychoanalytic interpretation can hardly ignore—(A) first-cousin union to be avoided; (B) conjugal/ sibling relationships the subject of ambiguity; and (C) Fanny's guilt—these naturally nonetheless raise another objection,[67] answering which provides another occasion for articulating an interpretative principle with wide retroactive application.

So: if we say that in any radical inquiry *pro*-gress involves a sort of *re*-gress, and thus that contending Jane Austen and Freud to be in some sense 'on the same line' entails the probability of childhood figuring, sooner or later, in her representations, this might be thought to expose us to the artillery arrayed to combat Janeism in Chapter I. A retort to (A), above, might be to quote a socio-historical 'fact': e.g. that, at the time of the goings-on at Mansfield, first-cousin marriage was neither uncommon nor prohibited in England.

---

[66] All part of the same thing, for Freud: his Gordian-knot-cutting way with this, is: human beings must desire their close relatives, for there would be no point forbidding so categorically what no-one wanted to do (1.247; 13.126). Such desires are thought to be among early memories that succumb to repression; conscious memory requires the jolt of Troll's avowal that when asked as a child whom he would marry, 'it did not occur to me that I would marry any woman but my own mother' (G.Groddeck: *Book of the It*, Gallimard 1963, Letter 10).

[67] Readers for whom the very suggestion that sibling incest taboo figures in Jane Austen's work is preposterous, may recall a chapter end in *Emma*: the heroine tells Mr Knightley she will dance with him since ' "..you know we are not really so much brother and sister as to make it at all improper" ', and he replies: ' "Brother and sister! no, indeed" ' (III.2.331).

One way of dealing with this would be to say, as has been said of the 'History' plays of Shakespeare, 'it is not the historical facts that matter, but what he made of them.'[68] On this view, the warrant to pass so directly from 'England'—even 'Jane Austen's England'—to 'Mansfield' cannot be granted. Corresponding to the difference between finding something in this book (*Mansfield Park*) and in other books, there is another still more important difference, which may be unsatisfactorily put as the difference between finding something in a book and finding it in the world. First-cousin marriage was probably no less common at the time of George IV than was, let us say, blindness at the time of Pericles, yet in the play, *Oedipus Rex*, the blindness of the seer, Tiresias, has powerful dramatic effect.

But the very terms of the reply are unsatisfactory, we speak of 'historical facts', but might be embarrassed if required to say exactly what or where they are. We think (cf. Chapter I pt. 2, section 6) we can say a book is 'realistic', or 'true to' our world, but on what terms can that world enter our discussion? Like the passage from England to Mansfield, the question supposes too direct a relation; we need first to ask if we know the world well enough to recognise whether something written about it is true; can we get nearer to it than our descriptions? Maybe all we can ask is whether a representation coheres with others; it is at least arguable that *Mansfield Park* tells us nothing directly about the world, any more than any other human creation can—even Freudian psychology.[69] And indeed, the world has this in common with the unconscious: as soon as we begin to speak of it our language orders it; the very act of knowing, it has been said, is a linguistic feat.

Thus—to expand here Chapter III's excursus (p. 117, n. 50) on the cultural cousinhood of Jane Austen and Sigmund Freud—if we say these two are on the same line, or that it is her world that he is the implacable analyst, all we mean is that they treat of the same world of representations. The question whether their representations are 'true' depends on a clear decision on a quite different question: whether any representations are. And that question is one which philosophy—to its scandal, perhaps—has not answered in a way that satisfies all parties.[70]

That cluster of three interrelated things we cannot avoid taking account of is *in this novel*, in *Mansfield Park*: that is the world we are talking about.

To start with the first of the three, the bit of the incest problem we are concerned with is the view (13.182/3) that the mating instinct cannot manifest

---

[68] Andrew Cairncross, Introduction to Arden ed. of *2 Henry VI*, Routledge 1995, p. 1.

[69] The question as to the status of the psychoanalytic warrant, as promised in the Introduction, is not to be lost sight of: Trilling thought Freud's work constituted a 'theory of mind itself' (Jones [1964], p. 11), suggesting upshots for philosophy—which claims to be about mind, not minds, let alone the world. The question may be asked: is the psyche (or even the sex) of which Freud writes, in the world?

[70] Engagement with this question is obviously beyond the present book's scope; but the idealist position (no facts apart from what anyone makes of them; il n'y a pas de hors d'oeuvre..) is perhaps espoused rather *blithely* by people concerned with the arts; like all philosophical positions, it has its pitfalls.

itself in the case of 'brothers and sisters, or of boys and girls brought up to-gether from infancy', where

> ..all the sensory stimuli of vision, hearing and touch have been dulled by use, trained to the calm level of affection, and deprived of their potency to arouse the erethistic excitement which produces sexual tumescence.

Since Freud felt that psychoanalytic findings made even this position (Have-lock Ellis') untenable, it is all the more interesting to find the opposing stands aired in a discussion at the very outset of Jane Austen's *Mansfield Park* (I.1.6/7), with reference to the cousins, who are long past infancy. Among factors militating against taking on Fanny, Sir Thomas 'thought . . . of his two sons—of cousins in love, &c.'; Mrs Norris declares such a thing ' "morally impossible" ', then jumps back to pick up a proof by induction (' "I never knew an instance of it" '); but this does not prevent her prudential conclusion—' "It is, in fact, the only sure way of providing against the **con-nection**" '—the necessity of which rather undermines the sureness of her initial *a priori* stand. These (what might be called comprehensive-risk) manoeuvres conclude her argument that ' "*that* is the least likely to happen; brought up, as they would be, always together like brothers and sisters" ': an irony of exceptional splendour, since happen it *does*, although they *are*..

It should next be noticed that the Ellis position is from the male point of view ('erethistic' may be neutral, but 'tumescence' seems to decide it.) Whilst remaining wary of underestimating Jane Austen's sophistication in any area, the principle argued for just now—no world other than *Mansfield Park* con-cerns us: a version of James' principle, granting authors their subject (Chapter II, p. 78)—can at once be put to work on what we may for the moment call another aesthetic peculiarity, or at least particularity, of that world, so setting on a broader theoretical base 'disappointment' in Jane Aus-ten heroes which, we recall, is an outcome of responding mistakenly to the invitation of her art.

Granting her her subject, we unfussily acknowledge that the level of inter-est Jane Austen's women have in her men is far greater than their author's interest in them:[71] again, the extreme is naturally to be found in *Mansfield Park*: for Fanny, the 'general nature of women' means nothing less than 'to adopt the opinions of the man she loved and respected, as her own' (367).

Jane Austen's artistic interest in men grew: in the two first-published no-vels they are either (Ferrars, Bingley) ciphers, or else (Willoughby certainly, to some extent Darcy[72]) rooted in rather second-hand sexual myth; Edmund,

---

[71] If such things may be compared: one being sexual, the other artistic; on the cusp is our finding 'natural' that some characters remain undeveloped—the iconic shorthand of Gen. Tilney's son-in-law—but 'believing' less readily in marriage between characters the object of very unequal artistic investment.

[72] Almost all we are told about Darcy is mere assertion: e.g. 'Darcy was clever' (*P & P* 16)—hard to support by illustration, perhaps: he says nothing very clever, and his behaviour in Kent is distinctly unclever.   Unless we

on a rising scale between Darcy and Mr Knightley, is a little nearer the latter. For us, the most interesting part of his portrayal is that the delicacy of sexual charge in his feelings for Fanny is associated with its being forbidden: early and quite late there are hints of Sir Thomas' apprehensions on this score; two examples: in the East Room interview with Fanny , we find the following exchange:

> 'Edmund I consider from his disposition and habits as much more likely to marry early than his brother. *He*, indeed, I have lately thought has seen the woman he could love, which, I am convinced, my eldest son has not. Am I right? Do you agree with me, my dear?'
> 'Yes, Sir.'
> It was gently, but it was calmly said, and Sir Thomas was easy on the score of the cousins. (II.1.317)

And at the II.10 ball, Edmund and Fanny dance together 'with such sober tranquillity as might satisfy any looker-on, that Sir Thomas had been bringing up no wife for his younger son' (279).[73]

The concern in these latish hints is substantially the same as Edmund's at the other end of the book: e.g. 'Edmund's friendship never failed her . . .Without any display of doing more than the rest, or any fear of doing too much..' (I.2.21); and he 'at length determined on a method of proceeding which would obviate the risk of his father's thinking he had done too much..' (I.4.37).[74] To put his feeling for Fanny *wholly* down to a wish to disobey father might be a bit cavalier—though since disobliging the family of one of the two parties is the result of practically all marriages in Jane Austen, are we to discount such a motive in his case?[75]

---

suppose that part of him does not want to be accepted by Elizabeth? That interpretation would, it is true, be buttressed by the slightest of gestures towards psychological complexity made right at the end of the novel, amongst his explanations of why he returned to Longbourn: ' "My real purpose was to see *you*, and to judge, if I could, whether I might ever hope to make you love me. My avowed one, or what I avowed to myself, was to see whether your sister were still partial to Bingley" ' (382).

The only other claim on our attention possessed by the men who so absorb that of Jane Austen's women, is the interesting fact that Ferrars, Brandon and Darcy all speak of their childhood (respectively: *S & S* 366 and 205 f., and *P & P* 369), whereas none of the heroines before Fanny does.

[73] Interesting questions arise from the detail of these two passages: of the first: to which of her uncle's (according to my count *five*) assertions does Fanny reply 'Yes'? (if she answered 'No', he would hardly not ask her which she was answering); of the second, could not the reaction of the putative looker-on be read as imagined by one of the dancers looked at—or both?

[74] 'Edmund did such things for Fanny as would give him no cause to fear he was doing too much', is one reading of p. 21; but there is 'Without', so the fear goes, and with it any certainty that he is aware of calculation; in the p. 37 example, there is no clear way between the proceeding and the thought behind it. Occurrences of this very sophisticated narrative ploy in *NA* are, incidentally, among reasons for supposing that novel was longer off the 'Shelve' at the end of Jane Austen's life than has been thought.

[75] He waits for his father's return as an alibi for his own admiration: ' "Go to my father if you want to be complimented. He will satisfy you. Ask your uncle what he thinks, and you will hear compliments enough; and though they may be chiefly on your person, you must . . . trust to his seeing as much beauty of mind in time . . . Your uncle thinks you are very pretty, dear Fanny–. . . Anybody but myself would have made something more of it . . . your uncle never did admire you till now–and now he does. Your complexion is so improved!– and you have gained so much countenance!–and your figure–Nay, Fanny, do not turn away about it–it is but an uncle. If you cannot bear an uncle's admiration.." ' etc., etc. (II.3.197/8).

Interpreting text in inverted commas involves weighing psychological probabilities about the character whose utterance it is. But it is *in the narration*—here we move to element (B) in our cluster requiring comment—that we find the plethora of expressions which play on the key sibling/cousin ambiguity:

> 'Now I must look at you, Fanny', said Edmund, with the kind smile of an affectionate brother. (II.5.222)
>
> ..it was not till it was over that she knew he was giving her the affectionate farewell of a brother. (III.6.374)

The meaning of smiles or farewells being harder to tie down than that of quoted speech, the question of *who* attributes brotherliness to them can only be decided by case: is it, here, (a) Edmund reminding himself to be no more than brotherly? or (b) Fanny reminding herself to infer no more than brotherliness? or (c) both?

If we opt for reading (a), two details must be noted: the first is that the relationship suggested by the sibling-term is twice used on the occasion of a physical act which can contain more than what is named: when he arrives in Portsmouth, she 'found herself pressed to his heart' as he says ' "My Fanny—my only sister—my only **comfort** now" ' (444); cf. Lady Bertram, when Fanny returns: ' "Dear Fanny! now I shall be **comfort**able" ' (447); when Fanny left Mansfield 'She **clung** to her aunt' (374); cf. Edmund's penultimate public affective attitude to his cousin the end of III.16: 'Fanny's friendship was all he had to **cling** to' (460).

The second detail—supposing we opt for (a) still—is that the term in Edmund's mind ('brother') denotes a kinship which, apart from a small category of Pharaohs, has always excluded marriage; Fanny by contrast always calls her cousin 'cousin'.

But this is highly ironical, in view of a fact we now notice formally: the importance (emblematised as in *S & S* and *P & P* by its site at the physical centre of the book, p. 235 in a work of 470 pp.) given to comparison of conjugal and sibling ties: the occasion for William and Fanny to talk of early years is

> ..a strengthener of love, in which even the conjugal tie is beneath the fraternal. Children of the same family, the same blood, with the same first associations and habits, have some means of enjoyment in their power, which no subsequent connections can supply; and it must be by a long and **unnatural** estrangement, by a divorce which no subsequent connection can justify, if such precious remains of the earliest attachments are ever entirely outlived.

In Fanny Price's psychical economy, that is, the brother/sister relationship represents the ideal, the very touchstone for others: to such an extent that when eventually we hear 'her **warm and sisterly** regard for [Edmund] would be foundation enough for wedded love' (470), 'warm and sisterly' is at least arguably a hendiadys.

In other words—to trump the occasion in Chapter I where Jane Austen was imagined reading *The Psychopathology of Everyday Life*—Fanny Price might have helped Freud with a question he admitted he had not answered ('Was will das Weib?') by telling him that what he said about first loves and final choices, in the passage (7.258) quoted at the start of this section, was not after all so strange.

For some readers nothing more preposterous can be imagined than a dialogue between a novel character and the founder of psychoanalysis. One may feel uncertain of the extent of one's licence, but is it after all so fanciful? What is it but to recall Freud's tribute to writers as forerunners and allies, and make capital of the position that these two writers belong to the same world of representations? Indeed, one upshot of that position—the object to be interpreted might itself contribute an interpretation—was foreseen in the Introduction (p. xxix, n. 52).

What is proof, if not coherence with what we know? Freud's daughter, aged eight and a half, dreamt that her twelve-year-old boyfriend formed part of the family, called her parents father and mother, and slept in the big bedroom 'like the boys'; Freud comments that her affection could not picture 'any other forms of companionship than those which were represented in the dream and which were based on her relation to her brothers' (4.208). *Mansfield Park* 'supports' this point.

But that hendiadys in *Mansfield Park* seems to be making a further point.

Freud makes no link in his published writings between incest-shyness and secondary sexual differences; however, such a link is suggested by the anthropologist quoted in Chapter I, in discussion of 'conscious and unconscious motivations which people [the word should be noted] may have for not committing incest': 'They [*sc.* 'people', still] may say they do not do it because the crops will fail if they do, or God may strike them dead, or [and here Fox's terms take on a particular colour] that *they don't like their sisters anyway*'.[76] The assumption is that the brothers do the (in this case negative) choosing. If procreation depends on male desire, would it not be needlessly uneconomic for both sexes to be incest-shy?[77]

It may be objected that Jane Austen was writing a novel not a contribution to anthropological research. But such categories are crude: there are cases of writers producing books that are greater as books than as novels (*Finnegans Wake*, perhaps?), and cases where a writer cannot help producing a novel-like object, even while intending to produce something 'objective' (Stendhal's *De*

---

[76] Fox, op. cit, p. 61 (my italics).

[77] This speculation—for which, naturally, no extravagant claims are made—supposes that nature played a role in setting the stage for the incest-problem by selecting a strain of incest-shy hominids; as it happens this fits in with Fox's view that being non-incestuous is an essential ingredient of our becoming human.

l'Amour?): the view that all Jane Austen work is 'personal' needs to be tempered with the realization that she had a non-personal interest in psychical structures; and 'It is in this depersonalization that art may be said to approach the condition of science'.[78]

Finally, if a point is being made about 'the general nature of women', it might be an unpalatable one for some: perhaps this has contributed to the Problem; perhaps the novelist was using something like what Freud calls the 'familiarity of the material' (14.124) for ancient audiences at Greek tragedies, with this difference: that the material at issue concerns 'something which is *secretly* familiar' (cf. Chapter I, p. 43)—that is, 'something familiar that has been repressed' (14.370). And we shall in fact find further support for this in what follows.

- 10 -

We are moving towards consideration of a specific use of 'nature' in *Mansfield Park*. The word therefore provides a good case for arguing a certain priority of specific-contextual over general-period meaning. When we find 'Nature had given [the Price family] no inconsiderable share of beauty' juxtaposed with Fanny's wonder at the fact 'that where **nature** had made so little **difference**' between Mrs Price and her sister, '**circumstances** should have made so much' (408), it would be short-sighted to deny that something begun long before this novel was thought up, a classic debate in the history of ideas, is more or less consciously alluded to. However, a certain short-sightedness is indispensable for close analysis: the wood is made of wood, but it is, one may with equal truth say, made of trees; it is from Jane Austen Studies being too long-sighted that the trees have been overlooked.

And this study's whole bias of starting from the results end first (Introduction p. xxiii) highlights local resonances within that debate. Such an approach finds more interesting in the present case to point out that the p. 408 contrast was prepared on p. 407 by another, about Fanny's and Henry's palate: '*She* was nice only from **natural** delicacy, but *he* had been brought up in a school of luxury and epicurism'; more interesting because this notation, while undeniably full of Rousseau etc, makes us think both of the Hill St. 'school for matrimony' which led Mary's aunt to have ' "little cause to love the state" ', her own view of it as ' "a manoeuvring business" ' (46), and of a play mooted for Mansfield (131), not staged until Richmond: *The School for Scandal*; it also sends us to the school-*room* (scene of early pains 'Miss Lee wondered at her ignorance', 14), where Edmund and Mary rehearse: when 'the scene was over' Fanny knows their performance will have '**nature** and feeling in it' (170).

The view that a point is being made about the nature of women is likewise supported by the fact that the III.6 notation is the third incidence of an

---

[78] T.S.Eliot, 'Tradition and the Individual Talent', in *Selected Essays*, ed. cit., p. 17.

almost identical expression, and in three successive chapters: in III.4 (353) Fanny distinguishes herself from the parsonage sisters' view of Henry's proposal by saying that she and they think ' "..very differently of the nature of women, if they can imagine a woman so very soon capable of returning an affection as this seems to imply.." '; and in III.5 (363), speaking of ' "having it in one's power to pay off the debts of one's sex" ', Mary tells her ' "it is not in woman's nature to refuse such a triumph." '

The extremely important upshot of all this, is that the famous sentence about Edmund becoming anxious to marry Fanny 'at the time when it was quite **natural** that it should be so . . . what could be more **natural** than the change?' (470), far from being, as the received account complains, a patched-up solution for the needs of a happy ending, has been long prepared, and is coherently interwoven with preoccupations already illustrated, by notations and significant juxtapositions at key points through the work: to such an extent, indeed, that we conclude nature to be not the least dynamic of the economies *Mansfield Park* explores.

Furthermore, the characters themselves would concede this, as is shown by their constantly referring to a related economy: to section 2's reference—Fanny's 'wonderful **good fortune**', the first ironic parallel with Miss Maria Ward's '**good luck**' in the novel's opening sentence (and eventually another 'hour of **good luck** came', 425: she gets to write an exciting episode in the novel that her good luck launched)—we may now add that, for Fanny, Mary is 'the **fortunate** creature . . . **mistress of** [Edmund's] **fate**' (420), the '**child** of **good luck**' (430); conversely, ' "**Lucky, lucky** girl" ' says Mary of Fanny (292), who refers to her own '**good fortune**' (when the Crawford chain will not go through the Price cross) on the same page as thinking of 'William's **good fortune**' (270); Edmund tells Henry ' "You are a **lucky** fellow" ' (241), Rushworth will be 'duped with . . . **good luck**' (464), etc., etc.

Sir Thomas' talk of Edmund's ' "**natural claims**" ', which Tom's extravagance wounded, shows that nature is related to another economy, found in notations about claims and expectations.

Here too we can fill out section 2's hint: Fanny reflects in the east room on 'the **claims** of her cousins to being obliged' (153); Edmund three pp. later tells her Mary's behaviour on what she had called the ' "cross evening" ' gives her ' "a very strong **claim** on my good will" ' (cf. 271); Yates has 'never been with those who thought much of parental **claims**' (177); and it is Crawford's rôle in the novel to articulate the growing feeling that the others do not seem ' "aware of [Fanny's] **claims** to notice" ' (229), in fact his own (cf. 353): for him to see Fanny again is for Sir Thomas ' "a request too **natural**, a **claim** too just to be denied" ' (321); we recall that in Edmund's estimation Henry ' "has the first **claim** on me" ' (351); Mary tells Fanny the Admiral's forwarding William's promotion is remarkable, given that there are ' "so many young men's **claims** to be attended to" ' (364), etc., etc.[79]

In a most important bridge notation, Edmund regrets the exclusion of the Grants on his father's return, because they ' "have a **claim**. They seem to **belong to us**" ' (196), which returns us to Fanny at the start: Edmund tells her that in going to the White House ' "You will **belong to us** almost as much as ever" ' (26).

The unifying factor in the economies so far illustrated is that they are all *profane*: indeed Maria's marriage and Edmund's ordination on Sir Thomas' return puts Mary in mind ' "of some of the old heathen heroes, who after performing great exploits in a foreign land, offered sacrifices to the gods on their safe return." ' (108).

Another of Mary's jokes; but she does preface this one with a request to him not to be ' "affronted" ', and the Oxonian ordinand replies 'with a serious smile'. It is a joke of a sophisticated historicist colour which would pass unnoticed in a novel today, but in its way—not the same way as 'rears and vices'—it is *risqué*.

For, as the time has come to recall from section 2, this chapter has emphasised such profane economies in order to correct the biographist reading of *Mansfield Park*. What we must now explore is the dynamic *relation between* these older economies, nature/fortune etc., and the (antipodal) economy of the manifest content.

The central concept of this economy is first implicit in a word occurring no less than four times, in various forms, on the two pages of the novel (6/7) which introduce Mrs Norris' idea of receiving Fanny: Sir Thomas' reaction is that 'a girl so brought up must be adequately **provided** for'; she then speaks of ' "doing every thing one could by way of **providing for** a child.." '; and he reacts with remarks about ' "the **provision** of a gentlewoman" '.

We shall return to resonances of this provision shortly, now noting simply three points: (a) repetition of the same idea gives a very different slant to the notation (already quoted) which immediately follows: to bring the cousins up like brothers and sisters is ' "the only sure way of **providing against** the connection" '; (b) these notations are related to three stages we see Fanny pass through: child, girl, gentlewoman; and (c) Sir Thomas returns to this last term in the instant of conceiving the idea of the vol.II ball: trusting that when his nephew and he see Fanny dance, they will ' "both think she acquits herself like a gentlewoman" ' (250).

In other words, Sir Thomas *has* been bringing up a wife for his son, *has* been '**rearing** a prime comfort for himself' (472). For himself, perhaps; but from his niece's point of view—and so the book's as a whole, because it is her

---

[79] As for expectations: Mrs Norris fixes on the White House 'To prevent its being expected' that Fanny will live there (28); Mrs Grant thinks ' "we are all apt to expect too much" ' (46); Maddox playing Anhalt is for Mary ' " by no means what I expected" ' (149); Henry ends 'what might ere long have raised expectations' in Julia (161), at Sotherton the question comes up of what younger sons can expect (92), etc., etc.

story—it is for her. Mrs Grant may wish 'to get any change for her sister' (205), but for Fanny herself, the book seems to ask: why, in 'this world of changes', should there be any change?

- 11 -

Before the II.5 dinner Fanny *imagines* her uncle 'a great while considering and deciding, and with very grave looks, and those grave looks directed to her, and at last decide against her'; on another occasion, she *imagines* 'Some very grave reproof, or at least the coldest expression of indifference' (II.7.250): on each such occasion his reaction is quite different from what she imagines; equally important, such imaginings are not limited to confrontations with her uncle, but are more or less particularised: before her ball (267), she suffers 'fears . . . of doing wrong and being looked at'; later, knowing Edmund is aware of Henry's proposal, 'she felt dreadfully guilty' (335); and after their conversation about it, she fears 'she had been doing wrong' (354); even in 'indulging herself' by talking of Mansfield to Susan, 'She hoped it was not wrong' (419). A related symptom appears on numerous occasions: in the vol. I riding-sequence, though disliking what she sees, 'She could not turn her eyes from the meadow, she could not help watching all that passed' (67); at the vol.II ball, seeing Edmund and Mary close to each other, she is 'not able to refrain entirely from observing them' (279). Finally, as an example of her characteristically self-excoriating reflexive verbs, when she thinks of Henry being with Edmund and Mary, it is with 'feelings so near akin to envy, as made her hate herself for having them' (413).

No further illustration will be needed to see that we have now come to element (C) on our section 9 list: Fanny's guilt, which, given the varied symptoms just illustrated, we may call a guilt-*complex*,[80] and which Freud can help us understand.

First, he found the sense of guilt was the invariable factor 'that transforms sadism into masochism' (10.175): *Mansfield Park*'s central preoccupation, section 1 announced, is the structure of Fanny's pain; as we remember the text itself tells us, it is the pain of her *mind*, much beyond that in her head, which is at stake.[81]

Pain, moreover, in the mind of *a gentlewoman*: it is the condition of such women (cf. Chapter III, p. 120) which particularly interest Freud, for it is suppression of *their* aggressiveness, 'prescribed for them constitutionally and imposed upon them socially', which 'favours the development of powerful masochistic impulses' (2.149).

---

[80] With due deference to *L & P*'s reserves about its theoretical usefulness: their article on the term recognises that it serves 'the descriptive purpose of singling out certain "groups of strongly emotional thoughts and interets" ' (and their quotation is from Freud: *SE* XV.109).

[81] What is sometimes (e.g. 4.243) called mental, and sometimes (e.g. 13.37 n.) moral masochism, distinguished from other forms by the pain not needing (a) to be physical, or (b) to be inflicted by the 'loved' person: bluntly, 'The suffering itself is what matters' (11.420).

So we find in *Mansfield Park* extension or refinement of the self-destructive instinct: in *Sense and Sensibility* (Chapter II, p. 86) father-religion was merely glimpsed; a link is now made between 'the heightened sadism of the super-ego to which the ego submits', and 'the ego's own masochism' (11.424). And if the essence of aggression is self aggression (*L & P* 20), the reason for the excessive reprobation in this novel should now be clear: it is because there is excessive *self*-reprobration.

We read Elizabeth Bennet's story in terms of Cinderella; Fanny Price's can be illuminated by another kind of old stories: *archaic* stories, or 'Family Romances' that children tell themselves:[82] for example, the feeling of being unloved by parents finds a vent in the idea

> ..often consciously recollected later from early childhood, of being a step-child or an adopted child . . . In this way, for instance, the young phan-tasy-builder can get rid of his forbidden degree of kinship with one of his sisters if he finds himself sexually attracted by her.   (7.222 and 224)

We need only reverse masculine/feminine pronouns here to get the situation in *Mansfield Park*, at the end of which Fanny is accepted as her uncle's daughter, yet without having to give up his son. To read on in the Freud:

> ..the child's imagination becomes engaged in the task of getting free from the parents of whom he now has a low opinion, and of replacing them by others, who as a rule are of higher social standing. He will make use in this connection of any opportune coincidences from his actual experience, such as his becoming acquainted with the Lord of the Manor or some landed proprietor if he lives in the country.

Such Romances 'correct' reality, then; dramatising ambivalent feelings towards parents/siblings, and fuelled from the unconscious, they also bear the mark of any unconscious formation, that of being a compromise: reflecting 'the desire to denigrate the parents from one angle while exalting them from another' (*L & P* 160).

For seasoned Jane Austen readers—those at least who acknowledge that she treats family relationships with *systematic* equivocation[83]—this should ring as many bells as the section 9 economies. In *Mansfield Park* we are told Mrs Price's disposition is '**naturally** easy and indolent, like Lady Bertram's'; she 'might have made just as good a woman of **consequence** as Lady Bertram, but Mrs Norris would have been a more respectable mother of nine children' (390). Such notations may be illuminated by a piece of psychoanaly-sis which has enjoyed some popularity: the so-called Kleinian theory of the

---

82 Moreover, old and archaic are linked: 'These consciously remembered mental impulses of childhood embody the factor which enables us to understand the nature of myths' (7.222).

83 From Marianne Dashwood, who we recall feels she knows Willoughby better than her half-brother, to Anne Elliot, who feels more at home with the Crofts than with her own father and sister.

'good and bad object'.[84] If Mrs Norris is a part of Sir Thomas, the fact that he cannot get away from her may be read as a figure for Fanny's experience.

This should also answer a possible objection to the effect that Fanny's guilt-complex is amply—'naturally'—warranted by the way in which she is represented as having been treated as a child. Extent of warrants, whether in humour or in larger questions of interpretation, has been a live issue in this study, and they need not be less required at this stage of it. A remarkable and persuasive detail, then, is that this stern-uncle/bad-aunt figure is *associated with* the supervalent character of Fanny's emotion: when, following the parsonage dinner invitation, her uncle in fact simply asks her if 4.20 will do for the carriage, ' "Yes, sir," was Fanny's humble answer, given with the feelings almost of a criminal towards Mrs. Norris' (221): in other words, cheated of all those 'grave looks', etc., from the uncle, she transfers her expectation of reproach to the aunt: the other element of her super-ego.[85]

Uncle/aunt being a concentration of Fanny's introjection is further testimony to Jane Austen's proto-analytic prescience. They are a 'naturalised' representation of a central Freudian discovery: the self-reproving agent is *essentially* supervalent; the super-ego displays 'a severity for which no model has been provided by the real parents' (15.441). Sir Thomas and Mrs Norris are not Fanny's real parents (he stands, we recall, 'in the place of her parents'); the real ones turn out to be harmless ciphers. A further subtlety is that something in her feeling for her 'natural' parents—in particular what arose from the 'so natural and motherly a joy' of Mrs Price's letter, and Fanny's feeling that if she had 'alienated Love', it must again have been 'her own **fault**' because she had wanted 'a larger share than any one among so many could **deserve**' (371)—turns out to have been illusive. For Mrs Price, 'The instinct of **nature** was soon satisfied' (389): in other words, kinship is not glorified *per se*; the real is, as it were, weighed up against the natural. This is clinched by the wry reappearance of a key verb when Fanny copes efficiently with Henry's sudden arrival in Portsmouth: 'Good sense, like hers, will always **act** when really called upon' (399): in her natural father's house, it seems, she *can*..

Section 1's term for this work's fundamental character—extreme—is in psychoanalytic terms the *supervalent*, then; indeed, as Edmund tells her on another occasion, ' "My dear Fanny, you feel these things a great deal too much" ' (262); a little later we learn she could not even think of her aunt Norris 'without reproaching herself for some little want of attention to her'—it was 'Fanny's disposition' (282).

---

84 Child's relation to the breast, metonym for the whole person; it can be traced back through Karl Abraham to Freud's hunch (Chapter III, p. 106 n. 25) about satisfying/hostile object being the same for the early feeder.

85 In 'Psychoanalysis and Legal Evidence', Freud compares criminal and hysteric: in both, he says, 'we are concerned . . . with something hidden . . . In the case of the criminal it is a secret which he knows and hides from you, whereas in the case of the hysteric it is a secret which he himself does not know either, which is hidden even from himself' (*SE* IX.108).

And thus we come to the nub of the help Freud affords to grasp Fanny's guilt-complex: the reason why self-reproaches are proof against 'rational' contradiction, is that they must be partly justified (13.116).

For guilt is invariably associated with repression—and specifically (another example of things sexual laying down a pattern for the rest) *one* repression: there is no doubt, declares Freud

> ..that it is connected with . . . incestuous wishes, and that it is justified by the persistence of those wishes in the unconscious.   (10.174)

Cinderella's story is about 'agonies and hopes which form the essential content of sibling rivalry': that is still the world of Elizabeth and sisters; but the reason why the tale 'replaces sibling relations with relations between step-siblings' may be that this is 'a device to explain and make acceptable an *animosity* which one wishes would not exist among true siblings':[86] my italics, for reversing not now the pronouns but the charge of the terms, we get the Mansfield drama: it is the *opposite* of animosity that Sir Thomas begins by hoping will not develop between the cousins.

So: on this reading, Fanny feels guilty towards Sir Thomas because she is in love with his son, and cannot say so.

But: does this do justice to *all* the facts? Is there, in her loving her cousin, material, as it were, for *enough* guilt? How is it that, even before meeting him, already on arrival at Mansfield, 'her **consciousness** of misery was . . . increased by the idea of its being a wicked thing for her not to be happy' (13)?

The section 9 list forms a *cluster* of elements: they cannot be considered in isolation from each other. Discussions so far have tacitly supposed that Fanny's guilt-complex—element (C)—draws its energy from element (A)—first-cousin union something to be avoided; but an equally weighty constituent is element (B): ambiguity in the terms used to describe sibling/conjugal ties.

Mansfield Park may be the first work in European literature to give such prominence to retracing a girl's experience from childhood to marriage; but all Jane Austen's novels ask—in various ways, more or less implicitly—questions about the relation between the original family and the new family generated by marriage.[87]

Another upshot of treating text as mimetic of mind will be to see text itself as supervalent. And the extreme/supervalent version of that question must be: if nature provides beauty, delicacy of taste, mind, feeling, etc., why not a partner? In other words, if cousins brought up together as brothers and sisters can feel the mating instinct, why not brothers and sisters themselves?

Why *any* change?

---

[86] Bettelheim, op. cit., p. 236.

[87] A version of it—why marriage entails leaving the original family—takes the form of Mr Elliot's explicit proposal to Anne Elliot that her name ' "might never change" ' (*P* II.8.188).

As preceding hints should have prepared the reader, this text does in fact glimpse that perspective; to 'see' it involves giving (what for some will be extreme) weight to the testimony of latent content, against manifest:

Section 6 could not quote all the 'firsts' in this novel; among those not illustrated the text describes Edmund (at the end of the book) as Fanny's 'first inclination'. But this is not strictly accurate: soon after arriving at Mansfield, having been comforted on the stairs by Edmund, we learn 'she loved him better than any body in the world *except William*' (my italics, naturally); the centre-point testimony supports this—conjugal tie beneath fraternal, etc.— and *the text*'s dive on the same page into Henry's thought about how he will 'excite the **first** ardours' of such a girl, is splendidly ambiguous, given that it is her avid listening *to William* that suggests this thought; as Henry himself thinks: 'Her affections were evidently strong. *To see her with her brother!*' (294, my italics).

It may be objected that we can read all this with the aid of the metaphor already given, under the light of Mary's comment ' "All are supplanted sooner or later" ': viz., as Fanny supplants Mary so Edmund supplants William;[88] or as Mrs Grant says, ' "if one scheme of happiness fails, **human nature** turns to another; if the **first** calculation is wrong, we make a **second** better; we find **comfort** somewhere" ' (46); whilst the 'unnatural estrangement' of the centre-point refers to Fanny and William, when the Henry drama is running, we learn of *Edmund's* point of view: 'Fanny estranged from him . . . was an unnatural state of things' (345).

But if William is supplanted, what are we to make of—as late as far into vol.III—the allusion to 'the little cottage . . . in which he and Fanny were to pass all their middle and latter life together' (III.7.375)?

In assessing what we are to make of it—meaning, what weight we give it— the following considerations, using the principle of putting a great deal into a small part, may be borne in mind:

First, that cottage is yet another of what may be called Fanny's virtual houses; second, the notation is also yet another ironic theatre-echo: the part almost played in *Lovers' Vows* is 'Cottager's Wife'. (Why does Jane Austen cast her in that part, if not to suggest that, just as the other actors find their rôles enabling—Henry and Maria to embrace; Rushworth to wear finery; Yates to rant; Mary to declare herself—Fanny is not excluded from the truth

---

88 One is certainly a sort of prototype for the other: William is 2nd lieutenant, Edmund a second son (' "well off for a cadet of even a Baronet's family" ' 226); at the centre-point William is 'opening all his heart to her', cf. Edmund telling Fanny all at a time when 'the heart must be opened' (453); William is 'in the king's service' long before Edmund had 'gone through the service' (340); the ostinato reference to Edmund's orders (89) are later echoed by William's (377, 378, 380, 388); in section 8 'absence' was said to be about Edmund's absence, but again William's has a kind of priority: 'she could not mention the number of years that he had been absent without tears in her eyes' (60, cf. 'so long absent and dearly loved brother' 232; similarly if Fanny's dancing possesses a sexual charge, William danced with her (250) long before Edmund (hence the interest of the figure for guilt, *supra*, p. 159, since William's question about her dancing is the new topic made necessary by realising Sir Thomas is near in II.7), etc. It may be added that the idea of adult relationships as inseparable from, or derived from, childhood ones, though perhaps banal nowadays, is itself for its period striking.

of the rôle? Are we not specifically told—and why else should we need to be?—' "she can say every word of it . . . for she could put Mrs. Grant right the other day in twenty places. Fanny, I am sure you know the part.." ' 172); third, advantage may also be taken of preceding demonstrations: section 6's general one that place-context always bears metaphorical significance, and section 5's specific one about carriages: tendentiously, we may say Fanny goes to Portsmouth with William but returns with Edmund; fourth and fifth, the linguistic detail of the notation: those who know the novel need reminding that the verb *were to* pass' is ambiguous for the first-time reader; then, the project (which the formulas invite us to suppose conceived before and re-evoked during the siblings' journey) is carefully unattributed to either character: no objection to the project is 'heard' from Fanny, leaving it open as to how far tacit consent depends upon the permanent ruin of her hopes for Edmund.

The narratological fullness of Fanny's silence is here at its height: all she cannot say, which the rest of the text obliges us to construct.

And the final upshot of text as in various and subtle ways mimetic of mind, will be that we may not go so far even as the 'technical innocence' grudgingly accorded Fanny (*supra*, p. 183). And after all, though in one sense as Henry says she ' "cannot speak or write a falsehood" ' (411), we recall that she herself is represented as thinking (in a characteristically exaggerated expression) 'She would rather die than tell the truth'. So the *most* charitable interpretation of what follows—a sample of half a dozen 'textual lies'—must be, as is said in *Emma* (II.2.166) 'there might be some truths not told..':

Fanny reacts without 'raptures' to the Portsmouth plan because, the text tells us, 'though never a great talker, she was always more inclined to silence when feeling most strongly' (369: n.b. *always*); how can this be squared with the bursts of eloquence we have had occasion to comment on: her rhapsodies on the stars (I.11), on the evergreen (II.4) on Edmund's chain (II.9), etc.?

When she is at Portsmouth, Mansfield Park is evoked as a place where 'every body had their due importance; every body's feelings were consulted' (392: n.b. *every*body); how can this be squared with the remark at the ball that she was 'totally unused to having her pleasure consulted' (280)?

The text tells us Fanny is pleased that Henry is present at the dinner in II.5 because 'every addition to the party must rather forward her favourite indulgence of being suffered to sit silent and unattended to' (223); how can this be squared with her reaction at the time of the play: contrasting herself with Mrs Grant, among others, as being 'sought for, and attended', whilst she herself is not ('*any thing*', the text underlines, 'would have been preferable to this', 160, my italics)?

She tells Edmund ' "I ought to believe you to be right rather than myself" ' (27); yet when Henry says her judgment is his rule of right, she replies ' "We have all a better guide in ourselves, if we would attend to it.." '—with again the specific addition '..than *any* other person can be" ' (412, my italics).

At the ball, we are told she 'so little understood her own claims' that it is a surprise to her when a page later she is summoned to open it (274/5); how is it then that she so understands them at the parsonage dinner where 'she must submit, as her own propriety of mind directed, in spite of her aunt Norris's opinion, to being the principal lady in company', etc. (223)?

Sixth and lastly, this dinner, now: in vol.I Mary mentions that Fanny ' "dined at the parsonage, with the rest of you, which seemed like being *out*" ' (48), yet when in vol. II Mrs Grant asks her to dine the text tells us 'This was so **new** an attention, so **perfectly new** a circumstance in the events of Fanny's life, that she was all surprise and embarrassment' (215). There seems to be a 'mistake', here.

But whose? The snag in supposing it the novelist's, is that she so very rarely commits what in film are called 'continuity' errors (any good Janeite will tell you the story of brother Edward asking her where she got those fruit-trees that blossom in midsummer, *E* III.6).

Readers reluctant to attribute her less sophistication than their own will on the contrary see here a greatly original narrative exploit. First, details in the notation alert us to links between this episode and key presences elsewhere: 'new' we have just seen; Lady Bertram tells her husband she has ' "something to tell you that will surprise you" '; when he has heard he says ' "The only surprise I can feel is that this should be the *first* time of its being paid" ' (218/9; n.b. the emphasis is Sir Thomas': other commentators have observed that Jane Austen was not above a little joke about her own mechanics, but I do not recall seeing it observed that she is capable of letting a character in on the joke.[89])

Then, not only is not-noticing-things a key theme in this text, but again we find an alibi for this incident elsewhere: Henry offers in II.7 to answer any inquiry William makes about Fanny's dancing; the narration next tells us that actually he 'could not for the life of him recall what her dancing had been, and rather took it for granted that she had been present than remembered any thing about her' (251).

So: are we meant to conclude Fanny did *not* dine at the parsonage before, and that it is *Mary*'s mistake? To apply in a thoroughgoing way interpretation of the whole work, including Mary, as a projection of Fanny's mind, could then lead us to imagine the text saying: 'I don't know which part of me is lying to the other'.[90]

---

[89] The idea that she here chuckles *with* Sir Thomas is supported by that character's jokes, both at Mrs Norris' expense: (1) on the occasion of this dinner he says to his wife her sister ' "perhaps may be prevailed on to spend the day with us" '; (2) Fanny's disfiguring tears lead him to tell Mrs Norris he ' "recommended the shrubbery as the dryest place" ' (323). Sir Thomas' rôle in histories of English prose style has also been overlooked: at the start of II.7, two sentences filling almost a page, of 104 and 106 words, evoke his thinking about Fanny and Henry; there is a longer sentence in *E* II.4.181/2 (170 words) but in Sir Thomas' meditations the foretaste of *The Golden Bowl* is almost palpable.

[90] As Robespierre does in Büchner's *Danton's Death* (Mermaid Drama 1963, p. 23).

Some readers might now feel this discussion needs some such corrective as the remark Hitchcock is said to have used in order to calm actresses who got hysterically frightened on the set by scenes in which they were acting: 'It's only a film'—after all, 'Mansfield Park never existed': in a sense the whole thing is a sort of lie.

That would be all very well, were it not that the 'textual lies' just illustrated (just a sample, it may be underlined, as in section 4's cases of technical innocence; additional cases should occur to readers when they next take up the novel) collectively making a disquieting impression, are commensurate with the uneasy relation between truth and not-truth elsewhere in the text, which is perhaps 'about' dishonesty in a further sense, then: in the sense that certain works of literature are partly about their own seductive mendacity; having mentioned (n. 89) the James novel in which the golden bowl is a figure for being taken in by what is flawed; this dinner-invitation may likewise be a *mise en abîme*.[91]

Some readers' thoughts may here turn to *Emma*: despite obvious differences (most important, the textual lie there seems more purely comic) we may reflect that because of the nature of the genre, although the dominant image in that work is blindness, we say that if we could have 'heard' Miss Bates properly at a first reading of the novel, there would be no mystery. It is therefore significant that at the only place in *Mansfield Park* when the text as it were *tells* us it has been lying, the occasion is given by something 'not heard': when at I.7.73 Edmund hears about the rose-cutting, he makes a series of indignant exclamations, and the text tells us 'Mrs. Norris was talking to Julia, and **did not hear**'; but her nephew does not let up on his remonstrances, whereupon we get this: ' "I am sure I do not know how it was to have been done better," cried Mrs. Norris, **unable to be longer deaf**..'

Similarly, when Edmund leaves Fanny after giving her the chain in II.9, her internal reaction to what he tells her is that 'it was a **stab**', although it had told her no more than what she knew, for it told of

> ..his own convictions and views. They were decided. He would marry Miss Crawford. It was a **stab**, in spite of every **long-standing expectation**.

But there is an exquisitely subtle ironic disjunction between this and the insistence which the text places on Fanny's 'modest claims', etc. (*vide* section 2). The upshot is that when she receives a letter from Mary, and the text represents her thinking Mary 'might love, but she did not deserve Edmund by any other sentiment' (367), we cannot but infer that she thinks she herself *does* (by virtue of what, we shall shortly see, along with a return to the remarkable 'stab').

---

91 Extension to a literary work of occurrence, somewhere in a painting, of its 'point': e.g. a tiny mirror in works by Metsys or Memling (cf. André Gide, *Oeuvres* for 1893, Pléiade ed., p. 41); in English, heart-point (more technically fess[e]-point), the central point in a shield .

Finally, Mary recounts in another letter the impact Edmund has made on her London friends: all were ' "much struck with his gentleman-like appearance" ', then more specifically a ' "Mrs. Fraser (no bad judge)" ', who had declared ' "..she knows but three men in town who have so good a person, height and air" ' (416). The exclamation Fanny makes to herself on this is: 'The woman who could speak of him, and speak only of his appearance!—What an unworthy attachment!'

But: if the reader accepts the upshot of section 7 (a strong sexual charge in her own view of Edmund[92]) this exclamation must certainly be called—with a handy expression that takes us to section 12—'holier than thou'.

- 12 -

It may be said that the argument of section 11 goes too far; in this final section of the chapter we shall see how far too far, in a specific area, *Mansfield Park* goes.

Unsurprisingly, it is again in a specific area of language that it goes too far; but what will now be illustrated starts in a sense elsewhere in the writer's processes than in her diction: if not actually in the ink that structuralism terrorises us into admitting literature is made of, then at the point where recourse to a symbolic system, such as an alphabet, acquires meaning: the moment when the hand, holding a feather dipped in that ink, decides on the size of the first letter of a word.

The words quoted in section 10 about Fanny's provision, her being provided for, etc., all appear, that is, in 'lower case'; but behind them all is the 'upper case'.

This becomes clear from the terms used in the judgments at the end of the book: the text contrasts 'the penalty' of 'this world'—'punishment, the public punishment of disgrace'—with what it refrains from 'presuming to look forward to': 'a juster appointment hereafter'; speaks of the 'no small portion of vexation and regret' that Crawford was indeed 'providing for himself' (468), and so on. The Christian scheme of Providence resonant here ('disgrace' is almost a technical term) has often been supposed extraneous authorial tub-thumping; it was the 'moral indignation' in *this* novel, we recall (Introduction, p. xx), which furnished the paradigm for the view that something must come from 'outside' the box.

But to continue the figure: behind *other* lower-case notations hitherto quoted—the light and the dark, penance, spare etc.—the upper case is lurking. Hence the section 1 allusion to 'serious' word-play as the nub of Jane Aus-

---

[92] Even in manifest content he is early presented as one of 'the sons very well-looking . . . well-grown and forward of their age' (13); if we recall the passage quoted in section 1 which describes 'The grandeur of the house' (14), we can also add to the overall testimony of the text's figuration a detail confirming the house symbolism (and recalling a figure with which *P & P* makes great play): two pages before, Fanny first impression is that the Bertram sons 'had all the grandeur of men in the eyes of their little cousin'.

ten's art; hence hints in the form of questions made in succeeding sections, now to be filled out.

Word-play, or—its equivalent in the perceptualist simulacrum—revived metaphor. For the moment, one example of each: when Lady Bertram's lymphatic resignation is contrasted with Fanny, who 'thought of the morrow', some readers may almost be *unable not* to think of 'Take no thought . . . for the morrow' (Matthew, 6.34). Likewise, Fanny being granted a fire in the East Room is an act which, for some readers, *cannot but* conjure up a particular figure (for drawing attention to what you have already done for someone by doing still more): 'heap coals of fire upon his head and the Lord shall reward thee' (Proverbs, 25.21/2).

So the source for these notations is the Authorized Version of the Bible. But the word 'source' does not do justice to what is at issue: the English A.V. is as much not outside Jane Austen's language *forms* as Freud's preoccupations are not outside the *content* which she makes those language forms carry.

The reader who has come as far as this in the book will not resent being reminded that just as dimensions of perceptualist suggestiveness (e.g. Chapter II, p. 83, n. 55) can be lost with the passage of time, so in our present area of concern, 1814 readers undeniably caught more meaning (conscious or unconscious): familiarity with the A.V. being now in large part lost, allusions must be spelt out, and—like an explained joke—the allusiveness must seem forced, over-conscious.

To ease the reader into that over-consciousness, three more examples. If Tom dies he will be 'cut off in the flower of his days' (434): somewhere behind this there is Psalm 103 ('for man, his days are as grass: as a flower of the field'); Edmund's question about Mary—' "where . . . shall we find a woman whom **nature** had so richly endowed?" ' (455)—recalls the question: 'Who can find a virtuous woman..?' (Proverbs, 31);[93] and Mrs Norris saying she is ' "the **last** person in the world to withhold my mite" '(6) is an (ironical) echo of 'the widow's mite' (Mark, 12)

Now: if the reader adopts in a thoroughgoing way the view of text as mimetic of Fanny's mind, such echoes can be read again as a consequence of Edmund having formed that mind: in other words, in the credible simulacrum, that circumstance plausibly contributes to this scriptural presence—in which, moreover, Edmund and his profession are constantly involved.[94]

---

93 Unless the reader has concluded this study to be evidence of an advanced case of psychosis (not impossible, literary criticism being as is well known the only civilized form of autobiography), given that the text continues 'for her price is far above rubies', one might conclude 'Rushworth' to be an alibi for the misprized 'Miss Price': was the apricot after all ' "so little worth the trouble of gathering" '? Is it ' "so valuable a fruit" ' (54)? Has not Fanny 'every recommendation of growing worth' (470)? Does not even Henry 'place a yet higher value of the sweetness of her temper' (468) etc.?

94 Another form of text's density evoking Fanny's psyche: lexical overlap between ordination and Edmund's objections to the theatre (reference to these is made by number):

(1) Sotherton chapel is ' "only for the **private** use of the family" ' (86); on the next page we hear of ' "the *private* **devotions** of such persons" '; and later Henry speaks to Fanny of someone ' "who sees and **worships** your merit . . . who loves you most **devotedly**" ' (344).

But this text—*Mansfield Park*—is a context, a particular organization of a particular selection; so the present reading can take further advantage from section 5's argument on context-dependence: not so much that there are 'too many' biblical resonances here (for the period), but that since it is coherent with what we know of Fanny—all the expressions connote preoccupations relating to her which we have seen elsewhere[95]—the coincidence is 'too great' between this linguistic feature and what the religiosity *carries*.

For that is all it does—as will be obvious if we now give a particularly dramatic example: when Edmund, warning Maria to desist from acting, hopes ' "It will not be necessary to send you to your *father's* judgment" ' (140), in the last three words an entire cultural system is implied: this becomes clear when, fifty pp. later, a gauge of the seriousness of the *end* of the play is found (join-ed incidentally to another instance of 'wipe') in a revived metaphor from this register—for Sir Thomas hopes to

..wipe away every outward memento of what had been, even to the destruction of every unbound copy of 'Lovers' Vows' . . . for he was burning all that met his eye..

*

To accept a view without accepting its consequences is philosophically 'soft': what has been illustrated has a 'hard' confirmatory converse, recourse to this biblical register being coherent with implications of section 9: Freud (F/F 252) specifically *linked* horror of incest, 'progressive renunciation' of animals' sexual liberty which human civilization involves, with the idea of the holy, and its invariable concomitant, sacrifice..

With that word in mind, Family Romances again become germane: a younger child is 'specially inclined to use imaginative stories . . . to rob those born before him of their prerogatives', and in a variant 'the hero and author

---

(2) Sir Thomas' absence, when the theatricals (almost) take place, corresponds to the absence of the priest, in the ordination theme, and the resonance for Fanny is clear from the loaded word contained in Sir Thomas' resolution 'to be the real and consistent patron of the selected child', at the start, to the 'patronage' and 'paternal abode' at the close. When Edmund speaks of ' "my father's house" ' (127), apart from the fact that he is referring to the place on the cover of the book, some readers will be almost unable not to complete the quotation ('In my father's house, there are many mansions', John, 14.2).

(3) Edmund going to a friend 'in the same **situation** as himself' (255, cf. also 92), refers to his being an ordinand, and when he says: ' "I have no idea but of residence" ' (247), the word has a technical sense. Even in manifest content Henry's aversion to 'permanence of abode' (41)—'there was nothing to call him elsewhere' (47) —contrasts with Edmund's 'calling'; he twice uses another word we have seen applied to Fanny's situation, when he speaks of ' "knowing that there was such a **provision** for me" ' (109); in the notation about the priest who forgets the importance of his cure ' "stepping out of his **place** to appear what he ought not to appear" ' (92) there is the space resonance in 'situation'.

(4) In section 6 we saw newness attainted: intimacy with Fanny results from Mary's 'desire of something new' (208): readers may here think of the Athenians who 'spent their time in nothing else but either to tell or hear some new thing' (Acts 17.21). (It may be added that the talk in I.9 of how ' "a good clergyman will be **useful**" ' when by his *presence* a congregation knows ' "his private character" ' (93), refers to the sacrament's efficacy having to be independent of the character of the priest: giving a 'character' is one of the few remnants of a culture which separates private and public virtue.)

[95] E.g. the notation about 'flower of his days' also recalls Fanny's flower-cutting ordeal; the 'widow' gives not a 'mite' to Fanny; and it is Fanny whom nature has 'richly endowed'.

returns to legitimacy himself while his brothers and sisters are eliminated by being bastardized' (7.224). Not only is Fanny's Romance a casebook-worthy illustration of this, but more remarkable still, it is that very term from the religious register that figures widely in this work. The details can be relegated to a note, where it will be seen that each occurrence is implicit with themes treated elsewhere.[96]

And not only is Fanny not excluded from this, but the two occurrences of the word which explicitly include her are occasions when she must please the interlopers: she might echo Rushworth's view ' "We did very well without them" ' when her uncle pressurises her to see Henry: ' "He leaves Northamptonshire so soon, that even this slight sacrifice cannot be often demanded" ' (331); and most significant when in II.9 Edmund, pressing her to wear Mary's chain, is sure she will ' "for only one night, if it *be* a sacrifice . . . upon consideration, make that sacrifice rather than give pain to one who has been so studious of your comfort" ' (263).

'Most significant', for who shall deny that, according to the terms of the plot, Fanny, though a queen, has her cross to bear? In other words (the title of William Penn's dissertation on sacrifice, become proverbial): no cross, no crown.

Those who feel this is interpretative zeal run amock must reckon with further textual facts: during the Portsmouth chapters various characters are eliminated, but (more Tom/Fanny parallels) just as the heroine does not 'die under the cure' (413), so Tom too narrowly escapes sacrifice. When his family 'were apprehensive for his lungs' (429), we hear an echo from the only other occurrence of the word in the novel: Tom wonders about Ravenshaw's real reasons for abandoning *Lovers' Vows*: ' "perhaps . . . he began to tremble for his credit and his lungs in the Baron" ' (123). Tom seems with dramatic irony to foresee his own future danger here.

A cross is moreover the figure behind the notation quoted in the foreword: what Tom says as he invites Fanny to dance, in order to escape another sort of play:

> 'A pretty modest request upon my word!' he indignantly exclaimed as they walked away. 'To want to **nail me to a card table** for the next two hours..'   (I.12.119)

---

[96] Sacrifice' in *MP* obeys (cf. 'unfold' in *P & P*) an equitable lexical distributism: Mary's joke about gods and heroes concerns sacrifices of Maria and Edmund; the novel's first occurrence of the word concerns Mrs Price's eagerness 'to regain the friends she had so carelessly sacrificed' (5) cf. the theme of characters thinking they can spare someone; when Fanny arrives at the Park, the Miss Bertrams 'had no idea of carrying their obliging manners to the sacrifice of any real pleasure' (36), recalling the instinct/civilization opposition; Tom's view that his sisters not playing Amelia can be ' "no sacrifice on their side, for it is highly comic" ' (133) recalls the irony in the idea that a rôle allowing a woman to declare her love might be comic; Mrs Norris' self-dramatising self-justification–'much exertion and many sacrifices to glance at in the form of hurried walks and sudden removals from her own fire-side' (188)–is the comic case; and Sir Thomas brings public/private into it when he assures Maria that 'long standing and public as was the engagement, her happiness must not be sacrificed to it' (200).

However 'she could not spare him': Tom returns to health transformed;[97] his sacrifice is purely symbolic. Likewise Lady Bertram, because as always, as we have seen, she 'would of course be spared' (253), the first of the cluster of occurrences of the word associated with the Portsmouth absence relates to her (to reconcile her to Fanny's departure Sir Thomas 'called it a sacrifice, and demanded it of her goodness and self-command as such', 371); she shows she really misses Fanny.

Each of the others really eliminated at the end—Henry, Maria, Mary, Mrs Norris—is associated with the word at the time of the Portsmouth episode.[98]

Most interesting, for our inquiry into Jane Austen's inquiry, in the three *women* sacrificed, again what is below is given greater prominence, and the Lydia Bennet theme reappears: ' "though Miss Crawford is in a manner at home, at the Parsonage" ', Mrs Norris had told Fanny; ' "you are not to be **taking place** of her" ' (221).

But Fanny is not content to be what Edmund told her she was: 'one of his two dearest', while Mary is 'the other!—the **first** !' (264), not content to have any but the first two dances with him kept for her (272): of all space-notations used by Mrs Norris, who 'grudged such an elevation to one whom she had been always trying to depress' (332), about Fanny's situation, the most memorable and absolute is when she tells her ' "Remember, wherever you are, you must be the lowest and last" ' (221). And she pays for it, since it turns out to be true that 'The last shall be first, and the first last' (Matthew, 20.16; this dictum, incidentally, is the moral of the story about labourers who have borne the burden in the heat of the day..)

It is now clear why Jane Austen 'permitted herself the licence' (Introduction, p. xxiv) of displacing the central event in the Christian calendar:

> Easter came—particularly late this year, as Fanny had most sorrowfully considered, on first learning that she had no chance of leaving Portsmouth till after it. (430)

Edmund writes that Fanny has to stay till someone fetch her after Easter (wounding her with allusion to improvements at Thornton Lacey, against the time when it will 'have a mistress', 423); Fanny vows never to wish for another letter, then ' "Not till after Easter!—How shall I bear it?" ' (424).

---

[97] Perhaps something draws back from fulfilment of Mary's wish for 'Edmund **the only son**' (430); nevertheless ' "**Lord** Edmund" ' (211, italics original) is a title Mary imagines him bearing; after all he will now always be 'there to mix **the wine and water**' for Fanny (66). As with the occurrence in one sentence of *S & S* of 'enthusiasm' and 'atone' (Chapter II, p. 87, n. 59), so in *MP* the appearance in the following sentence of two words linked in our argument—' "and a sermon at **Christmas** and **Easter**, I suppose, will be the sum total of **sacrifice**" ' (226) makes one wonder again about author's guile. Another page in *MP* (265) juxtaposes 'The enthusiasm of a woman's love' with 'blessed' and 'blessedness'.

[98] For Henry, 'the temptation of immediate pleasure was too strong for a mind unused to make any sacrifice to right' (467); Maria, 'in sacrificing such a situation' (454) guilty of nothing but folly; Mary's affection for Edmund is ' "not equal to sacrifices, which, in fact, I am scarcely justified in asking" ' (422); and Mrs Norris boasts of having to 'sacrifice every other pleasure to that of being useful' to the Bertrams (373).

Earlier trials adumbrate this: after the I.7 riding scene coachman contrasts Mary's skill with Fanny's beginning ' "six years ago come next **Easter**" ' (69); Edmund spoke of ' "limiting the exhibition" ' (155) of the theatricals, but it is the **east** room that becomes the theatre of Fanny's severest trial: to watch Edmund and Mary rehearsing their *Lovers' Vows* together is 'a very **suffering** exhibition' (170):[99] so Fanny deserves Edmund by suffering; what she learnt in the schoolroom were indeed 'lessons of affliction' (459). And indeed, we recall, for Freud love involves 'a sacrifice of the self'.

But to return to Edmund's II.9 injunction—' "make that sacrifice rather than give pain" ' to Mary (p. 206, *supra*)—we must add an important supplement to the stand that *Mansfield Park* explores the structure of Fanny's pain: it is an *ironic* structure, as it is a guilt *complex*: though the extreme figuration of the pain she receives may not have been consciously noticed, her readiness to suffer has actually fuelled her unpopularity. This may partly be for reasons section 1 tried to elucidate, but also to avoid seeing the pain she *gives*.

Edmund himself is not eliminated; but he must suffer. For a start, symbolically, he is not excluded from the 'sacrifices' at the time of Portsmouth:

> He too had a sacrifice to make to Mansfield Park . . . he could not leave his father and mother just when every body else of most importance to their comfort, was leaving them.   (373[100])

We are further specifically told Fanny enjoys his pain—on not one but two occasions: (a) interestingly near a bout of her own masochism (p. 195, *supra*): it was 'barbarous to be happy when Edmund was suffering. Yet some happiness must and would arise, from the very conviction, that he did suffer' (279); (b) later, after a paragraph in which the word 'happy' is again used, four times about her, she knows that Edmund on the contrary is far from happy,

> ..suffering from disappointment and regret, grieving over what was, and wishing for what could never be. She knew it was so, and was sorry; but it was with a sorrow so founded on satisfaction..   (etc., 461)

---

[99] Since Easter is so late as to be in May, an otherwise quite gratuitous remark of Edmund's—' "We may sometimes take greater liberties in November [the 'black month' of Sir Thomas' return] than in May" ' (II.4. 212)—receives an explanation (the liberty in question there was ' "sitting down for a few minutes" '. Mary replies that he does not know ' "how much we have been **suffering**, nor what **chills** we have felt" '; and Mrs Grant wishes it had been ' "a good sharp **east** wind blowing on you" '.

[100] Cf. 'Therefore shall a man leave his father and his mother, and shall cleave to his wife' (Genesis 2. 24). Given that the path taken in the Sotherton wilderness is described as ' "a very serpentine course" ' (94), that Edmund and Mary tell the jealous Fanny, after their windings, they 'had been sitting down under one of the trees' (103), and that the eventual way in which Edmund finds 'improvement in his spirits' is by 'wandering about and sitting under trees with Fanny all the summer evenings' (462), there is clearly another wish-fulfilment here, this one borrowing some of its paradisiac force from Genesis. Indeed Fanny finally sees *everything* 'take place . . . in the way she could desire' (280). And in the context of her author's inquiry, what she becomes for Edmund is inseparable from what she becomes for his parent, as a minor earlier wish-fulfilment goes some way to make clear: 'would he only have smiled upon her and called her "my dear Fanny"..' (33); on his return from abroad, 'perceiving her, [he] came forward with a kindness which astonished and penetrated her, calling her his dear Fanny, kissing her affectionately' (etc.,178).

It further seems she is partly responsible for this suffering, for we learn that when the gentle girl (who dreads taking a liberty with her uncle, and once asked Edmund to ' "Excuse the liberty, but.." ', 269) is finally 'at liberty to speak openly', she feels

> ..more than justified in adding to his knowledge of [Mary's] real character, by some hint of what share his brother's state of health might be supposed to have in her wish for a complete reconciliation.   (459)[101]

This (retaliative) use to which she puts her liberty, follows hard on his final unconscious wounding of her, when he speaks for one last time of 'how delightful nature had made..'—Mary—so she is perhaps less hurting *him* than, so to speak, stabbing *Mary* in the back as she makes her exit from the novel.

'So to speak', but as the reader may recall from a passage quoted at this chapter's head and at the end of section 11, there is a 'stab' in the text.

A strong word,[102] between which and the word 'gentle' there is again complete disjunction.[103] In presenting its material this study has had to manage a balancing-act between illustration of lexical dispositions and description of their effect, but in this instance the effect is clear: once all the characters closely connected with Fanny are agreed that she is gentle, the word can disappear from the text, for her enemies are moving towards their elimination.

This affords us a last gauge of *Mansfield Park*'s symbolic relation to the Jane Austen oeuvre: in final, decisive abrogation of the received account's picture of Fanny, it was after all to be expected that in a paradigmatically passive heroine, whose aggression is merely suppressed, we should find further testimony that there is always something aggressive in the sexual.

And with that, together with 'stab', in mind, we return to a last 'detail' ('an explanation must be found for *every* detail'): for Fanny to get her own place, Maria proves unworthy of being a *Miss Bertram* and Mary of being *Mrs* Bertram. If it be acknowledged that, in 'mythical' terms, Mary and Maria have the same name (and the link is 'naturalised' by Fanny's double displacement, becoming daughter of the father and wife of the son) as if two Marys were not enough, there is a third Mary, reference to whose annihilation is

---

101 This in spite of a further remarkable textual contradiction—for it must now be pointed out that even the idea of Tom dying *occurs* to Fanny *before* Mary's letter (III.9.433-5), and is then *projected onto* Mary, thus: 'to her selfishness and vanity it would be good luck to have Edmund the only son' (430).

102 Most readers, hard put to it to imagine a circumstance in which Jane Austen could even have occasion for it, would tell you she does not; but the action it performs is present in the scene just quoted: though Edmund first says he cannot consider Mary ' "as meaning to wound my feelings" ' (456), he later admits ' "she had been inflicting deeper wounds in almost every sentence" '.

103 Only an enthusiast's exaggerated consciousness will welcome exhaustive account of words' career across a Jane Austen text; but even a page before the end of this chapter it must be said that 'gentle' has an exceptionally interesting one: Sir Thomas' hope that Fanny acquit herself like a gentlewoman (250) is the first occurrence of the word (since his plan for *provision* of a gentlewoman); the 'stab' passage follows shortly after (264); then in the course of the next hundred pages 'gentle' appears no less than twelve times (269, 276, 293, 294 [twice], 296, 317, 327, 328, 329, 351 and 359) in the hands of Edmund, Henry, Mary, Sir Thomas, and less precisely identifiable agencies (276 is perhaps an observer at the ball, and 269 perhaps a self-image of Fanny's own); it then stops—the last recourse to it being Mary's, when she calls the heroine ' "Good, gentle Fanny" '.

reserved for Portsmouth: Fanny's real sister, her mother's tenth child, who died after Fanny left for Mansfield.

Whatever can be the point of this Mary—who according to 'realist' decorum assumes decidedly far too much weight, too late in the story?—unless it be the knife, which, it will be recalled, she left to Susan, replacing which binds Susan to Fanny, (and which, it may also be recalled, is the last 'act' in the novel: 'an act *of kindness*' it is called: my italics); again, what clinches this is the detail in the detail: Betsey has the bad taste to prefer the **new** knife that Fanny buys her—she accepts it 'with great delight, its **newness** giving it every advantage over the other that could be desired' (397).

*

If the field-day of registers we began by illustrating in section 1 is no more than an alibi for one particular register (the biblical); if *Mansfield Park* is not a moral story but a psychological myth; if Easter is an alibi for Fanny Price clearing the board for herself; and if the sacrifice of the characters is the Price Fanny is paid by them for having sacrificed her to their pleasure, as her guilt at loving Edmund is an alibi for her first inclination—if all this is so, then the case for the centrality of figuration in Jane Austen has, in an interpretation of a third successive work, been upheld.

And returning to the terms of this study's preface, it may now be said that if for some the encounter it proposes must have been preposterous, offensive or sacrilegious, for others it will have erred, as an interpretation, on the side of timidity: for on a psychoanalytic reading, there is an utter inevitability in Fanny's guilt taking the form of religiosity. The view that projection is the essence of religion (projection of the father onto the cosmos) is not the least of the blows Freud dealt to a sacred subject—family relations: good behaviour is an attempt 'to appease the father by deferred obedience' (13.206). Indeed, for Freud, religion is itself an alibi: 'acceptance of the universal neurosis spares [believers] the task of constructing a personal one' (12.227). And if *that* be accepted, it follows that Fanny's religion, her pain—what this astonishing work is about—*is* her sexuality.

*

Appendix: Jane Austen, Psychoanalysis, and the Critics

Until very recently, psychoanalytic terminology has been exceedingly rare in Jane Austen Studies.[1] Liddell (1963) sees in Edmund's behaviour with Mary the novelist's memories of a loved brother led astray by a fascinating cousin (Eliza de Feuillide), and comments 'It may be that personal experience has not always been sufficiently sublimated';[2] Hodge (1972) declares *Pride and Prejudice* 'could be, and has been described as a wish-fulfilment story';[3] and two 1980s critics have recourse to a recondite term (which, with the greatest respect, one cannot but wonder whether they fully understand): Halperin that certain chapters of *Mansfield Park* show 'the novelist's neurasthenia growing by leaps and bounds'; and Honan that 'Mary [Crawford] is small, well-formed, pretty and neurasthenic'.[4]

In the same vein of fleeting allusions to what seems to call for longer treatment, mention may be made of a 1990 book which makes a fugitive reference to incest in *Mansfield Park*.[5]

Much longer ago (1939 & 1957) two articles by Geoffrey Gorer appeared[6] in which promising remarks are made (e.g. the sisters in *S & S* 'seem like the split facets of a single personality'[7]); but these one-off assertions are never followed up, and the 1957 article's title gives the tone of the project (probably what readers expected from the present study): relating or attempting to

---

[1] The 20th century's most influential academic critic (who half-promised, but never produced, a book on her) avowed nothing but scorn for psychoanalysis: e.g. 'Hawthorne's psychology, a striking achievement of intuition, anticipates. . .what are supposed to be modern findings' (Leavis, op. cit., p. 145); Empson, quoted occasionally in this study, was another persuasion, and close to Freud's essence in 'verbal analysis'. This is often said to work best on short poems, but is mere length behind the implication that novels contain more 'filling' than verse? There seems no exactly analogous state of affairs in other arts: we do not suppose there is more dispensable matter in larger musical or architectural works than in smaller. Rieff's view is that restoring the importance of detail is a key achievement of application–to any discipline–of psychoanalysis, itself in his view 'a kind of literary criticism' (op. cit., pp. 134/145). A whole district of contemporary art-connoisseurs is Morellian in inspiration (*vide* Chapter I, p. 46); one may regret that the lesson has remained relatively unlearnt outside Bond Street, and that no literary critic of Empson's stature has appeared with the torch.

[2] Liddell, op. cit., pp. 63/4.

[3] Hodge, op. cit., p. 50. Naturally this is not a complete account of occasional recourses to such terms, which in any case are not specific to psychoanalysis: e.g. Blythe mentions a 'strange unconscious unity' between Emma and Mr Knightley (op. cit., p. 21), Wright mentions 'how large a part unconsciousness plays in [Emma's] relation to Mr Knightley' (op. cit., p. 140), etc.

[4] Halperin, op. cit., p. 240, Honan, op.cit., p. 339. (The now obsolescent term denotes a condition caused by inadequately discharged sexual tension as a result of masturbation.)

[5] Richard Handler and Daniel Segal: *Jane Austen and the Fiction of Culture*, University of Arizona, 1990.

[6] (1) 'The Myth in Jane Austen' Life and Letters Today, no.21, May 1939, reprinted in *Five Approaches of Literary Criticism*, ed. W.Scott, Macmillan N.Y.1962; (2) 'Poor Honey: some notes on Jane Austen and her mother', London Magazine no.8, Aug.1957, reprinted in *The Danger of Equality, and other essays*, Cresset 1966.

[7] Gorer (1962) p. 97.

relate Jane Austen's family life to the constellations in the novels, and this in a manner for which the word 'cavalier' would be an understatement.[8]

As Gorer's articles have no critical upshot, allusion to them might appear pointless, were it not that his approach has reappeared in studies of the last ten years. Indeed James Thompson (1988) compounds its vices: there is sheer unblushing unsupported hypothesis about the life—'Jane Austen appears to have idealized her father, seeking to share his love of words, as she was free to roam in his study'[9]—there is the Janeite ploy of using what has been admitted to be hypothesis, to fuel understanding of the work—'Though conjectural, this projection of Austen's early family history parallels that of the Bennet family'[10]—and there is the attempt to bludgeon non-existent facts into service:

> *Though* the evidence is slight (from memories by relatives written after Austen was dead and from the letters that her sister Cassandra did not burn) *and the argument highly speculative*, this pattern of narcissism *must* have had part of its origin in Jane Austen herself . . . There is *little factual evidence* about Austen's childhood, *but* from the patterns established in Kohnt's clinical evidence, Austen's parents *ought to have been* distant and withdrawn'.[11]

Psychoanalytic Janeism colours a 1989 study: 'If we assume that there are portions of Austen's own hidden self in all heroines, whether transcended or not, we need to examine some of the subversive attitudes of these heroines.'[12]

Mary Evans' thesis, stated at the end of her 1993 essay—'all Jane Austen's fiction could be illuminated by, and illuminate, Freud's ideas'[13]—is exactly the one this inquiry tries to explore; substantiation of it is, however, disappointingly meagre. Given the potential bombshell under her arm, it seems extraordinary that so much of the article should be taken up with mere plot summary; it is full of critical solecisms which one might think her 'approach' had permanently outmoded (apart from Crawford and Maria 'Nobody . . . actually does anything in *Mansfield Park* . . . Austen's fiction is

---

[8] An example of the strategy: we are first told (1962, p. 93) that in three novels 'the heroine actively dislikes her mother' (this might just do for Elizabeth Bennet, but hardly for the Dashwoods or Fanny Price); by the next page interest has accrued: we now get 'This central myth—the girl who hates and despises her mother.'

[9] James Thompson: *Between Jane Austen and the World: The Novels of Jane Austen*, Pennsylvania State University Press, 1988, pp. 124/5.

[10] Ibid., p. 125.

[11] Ibid., p. 124 (my italics). Cf. 'There is not one reference to Wollstonecraft in Austen's writings, either her fiction or correspondence. Since most of Austen's letters have been lost or were destroyed it is entirely possible that she did comment on this controversial author; if so, her remarks undoubtedly expressed censure or disapproval' (Roberts, op. cit., p. 156). Who would not be sorry to have missed that?

[12] Alison G. Sulloway: *Jane Austen and the Province of Womanhood*, University of Pennsylvania, 1989, p. 49. Readers who suppose extinct the high-handed ways with texts illustrated in Chapter I, must be disabused: 'When Mr Austen relinquished his ecclesiastical living in favour of James and then retired to Bath, James coolly bargained for all the household goods at Steventon, for the books, pictures and silverware, in exactly the same cheap and contemptuous way as did the John Dashwoods in *Sense and Sensibility*' (p. 102). Did they?

[13] Mary Evans, op. cit., p. 54.

singularly lacking in decisive action, deliberate choice'[14]); and the character lighted upon to illustrate the 'many moments of unerring prediction of the themes of psychoanalysis'[15] is not the work's heroine, but Crawford: an odd, one would have thought unpromising, choice—and indeed with only one single short essay of Freud's turned to account (PFL 7.248-60),[16] the 'illumination', when it comes, turns out to consist in precisely the sort of psychological explanation for which we do not need his help: viz. 'Jane Austen, quite as much as Freud, understood that human beings are often powerless in the face of their emotions'.[17]

Finally, Tara Ghoshal Wallace published a study in 1995 that may or may not be a contribution to critical theory and/or the psychology of reading, but does not appear to have much to do with the work of the novelist whose name figures on the cover of her book: for though we are informed on the first page that 'Austen both empowers women and critiques women's assumption of power',[18] that her novels 'are more than artefacts of self-reflexivity', but rather that 'they challenge and enable' us 'to move beyond a deconstructive dismantling of her texts'[19] (matters on which readers must make up their own minds) the upshot of the study relates to their 'authorship'—or rather, for there is scarcely any such simple concept wielded, it is to 'the problematics of authorship encoded in her work.'[20]

In fact, for all this fantastic display of contemporary catch-phrase (indeed for all her 'Austen') Wallace is a *Janeite*: though if this authorship 'liberates as well as compromises Austen's desire for feminine power',[21] even the final Janeite lesson is thin, for what we eventually learn on the last page is this:

Austen wants, I believe, to return herself to the text . . . To do so, she deliberately writes out (*not* encodes) her personal ambivalences about fat or ugly women.[22]

---

[14] Ibid., p. 47. The article abounds in schoolgirlish turns of phrase: concerning the point in the novel when the Crawfords are introduced: 'Readers must *put their own gold stars* by these pages', in hypotheses about artistic intentions which Evans is not in a position to know: e.g. 'Austen *does her best* to remind us that patriarchal authority is absent' (my italics), and the old chestnut about the limits of the novelist's imagination reappears: speaking of two male characters in *MP*, 'It might well be that Jane Austen felt that she did not know *how* men talked to each other, and thus had no confidence in manufacturing their conversation' (pp. 37 & 40).

[15] Ibid., p. 46.

[16] Hardly better is John Wiltshire's *Jane Austen and the Body* (C.U.P. 1992) where three very short Freud quotations—from *The Psychopathology of Everyday Life*, the *Introductory Lectures*, and (in a note) *On Narcissism*—are submerged by a flood of Cixous, Clément, Merleau-Ponty, Foucault, Kristeva, etc.

[17] Ibid., p. 50. Evans' opening sentence, 'Jane Austen does not, in any of her novels, invite her readers to speculate about the potency—or otherwise—of her male characters', could certainly be challenged in the case of John Thorpe (e.g. *NA* I.9.62; I.10.76; I.12.96 etc.).

[18] *Jane Austen and Narrative Authority*, Macmillan 1995, p. 1.

[19] Ibid.

[20] Ibid.

[21] Ibid.

[22] Ibid., p. 116.

References

Numerals in bold refer to pages in this study on which the following are quoted.

Ahearn, Edward J.: *Marx and Modern Fiction*, Yale U.P. 1989. **36n.**

Auden, W.H.: *Collected Shorter Poems*, Faber and Faber 1966. **12n.**

Auerbach, Erich: *Mimesis*, Princeton 1953. **83n.**

Austen, Jane: *The Oxford Illustrated Jane Austen*, ed. R.W.Chapman, O.U.P. 1953, rev. Mary Lascelles and B.C.Southam. *Passim*; see Indexes
—— *Jane Austen's Letters to her Sister Cassandra and Others*, ed. R.W.Chapman, O.U.P. 1932. **xvi n.**, **xxvii n.**, **30n.**, **41n.**, **47n.**, **124n.**
—— *Mansfield Park* trans. by Denise Getzler, Christian Bourgois 1982. **40n.**

Austen-Leigh, James: *A Memoir of Jane Austen* (1870), reprinted in Penguin ed. of *P*. **23n.**, **27**, **34**

Austen-Leigh, William and R.A.: *Jane Austen, Her Life and Letters*, Smith, Elder & Co., 1913. **26**

Ayer, A.J.: *Wittgenstein*, Penguin 1986. **146n.**

Ayers, M.R.: *Locke*, R.K.P. 1991. **39n.**

Bailey, John: *Introductions to Jane Austen*, O.U.P. 1931. **31**

Barfoot, C.C.: *The Thread of Connection: Aspects of Fate in the Novels of Jane Austen and Others*, Rodopi (Amsterdam) 1982. **24**

Belsey, Catherine: *Critical Practice*, Methuen 1980. **40**

Berlin, Isaiah: *Karl Marx*, Gallimard 1962. **144n.**

Bettelheim, Bruno: *The Uses of Enchantment*, Peregrine 1978. **126n.**, **198**

Blythe, Ronald: Introduction, Penguin ed. of *E*, 1966. **31**, **213**

Booth, Wayne C.: *The Rhetoric of Fiction*, Chicago U.P. 1961. **24n.**, **78**

Borges, Jorge Luis: *Labyrinths*, Penguin 1970. **39n.**

Boswell, James: *Life of Samuel Johnson*, Everyman 1939. **xvi n**, **3n**, **18**, **167n.**

Bradbury, Malcolm: 'Jane Austen's *Emma*' in *Emma, A Casebook*, Macmillan 1970. **34**

Brown, J.A.C.: *Freud and the Post-Freudians*, Penguin 1961. **119**

Büchner, Georg: *Danton's Death*, tr. C.R.Mueller, Mermaid Drama 1963. **201**

Butler, Marilyn: in *Northanger Abbey: A Casebook*, Macmillan 1976 (revised version. of orig. pub. in *Jane Austen and The War of Ideas*, O.U.P. 1975.) **36n.**

Cairncross, Andrew: Introduction, Arden ed. of *2 Henry VI*, Routledge 1969. **187**

Cecil, Lord David: Introduction, 'Sir Charles Grandison', O.U.P. 1981. **xxi n**.

Chandler, Alice: 'A Pair of Fine Eyes', *Studies in the Novel* no. 7, 1975. **82n.**

Chapman, R.W.: *Jane Austen: Facts and Problems*, O.U.P. 1948. **xxiii**, **35**, **40n.**

Ciardi, J.: 'A Burble Through the Tulgey Wood' in *Aspects of Alice*, Penguin 1974. **81**

Clark, R.W.: *Freud: the Man and the Cause*, Jonathan Cape 1980. **20**

Craik, Wendy: *Jane Austen, the Six Novels*, Methuen 1965. **26**, **31**

Donoghue, Denis: 'A View of *Mansfield Park*', in *Critical Essays on Jane Austen*, R.K.P. 1968. **31**

Doody, Margaret Anne: Introduction, Penguin ed. of *S & S*, 1990. **29n.**, **33n.**

Doolittle, Hilda: *Tribute to Freud*, Carcanet Press 1971. **129n.**

Drabble, Margaret: Introduction, *Minor Works*, Penguin ed. 1974. **xiv**
Duckworth, Alistair: *The Improvement of the Estate*, Baltimore U. P. 1971. **26, 32,**
    115n., 169n.
Edel, Leon: *Literary Biography*, Rupert Hart-Davis 1957. **xxviii n.**
Ehrenzweig, Anton: *The Hidden Order of Art*, Paladin 1970. **39**
Einstein, Albert: *Relativity, the Special and the General Theory, a popular*
    exposition, Methuen 1960. **146n., 172n.**
Eliot, T.S.: *Selected Essays*, Faber and Faber 1951. **xxi, 192**
――――― *Collected Poems*, Faber and Faber 1963. **178n.**
Empson, William: *Seven Types of Ambiguity*, Pelican 1973. **46, 53, 165n., 213n.**
Evans, Ifor: *A Short History of English Literature*, Pelican 1940. **xiv, 45n.**
Evans, Mary: 'Henry Crawford and the sphere of love in *Mansfield Park*',
    '*Mansfield Park*', Open U.P. 1993. **28n., 29n., 92n., 213/4 + n.**
Eysenck, H.J.: *The Decline and Fall of the Freudian Empire*, Penguin 1985. **xvi, 9**
Forster, E.M.: *Aspects of the Novel*, Pelican 1962. **131**
Fox, Robin: *Kinship and Marriage*, Pelican 1984. **14, 191 + n.**
Fraser, G.S.: *The Modern Writer and His World*, Pelican 1970. **xiv, 32, 45n.**
Freud, Sigmund: *Standard Edition of the Complete Psychological Works*, trans.
    and ed. by James Strachey. ***Passim***; see Indexes
――――― *The Complete Letters of Sigmund Freud to Wilhelm Fliess*, trans. & ed. by
    Jeffrey Moussaieff Masson, Belknap Harvard 1985. **xxvi n., 5, 8, 9nn.,**
    20, 22n., 66n., 67, 71, 116n., 136, 145, 163, 164, 165n., 205
――――― *The Freud/Jung Letters*, ed. William McGuire, abr. Alan McGlashan,
    Picador 1979. **2, 8n., 12, 43**
Frye, Northrop: *Fearful Symmetry*, Princeton 1969. **xxii**
Garis, Robert: 'Learning, Experience and Change', in *Critical Essays on Jane*
    Austen, R.K.P. 1968. **28**
Gibbons, Stella: *Cold Comfort Farm*, Longman 1932. **139n.**
Gilbert, Sandra, and Gubar, Susan: *The Madwoman in the Attic: the Woman*
    Writer in the Nineteenth Century Literary Imagination, Yale U.P. 1979. **33**
Gombrich, E.H.: *Meditations on A Hobbyhorse*, Phaidon 1963. **44n., 166**
Gorer, Geoffrey: 'The Myth in Jane Austen', *Life & Letters Today* no.21, May 1939
    repr. *Five Approaches of Literary Criticism*, Macmillan N.Y. 1962. **213 + n.**
――――― 'Poor Honey: Some Notes on Jane Austen and her Mother', *London Maga-*
    zine no.8, Aug. 1957; repr. *The Danger of Equality*, Cresset 1966. **213 + n.**
Groddeck, Georg: *Le Livre du Ca*, tr. L.Jumel, Gallimard 1963. **80, 186n.**
Grey, J.David: *Jane Austen Handbook*, Athlone Press 1986. **27n.**
Halperin, John: *The Life of Jane Austen*, Harvester 1984. **29, 31 + n., 33, 213**
Hamlyn, D.W.: *Metaphysics*, C.U.P. 1984. **172n.**
Handler, Richard, and Segal, Daniel: *Jane Austen and the Fiction of Culture*,
    University of Arizona Press 1990. **213**
Harding, D.W.: 'Regulated Hatred: An Aspect of the Work of Jane Austen',
    Scrutiny 1940. **34**
Hardwick, Elizabeth: Afterword, *Northanger Abbey*, Signet ed. 1965. **xxi n.**
Hardy, Barbara: *Jane Austen*, Peter Owen 1975. **45n.**
Harth, Eric: *Windows on the Mind*, Pelican 1982. **71n.**
Harris, Jocelyn: *Jane Austen's Art of Memory*, C.U.P. 1989. **25n.**
Hartley, L.P.: Address (1965), J.A. Society Reports, Wm. Dawson & Sons. **34**
Hawkridge, Audrey: *Jane Austen in Hampshire*, Hampshire Co. Council 1995. **38n.**
Hazlitt, William, quoted in Rossiter, A.P.: *Angel With Horns*, Longman 1970. **141n.**

Heisenberg, Werner: *Physics and Philosophy*, Penguin 1990. **146n.**
Hodge, J.: *The Double Life of Jane Austen*, Hodder & Stoughton 1972. **25, 28, 213**
Honan, Park; *Jane Austen: Her Life*, Weidenfeld and Nicholson 1987. **xx, 213**
Hough, Graham: *The Dream and the Task*, Duckworth 1963. **34, 41n.**
Hughes, H.Stuart: *Consciousness and Society*, Paladin 1974. **129**
James, Henry: *Selected Literary Criticism*, Peregrine 1968. **xxii, 72, 78, 188**
―――― 'The Lesson of Balzac', in *The House of Fiction*, Greenwood Press 1957. **36**
―――― *The Wings of the Dove*, Penguin 1966. **117n.**
James, William: *Varieties of Religious Experience*, Fontana 1974. **21n.**
Johnson, Claudia L.: *Jane Austen, Women, Politics and the Novel*, Chicago
    U.P. 1987. **32n.**
Jones, Ernest: *Sigmund Freud, Life and Work*, 3 vol. ed. Hogarth 1953, 1955 and
    1957; Penguin ed. abr. by Lionel Trilling and Steven Marcus, 1974. **xvii,
    1, 7, 8, 10n., 11, 12 + n., 14, 20n., 66, 106, 111, 129, 139, 187**
Joyce, James: *Ulysses*, Penguin 1969. **34n.**
Jung, C.G.: *Analytical Psychology: Its Theory and Practice*, R.K.P. 1976. **67**
―――― *Memories, Dreams, Reflections*, Fontana 1961. **1**
―――― *Modern Man in Search of a Soul*, R.K.P. 1947. **38**
Kaplan, Deborah: *Jane Austen Among Women*, Johns Hopkins U.P. 1992. **xxi n.**
Kermode, Frank: *Renaissance Essays*, Fontana 1973. **xxix n.**
Kirk, G.S.: *The Nature of Greek Myths*, Pelican 1974. **43n.**
Kirkham, Margaret: *Feminism and Fiction*, Harvester Press 1983. **36n., 41n.**
Kris, Ernst: *The Origins of Psychoanalysis*, Imago 1954. **108**
―――― *Psychoanalytic Explorations in Art*, Schocken 1971. **21n.**
Kroeber, Karl: *Styles in Fictional Structure*, Princeton U.P. 1971. **42, 45**
Lacan, Jacques: *L'Ethique de la Psychanalyse*, Seuil 1986. **10n., 71n., 165 + n.**
―――― *Le Moi dans la Théorie et dans la Technique de la Psychanalyse*, 1976.**11n.**
―――― *Les Quatre Concepts Fondamentaux de la Psychanalyse*, 1973. **10n., 22n.,
    71n., 72**
Lacey, A.R.: *A Dictionary of Philosophy*, R.K.P. 1986. **10**
Lane, Maggie: *Jane Austen and Food*, Hambledon Press 1995. **26, 29n.**
Laplanche, J.; Pontalis, J.-B.: *The Language of Psychoanalysis*, translated by
    Donald Nicholson-Smith, Hogarth 1973, from orig. French *Le Vocabulaire
    de la Psychanalyse*, Presses Universitaires de France 1967. **Passim**
Lascelles, Mary; *Jane Austen and her Art*, O.U.P. 1939. **25, 30/1/2, 37, 45n., 123**
Lauber, John: *Jane Austen*, Twayne 1993. **xx n.**
Leavis, F.R.: *The Great Tradition*, Pelican 1967. **xiv n., 213n.**
Leavis, Q.D.: 'A Critical Theory of Jane Austen's Writings', *Scrutiny* 1941. **xxviii n.**
Lerner, Laurence: *The Truth-Tellers*, Chatto and Windus 1967. **32**
Levin, Harry: *The Gates of Horn*, O.U.P. 1963. **xxviii n.**
Lewes, George Henry: 'The Novels of Jane Austen', *Blackwood's* July 1859. **xiii**
Lewis, C.S.: *The Allegory of Love*, Galaxy 1958. **143n.**
Liddell, Robert: *The Novels of Jane Austen*, Longman 1963. **33, 35 + n., 36, 213**
Litz, A.Walton: *Jane Austen, A Study of Her Artistic Development*, Chatto and
    Windus 1965. **xx, 29n.**
Llewelyn, Margaret: *Jane Austen, A Character Study*, Kimber 1977. **xxi n.**
Lodge, David: 'The Novelist at the Crossroads', in *The Novel Today*, Fontana
    1977. **24n., 41n.**
―――― Introduction, *Emma: A Casebook*, Macmillan 1969. **28, 45n.**
Lomas, Peter: *The Limits of Interpretation*, Pelican 1987. **12, 19, 145n.**

Lucas, Victor: *Jane Austen*, Pitkin 1996. **41n.**

Macaulay, Thomas Babington: 'Madame d'Arblay', in *Critical and Historical Essays*, Longman 1857. **xiii, 42**

MacDonagh, Oliver: *Jane Austen, Real and Imagined Worlds*, Yale U.P. 1991. **27n.**

Magee, Bryan: *Modern British Philosophy*, Paladin 1971. **28**

Mansfield, Katherine: quoted in Lascelles, Mary, q.v. **35**

Marcus, Steven: 'Freud and Dora', in *In Dora's Case*, Virago 1985. **20**

Maugham, W.S.: *The Summing-Up*, Pan 1976. **5n., 21**

McGuinness, Brian: *Wittgenstein, A Life*, Penguin 1990. **137n.**

McMaster, Juliet: 'Jane Austen on Love', University of Victoria English Literary Monographs, No.13, 1978. **24 + n., 41n.**

Mooneyham, Laura G.: *Romance, Language and Education in Jane Austen's Novels*, Macmillan 1988. **31n.**

Morgan, Susan: *In the Meantime, Character and Perception in Jane Austen's Fiction*, Chicago U.P. 1980. **32**

Mudrick, Marvin: *Irony as Defense and Discovery*, Princeton 1952. **29n., 77n.**

Nabokov, Vladimir: *Lectures on Literature*, Picador 1983. **29n.**

Nardin, Jane: *Those Elegant Decorums*, N.Y. State U.P. 1973. **32**

O'Hear, Anthony: *What Philosophy Is*, Penguin 1988. **146n.**

Ortega y Gasset, José: *On Love... Aspects of A Single Theme*, trans. from Spanish, (Revista de Occidente 1941) by Toby Talbot, Jonathan Cape 1964. **1**

Page, Norman: *The Language of Jane Austen*, Blackwell 1972. **26, 27, 29, 42 + n.**

Paris, Bernard J.: *Character and Conflict in Jane Austen's Novels*, Harvester 1979. **xxi n., 28**

Pears, David: *Wittgenstein*, Fontana 1971. **8**

Phillipps, K.C.: *Jane Austen's English*, André Deutsch 1969. **xv**

Piozzi, Hesther: *Anecdotes of Samuel Johnson*, ed. A. Sherbo, O.U.P. 1974. **18**

Popper, Karl: *Conjectures and Refutations*, R.K.P. 1978. **11**

Pound, Ezra: *Literary Essays*, Faber and Faber 1960. **27**

Price, H.H., quoted in *A Critical History of Western Philosophy*, ed. D.J.O'Connor, Free Press 1964. **172n.**

Quinton, Anthony, quoted in Magee, Bryan, q.v. **161n.**

Raleigh, Walter, quoted in Rossiter, A.P.: *Angel With Horns*, Longman 1970. **139**

Reddy, T.V.: *Jane Austen and the Matrix of Matrimony*, Bohra 1987. **31n.**

Rhees, Rush: Preface, Wittgenstein's *Lectures and Conversations on Aesthetics, Psychology & Religious Belief*, Blackwell 1966. **13n., 39**

Richardson, Samuel: *Sir Charles Grandison* (1754). **xxiii, 23, 47**

Ricoeur, Paul: *De L'Interprétation*, Seuil 1965. **xxii, 11, 13n., 46, 81**

Rieff, Philip: *Freud: The Man and the Moralist*, Chicago U.P. 1959. **xvi, xxv, 2, 7, 8, 19, 22, 123, 132, 213n.**

Roazen, Paul: *Freud and His Followers*, Peregrine 1969. **2, 7**

Roberts, Warren: *Jane Austen and the French Revolution*, Athlone 1995. **32, 213 + n**

Rycroft, Charles: *Psychoanalysis and Beyond*, Chatto and Windus 1985. **xvi, xvii**

—— *The Innocence of Dreams*, O.U.P. 1981. **67**

—— *Critical Dictionary of Psychoanalysis*, Penguin 1972. **105 n., 111, 126 + n.**

Russell, Bertrand: *The Problems of Philosophy*, Butterworth 1912. **143, 161n.**

Sachs, Hanns: *Freud: Master and Friend*, Imago 1945. **8n., 90**

Sales, R.: *Jane Austen and Representations of Regency England*, R.K.P. 1996. **28n.**

Schorer, Mark: 'The Humiliation of Emma Woodhouse', in *Jane Austen, A Collection of Critical Essays*, Prentice Hall Inc. 1963. **29, 31**

219

Shannon, Edgar: 'Emma: Character and Construction', PMLA. LXXI 1956. **32**
Smith, Leroy W.: *Jane Austen and the Drama of Women*, Macmillan 1983. **42n.**
Southam, B.C.: Introduction, *Jane Austen: The Critical Heritage*, R.K.P. 1968. **28**
───── 'The Seventh Novel', in *Jane Austen's Achievement*, Macmillan 1976. **32**
Spacks, P.M.: *The Female Imagination*, Allen and Unwin 1976. **100n.**
Spinoza, Baruch: *Theological-Political Tractatus* (1670). **xxii n.**
Stewart, J.I.M.: 'Tradition and Miss Austen', in *Critical Essays on Jane Austen*,
 R.K.P. 1968. **25**
Storr, Anthony: *The Dynamics of Creation*, Penguin 1976. **21**
Sulloway, A.: *Jane Austen and the Province of Womanhood*, Pa. U.P. 1989. **214**
Szasz, Thomas: *The Myth of Mental Illness*, Secker and Warburg 1962. **5**
Tanner, Tony: *Jane Austen*, Macmillan 1986. **xv n.**, **25-7**, **31**, **40n.**, **53/4**, **60**, **77n.**
A.G.Tansley, Royal Society Obituary Notices, vol.3. **139**
Thomson, Robert: *Pelican History of Psychology*, Penguin 1962. **xxvi n.**
Thompson, James: *Between Jane Austen and World*, Pa. State UP. 1988. **213**
Trilling, Lionel: *Beyond Culture*, Secker and Warburg 1966. **xix**
────── *The Liberal Imagination*, Mercury 1961. **19**
Van Ghent, D.: *The English Novel, Form and Function*, Harper & Row 1967. **138n.**
Wallace, Tara Ghoshal: *Jane Austen and Narrative Authority*, Macmillan 1995. **215**
Watson, George: *The Literary Critics*, Penguin 1962. **139n.**
Warnock, Geoffrey: *Berkeley*, Blackwell 1982. **166n.**
Washington, P.: Introduction, *Sanditon & Other Stories*, Everyman 1996. **xxiii n.**
Watt, Ian: Introduction, *Jane Austen, A Collection of Critical Essays*,
 Prentice Hall Inc. 1963. **26**, **41n.**
Whyte, L.L.: *The Unconscious Before Freud*, J.Friedmann 1979. **xvi n.**, **8n.**, **122**
Williams, M.: *Jane Austen: Six Novels and their Methods*, Macmillan 1986. **32n.**
Wilson, Edmund: 'A Long Talk About Jane Austen', in *Jane Austen, A Collection
 of Critical Essays*, Prentice Hall Inc. 1963. **29n.**
Wiltshire, John: *Jane Austen and the Body*, C.U.P. 1992. **215**
Wittgenstein, Ludwig: *The Blue and Brown Books*, Blackwell 1972. **xxi n.**
────── *On Certainty*, do. 1969. **xviii**, **72n.**
────── *Philosophical Grammar*, do. 1974. **xviii**
────── *Philosophical Investigations*, do. 1968. **xviii**, **26**, **30n.**, **33n.**, **37/8 + n.**, **40**,
 72n., **133**
────── *Tractatus*, (do.) **36**
────── *Remarks on the Foundations of Mathematics*, Macmillan 1956. **146n.**
Wölfflin, Heinrich: *Principles of Art History*, Dover 1950. **xxvii n.**
Wollheim, Richard: *Art And Its Objects*, Peregrine 1975. **xiv**, **xxiv**, **19**, **37/8**, **45n.**
────── *Freud*, Fontana 1971. **3n.**
────── Introduction, *The Image in Form: Selected Writings of Adrian Stokes*,
 Penguin 1972. **37n.**
Wood, Nigel: Introduction, *'Mansfield Park'*, Open U.P. 1993. **27n.**
Woolf, Leonard: *Beginning Again: Autobiography of the Years 1911-18*, Hogarth
 1964. **114**
Woolf, Virginia: 'Jane Austen at Sixty', Nation & Athenæum Dec.15 1923. **xxvi**, **46**
Wright, Andrew: *Jane Austen's Novels*, Penguin 1962. **24**, **32**, **40n.**, **77**, **213**
Wright, Elizabeth: *Psychoanalytic Criticism*, Methuen 1984. **20**

INDEX 1: Sigmund Freud's Works

INDEX 2: Jane Austen's Works

INDEX 3: thematic & interpretative terms

Readers using indexes 3 and 4 are reminded that a considerable degree of overlap—between terms belonging to the literary-critical register, on the one hand, and to the terminology of psycho-analysis, on the other—is an inevitable result of the overall point this book seeks to establish. It has nevertheless seem-ed desirable to separate, for purposes of reference at least, entries in these listings which by their nature have very general pertinence (e.g. *language*, in Index 3) from those that tend to the extreme-ly specific (e.g. *scotoma*, in Index 4).